Feminist Frameworks

FEMINIST FRAMEWORKS

Alternative Theoretical Accounts
of the Relations between Women and Men

Alison M. Jaggar
Associate Professor of Philosophy
University of Cincinnati

Paula Rothenberg Struhl
Associate Professor of Philosophy
The William Paterson College
of New Jersey

McGraw-Hill Book Company

New York   St. Louis   San Francisco   Auckland
Bogotá   Düsseldorf   Johannesburg   London   Madrid
Mexico   Montreal   New Delhi   Panama   Paris
São Paulo   Singapore   Sydney   Tokyo   Toronto

FEMINIST FRAMEWORKS:
Alternative Theoretical Accounts
of the Relations between Women and Men

This book was set in Times Roman by University Graphics, Inc.
The editors were Jean Smith, Rhona Robbin, and Laura D. Warner;
the cover was designed by Judith Michael;
the production supervisor was Milton J. Heiberg.
Fairfield Graphics was printer and binder.

See Acknowledgments on pages 319–322.
Copyrights included on this page by reference.

Library of Congress Cataloging in Publication Data
Main entry under title:

Feminist frameworks.

    Includes bibliographies and index.
    1. Feminism—United States—Addresses, essays,
lectures. 2. Sexism—Addresses, essays, lectures.
3. Social institutions—Addresses, essays, lectures.
4. Women's rights—Addresses, essays, lectures.
5. Social change—Addresses, essays, lectures.
I. Jaggar, Alison M.   II.   Struhl, Paula Rothenberg.
HQ1426.F47   301.41   77-11069
ISBN 0-07-032250-3

Contents

Part II: Alternative Feminist Frameworks

Part III: Practice: The Implications of the Theories

Introduction

FEMINIST THEORY AND FEMINIST PRACTICE

This book is about the relations between women and men in our society. It presents various accounts both of what those relations are and of how they ought to be changed. The book springs from several sources. It comes out of our deep belief, as feminists, that changes are urgently required in the position of women. It springs also from our conviction, as philosophers, that the presuppositions and implications of any proposed changes need to be worked out very carefully. Finally, it is motivated by our recognition, as activists, that not only must our activity be guided by theory but our theory must be evaluated by its success in practice.

To say that change is needed is hardly controversial. But what kinds of changes should be made? Even within the feminist movement there are sharp disagreements. Topics such as reverse discrimination, lesbianism, marriage, wages for housework, and even the equal rights amendment are bitterly disputed. We believe that such specific social issues can be considered fruitfully only within the context of a comprehensive theory of the good society and women's place within it. Against this theory we must measure our existing institutions, studying how they function and what effects they have on people's lives; for until we have acquired a thorough understanding of the nature of the society in which we live, we shall not be able to determine the kinds of changes that must be made in the interests of us all. Our book is designed to present a number of the theories that contemporary feminists defend and to show how they generate very different recommendations for resolving the central issues of feminism.

Why do we say that a comprehensive theory of society is required, and how should we determine which of the several competing theories (if any) is true? In our introduction, we shall suggest some answers to these questions.

THE NEED FOR A COMPREHENSIVE FRAMEWORK

Most people recognize that any recommendation for social change rests on certain presuppositions, ordinarily called "philosophical," including beliefs about social authority, human fulfillment, freedom, and justice. What is less widely recognized, however, is that even apparently straightforward *descriptions* of a social situation also make presuppositions. These are presuppositions regarding the choice of categories or concepts which will be the most useful in bringing out those features of the situation which deserve emphasis. For example, to say that women suffer from job discrimination is to presuppose (among other things) that certain procedures for assigning jobs are appropriate and that others are inappropriate; to say that women are exploited is (usually) to presuppose some version of Marxian economic theory; to say that women are oppressed is to presuppose a certain view of justice and equality. Many philosophers argue that all descriptions of reality are, in this way, "theory-laden."

To bring out the point that social facts exist only within a certain theoretical context, we shall sometimes talk of social theories as "conceptual frameworks" and sometimes just as "frameworks."

The theoretical presuppositions of our ordinary ways of thinking and talking are not always conscious. A large part of the feminist critique of contemporary society has consisted in uncovering the presuppositions of those who deny the need for change. Often, a demonstration of the antidemocratic nature of these presuppositions has been sufficient in itself to incite pressure for change. But still there remains the question of precisely what changes should be made. It is to answer this question that feminists have felt the need to construct a new theoretical framework in which to locate our critique of the contemporary position of women and our recommendations for how that position should be altered.

A comprehensive theory of the position of women in society is necessary to feminists for several reasons. Most obviously, feminists need an alternative to the views that we criticize; indeed, if what we have said earlier is correct, the beginnings of feminist theory will necessarily be presupposed in any feminist attempt at social criticism. But it is important that feminist theory be carefully worked out and its implications thoroughly explored. Only by doing this can we ensure that our recommendations for change in one area are consistent with our recommendations in another area, and that both are consistent with our deeper beliefs about human nature and human fulfillment. In addition, we need a comprehensive account of our present situation in the world, its strengths and weaknesses, and the possibilities for improving it or changing it entirely. An incomplete understanding of women's contemporary situation will prompt us to direct our energies wrongly, so that no matter how hard we struggle we shall make little or no progress. Perhaps we shall end up proposing piecemeal solutions to a problem that requires systematic revision. If the problem pervades the entire system under which we live, attempts to reform individual institutions will ultimately fail or, worse yet, cause even more serious problems in other parts of society. By failing to develop a complete analysis of women's situation, we may well mistake a symptom of the illness for its cause and "cure" the patient's fever only to have her succumb to a massive infection that goes undiagnosed.

Thus we see that a feminist framework has a dual aspect. Simultaneously, it offers a *de*scription of women's oppression and a *pre*scription for eliminating it. It is empirical insofar as it examines women's experience in the world; but it is normative insofar as it characterizes certain features of that experience as oppressive and offers a new vision of justice and freedom for women.

One main purpose of this book is to present several different theoretical frameworks for understanding women's situation, showing how different diagnoses of what is wrong with the present necessarily generate different proposals for the future and how, therefore, descriptions of the present and prescriptions for the future are interdependent. Having understood these theories, we must determine which of them is most adequate.

DETERMINING THE ADEQUACY OF A FEMINIST FRAMEWORK

Space does not allow for a thorough discussion of this difficult question. We editors do believe strongly that one framework is *not* as good as another, that all descriptions of social reality are not equally valid, and that some societies are better structured than others to allow for human fulfillment. But to formulate the precise criteria for the adequacy of a comprehensive social theory is too ambitious an undertaking for this brief introduction. The remarks that follow are necessarily very general.

In part, a theory of women's position in society is evaluated like an ordinary empirical theory—that is to say, by its success in explaining reality and in enabling us to control it. Thus, feminist theories, like all theories, are tested in part by comparison of their claims with the facts of experience. In doing this, however, we must bear in mind that the facts of experience do not present themselves immediately to us; rather, they are known only in terms of a conceptual framework which acts like a filter, in that it emphasizes some features of our experience while ignoring other aspects or even rendering them invisible. This is a special danger in attempting to describe women's situation: Shulamith Firestone begins *The Dialectic of Sex* with the claim that "sex class is invisible," and that a large part of the feminist task is precisely to make it visible. A successful feminist theory must provide us with the conceptual tools for describing our experiences as women and men in the world today, including experiences of which we may hardly have been aware before encountering the theory.

Besides describing social reality, feminist theory must also explain it. Thus, it must help us assess the role played by our biology in shaping various social institutions, and it must enable us to determine how these institutions interact with each other. Only by providing a comprehensive explanation of the deeper causes of women's subordination can a feminist theory function as the guide we need to direct our struggles for social change. In part, then, the adequacy of a feminist explanation of the deeper causes of women's subordination is determined by how well it works in the practical struggle for our own liberation.

Yet the evaluation of a feminist framework is not entirely a practical matter. We have said that the best feminist framework is ultimately the one which most successfully points the way to women's (and thereby human) liberation. It follows that in order to evaluate feminist theories, we require not only an awareness of our own experience, together with a deep understanding of its biological and social genesis, but also a clear notion of what constitutes liberation.

Rather than viewing a feminist theory as setting up a blueprint for the position of women in some future utopia, we believe that it is more helpful to view such a theory as attempting to discover the conditions under which women will be able to exercise significantly free choice about our own future position in society. On this view, liberation ceases to be imagined as some clearly defined end state and is viewed instead as a continual process. To look at feminist theories in this way helps to avoid very abstract speculations about the ultimate nature of liberation and encourages us to focus instead on the specific social institutions which limit our choices. We may then evaluate feminist frameworks according to their success in identifying the conditions which prevent women from freely choosing which of our potentialities we wish to fulfill.

INTRODUCING THE FEMINIST FRAMEWORKS

If we view feminist theories as searching for the conditions which restrict women's freedom to determine our own lives, we have a convenient way of distinguishing between the various theories presented in this book. We have selected five theories or frameworks, only four of which would ordinarily be described as feminist. The first theory, conservatism, attempts to defend women's position in contemporary society by arguing that it is in accord with some kind of biological imperative; hence, conservatives believe that, for women, freedom is something like the knowledge and acceptance of biological necessity. Liberal feminists, on the contrary, argue that liberation for women requires that we have opportunities for education and professional advancement which are equal with those of men. Traditional Marxist feminists believe that the liberal analysis is too superficial: for them, women's oppression is merely a symptom of the pervasive oppression endemic to a class society. Hence, they argue that liberation for women would be achieved with the achievement of a classless society. Radical feminists deny this claim. They believe that the oppression of women may exist within any type of economic system. For them, the liberation of women requires the abolition of the social institution of gender, if not, indeed, the elimination of the biological fact of sex itself. Finally, the socialist feminist reestablishes the classical Marxist connection between class society and sexism but denies the contention that sexism is the less fundamental. For the socialist feminist, women will not be able freely to determine the conditions of our own lives without the elimination both of class society and of the institution of gender.

This initial characterization of the frameworks with which we are going to deal is not intended to sum up all the differences between them. The frameworks are complex, and a careful study of them will inevitably reveal inaccuracy in what we have just said. What this characterization does, however, is illustrate the way in which feminist theory building can be viewed as a dialogue, each theory constructed in order to remedy apparent deficiencies in earlier accounts. Our order of exposition reflects this historical development. This is not to say, of course, that the last theory, socialist feminism, is accepted as any kind of orthodoxy in the women's movement (although we do see increasing acceptance of it and although we ourselves do believe that some version of socialist feminism offers the best hope of providing an adequate conceptual framework for women's liberation). As we remarked, each of the theories presented here currently has its adherents. Indeed, it was precisely the existence of so many feminist frameworks, generating so many acrimonious debates and splits in the women's movement, which partly motivated this book. We should like our book to encourage and facilitate the critical evaluation of the presuppositions and implications of the competing feminist frameworks and hence to contribute to the construction of a fully adequate theory.

THE STRUCTURE OF THE BOOK

The overall structure of this book is designed to facilitate an understanding of the interconnection between specific recommendations for change and their theoretical presuppositions. Part I attempts to show how contemporary social arrangements for organizing various aspects of our lives fail to promote personal happiness and fulfillment. In constructing this section, we have drawn upon the experience of persons of different sexes, ages, and ethnic backgrounds. We have been particularly concerned to show that there are problems in the areas of work, the family, and sexuality, since those are the areas through which we shall examine the feminist frameworks that we present.

Part II of the book presents the major theoretical frameworks within which those problems are examined. We have already mentioned what the frameworks are: conservatism, liberalism, traditional Marxism, radical feminism, and socialist feminism. These theories are presented through the use of selections from classic statements by major proponents of the views.

Finally, in Part III, the feminist frameworks are applied to the problems raised at the outset of the book (work, family, and sexuality), thus demonstrating the alternative solutions generated by different theoretical frameworks. This organization is intended to show the reader how the theories function with respect to specific and concrete issues and to demonstrate the striking differences between the theories when they are employed to solve specific problems of daily life. We hope that this structure will help the reader to avoid treating either the theories or the solutions which they generate in isolation from each other.

IN ACKNOWLEDGMENT

We wish to thank everyone who helped in the preparation of this book. We are especially grateful to Jayne Broughton, The Free Public Library of Montclair, N.J., Barbara Edmondson, Carolyn Shafer, Donna Parisi, Ann McKiernan, Audrey Pelham, Rhona Robbin, Jean Smith, the MAP Women's Study Group, Barbara Chasin, Jill Stone, Laura Warner, Milton Heiberg, Judith Michael, Lillian Margot, Greg, Sharon, David, and Teresa. Thanks also to Sumita, Karuna, and Karl (who enjoyed the pasting), and to our students at The William Paterson College of New Jersey and the University of Cincinnati.

Alison M. Jaggar
Paula Rothenberg Struhl

Part I

The Problem

THE NEED FOR WOMEN'S AND MEN'S LIBERATION

Sex prejudice has been the chief hindrance in the rapid advance of the woman's rights movement to its present status, and it is still a stupendous obstacle to be overcome.

This world taught woman nothing skillful and then said her work was valueless. It permitted her no opinions and said she did not know how to think. It forbade her to speak in public, and said the sex had no orators. It denied her the schools, and said the sex had no genius. It robbed her of every vestige of responsibility and then called her weak. It taught her that every pleasure must come as a favor from men, and when to gain it she decked herself in paint and fine feathers, as she had been taught to do, it called her vain.

Carrie Chapman Catt, 1902

We are born into the world as females and males and then we learn to be women and men. Our society defines what it means to be a woman and a man, and then its institutions administer the necessary lessons. But what we are taught as we grow up depends on other factors as well. Sex role stereotyping takes place within the context of race and class. In other words, the kinds of things we learn and the kinds of experience we have will depend first upon whether we are female or male but in addition will be affected by whether we are black, white, yellow, or red and whether we are rich or poor. At times, these factors will be compounded by yet another factor, namely, age.

The effects of sex, race, and class are so pervasive that it is often difficult to recognize the enormous role they play in shaping the kinds of choices available to us. It is both their comprehensive nature and their strength that have often led people to mistakenly attribute certain characteristics, abilities, and deficiencies to "natural" disposition rather than social conditioning. The articles that appear in Part I are designed to focus our attention on the experiences we have living in contemporary American society. In addition, they can help us remember some of the lessons we learned, in school and out, while we were growing up. What kinds of things were we encouraged to believe about ourselves and each other? Why do we hold these beliefs? What effect do they have on how we treat others and how we expect to be treated? What is the relation between the treatment we receive, the beliefs and values we are taught, and the expectations we form with respect to our futures? These questions are really questions about the effect of ideology. In Part I, Sandra and Daryl Bem explain ideology by talking about the fish who, being entirely submerged in water, never realizes that she is wet. Because we take so much of what happens to us for granted, because the way things are seems so "natural," we may be very much like that fish—all wet without even knowing it.

Several years ago *Psychology Today* magazine did a survey concerning women and work. According to its findings, 95 percent of the women who work are discriminated against, that is, are paid less than a man for doing the same or a comparable job. Unfortunately this statistic will not come as a surprise to many of us. As indicated by the figures in the work tables included in Part I, women workers have been doing badly for a long time, and (in spite of all the attention that the women's movement has received over the past decade) women workers are doing worse now than ever before. In 1970 the income received by full-time women workers amounted to just 59 percent of what a male worker would get; by 1973 that figure had dropped to 57 percent. Even more disturbing, while 95 percent of women workers are discriminated against, only 8 percent actually believe they are discriminated against. The lack of correlation between the way women workers are actually treated on the job and the way we perceive our work experience is one of the many phenomena that prompt us to ask about the force of ideology. Why is it that women who are the subject of outrageous discrimination in the field of employment often fail to either recognize that discrimination or act to change it? Perhaps the answer lies in what women believe to be their real role in life. As so many of the articles in Part I demonstrate, women are raised to be wives and mothers. Most of the messages we receive from our parents, teachers, and friends, as well as what we see on television and in films, set this idea firmly before us. No wonder, then, that women are not always quick to recognize inequitable treatment by their employers. Believing that men are supposed to be the breadwinners and women are primarily wives and mothers, some women workers treat their salaried job as a secondary activity. The force of ideology can hide from them the true extent of the discrimination they experience—and thus can rob both these women and their husbands of their rightful family wage. Ideology can be both powerful and dangerous, as this one example shows.

While all women find themselves at a disadvantage when seeking employment and in the wages and benefits they receive, some women have more touble than others. The woman who is overweight, or older, the woman who has young children, the woman who is unattractive by society's standards, all find even more obstacles in their path. Third-world women, women who are black, chicana, or Latin, suffer especially severe discrimination. As the last table in the section "Women in the Work

Force: Five Tables" indicates, white women are paid less than men, white or black, and black women earn least of all. Two articles in Part I, "Older Working Women" and "Black Women and the Market," paint a picture of the insulting and humiliating kinds of discrimination often experienced by these women.

At the same time that the ideology we have been examining—that is, beliefs about the proper roles for the sexes—gives both women and men reasons for deemphasizing the importance of women's paid labor, it places an unduly heavy emphasis on men's work. If our society evaluates a woman's success in terms of the man or men she attracts, it evaluates the man's success in terms of his ability to provide for his wife and children. The resulting effect is summed up in the title of one of the essays that appear in Part I, "Measuring Masculinity by the Size of a Paycheck." This piece focuses on some of the special pressures that men experience because of sex role stereotyping. Sex roles are reciprocal. Men pay a price in their own lives for the way that society teaches them and us to define femininity.

But sex roles are not entirely inflexible. They are modified constantly, often subtly, by changes in the society at large and particularly by changes in the economic needs of the society. As a result of the spiraling costs of living, the modern family seems increasingly able to tolerate the idea of both husband and wife working—at least until the children come along or after the children are grown. It is not uncommon to hear young women who are married or are about to be married announce proudly, as proof of their liberated relationship, that their husbands or fiancés have told them they can have a career or go out to work if they really want to. (Just imagine how it would sound if a young man made a similar announcement: "My girlfriend promised that I can keep working after our marriage if I really want to.") In any case, even where by mutual agreement both members of the family work, it is usually the case that the husband's job begins at 8:30 or 9 and ends at 5 or 5:30 in the evening. The woman's working hours extend pretty much from waking up in the morning to going to sleep at night. In "The Politics of Housework," Pat Mainardi talks about what happened when she decided to challenge the unequal distribution of housework in her family. Like many women, she found that her husband was willing to help her with "her work"—but only under certain very carefully worked-out conditions. Interesting, isn't it, that in so many relationships, when a man does something as simple as washing his own lunch dishes, he is "helping her with her work"? How did *his* lunch dishes get to be "*her* work" in the first place?

When children come along, the brunt of the responsibility for caring for them usually falls on the mother. This creates a situation that has bad consequences for both the woman and the child. What is ballyhooed as the crowning event in a woman's life in reality makes more demands on her strength and energy and leaves her less time for herself than she ever imagined. In "The Liberation of Children," Deborah Babcox touches upon some of the realities of motherhood that are leading some young women to question having children at all. Not long ago, a nationally syndicated columnist asked her readers whether they would have children if they had it to do over again. The overwhelming majority said no. Nonetheless the mystique attached to motherhood remains strong, so strong that in light of it the choice to have children hardly qualifies as one which is made freely and consciously by most people. Urging people not to have children until they have considered the pros and cons very carefully is still regarded as sacrilege by many people.

One of the central issues that have been raised by the women's movement involves the definition of work. As anyone who has kept house knows, shopping for groceries, washing clothes, planning and preparing meals, cleaning house, and caring for children are hard work. These chores have to be done every day of the week and every day of the year. There are no holidays from laundry or meal planning and preparation. There is no weekend off and no overtime pay. What's more, most if not all work that is done in the home has a peculiar quality to it: it never gets done. Almost as soon as the dishes are washed and dried or unloaded from the dishwasher, they are used again. No sooner is breakfast over than it's time to think about lunch, or dinner, or tomorrow's dinner. Hours are spent washing and ironing clothes, but the laundry basket will probably be half filled again before today's wash is put away. For most of us, performing the chores necessary to keep us going is demanding and difficult—for some it is almost impossible. In "I Just Don't Know If I Can Make It" a young welfare mother talks about the constant struggle to survive that constitutes her life. The account she gives of trying to provide for herself and her child points out one of the ways that the particular problems we face as women can be compounded by our class position. The less we have to spend, the harder we have to work to spend it.

And so much of the American dream revolves around consuming. When we are small girls, we learn to define happiness in terms of the plastic dishes and miniature kitchens that wait for us under the Christmas tree. While boys receive toy trains and building sets, we are given tiny baby carriages for our dolls and toy vacuum cleaners so that we can be "just like Mommy." No wonder that by the time we are grown up we have acquired the habit of investing a lot of energy in buying household items and have actually learned to get satisfaction from buying a new mop, pot, or casserole. In "With an Eye to the Future," which appeared originally in *Modern Bride* magazine, the author skillfully accommodates aspects of the new women's consciousness to the values and needs of a consumer society. Recognizing the emphasis placed by the women's movement on independence and planning for our own future, the author exhorts us to express this independence by purchasing our cookware, china, and crystal even before we have met Mr. Right.

The pressure to buy and show extends to us all, and it comes at a terrible price, as the women who wrote "Black Women in Revolt" seek to demonstrate. Food money is spent on clothes, men lose their own self-esteem and that of their wives and children because they cannot spend enough—the pressure exists for us all, but it affects black and white, rich and poor, in its own special ways, as the articles in Part I show.

Boy children learn early that they will have to develop their skills and abilities if they are to get a good job and become successful providers for their families. Girl children learn, too, that their success will depend on their ability to develop their potential—but the emphasis here will not be so much on what they do as on how they look.

From an early age we scrutinize our bodies and our faces and try to figure out how to package them in a pleasing way. Some will object immediately: What's wrong with looking good? This is a fair question. There's nothing wrong with looking good, but the real question is: What does it take to make you feel good about how you look? For so many of us, our body becomes an object to transform. We wear shoes that keep us from walking easily and never let us run. We wear clothes that make it difficult to sit comfortably and never let us climb up or bend down. We do our hair in styles that destroy its natural texture and color, and then we must stay out of the sun or sleep sitting up to protect it. Before long we have no sense of how our own body and our own face feel. We have become our packaging and will spend our lives dieting and painting and curling and creaming, telling ourselves how much we enjoy "looking good" and never daring to stop for fear that we'll get old and fat and ugly. In "Mirror, Mirror" and "It Hurts to Be Alive and Obsolete" two women, one in her twenties and the other in middle age, tell us about growing up and growing older in American society.

The kind of packaging we have been talking about, and the kind of sex role stereotyping we have been exploring, have consequences for every aspect of our lives. This includes the most intimate parts of our lives, namely, our sexual encounters. In the article about sexual fantasies included in Part I we see some concrete consequences of the way we have been taught to define ourselves and our roles as women and men. If contemporary sex studies are accurate, we as women feel guilty about our sexual feelings and our sexual fantasies. Many of us are real strangers to our own bodies, and some of us regard sex more as something we do for our boyfriends or husbands than as something we do for our mutual pleasure. We are taught that the only acceptable sex occurs between members of opposite sexes, and so we feel guilty and frightened when we experience sexual feelings for other women (and most women do). Our fantasies revolve around "being taken by force" or doing sexual charity work. In both cases our fantasies allow us to experience pleasure without taking any responsibility for it, because that, of course, would be unfeminine.

The other side of the picture is painted by Jack Litewka in his highly personal account of reaching sexual manhood in America. He writes about the pressures on men to perform sexually and about the really tragic consequences that sex role stereotyping and sexual packaging can have on relations between women and men.

Not only is the emphasis on artificial conceptions of beauty and sexuality detrimental to fulfilling human relations; it can, as Susan Radner writes, be downright deadly. As the number of women who are diagnosed as having breast cancer skyrockets, the culture's definition of femininity and its tendency to measure women's worth by their sexual apparatus become a life-and-death matter for many women.

We are what we earn. We are what we buy. We are what we spend. We are our bodies objectified and packaged according to the sexual stereotype. In allowing the stereotype to run our lives as women and as men, we destroy rather than enhance our health and our happiness. Relationships occur between socially defined roles rather than between complete and mature adult human beings. The roles defined by contemporary society create the kind of financial, emotional, and sexual dependency of women on men that makes a really satisfying relationship between people difficult if not impossible. It makes us judge ourselves and evaluate each other by the wrong criteria and then live out our lives in ways that leave us feeling empty and frustrated. The question is: Why?

In the next section we shall begin exploring various answers to that question by placing the ordinary experience of all of us within the context of systematic feminist theories. These theories seek to explain the way in which society defines what it means to be a woman and what it means to be a man. Once we understand in whose interests it is that we define the roles in this way, we will know something about how to change them.

Homogenizing the American Woman:
The Power of an Unconscious Ideology

Sandra L. Bem and Daryl J. Bem

> In the beginning God created the heaven and the earth. . . . And God said, Let us make man in our image, after our likeness; and let him have dominion over the fish of the sea, and over the fowl of the air, and over the cattle, and over all the earth. . . . And the rib, which the Lord God had taken from man, made he a woman and brought her unto the man. . . . And the Lord God said unto the woman, What is this that thou hast done? And the woman said, The serpent beguiled me, and I did eat. . . . Unto the woman God said, I will greatly multiply thy sorrow and thy conception; in sorrow thou shalt bring forth children; and thy desire shall be to thy husband, and he shall rule over thee. (Gen. 1, 2, 3)

There is a moral to that story. St. Paul spells it out even more clearly.

> For a man . . . is the image and glory of God; but the woman is the glory of the man. For the man is not of the woman, but the woman of the man. Neither was the man created for the woman, but the woman for the man. (1 Cor. 11)

> Let the woman learn in silence with all subjection. But suffer not a woman to teach, nor to usurp authority over the man, but to be in silence. For Adam was first formed and then Eve. And Adam was not deceived, but the woman, being deceived, was in the transgression. Notwithstanding, she shall be saved in childbearing, if they continue in faith and charity and holiness with sobriety. (1 Tim. 2)

Now one should not assume that only Christians have this kind of rich heritage of ideology about women. So consider now, the morning prayer of the Orthodox Jew:

> Blessed art Thou, oh Lord our God, King of the Universe, that I was not born a gentile.

> Blessed art Thou, oh Lord our God, King of the Universe, that I was not born a slave.

> Blessed art Thou, oh Lord our God, King of the Universe, that I was not born a woman.

Or, consider the Koran, the sacred text of Islam:

> Men are superior to women on account of the qualities in which God has given them preeminence.

Because they think they sense a decline in feminine "faith, charity, and holiness with sobriety," many people today jump to the conclusion that the ideology expressed in these passages is a relic of the past. Not so, of course. It has simply been obscured by an equalitarian veneer, and the same ideology has now become unconscious. That is, we remain unaware of it because alternative beliefs and attitudes about women, until very recently, have gone unimagined. We are very much like the fish who is unaware of the fact that his environment is wet. After all, what else could it be? Such is the nature of all unconscious ideologies in a society. Such, in particular, is the nature of America's ideology about women.

What we should like to do in this paper is to discuss today's version of this same ideology.

When a baby boy is born, it is difficult to predict what he will be doing 25 years later. We can't say whether he will be an artist, a doctor, a lawyer, a college professor, or a bricklayer, because he will be permitted to develop and fulfill his own unique potential—particularly, of course, if he happens to be white and middle class. But if that same newborn child happens to be a girl, we can predict with almost complete confidence how she is likely to be spending her time some 25 years later. Why can we do that? Because her individuality doesn't have to be considered. Her individuality is irrelevant. Time studies have shown that she will spend the equivalent of a full working day, 7.1 hours, in preparing meals, cleaning house, laundering, mending, shopping and doing other household tasks. In other words, 43 percent of her waking time will be spent in activity that would command an hourly wage on the open market well below the federally set minimum for menial industrial work.

Of course, the point really is not how little she would earn if she did these things in someone else's home. She will be doing them in her own home for free. The point is that this use of time is virtually the same for homemakers with college degrees and for homemakers with less than a grade-school education, for women married to professional men, and for women married to blue-collar workers. Actually, that's understating it slightly. What the time study really showed was that college-educated women spend slightly *more* time cleaning their houses than their less-educated counterparts!

Of course, it is not simply the full-time homemaker whose unique identity has been rendered largely irrelevant. Of the 31 million women who work outside the home in our society, 78 percent end up in dead-end jobs as clerical workers, service workers, factory workers, or sales clerks, compared to a comparable figure of 40 percent for men. Only 15 percent of all women workers in our society are classified by the Labor Department as professional and technical workers, and even this figure is misleading—for the single, poorly-paid occupation of non-college teacher absorbs half of these women, and the occupation of nurse absorbs an additional quarter. In other words, the two jobs of teacher and nurse absorb three-quarters of all women classified in our society as technical or professional. That means, then, that fewer than 5 percent of all professional women—fewer than 1 percent of all women workers—fill those positions which to most Americans connote "professional": physician, lawyer, engineer, scientist, college professor, journalist, writer, and so forth.

Even an I.Q. in the genius range does not guarantee that a woman's unique potential will find expression. There was a famous study of over 1,300 boys and girls whose I.Q.'s averaged 151.[1] When the study began in the early 1900s, these highly gifted youngsters were only ten years old, and their careers have been followed ever since. What are they today? 86 percent of the men have now achieved prominence in professional and managerial occupations. In contrast, only a minority of the women were even employed. Of those who were, 37 percent were nurses, librarians, social workers, and non-college teachers. An additional 26 percent were secretaries, stenographers, bookkeepers, and office workers! Only 11 percent entered the higher professions of law, medicine, college teaching, engineering, science, economics, and the like. And even at age 44, well after all their children had gone to school, 61 percent of these highly gifted women remained full-time homemakers. Talent, education, ability, interests, motivations: all irrelevant. In our society, being female uniquely qualifies an individual for domestic work—either by itself or in conjunction with typing, teaching, nursing, or (most often) unskilled labor. It is this homogenization of America's women which is the major consequence of our society's sex-role ideology.

It is true, of course, that most women have several hours of leisure time every day. And it is here, we are often told, that each woman can express her unique identity. Thus, politically interested women can join the League of Women Voters. Women with humane interests can become part-time Gray Ladies. Women who love music can raise money for the symphony. Protestant women play canasta; Jewish woman play mah-jongg; brighter women of all denominations and faculty wives play bridge.

But politically interested *men* serve in legislatures. *Men* with humane interests become physicians or clinical psychologists. *Men* who love music play in the symphony. In other words, why should a woman's unique identity determine only the periphery of her life rather than its central core?

Why? Why nurse rather than physician, secretary rather than executive, stewardess rather than pilot? Why faculty wife rather than faculty? Why doctor's mother rather than doctor? There are three basic answers to this question: (1) discrimination; (2) sex-role conditioning; and (3) the presumed incompatibility of family and career.

Discrimination

In 1968, the median income of full-time women workers was approximately $4,500. The comparable figure for men was $3,000 higher. Moreover, the gap is widening. Ten years ago, women earned 64 percent of what men did; that percentage has now shrunk to 58 percent. Today, a female college graduate working full-time can expect to earn less per year than a male high-school dropout.

There are two reasons for this pay differential. First, in every category of occupation, women are employed in the lesser-skilled, lower-paid positions.

---

[1]L. M. Terman and M. H. Oden, *The Gifted Group at Mid-Life: Thirty-Five Years' Follow-up of the Superior Child,* Genetic Studies of Genius, V (Stanford, Calif.: Stanford University Press, 1959).

Even in the clerical field, where 73 percent of the workers are women, females are relegated to the lowest status positions and hence earn only 65 percent of what male clerical workers earn. The second reason for this pay differential is discrimination in its purest form: unequal pay for equal work. According to a survey of 206 companies in 1970, female college graduates were offered jobs which paid $43 per month less than those offered to their male counterparts in the same college major.

New laws should begin to correct both of these situations. The Equal Pay Act of 1963 prohibits employers from discriminating on the basis of sex in the payment of wages for equal work. In a landmark ruling on May 18, 1970, the U.S. Supreme Court ordered that $250,000 in back pay be paid to women employed by a single New Jersey glass company. This decision followed a two-year court battle by the Labor Department after it found that the company was paying men selector-packers 21.5 cents more per hour than women doing the same work. In a similar case, the Eighth Circuit Court of Appeals ordered a major can company to pay more than $100,000 in back wages to women doing equal work. According to the Labor Department, an estimated $17 million is owed to women in back pay. Since that estimate was made, a 1972 amendment extended the Act to cover executive, administrative, and professional employees as well.

But to enjoy equal pay, women must also have access to equal jobs. Title VII of the 1964 Civil Rights Act prohibits discrimination in employment on the basis of race, color, religion, national origin—and sex. Although the sex provision was treated as a joke at the time (and was originally introduced by a Southern Congressman in an attempt to defeat the bill), the Equal Employment Opportunities Commission discovered in its first year of operation that 40 percent or more of the complaints warranting investigation charged discrimination on the basis of sex.[2]

Title VII has served as one of the most effective instruments in helping to achieve sex equality in the world of work. According to a report by the E.E.O.C., nearly 6,000 charges of sex discrimination were filed with that agency in 1971 alone, a 62 percent increase over the previous year.

But the most significant legislative breakthrough in the area of sex equality was the passage of the Equal Rights Amendment by both houses of Congress in 1972. The ERA simply states that "Equality of rights under the law shall not be denied or abridged by the United States or by any state on account of sex." This amendment has been introduced into every session of Congress since 1923, and its passage now is clearly an indication of the changing role of the American woman. All of the various ramifications are hard to predict, but it is clear that it will have profound consequences in private as well as public life.

Many Americans assume that the recent drive for equality between the sexes is primarily for the benefit of the middle-class woman who wants to seek self-fulfillment in a professional career. But in many ways, it is the woman in

[2]C. Bird, *Born Female: The High Cost of Keeping Women Down* (New York, Pocket Books, 1969).

more modest circumstances, the woman who *must* work for economic reasons, who stands to benefit most from the removal of discriminatory barriers. It is *she* who is hardest hit by unequal pay; it is *she* who so desperately needs adequate day-care facilities; it is *her* job which is often dead-ended while her male colleagues in the factory get trained and promoted into the skilled craft jobs. And if both she and her husband work at unfulfilling jobs eight hours a day just to make an adequate income, it is still *she* who carries the additional burden of domestic chores when they return home.

We think it is important to emphasize these points at the outset, for we have chosen to focus our remarks in this particular paper on those fortunate men and women who can afford the luxury of pursuing self-fulfillment through the world of work and career. But every societal reform advocated by the new feminist movement, whether it be the Equal Rights Amendment, the establishment of child-care centers, or basic changes in America's sex-role ideology, will affect the lives of men and women in every economic circumstance. Nevertheless, it is still economic discrimination which hits hardest at the largest group of women, and it is here that the drive for equality can be most successfully launched with legislative and judicial tools.

Sex-Role Conditioning

But even if all discrimination were to end tomorrow, nothing very drastic would change. For job discrimination is only part of the problem. It does impede women who choose to become lawyers or managers or physicians. But it does not, by itself, help us to understand why so many women "choose" to be secretaries or nurses rather than executives or physicians; why only 3 percent of ninth-grade girls as compared to 25 percent of the boys "choose" careers in science or engineering; or why 63 percent of America's married women "choose" not to work at all. It certainly doesn't explain those young women whose vision of the future includes only marriage, children, and living happily ever after; who may, at some point, "choose" to take a job, but who almost never "choose" to pursue a career. Discrimination frustrates choices already made. Something more pernicious perverts the motivation to choose.

That "something" is an unconscious ideology about the nature of the female sex, an ideology which constricts the emerging self-image of the female child and the nature of her aspirations from the very beginning; an ideology which leads even those Americans who agree that a black skin should not uniquely qualify *its* owner for a janitorial or domestic service to act as if the possession of a uterus uniquely qualifies *its* owner for precisely such service.

Consider, for example, the 1968 student rebellion at Columbia University. Students from the radical Left took over some administration buildings in the name of equalitarian ideals which they accused the university of flouting. Here were the most militant spokesmen one could hope to find in the cause of equalitarian ideals. But no sooner had they occupied the buildings than the male militants blandly turned to their sisters-in-arms and assigned them the task of preparing the food, while they—the menfolk—would presumably plan future strategy. The reply these males received was the reply that they deserved—we will leave that to your imagination—and the fact that domestic tasks behind the barricades were desegregated across the sex line that day is an everlasting tribute to the class consciousness of these ladies of the Left. And it was really on that day that the campus women's liberation movement got its start—when radical women finally realized that they were never going to get to make revolution, only coffee.

But these conscious co-eds are not typical, for the unconscious assumptions about a woman's "natural" talents (or lack of them) are at least as prevalent among women as they are among men. A psychologist named Phillip Goldberg demonstrated this by asking female college students to rate a number of professional articles from each of six fields.[3] The articles were collated into two equal sets of booklets, and the names of the authors were changed so that the identical article was attributed to a male author (e.g., John T. McKay) in one booklet and to a female author (e.g., Joan T. McKay) in the other booklet. Each student was asked to read the articles in her booklet and to rate them for value, competence, persuasiveness, writing style, and so forth.

As he had anticipated, Goldberg found that the identical article received significantly lower ratings when it was attributed to a female author than when it was attributed to a male author. He had predicted this result for articles from professional fields generally considered the province of men, like law or city planning, but to his surprise, these women also downgraded articles from the fields of dietetics and elementary-school education when they were attributed to female authors. In other words, these students rated the male authors as better at everything, agreeing with Aristotle that "we should regard the female nature as afflicted with a natural defectiveness." Such is the nature of America's unconscious ideology about women.

When does this ideology begin to affect the life of a young girl? Research now tells us that from the day a newborn child is dressed in pink, she is given "special" treatment. Perhaps because they are thought to be more fragile, six-month-old infant girls are actually touched, spoken to, and hovered over more by their mothers while they are playing than are infant boys.[4] One study even showed that when mothers and babies are still in the hospital, mothers smile at, talk to, and touch their female infants more than their male infants at two days of age.[5] Differential treatment can't begin much earlier than that.

As children begin to read, the storybook characters become the images and the models that little boys and little girls aspire to become. What kind of role does the female play in the world of children's literature? The fact is that there aren't even very many females in that world. One survey[6] found that five times as many males as females appear in the titles of children's books; the fantasy world of

[3]Phillip Goldberg, "Are Women Prejudiced Against Women?" *Transaction* 5 (April 1968), 28–30.

[4]S. Goldberg and M. Lewis, "Play Behavior in the Year-old Infant: Early Sex Differences," *Child Development* 40 (1969), 21–31.

[5]E. B. Thoman, P. H. Leiderman, and J. P. Olson, "Neonate-Mother Interaction during Breast Feeding," *Developmental Psychology* 6 (1972), 110–118.

[6]E. Fisher, "The Second Sex, Junior Division," *The New York Times Book Review,* May 1970.

Doctor Seuss is almost entirely male; and even animals and machines are represented as male. When females do appear, they are noteworthy primarily for what they do *not* do. They do not drive cars, and they seldom even ride bicycles. In one story in which a girl does ride a bicycle, it's a two-seater. Guess where the girl is seated! Boys in these stories climb trees and fish and roll in the leaves and skate. Girls watch, fall down, and get dizzy. Girls are never doctors, and although they may be nurses or librarians or teachers, they are never principals. There seemed to be only one children's book about mothers who work, and it concludes that what mothers love "best of all" is "being your very own Mommy and coming home to you." And although this is no doubt true of many daddies as well, no book about working fathers has ever found it necessary to apologize for working in quite the same way.

As children grow older, more explicit sex-role training is introduced. Boys are encouraged to take more of an interest in mathematics and science. Boys, not girls, are usually given chemistry sets and microscopes for Christmas. Moreover, all children quickly learn that mommy is proud to be a moron when it comes to math and science, whereas daddy is a little ashamed if he doesn't know all about such things. When a young boy returns from school all excited about biology, he is almost certain to be encouraged to think of becoming a physician. A girl with similar enthusiasm is usually told that she might want to consider nurse's training later on, so she can have "an interesting job to fall back upon in case—God forbid—she ever needs to support herself." A very different kind of encouragement. And any girl who doggedly persists in her enthusiasm for science is likely to find her parents as horrified by the prospect of a permanent love affair with physics as they would be either by the prospect of an interracial marriage or, horror of horrors, no marriage at all. Indeed, our graduate women report that their families seem convinced that the menopause must come at age 23.

These socialization practices take their toll. When they apply for college, boys and girls are about equal on verbal aptitude tests, but boys score significantly higher on mathematical aptitude tests—about 60 points higher on the College Board Exams.[7] Moreover, for those who are convinced that this is due to female hormones, it is relevant to know that girls improve their mathematical performance if the problems are simply reworded so that they deal with cooking and gardening, even though the abstract reasoning required for solution remains exactly the same.[8] That's not hormones! Clearly, what has been undermined is not a woman's mathematical ability, but rather her confidence in that ability.

But these effects in mathematics and science are only part of the story. The most conspicuous outcome of all is that the majority of America's women become full-time homemakers. And of those who do work, nearly 80 percent end up in dead-end jobs as clerical workers, service workers, factory workers, or sales clerks. Again, it is this "homogenization" of America's women which is the major consequence of America's sex-role ideology.

[7]For example, R. Brown, *Social Psychology* (New York: Free Press, 1965).
[8]G. A. Milton, "Sex Differences in Problem Solving as a Function of Role Appropriateness of the Problem Content," *Psychological Reports* 5 (1959), 705–708.

The important point is not that the role of homemaker is necessarily inferior, but rather that our society is managing to consign a large segment of its population to the role of homemaker—either with or without a dead-end job—solely on the basis of sex just as inexorably as it has in the past consigned the individual with a black skin to the role of janitor or domestic. The important point is that in spite of their unique identities, the majority of American women end up in virtually the *same* role.

The socialization of the American male has closed off certain options for him, too. Men are discouraged from developing certain desirable traits such as tenderness and sensitivity, just as surely as women are discouraged from being assertive and, alas, "too bright." Young boys are encouraged to be incompetent at cooking and certainly child care, just as surely as young girls are urged to be incompetent at math and science. The elimination of sex-role stereotyping implies that each individual would be encouraged to "do his own thing." Men and women would no longer be stereotyped by society's definitions of masculine and feminine. If sensitivity, emotionality, and warmth are desirable *human* characteristics, then they are desirable for men as well as for women. If independence, assertiveness, and serious intellectual commitment are desirable *human* characteristics, then they are desirable for women as well as for men. Thus, we are not implying that men have all the goodies and that women can obtain self-fulfillment by acting like men. That is hardly the utopia implied by today's feminist movement. Rather, we envision a society which raises its children so flexibly and with sufficient respect for the integrity of individual uniqueness that some men might emerge with the motivation, the ability, and the opportunity to stay home and raise children without bearing the stigma of being peculiar. Indeed, if homemaking is as glamorous as women's magazines and television commercials would have us believe, then men, too, should have that option. And even if homemaking isn't all that glamorous, it would probably still be more fulfilling for some men than the jobs in which they now find themselves forced because of their role as breadwinner. Thus, it is true that a man's options are also limited by our society's sex-role ideology, but as the "predictability test" reveals, it is still the woman in our society whose identity is rendered irrelevant by America's socialization practices.

Further Psychological Barriers

But what of the woman who arrives at age 21 still motivated to be challenged and fulfilled by a growing career? Is she free to choose a career if she cares to do so? Or is there something standing even in her way?

There is. Even the woman who has managed to finesse society's attempt to rob her of her career motivations is likely to find herself blocked by society's trump card: the feeling that one cannot have a career and be a successful woman simultaneously. A competent and motivated woman is thus caught in a double-bind which few men have ever faced. She must worry not only about failure, but also about success.

This conflict was strikingly revealed in a study which required college women to complete the following story: "After first-term finals, Anne finds herself at the top of her medical-school class."[9] The stories were then examined for concern about the negative consequences of success. The women in this study all had high intellectual ability and histories of academic success. They were the very women who could have successful careers. And yet, over two-thirds of their stories revealed a clear-cut inability to cope with the concept of a feminine, yet career-oriented, woman.

The most common "fear-of-success" stories showed fears of social rejection as a result of success. The women in this group showed anxiety about becoming unpopular, unmarriageable, and lonely:

> Anne starts proclaiming her surprise and joy. Her fellow classmates are so disgusted with her behavior that they jump on her in a body and beat her. She is maimed for life.

> Anne is an acne-faced bookworm. . . . She studies twelve hours a day, and lives at home to save money. "Well, it certainly paid off. All the Friday and Saturday nights without dates, fun—I'll be the best woman doctor alive." And yet a twinge of sadness comes through—she wonders what she really has. . . .

> Anne doesn't want to be number one in her class. . . . She feels she shouldn't rank so high because of social reasons. She drops to ninth and then marries the boy who graduates number one.

In the second "fear-of-success" category were stories in which the women seemed concerned about definitions of womanhood. These stories expressed guilt and despair over success and doubts about their femininity and normality:

> Unfortunately Anne no longer feels so certain that she really wants to be a doctor. She is worried about herself and wonders if perhaps she is not normal. . . . Anne decides not to continue with her medical work but to take courses that have a deeper personal meaning for her.

> Anne feels guilty. . . . She will finally have a nervous breakdown and quit medical school and marry a successful young doctor.

A third group of stories could not even face up to the conflict between having a career and being a woman. These stories simply denied the possibility that any woman could be so successful:

> Anne is a code name for a nonexistent person created by a group of med students. They take turns writing for Anne. . . .

> Anne is really happy she's on top, though Tom is higher than she—though that's as it should be. Anne doesn't mind Tom winning.

> Anne is talking to her counselor. Counselor says she will make a fine nurse.

[9]M. S. Horner, "Fail: Bright Women," *Psychology Today,* November 1969.

By way of contrast, here is a typical story written not about Anne, but about John:

> John has worked very hard and his long hours of study have paid off. . . . He is thinking about his girl, Cheri, whom he will marry at the end of med school. He realizes he can give her all the things she desires after he becomes established. He will go on in med school and be successful in the long run.

Nevertheless, there were a few women in the study who welcomed the prospect of success:

> Anne is quite a lady—not only is she top academically, but she is liked and admired by her fellow students—quite a trick in a man-dominated field. She is brilliant—but she is also a woman. She will continue to be at or near the top. And . . . always a lady.

Hopefully the day is approaching when as many "Anne" stories as "John" stories will have happy endings. But notice that even this story finds it necessary to affirm repeatedly that femininity is not necessarily destroyed by accomplishment. One would never encounter a comparable story written about John who, although brilliant and at the top of his class, is "still a man, still a man, still a man."

It seems unlikely that anyone in our society would view these "fear-of-success" stories as portraits of mental health. But even our concept of mental health has been distorted by America's sex-role stereotypes. Here we must indict our own profession of psychology. A recent survey of seventy-nine clinically-trained psychologists, psychiatrists, and social workers, both male and female, revealed a double standard of mental health.[10] That is, even professional clinicians have two different concepts of mental health, one for men and one for women; and these concepts parallel the sex-role stereotypes prevalent in our society. Thus, according to these clinicians, a woman is to be regarded as healthier and more mature if she is: more submissive, less independent, less adventurous, more easily influenced, less aggressive, less competitive, more excitable in minor crises, more susceptible to hurt feelings, more emotional, more conceited about her appearance, less objective, and more antagonistic toward math and science! But this was the very same description which these clinicians used to characterize an unhealthy, immature man or an unhealthy, immature adult (sex unspecified)! The equation is clear: Mature woman equals immature adult.

Given this concept of a mature woman, is it any wonder that few women ever aspire toward challenging and fulfilling careers? In order to have a career, a woman will probably need to become relatively more dominant, independent,

[10]I. K. Broverman et al., "Sex-Role Stereotypes and Clinical Judgments of Mental Health," *Journal of Consulting and Clinical Psychology* 34 (1970), 1–7.

adventurous, aggressive, competitive, and objective, and relatively less excit-able, emotional and conceited than our ideal of femininity requires. If she were a man (or an adult, sex unspecified), these would all be considered positive traits. But because she is a woman, these same traits will bring her disapproval. She must then either be strong enough to have her "femininity" questioned; or she must behave in the prescribed feminine manner and accept second-class status, as an adult and as a professional.

And, of course, should a woman faced with this conflict seek professional help, hoping to summon the strength she will need to pursue her career goals, the advice she is likely to receive will be of virtually no use. For, as this study reveals, even professional counselors have been contaminated by the sex-role ideology.

It is frequently argued that a 21-year-old woman is perfectly free to choose a career if she cares to do so. No one is standing in her way. But this argument conveniently overlooks the fact that our society has spent 20 years carefully marking the woman's ballot for her, and so it has nothing to lose in that 21st year by pretending to let her cast it for the alternative of her choice. Society has controlled not her alternatives (although discrimination does do that), but more importantly, it has controlled her motivation to choose any but one of those alternatives. The so-called freedom-to-choose is illusory, and it cannot be invoked to justify a society which controls the woman's motivation to choose.

Biological Considerations

Up to this point, we have argued that the differing life patterns of men and women in our society can be chiefly accounted for by cultural conditioning. The most common counterargument to this view, of course, is the biological one. The biological argument suggests that there may really be inborn differences between men and women in, say, independence or mathematical ability. Or that there may be biological factors beyond the fact that women can become pregnant and nurse children which uniquely dictate that they, but not men, should stay home all day and shun serious outside commitment. What this argument suggests is that maybe female hormones really are responsible somehow. One difficulty with this argument, of course, is that female hormones would have to be different in the Soviet Union, where one-third of the engineers and 75 percent of the physicians are women.[11] In America, by way of contrast, women constitute less than 1 percent of the engineers and only 7 percent of the physicians. Female physiology *is* different, and it may account for some of the psychological differences between the sexes, but America's sex-role ideology still seems primarily responsible for the fact that so few women emerge from childhood with the motivation to seek out any role beyond the one that our society dictates.

But even if there really were biological differences between the sexes along these lines, the biological argument would still be irrelevant. The reason can best be illustrated with an analogy.

Suppose that every black American boy were to be socialized to become a

[11]N. D. Dodge, *Women in the Soviet Economy* (Baltimore: Johns Hopkins Press, 1966).

jazz musician on the assumption that he was a "natural" talent in that direction; or suppose that parents and counselors should subtly discourage him from other pursuits because it is considered "inappropriate" for black men to become physicians or physicists. Most Americans would disapprove. But suppose that it *could* be demonstrated that black Americans, *on the average,* did possess an inborn better sense of rhythm than white Americans. Would *that* justify ignoring the unique characteristics of a *particular* black youngster from the very beginning and specifically socializing him to become a musician? We don't think so. Similarly, as long as a woman's socialization does not nurture her uniqueness, but treats her only as a member of a group on the basis of some assumed *average* characteristic, she will not be prepared to realize her own potential in the way that the values of individuality and self-fulfillment imply that she should.

The Presumed Incompatibility of Family and Career

If we were to ask the average American woman why she is not pursuing a full-time career, she would probably not say that discrimination had discouraged her; nor would she be likely to recognize the pervasive effects of her own sex-role conditioning. What she probably would say is that a career, no matter how desirable, is simply incompatible with the role of wife and mother.

As recently as the turn of the century, and in less technological societies today, this incompatibility between career and family was, in fact, decisive. Women died in their forties and they were pregnant or nursing during most of their adult lives. Moreover, the work that a less technological society requires places a premium on mobility and physical strength, neither of which a pregnant woman has a great deal of. Thus, the historical division of labor between the sexes—the man away at work and the woman at home with the children—was a biological necessity. Today it is not.

Today, the work that our technological society requires is primarily mental in nature, women have virtually complete control over their reproductive lives; and most important of all, the average American woman now lives to age 74 and has her last child before age 30. This means that by the time a woman is 35 or so, her children have more important things to do with their daytime hours than to spend them entertaining some adult woman who has nothing fulfilling to do during the entire second half of her life span.

But social forms have a way of outliving the necessities which gave rise to them. And today's female adolescent continues to plan for a nineteenth-century life style in a twentieth-century world. A Gallup poll has found that young women give no thought whatever to life after forty.[12] They plan to graduate from high school, perhaps go to college, and then get married. Period!

The Woman as Wife

At some level, of course, this kind of planning is "realistic." Because most women do grow up to be wives and mothers, and because, for many women, this

---

[12]G. Gallup and E. Hill, "The American Woman," *The Saturday Evening Post,* 22 December 1962, pp 15–32.

means that they will be leaving the labor force during the child-rearing years, a career is not really feasible. After all, a career involves long-term commitment and perhaps some sacrifice on the part of the family. Furthermore, as every "successful" woman knows, a wife's appropriate role is to encourage her husband in *his* career. The "good" wife puts her husband through school, endures the family's early financial difficulties without a whimper, and, if her husband's career should suddenly dictate a move to another city, she sees to it that the transition is accomplished as painlessly as possible. The good wife is selfless. And to be seriously concerned about one's own career is selfish—if one is female, that is. With these kinds of constraints imposed upon the work life of the married woman, perhaps it would be "unrealistic" for her to seriously aspire toward a career rather than a job.

There is some evidence of discontent among these "selfless" women, however. A 1962 Gallup poll revealed that only 10 percent of American women would want their daughters to live their lives the way they did.[13] These mothers wanted their daughters to get more education and to marry later. And a 1970 study of women married to top Chicago-area business and professional men revealed that if these women could live their lives over again, they would pursue careers.[14]

Accordingly, the traditional conception of the husband-wife relationship is now being challenged, not so much because of this widespread discontent among older, married women, but because it violates two of the most basic values of today's college generation. These values concern personal growth, on the one hand, and interpersonal relationships on the other. The first of these emphasizes individuality and self-fulfillment; the second stresses openness, honesty, and equality in all human relationships.

Because they see the traditional male-female relationship as incompatible with these basic values, today's young people are experimenting with alternatives to the traditional marriage pattern. Although a few are testing out ideas like communal living, most seem to be searching for satisfactory modifications of the husband-wife relationship, either in or out of the context of marriage. An increasing number of young people claim to be seeking fully equalitarian relationships and they cite examples like the following:

Both my wife and I earned college degrees in our respective disciplines. I turned down a superior job offer in Oregon and accepted a slightly less desirable position in New York where my wife would have more opportunities for part-time work in her specialty. Although I would have preferred to live in a suburb, we purchased a home near my wife's job so that she could have an office at home where she would be when the children returned from school. Because my wife earns a good salary, she can easily afford to pay a housekeeper to do her major household chores. My wife and I share all other tasks around the house equally. For example, she cooks the meals, but I do the laundry for her and help her with many of her other household tasks.

[13]Ibid.
[14]M. Ringo, "The Well-placed Wife" (Chicago: John Paisios & Associates, 332 South Michigan Ave., Unpublished manuscript).

Without questioning the basic happiness of such a marriage or its appropriateness for many couples, we can legitimately ask if such a marriage is, in fact, an instance of interpersonal equality. Have all the hidden assumptions about the woman's "natural" role really been eliminated? Have our visionary students really exorcised the traditional ideology as they claim? There is a very simple test. If the marriage is truly equalitarian, then its description should retain the same flavor and tone even if the roles of the husband and wife were to be reversed:

Both my husband and I earned college degrees in our respective disciplines. I turned down a superior job offer in Oregon and accepted a slightly less desirable position in New York where my husband would have more opportunities for part-time work in his specialty. Although I would have preferred to live in a suburb, we purchased a home near my husband's job so that he could have an office at home where he would be when the children returned from school. Because my husband earns a good salary, he can easily afford to pay a housekeeper to do his major household chores. My husband and I share all other tasks around the house equally. For example, he cooks the meals, but I do the laundry for him and help him with many of his other household tasks.

Somehow it sounds different, and yet only the pronouns have been changed to protect the powerful! Certainly no one would ever mistake the marriage *just* described as equalitarian or even very desirable, and thus it becomes apparent that the ideology about the woman's "natural" place unconsciously permeates the entire fabric of such "pseudo-equalitarian" marriages. It is true the wife gains some measure of equality when she can have a career rather than have a job and when her career can influence the final place of residence. But why is it the unquestioned assumption that the husband's career solely determines the initial set of alternatives that are to be considered? Why is it the wife who automatically seeks the part-time position? Why is it *her* housekeeper rather than *their* housekeeper? Why *her* household tasks? And so forth throughout the entire relationship.

The important point is not that such marriages are bad or that their basic assumptions of inequality produce unhappy, frustrated women. Quite the contrary. It is the very happiness of the wives in such marriages that reveals society's smashing success in socializing its women. It is a measure of the distance our society must yet traverse toward the goal of full equality that such marriages are widely characterized as utopian and fully equalitarian. It is a mark of how well the woman has been kept in her place that the husband in such a marriage is almost always idolized by women, including his wife. Why? Because he "permits her" to squeeze a career into the interstices of their marriage as long as his own career is not unduly inconvenienced. Thus is the white man blessed for exercising his power benignly while his "natural" right to that power forever remains unquestioned. Such is the subtlety of America's ideology about women.

In fact, however, even these "benign" inequities are now being challenged. More and more young couples really are entering marriages of full equality, marriages in which both partners pursue careers or outside commitments which carry equal weight when all important decisions are to be made, marriages in which both husband and wife accept some compromise in the growth of their respective careers for their mutual partnership. Certainly such marriages have more tactical difficulties than more traditional ones: It is simply more difficult to coordinate two independent lives rather than one-and-a-half. The point is that it is not possible to predict ahead of time *on the basis of sex,* who will be doing the compromising at any given point of decision.

It should be clear that the man or woman who places career above all else ought not to enter an equalitarian marriage. The man would do better to marry a traditional wife, a wife who will make whatever sacrifices his career necessitates. The woman who places career above all else would do better—in our present society—to remain single. For an equalitarian marriage is not designed for extra efficiency, but for double fulfillment.

The Woman as Mother

In all marriages, whether traditional, pseudo-equalitarian or fully equalitarian, the real question surrounding a mother's career will probably continue to be the well-being of the children. All parents want to be certain that they are doing the very best for their children and that they are not depriving them in any important way, either materially or psychologically. What this has meant recently in most families that could afford it was that mother would devote herself to the children on a full-time basis. Women have been convinced—by their mothers and by the so-called experts—that there is something wrong with them if they even want to do otherwise.

For example, according to Dr. Spock, any woman who finds full-time motherhood unfulfilling is showing "a residue of difficult relationships in her own childhood."[15] If a vacation doesn't solve the problem, then she is probably having emotional problems which can be relieved "through regular counseling in a family social agency, or if severe, through psychiatric treatment . . . Any mother of a pre-school child who is considering a job should discuss the issues with a social worker before making her decision." The message is clear: If you don't feel that your two-year-old is a stimulating, full-time, companion, then you are probably neurotic.

In fact, research does not support the view that children suffer in any way when mother works. Although it came as a surprise to most researchers in the area, maternal employment in and of itself does not seem to have any negative effects on the children; and part-time work actually seems to benefit the children. Children of working mothers are no more likely than children of non-working mothers to be delinquent or nervous or withdrawn or antisocial; they are no more likely to show neurotic symptoms; they are no more likely to perform poorly in school; and they are no more likely to feel deprived of their mothers' love. Daughters of working mothers are more likely to want to work themselves, and,

[15]B. Spock, "Should Mothers Work?" *Ladies' Home Journal,* February 1963.

when asked to name the one woman in the world that they most admire, daughters of working mothers are more likely to name their own mothers![16] This is one finding that we wish every working woman in America could hear because the other thing that is true of almost every working mother is that she *thinks* she is hurting her children and she feels guilty. In fact, research has shown that the worst mothers are those who would like to work, but who stay home out of a sense of duty.[17] The major conclusion from all the research is really this: What matters is the quality of a mother's relationship with her children, not the time of day it happens to be administered. This conclusion should become as no surprise; successful fathers have been demonstrating it for years. Some fathers are great, some fathers stink, and they're all at work at least eight hours a day.

Similarly, it is true that the quality of substitute care that children receive while their parents are at work also matters. Young children do need security, and research has shown that it is not good to have a constant turnover of parent-substitutes, a rapid succession of changing baby-sitters or housekeepers.[18] Clearly, this is why the establishment of child-care centers is vitally important at the moment. This is why virtually every woman's group in the country, no matter how conservative or how radical, is in agreement on this one issue: that child-care centers ought to be available to those who need them.

Once again, it is relevant to emphasize that child-care centers, like the other reforms advocated, are not merely for the benefit of middle-class women who wish to pursue professional careers. Of the 31 million women in the labor force, nearly 40 percent of them are working mothers. In 1960, mothers constituted more than one-third of the total woman labor force. In March 1971, more than 1 out of 3 working mothers (4.3 million of them) had children under 6 years of age, and about half of these had children under 3 years of age. And most of these women in the labor force—like most men—work because they cannot afford to do otherwise. Moreover, they cannot currently deduct the full costs of child care as a business expense as the executive can often deduct an expensive car. At the moment, the majority of these working women must simply "make do" with whatever child-care arrangements they can manage. Only 6 percent of their children under 6 years of age currently receive group care in child-care centers. *This* is why child-care centers are a central issue of the new feminist movement. This is why they are not just an additional luxury for the middle-class family with a woman who wants to pursue a professional career.

But even the woman who is educationally and economically in a position to pursue a career must feel free to utilize these alternative arrangements for child care. For once again, America's sex-role ideology intrudes. Many people still assume that if a woman wants a full-time career, then children must be unimpor-

[16]F. I. Nye and L. W. Hoffman, *The Employed Mother in America* (Chicago: Rand McNally, 1963).

[17]M. R. Yarrow et al., "Child-rearing in Families of Working and Non-Working Mothers," *Sociometry* 25 (1962), 122–140.

[18]E. E. Maccoby, "Effects upon Children of Their Mothers' Outside Employment," in *Work in the Lives of Married Women* (New York: Columbia University Press, 1958).

tant to her. But of course, no one makes this assumption about her husband. No one assumes that a father's interest in his career necessarily precludes a deep and abiding affection for his children or a vital interest in their development. Once again, America applies a double standard of judgment. Suppose that a father of small children suddenly lost his wife. No matter how much he loved his children, no one would expect him to sacrifice his career in order to stay home with them on a full-time basis—even if he had an independent source of income. No one would charge him with selfishness or lack of parental feeling if he sought professional care for his children during the day.

It is here that full equality between husband and wife assumes its ultimate importance. The fully equalitarian marriage abolishes this double standard and extends the same freedom to the mother. The equalitarian marriage provides the framework for both husband and wife to pursue careers which are challenging and fulfilling and, at the same time, to participate equally in the pleasures and responsibilities of child-rearing. Indeed, it is the equalitarian marriage which has the potential for giving children the love and concern of two parents rather than one. And it is the equalitarian marriage which has the most potential for giving parents the challenge and fulfillment of two worlds—family and career—rather than one.

In addition to providing this potential for equalized child care, a truly equalitarian marriage embraces a more general division of labor which satisfies what we like to call "the roommate test." That is, the labor is divided just as it is when two men or two women room together in college or set up a bachelor apartment together. Errands and domestic chores are assigned by preference, agreement, flipping a coin, alternated, given to hired help, or—perhaps most often the case—left undone.

It is significant that today's young people, so many of whom live precisely this way prior to marriage, find this kind of arrangement within marriage so foreign to their thinking. Consider an analogy. Suppose that a white male college student decided to room or set up a bachelor apartment with a black male friend. Surely the typical white student would not blithely assume that his black roommate was to handle all the domestic chores. Nor would his conscience allow him to do so even in the unlikely event that his roommate would say: "No, that's okay. I like doing housework. I'd be happy to do it." We suspect that the typical white student would still not be comfortable if he took advantage of this offer because he and America have finally realized that he would be taking advantage of the fact that such a roommate had been socialized by our society to be "happy" with such obvious inequity. But change this hypothetical black roommate to a female marriage partner, and somehow the student's conscience goes to sleep. At most it is quickly tranquilized by the comforting thought that "she is happiest when she is ironing for her loved one." Such is the power of an unconscious ideology.

Of course, it may well be that she *is* happiest when she is ironing for her loved one.

Such, indeed, is the power of an unconscious ideology.

Women in the Work Force: Five Tables

The Female Labor Force

	Female labor force as per cent of total labor force	Female labor force as per cent of female population		Employed married women as per cent of female labor force
		Total	Married	
1890	16	18	5	14
1900	18	20	6	15
1910	21	24	11	15
1920	20	23	9	23
1930	22	24	12	29
1940	25	27	17	36
1950	29	31	25	52
1960	33	35	32	60
1970	38	43	41	63

Sources: U.S. Bureau of the Census, *Statistical Abstract of the United States: 1973* (Washington, D.C., 1973), pp. 219, 221, 222; U.S. Bureau of the Census, *Historical Statistics of the United States; Colonial Times to 1957* (Washington, D.C., 1961), pp. 71, 72; U.S. Bureau of the Census, *Fifteenth Census of the United States: 1930–Population*, vol. IV, *Occupations* (Washington, D.C., 1933), p. 69; Joseph A. Hill, *Women in Gainful Occupations, 1870–1920*, Census Monographs, IX (Washington, D.C., 1929), pp. 52, 76; Sophonisba P. Breckinridge, *Women in the Twentieth Century: A Study of Their Political, Social and Economic Activities* (New York, 1933), pp. 116, 117.

The Income of Women Is One-third of the Income of Men

	Men	Women	Women's income as a percentage of men's
1947	$2,230	$1,017	46%
1950	2,570	953	37
1960	4,081	1,262	31
1970	6,670	2,237	34
1973	8,056	2,796	35

Note: This table only includes people who received some money income during the year. *Income* refers to everything from salaries to welfare benefits to interest on bonds. These data refer to total money income for men and women over 14 years of age expressed in median dollars for each year. These figures are lower than those you generally see since government statisticians prefer to display the incomes of full-time, year-round workers.

Women Working Full-time Earn Less than Men and the Gap Between Men and Women Is Increasing

	Women	Men	Women's income as a percentage of men's
1955	$2,719	$ 4,252	64%
1960	3,293	5,417	61
1965	3,823	6,375	60
1970	5,403	9,104	59
1973	6,488	11,468	57

Note: The data are for year-round, full-time workers and their median income for the year. By 1973, women workers were reduced to 57% of the income of men workers. For every dollar a man earned, women earned fifty-seven cents. The Bureau of the Census defines a full-time worker as a person who worked 35 hours or more a week for 50–52 weeks.

Even Today with the Same Job Category Women Earn Less than Men

	Women's income as a percentage of men's	
	1970	1973
Professionals	67%	64%
Managers	56	53
Clerical workers	67	61
Sales workers	43	38
Operatives	59	56
Service workers	57	58
All occupations	60	57

Note: These data are for year-round, full-time workers, and the percentages are based on the median salary figures for women and men.

Some Facts about Blacks and Whites, Women and Men in 1973

White men had higher median income than black men and both white and black women [year round, full time workers].

		Black men	$7,593
White men	$11,800	White women	6,598
		Black women	5,595

Unemployment rates were higher for women than men in each group.

White women	5.3%	Black women	11.1%
White men	3.7	Black men	7.9

Within each group, about the same percentage of men and women [20 to 24 years of age] had finished high school.

White women	85%	Black women	72%
White men	85	Black men	70

White men are more likely to finish college than white women

White women	15.5%	White men	22.6%

but there is little difference between the number of black men and women who finish college

Black women	8.5%	Black men	8.0%

Black Women and the Market

Michelle Russell and Mary Jane Lupton

"She picked very fast and very clean, and with an air of scorn, as if she despised both the work and the disgrace and humiliation of the circumstances in which she was placed." The worker is Cassy, the defiant mistress of Simon Legree, who has come down to the cotton fields to get away from the master's house and from the other two jobs black women were forced to do under slavery: domestic work and prostitution.

Uncle Tom's Cabin was written in 1852, nine years before the outbreak of the war between the North and the South over who would continue to control the destiny of black people in America. The victory of the North ended slavery as an institution but left black women far from free.

If the historic life rhythm of the masses of black men takes shape from the beat of sledge hammers in construction gangs and work camps and the pounding of machines in factories, the beat of black women's special oppression rises in the time they have been forced to do on the production line as breeders for the domestic slave market, as the sexual prey of white men, and in the washboard grind of cleaning their bosses dirty linen and nourishing their future oppressors at their breasts. Before the Civil War "the field woman was a laborer beside her man, a begetter of children . . . If she rose in social status then she became a mammy to the white children." (See Pat Robinson's article in *Black Women*.)

The passage of the thirteenth amendment simply expanded the social contexts in which the same kind of female slave-labor could be extracted from black women. Many of the house and field functions merged, so that the paid domestic tended the crops as well as the children. If a woman's "paid" job was that of wetnurse to white babies, then she had to be constantly pregnant, just as under slavery she was perpetually employed in producing more "chattel."

The migration of blacks to the northern urban areas during the periods of the two world wars changed little for the black woman. She remained MEAT FOR SALE. Before hiring black women as salesgirls, managers would circulate questionnaires to their white clientele to see if such a move would lose valuable customers. Women were allowed into the factories as blue-collar semi-skilled workers when there were labor shortages; but their desperation was used to pay them the least and to keep black and non-black males from demanding higher wages for the same work. And, of course, in domestic work, where the majority of employed black women find themselves, there is no minimum wage requirement employers have to meet, no benefits such as health insurance, overtime, or vacation coverage demanded by law. As under slavery, all the rules are set by the missus or the master of the house. And there is no way these rules can be anything but degrading.

The tale most often passed on from mother to daughter in black communities, to teach the child what to expect from life, deals with rape by white men. The "normal" circumstances in which this occurs are dramatized by Richard Wright in a story called "Man of All Work." It is about a typical black family. The husband, Carl, is out of work; his wife, Lucy, is recovering from having her second child. They need money desperately and Carl, who is a cook, can only find cook's work in the "Female Help Wanted" column, where there is a "Cook–Housekeeper Job." The job sounds simple, so, much to Lucy's objection, Carl puts on one of her dresses and answers the ad. The employers, the Fairchilds, take "Lucy" at face value. First, Mrs. Fairchild gets "Lucy" to help her with her bath. Then home comes David, who tries to seduce the new maid like he's done successfully in the past. This time the "colored girl" puts up such a fight she nearly breaks Mr. Fairchild's arm. The wife comes home and, in jealousy, shoots the maid. A doctor, a friend of the family, comes to examine the patient. The truth is learned and "Lucy" is paid $200 to keep his mouth shut. Carl goes home. ". . . Carl, promise me you'll never do anything like that again." ". . . Ha, ha, Lucy, you don't have to ask. I was a woman for almost six hours and it almost killed me. Two hours after I put that dress on I thought I was going crazy. I don't know how you women manage it." Their immediate predicament is solved. But the real Lucy, as soon as she's strong, will wear that dress again. And she will have to manage.

To keep pushing is hard. Frances Beal points out in her well-known essay, "Double Jeopardy: To Be Black and Female," that wage scale has always been lower for black women than any other group in the work force. In 1967, yearly median wages looked like this: White Males—$6704; Non-White Males—$4277; White Females—$3991; Non-White Females—$2861. And this is only if she is "lucky" enough to find a job. Unemployment is also higher among black women than for any other group. Black women work. All black women work. They work hard long hours under wretched conditions—in the home, on the street—to keep body and soul together, raise their own and other's children, and make communities of ghettoes. But they don't get wages for work done.

The only material asset black women have to offer the labor market is themselves. As blues singer Bessie Jackson testified in the 1920's:

> I need shoes on my feet, clothes on my back
> That's why I'm walkin these streets all dressed in black
> I got to make my livin', don't care where I go
> They got a store on the corner where they're sellin' stuff cheap
> I got a market 'cross the street where I sell my meat
> But Tricks ain't walkin', Tricks ain't walkin' no more.

If they resort to selling their bodies for food, they are called prostitutes. If they use the fruit of their wombs, their children, as a claim on the State to help them survive, they are called culturally deprived parasites. The only way their participation in the economy is sanctioned is as consumers; the only official recognition of their existence comes in the form of the welfare system. Trapped in ghettoes, still a domestic, the welfare mother is paid below minimum wages for her labor, refused ADC benefits if she has too many children for the system to control. But her historic role—providing much of the labor which built the system in the first place—is denied. When she has organized against her colonizers, forming groups such as NWRO, demanding a guaranteed income, fighting for legitimacy as a raiser of children through community control of the school struggles, the system has tried to "retrain" her to think of herself as a "para-professional" instead of a mammy, maid, or prostitute. But how significant is this change?

In the New York City schools alone there are over 15,000 para-professionals, perhaps 95% of them Black or Puerto Rican. Most of them only earn between $1800 and $2400 a year. "Ironically, these jobs were first opened up to give the poor a chance to lift themselves out of poverty and also to help them get off welfare. But four years later, the para-professionals are still earning the same hourly rate and are still working under the same conditions." (Dulce Garcia in *Up From Under,* August, 1970).

The consciousness of black women who are placed in paraprofessional programs is not dulled or blunted by the system's mystification. If anything, their appreciation of their exploitation is sharpened. Recently, a class of women in training to become elementary teacher's aides was asked what the term "paraprofessional" meant to them. Here are a few of their answers: "Second best; Off the street; Next to nothing; Teacher's maid, not teacher's aide."

A more extensive political analysis of the black woman's position as a paraprofessional is offered by Cleo Silvers (*Up from Under,* August 1970). She writes: "Our job would be to act as representatives of the community inside their agencies, to interpret things about our people and our community that the professionals did not understand . . . We would gather data that they would never be able to get from our people . . . We were supposed to learn to do the tedious paperwork which the professionals did not want to do . . . Most important, we would act as buffers between our people, who are angry and absolutely disgusted with having exploiters in their midst." These experiences comprise a brutal and stark reality. They epitomize what it means to be simultaneously female in a feudal setting, black in a white racist environment, a colonial tool, and a worker under capitalism.

Employment alone will not change the colonial relationship of black people to Anglo-American society. The struggle is for control—a control that will only come through revolution. For the black woman, control of her body, the social production it engages in, and the ends to which that production is put is what the battle has been and continues to be about. It is the same fight that all black people must wage: for the annihilation of slavery in all its forms and the initiation of a new rhythm of life.

Older Working Women

Joyce Maupin Berkeley

Women live too long. We live past the age where we can find employment, we receive meager pensions or none at all, we survive without the companionship, housing, food or medical care which make a long life satisfying.

At forty we grow old in the job market, but we continue living and working. The Women's Bureau Handbook on Women Workers states that women 45 to 64 are "most likely" to work year round. The unemployment rate for this age group is low but of 263,000 reported unemployed ("reported unemployed" means that you qualify for unemployment insurance) many have been looking for work for more than six months and "many more thousands may have given up."

Unemployment

The Senate Special Committee on Aging reports that in the last four years there has been a 22 per cent rise in the unemployment rate of persons over 45. This figure does not reflect the involuntary dropouts who don't qualify for benefits and are not counted, or others who "may have given up." The hidden unemployment of women over 45 is estimated at three times the official rate.

What happens to the involuntary dropouts? They find a little work—Christmas sales, baby sitting, cleaning—you are never too old for housework, 10 per cent of women earning a living at housework are over 65 years of age. Somehow these women hang on until, at age 62, they qualify for social security benefits—a benefit which will be 20 per cent lower than the one they would get if they could wait until age 65.

A lucky 10 per cent of working women qualify for a payment under some type of private pension plan, but these payments are usually small. Private pension plans resemble lotteries—there are only a few winners.

These plans are built on the assumption that most workers will quit or get laid off long before they reach 65. Pension plans are not portable, benefits cannot be carried from one job to another.

Pension funds are not put in a safe place. They may disappear in bad investments, or they may in any case be insufficient to pay promised benefits. The amount of the pension, if you get one, depends upon length of service. Women, due to periods of voluntary or involuntary dropout, rarely have enough tenure to qualify. When they do get a pension, payments average less than half of those received by men.

The meager amount of social security benefits, averaging $140 a month for single women, may explain why a large number of women over 65, and even over 70, are still in the work force.

Be Adaptable

Age discrimination is less evident in unskilled jobs which pay the minimum—or less. Older women are rarely employed, even if they are qualified, in skilled jobs which pay better wages.

The Handbook on Women Workers suggests that women be "adaptable and flexible in their attitudes—willing to learn and make necessary changes . . . alert to new job opportunities and new training programs. Only if they are fully prepared by education, training, and the willingness to learn anew, will they be ready for the challenges and demands of tomorrow's society." This advice will not help the woman past 45, who rarely is offered an interview or even an application form.

Mature women, or senior citizens (it's not nice to say old), evidently do adapt because they continue to survive. As long as they can still get around they survive in little cubicles in rooming houses or rundown hotels, preparing a single meal on an illegal hot plate. They survive their husbands but in very few instances (about 2 per cent) do they receive any part of the husband's pension benefit.

Measuring Masculinity by the Size of a Paycheck

Robert E. Gould, M.D.

Is Bobby Murcer a $100,000 ballplayer? Did Tom Seaver earn a raise above his $120,000 off his 21–12 record? How much is rookie Jon Matlack worth on the open market?

Lead paragraph from a *New York Post* news story, January 10, 1973

In our culture money equals success. Does it also equal masculinity? Yes—to the extent that a man is too often measured by his money, by what he is "worth." Not by his worth as a human being, but by what he is able to earn, how much he can command on the "open market."

In my psychiatric practice I have seen a number of male patients through the years, of all ages, who have equated moneymaking with a sense of masculinity. Peter G., for example. He was 23 years old, very inhibited, and socially inept. Raised in a strict, religious home, he had had very little contact with girls and virtually no dating experience until his second year of college. He was sure that no woman would find him attractive unless he was making good money. In analysis it became evident that he was painfully insecure and unsure of his abilities in *any* area. Money was his "cover": if he flashed a roll of bills, no one would see how little else there was to him. He needed expensive clothes, a big sporty car, and a thick wallet; all these were extensions of his penis. Money would show women he could give them what they needed, and thereby get him what he thought he needed, "a beautiful girl with big boobs." His idea that women were essentially passive and looking to be taken care of by a big, strong male demanded that he "make" good money before he could "make" the woman of his dreams.

This kind of thinking is often reinforced by both men and women who have bought the myth that endows a moneymaking man with sexiness and virility, and is based on man's dominance, strength, and ability to provide for and care for "his" woman. We have many cultural models of this unrealistic and frequently self-defeating image of masculinity. Hollywood has gone a long way to reflect and glorify it in such figures as the John Wayne-style cowboy, the private eye, war hero, foreign correspondent, lone adventurer—all "he-men" (a phrase that in its redundancy seems to "protest too much") who use physical strength, courage, and masculine wiles to conquer their worlds, their villainous rivals, and their women. *Money* rarely has anything to do with it.

But in real life in the 1970s, few women have much concern about men like that. After all, there are few frontiers to conquer, or international spy rings to crack, or glorious wars to wage. All that is left for the real-life, middle-class man is the battle for the bulging wallet.

This measure of one's "masculinity quotient" becomes a convenient fall-back to those who have a weak sense of self and who doubt their innate ability to attract women. Because it is hard for these men to face their inadequacies and the anxieties that would follow, they strive for money as a panacea for all their personal ills.

For them, money alone separates the men from the boys. I have even seen youngsters drop out of school to make money, just to prove their manhood.

For their part, women have been taught that men who achieve success are the best "catches" in the marriage market. Women have also been taught that the right motives for marriage are love and sexual attraction. Thus, if a woman wants to marry a man with money, she has to believe she loves him; that he is sexually appealing—even if the real appeal is his money. She has to convince herself—and him—that it's the man behind the money that turns her on. Many women *learn* to make this emotional jump: to feel genuinely attracted to the man who makes it big, and to accept the equation of moneymaking power with sexual power.

There are many phenomenally wealthy men in the public eye who are physically unattractive by traditional criteria; yet they are surrounded by beautiful women and an aura of sexiness and virility. A woman in the same financial position loses in attractiveness (at least if she is *earning* the money rather than spending an inheritance); she poses a threat to a man's sense of masculinity. As I once heard a sociologist say: men are unsexed by failure, women by success.

Yet why is it that many men who have met the moneymaking standards are still not sure of their masculinity? Quite simply because money is—and always was—a pretty insecure peg on which to hang a masculine image.

Take Jerry L., a stockbroker. He lost most of his money three years ago during a very bad spell in the market. Distraught as he was over the financial loss, he was devastated over the sexual impotence which followed in its wake. This direct one-to-one relationship may seem awfully pat, but its validity can be attested to by many men (and "their" women) who have gone through serious financial setbacks. Even a temporary inability to provide properly for his family and to justify himself with his checkbook makes such a man feel totally "worthless."

When Jerry L. recouped most of his losses in the course of the next two years, he did *not* regain his previous sexual potency. The experience had made it impossible for him ever again to rely *solely* on money as proof of his masculinity.

The most extreme and dramatic reaction to personal financial loss is suicide. I have seen several men to whom great losses of money represented such a great loss of self, of ego, and ultimately of masculine image, that life no longer seemed worth living.

The situation becomes even more complicated when "the head of the house" is competing against his wife's paycheck as well as his own expectations. Recently, economic realities have made the two-paycheck family respectable. This is tolerable to Jack as long as he can provide for his family and Jill only earns enough to make all the "little extras" possible.

Given current salary inequities, it is unlikely that she will threaten his place as number-one breadwinner. But if she does, if she can make *real money,* she is co-opting the man's passport to masculinity (thus the stereotype of the successful woman being too masculine, too competitive, too unfeminine), and he is effectively castrated.

Thus it is vital that the woman be "kept in her place," which is classically "in the home," so that her second-class status assures him of his first place. Many divorces and breakups that are blamed on "conflict of careers" often mean nothing more than a wife who would not give up her career (and earning ability) in deference to her husband's.

I know plenty of men who are sufficiently "enlightened" intellectually to accept the idea that a woman has as much right (and power) to make money as a man does. But in practice emotionally—when it comes to *their* wives—these men often feel threatened and emasculated. Because he is unable to see this in himself, such a man expresses his anxiety by forcing a "conflict" with the woman in some other area of their relationship, like dealing with in-laws or running the house, where there is, in fact, no conflict. In this way he deflects attention from his problem but also precludes adequate resolution of it in their relationship.

There is no other common male defense against the income-producing woman. No matter how much she makes, he still maintains she doesn't "understand" money, calling upon the stereotyped image of the cute little wife who can't balance the checkbook. He doesn't have to look further for reassurance than the insurance company, for example, that appeals to a husband's protector-provider definition of himself with pictures of helpless widows and children, and the caption "What will happen to them after you're gone?"

Marty B. was caught in this bind. A successful doctor, he divided his time between research, which he found enjoyable but not very rewarding financially, and the practice of internal medicine, which was more lucrative but not so enjoyable. Marty felt it a strain to deal with many diverse people; he was more comfortable with animal research, which also fulfilled his creative talents and led to his writing a number of solid scientific papers. So far, so good. But then Marty's wife, Janet, an actress who had had only middling success, became an actors' agent and clicked right away.

Soon, Janet began to earn more money than Marty. At first he joked about it with her and even with close friends, but, as it turned out later, the joking was uneasy, and laden with anxiety. Marty decided to increase his patient practice at the expense of his research. He forced himself to make more money—when he actually needed less, thanks to Janet's high income.

They began quarreling about many small things—arguments without resolutions because they had nothing to do with the real issue: that her new money-making powers were a threat to his masculinity.

Marty and Janet came to see me because they were considering separating after eight years of a happy marriage. After a number of sessions, it became clear that Marty felt that Janet's success meant she didn't need him any more; that he had been diminished as "the man of the house." This was not easy for Marty to admit; he had always claimed he was happy to see Janet doing what she wanted to professionally. But this was the first time he had to face her actually succeeding at it. Marty agreed, with some ambivalence, to go into psychoanalytic therapy. As therapy evolved, his problem with "masculinity" emerged even more clearly. He had never felt comfortable competing with men; this was a contributing factor to his going into animal research. He really received very little gratification from his medical practice, but he needed to make a lot of money to feel competent as a man. He resented Janet's success but since he was not aware that his manhood was threatened, he found "other" things to complain and argue about. After three years of therapy and six months of a trial separation, Marty worked through his problems. Their marriage and Janet's success both survived.

There are many marriages with similar tension that don't survive. Often neither husband nor wife is aware of how profoundly money and masculinity are equated, or of how much a husband's financial security may depend on having a dependent wife.

But are the old rules working as they once did? Increasing numbers of men making good money are not feeling the strong sense of masculinity it used to provide. A man can buy an expensive car and still get stalled in traffic; how powerful does he feel then? Money seems in danger of losing its omnipotence. In a complicated world, the formerly "almighty" dollar has all too few magical properties.

As a result, we may have to begin dealing with the fact that money has been an artificial symbol of masculinity all along, that we invested it with power and that, like brute strength, it can no longer get us where we want to go.

I suspect we will have to give up the whole idea of "masculinity" and start trying to find out about the real male person. We may find that masculinity has more to do with man's sensitivity, with the nature of his emotional capacity to respond to others, than it has to do with dominance, strength, or ability to "provide for" a woman materially—especially if she isn't pretending to be helpless any more.

Some day soon virility may be the measure of how well a man relates to a woman as an equal, and masculinity will be equated not with moneymaking prowess but with a man's power to feel, express, and give love. That might just possibly be worth much more than money.

The Politics of Housework

Pat Mainardi

Though women do not complain of the power of husbands, each complains of her own husband, or of the husbands of her friends. It is the same in all other cases of servitude; at least in the commencement of the emancipatory movement. The serfs did not at first complain of the power of the lords, but only of their tyranny.

John Stuart Mill
On the Subjection of Women

Liberated women—very different from women's liberation! The first signals all kinds of goodies, to warm the hearts (not to mention other parts) of the most radical men. The other signals—*housework*. The first brings sex without marriage, sex before marriage, cozy housekeeping arrangements ("You see, I'm living with this chick") and the self-content of knowing that you're not the kind of man who wants a doormat instead of a woman. That will come later. After all, who wants that old commodity anymore, the Standard American Housewife, all husband, home and kids. The New Commodity, the Liberated Woman, has sex a lot and has a Career, preferably something that can be fitted in with the household chores—like dancing, pottery, or painting.

On the other hand is women's liberation—and housework. What? You say this is all trivial? Wonderful! That's what I thought. It seemed perfectly reasonable. We both had careers, both had to work a couple of days a week to earn enough to live on, so why shouldn't we share the housework? So I suggested it to my mate and he agreed—most men are too hip to turn you down flat. "You're right," he said. "It's only fair."

Then an interesting thing happened. I can only explain it by stating that we women have been brainwashed more than even we can imagine. Probably too many years of seeing television women in ecstasy over their shiny waxed floors or breaking down over their dirty shirt collars. Men have no such conditioning. They recognize the essential fact of housework right from the very beginning. Which is that it stinks. Here's my list of dirty chores: buying groceries, carting them home and putting them away; cooking meals and washing dishes and pots; doing the laundry, digging out the place when things get out of control; washing floors. The list could go on but the sheer necessities are bad enough. All of us have to do these things, or get some one else to do them for us. The longer my husband contemplated these chores, the more repulsed he became, and so proceeded the change from the normally sweet considerate Dr. Jekyll into the crafty Mr. Hyde who would stop at nothing to avoid the horrors of—*housework*. As he felt himself backed into a corner laden with dirty dishes, brooms, mops, and reeking garbage, his front teeth grew longer and pointier, his fingernails haggled and his eyes grew wild. Housework trivial? Not on your life! Just try to share the burden.

So ensued a dialogue that's been going on for several years. Here are some of the high points:

"I don't mind sharing the housework, but I don't do it very well. We should each do the things we're best at."

Meaning: Unfortunately I'm no good at things like washing dishes or cooking. What I do best is a little light carpentry, changing light bulbs, moving furniture *(how often do you move furniture?).*

Also Meaning: Historically the lower classes (black men and us) have had hundreds of years experience doing menial jobs. It would be a waste of manpower to train someone else to do them now.

Also Meaning: I don't like the dull stupid boring jobs, so you should do them.

"I don't mind sharing the work, but you'll have to show me how to do it."

Meaning: I ask a lot of questions and you'll have to show me everything everytime I do it because I don't remember so good. Also don't try to sit down and read while I'm doing my jobs because I'm going to annoy hell out of you until it's easier to do them yourself.

"We used to be so happy!" (Said whenever it was his turn to do something.)

Meaning: I used to be so happy.

Meaning: Life without housework is bliss. *(No quarrel here. Perfect agreement.)*

"We have different standards, and why should I have to work to your standards. That's unfair."

Meaning: If I begin to get bugged by the dirt and crap I will say "This place sure is a sty" or "How can anyone live like this?" and wait for your reaction. I know that all women have a sore called "Guilt over a messy house" or "Household work is ultimately my responsibility." I know that men have caused that sore—if anyone visits and the place *is* a sty, they're not going to leave and say, "He sure is a lousy housekeeper." You'll take the rap in any case. I can outwait you.

Also Meaning: I can provoke innumerable scenes over the housework issue. Eventually doing all the housework yourself will be less painful to you than trying to get me to do half. Or I'll suggest we get a maid. She will do my share of the work. You will do yours. It's women's work.

"I've got nothing against sharing the housework, but you can't make me do it on your schedule."

Meaning: Passive resistance. I'll do it when I damned well please, if at all. If my job is doing dishes, it's easier to do them once a week. If taking out laundry, once a month. If washing the floors, once a year. If you don't like it, do it yourself oftener, and then I won't do it at all.

"I *hate* it more than you. You don't mind it so much."

Meaning: Housework is garbage work. It's the worst crap I've ever done. It's degrading and humiliating for someone of *my* intelligence to do it. But for someone of *your* intelligence . . .

"Housework is too trivial to even talk about."

Meaning: It's even more trivial to do. Housework is beneath my status. My purpose in life is to deal with matters of significance. Yours is to deal with matters of insignificance. You should do the housework.

"This problem of housework is not a man-woman problem! In any relationship between two people one is going to have a stronger personality and dominate."

Meaning: That stronger personality had better be *me.*

"In animal societies, wolves, for example, the top animal is usually a male even where he is not chosen for brute strength but on the basis of cunning and intelligence. Isn't that interesting?"

Meaning: I have historical, psychological, anthropological, and biological justification for keeping you down. How can you ask the top wolf to be equal?

"Women's liberation isn't really a political movement."

Meaning: The Revolution is coming too close to home.

Also Meaning: I am only interested in how *I* am oppressed, not how I oppress others. Therefore the war, the draft, and the university are political. Women's liberation is not.

"Man's accomplishments have always depended on getting help from other people, mostly women. What great man would have accomplished what he did if he had to do his own housework?

Meaning: Oppression is built into the System and I, as the white American male receive the benefits of this System. I don't want to give them up.

Postscript

Participatory democracy begins at home. If you are planning to implement your politics, there are certain things to remember.

1 He *is* feeling it more than you. He's losing some leisure and you're gaining it. The measure of your oppression is his resistance.

2 A great many American men are not accustomed to doing monotonous repetitive work which never ushers in any lasting let alone important achievement. This is why they would rather repair a cabinet than wash dishes. If human endeavors are like a pyramid with man's highest achievements at the top, then keeping oneself alive is at the bottom. Men have always had servants (us) to take care of this bottom strata of life while they have confined their efforts to the rarefied upper regions. It is thus ironic when they ask of women—where are your great painters, statesmen, etc? Mme. Matisse ran a millinery shop so he could paint. Mrs. Martin Luther King kept his house and raised his babies.

3 It is a traumatizing experience for someone who has always thought of himself as being against any oppression or exploitation of one human being by another to realize that in his daily life he has been accepting and implementing (and benefiting from) this exploitation; that his rationalization is little different from that of the racist who says "Black people don't feel pain" (women don't mind doing the shitwork); and that the oldest form of oppression in history has been the oppression of 50 percent of the population by the other 50 percent.

4 Arm yourself with some knowledge of the psychology of oppressed peoples everywhere, and a few facts about the animal kingdom. I admit playing top wolf or who runs the gorillas is silly but as a last resort men bring it up all the time. Talk about bees. If you feel really hostile bring up the sex life of spiders. They have sex. She bites off his head.

The psychology of oppressed people is not silly. Jews, immigrants, black men, and all women have employed the same psychological mechanisms to survive: admiring the oppressor, glorifying the oppressor, wanting to be like the oppressor, wanting the oppressor to like them, mostly because the oppressor held all the power.

5 In a sense, all men everywhere are slightly schizoid—divorced from the reality of maintaining life. This makes it easier for them to play games with it. It is almost a cliché that women feel greater grief at sending a son off to war or losing him to that war because they bore him, suckled him, and raised him. The men who foment those wars did none of those things and have a more superficial

estimate of the worth of human life. One hour a day is a low estimate of the amount of time one has to spend "keeping" oneself. By foisting this off on others, man gains seven hours a week—one working day more to play with his mind and not his human needs. Over the course of generations it is easy to see whence evolved the horrifying abstractions of modern life.

6   With the death of each form of oppression, life changes and new forms evolve. English aristocrats at the turn of the century were horrified at the idea of enfranchising working men—were sure that it signaled the death of civilization and a return to barbarism. Some working men were even deceived by this line. Similarly with the minimum wage, abolition of slavery, and female suffrage. Life changes but it goes on. Don't fall for any line about the death of everything if men take a turn at the dishes. They will imply that you are holding back the Revolution (their Revolution). But you are advancing it (your Revolution).

7   Keep checking up. Periodically consider who's actually *doing* the jobs. These things have a way of backsliding so that a year later once again the woman is doing everything. After a year make a list of jobs the man has rarely if ever done. You will find cleaning pots, toilets, refrigerators and ovens high on the list. Use time sheets if necessary. He will accuse you of being petty. He is above that sort of thing—(housework). Bear in mind what the worst jobs are, namely the ones that have to be done every day or several times a day. Also the ones that are dirty—it's more pleasant to pick up books, newspapers etc. than to wash dishes. Alternate the bad jobs. It's the daily grind that gets you down. Also make sure that you don't have the responsibility for the housework with occasional help from him. "I'll cook dinner for you tonight" implies it's really your job and isn't he a nice guy to do some of it for you.

8   Most men had a rich and rewarding bachelor life during which they did not starve or become encrusted with crud or buried under the litter. There is a taboo that says that women mustn't stain themselves in the presence of men: we haul around 50 pounds of groceries if we have to but aren't allowed to open a jar if there is someone around to do it for us. The reverse side of the coin is that men aren't supposed to be able to take care of themselves without a woman. Both are excuses for making women do the housework.

9   Beware of the double whammy. He won't do the little things he always did because you're now a "Liberated Woman," right? Of course he won't do anything else either . . .

I was just finishing this when my husband came in and asked what I was doing. Writing a paper on housework. Housework? he said, *Housework?* Oh my god how trivial can you get. A paper on housework.

Little Politics of Housework Quiz

The lowest job in the army, used as punishment is: a) working 9–5; b) kitchen duty (K.P.).

When a man lives with his family, his: a) father b) mother does his housework.

When he lives with a woman, a) he b) she does the housework.

A) his son b) his daughter learns preschool how much fun it is to iron daddy's handkerchief.

From the *New York Times,* 9/21/69: "Former Greek Official George Mylonas pays the penalty for differing with the ruling junta in Athens by performing household chores on the island of Amorgos where he lives in forced exile" (with hilarious photo of a miserable Mylonas carrying his own water). What the *Times* means is that he ought to have a) indoor plumbing b) a maid.

Dr. Spock said *(Redbook 3/69):* "Biologically and temperamentally I believe, women were made to be concerned first and foremost with child care, husband care, and home care." Think about: a) *who* made us b) why? c) what is the effect on their lives d) what is the effect on our lives?

From *Time* 1/5/70, "Like their American counterparts, many housing project housewives are said to suffer from neurosis. And for the first time in Japanese history, many young husbands today complain of being henpecked. Their wives are beginning to demand detailed explanations when they don't come home straight from work and some Japanese males nowadays are even compelled to do housework." According to *Time,* women become neurotic: a) when they are forced to do the maintenance work for the male caste all day every day of their lives or b) when they no longer want to do the maintenance work for the male caste all day every day of their lives.

The Liberation of Children

Deborah Babcox

A friend of mine called me recently, disturbed about her brother's wife. The woman had given birth to a baby several weeks before, and when she got home from the hospital, she had slipped into a state of utter depression. She cried all the time and was very irritable, insisting that she was too weak to take care of the baby and certainly couldn't manage the housework. Her mother and mother-in-law had been going over every day to help, but they were beginning to feel she should snap out of it. Would I go over with her and try to talk to the woman?

I went reluctantly—I had never known the woman well—and it was worse than I could have imagined. She was listless, uninterested in the baby, and generally distracted. She kept getting up to walk idly about the room, forgetting what she'd been saying. Twice while we were there she burst into tears when her mother-in-law asked her to do something—hold the baby for a minute, or get some coffee cups from the cupboard. "How can you stand it!" she wailed to me. "A baby takes over your life . . . I can't even take a shower with it in the house!"

I had remembered the woman as being a reasonable person, not unusually self-centered or unstable, and while many women are afflicted with similar feelings after having a baby, she was obviously suffering from this depression more than most. I left the house feeling very depressed myself . . . for both the mother and the baby. The mother's condition seemed to border on real mental illness, but her family was treating her as if she were a spoiled child who would snap out of it at any time. I didn't know if they would ever seek treatment for her, and if they didn't, what would happen to the child? He already seemed strangely subdued, not a very responsive baby. I hated to think of him growing up bewildered and hurt, an unwitting victim of his mother's situation. So many people—most of my friends, in fact—complain all the time about the horrible things their mothers did (or do) to them, and few of them have been able to come to terms with their feelings about it even as supposedly mature adults.

And for perhaps the first time, I really began to connect that with my difficulties with my children. Heaven knows I understood the emotions of the woman whose house I had just left all too well. I remember vividly standing in my doorway, tears streaming down my cheeks, as I watched my mother leave for her home 1,000 miles away, leaving me alone for the first time with my new-born son. I was 26, quite well aware of the responsibilities involved in having a child and of the limitations that would be placed on my freedom. I had wanted—longed—to have that baby, but somehow all the education and thinking in the world can't prepare you for the gut-level realization of how a baby imprisons you with its dependence.

The difference between us was really only one of degree. I had, in the end, learned to cope, and even accept the idea that I had to do housework, and I didn't have much confidence that she would. Even now, I don't always find life easy with my two wild little boys, but I am charmed by them anyway. We enjoy each other, and I would rather stay home and take care of them than do most other jobs I can think of.

Even so, there are days when their sheer energy makes for inevitable conflict. Once, when he was about two years old, my older son came in early to our bedroom to lie down beside me and drink his bottle. After a few minutes of lying there, humming to himself, he sat up and looked at me with a surprised expression. "You *are* a nice Mommy!" he said. Evidently he had gone to bed feeling about me exactly as I had felt about him—that I was a monster! And we both had recovered our good nature during the night, because by the morning I thought him delightful, too. But there are still more days than I care to think about when everything in the household falls apart and I feel like taking to my bed and pulling the covers over my head, grieving in my heart for the injury I have that day done my children. Why me? Why should I feel so deeply this all-encompassing responsibility for them that is sometimes so corrosive?

I do know that it is very much a part of our tradition. When the first child-raising literature began to appear in America at the beginning of the nineteenth century great emphasis was placed on the exclusive role of the mother in the forming of her child's character. Industrialization and urbanization were accelerating, and the role of the father and of men in general in the upbringing of children was declining markedly. Women were taking over most of the teaching of young children in the newly established public school system, and more and more fathers worked out and away from their homes.

In the nineteenth century, of course, the moral character of the developing child was the mother's crucial responsibility. (The essential depravity of the child had to be overcome by her loving guidance and the purity of her example.) These days we are more modern: mothers are only responsible for the child's adjust-ment to society and its intelligence. Thus, Dr. Spock warns in his new book that women had best forget about "liberation" and stay home with the children, or society will suffer. And Burton White at Harvard finds that superior ability in school is the result of a child's having been nurtured by a "super-mother" who lavishes love and attention and conversation on her small baby.

All of this may be quite true, but at what price do we place such exclusive responsibility on the mother for the child's well-being? Almost everyone I grew up with resented their mothers terribly; almost every young mother I know resents in some degree her children's dependence on her. It seems to me that it places intolerable burdens on both mothers and children to bind them so closely together, and both are hurt by it. Dr. Spock is wrong, though the problem he speaks to is a real one. He sees that children are growing up in this society without the emotional support they need to be healthy adults. But the source of that difficulty is not that women are too free: it lies in the fact that they are still too restricted by the exclusive bonds of child-care to be good mothers. To raise a child to be self-confident, loving, curious, and capable of autonomous behavior is extremely difficult. It requires a great deal of self-control, understanding, and love, and one mother in this kind of family (a nuclear family) with the father gone most of the time, is most likely to lack just those qualities.

There is no reason that men and women should not share the care of their children to the benefit of all concerned; neither men or women are more biologically suited for doing dishes or deciding whether a child should wear its boots, and it's unfair to make these things the exclusive responsibility of the mother. It is unfair to women, who are then forced to live through other people's lives and devote themselves to the day-to-day well-being of the other members of the family. It is also unfair, and probably destructive, to the children. Since it is the mother who is alone with the children most in the circumstances in which most of us now live, and since it is she whose life is most restricted by them, she is naturally the one most likely to injure them.

And how can a girl growing up in this society fail to be ambivalent about motherhood? She is ceaselessly exhorted to be attractive, tend to her makeup and hair color, be smart but not too smart, get a good job, but only so as to be able to meet eligible men—all for what? Why, to get married to stay home and take care of baby, in soap-powder bliss. Even those of us who scoff at these images are affected by them; they subtlely contribute to our expectations of ourselves and our future lives. We imagine ourselves the impeccable housewives in all the TV ads, perhaps with part-time jobs, contented, sweet-smelling babies and self-cleaning ovens to make our lives manageable—or even that hackneyed favorite, the lovely wife greeting her husband at the door every evening with his slippers and a drink. Most women find out very quickly that babies don't permit that kind of nonsense, and that working with children is no picnic. It's difficult to provide for them during the day, and then there's all that housework to do in the evenings—which all of our "modern conveniences" have done little to make more convenient. And the realization that your life is no longer your own is often quite a startling one, trite as that may sound to unmarried, non-mothers (who always think, "Oh, that won't happen to me. . . .").

But I think that life in our small families is often quite difficult for men, too, and when a woman who finds that her life is hard turns to her husband for sympathy and help she may find herself rebuffed. A young man may find the financial responsibility of his family burdensome. Perhaps he hadn't realized, either, how his freedom would be restricted. He will probably often come in from a demanding job, expecting to relax, watch TV, and be comforted by his loving family, only to find that his wife has been waiting all day for him to come home so *she* could relax. Chances are that each feels he or she has the harder life, and that the other should understand and be sympathetic. Both parents will probably have expectations of each other and of the children that they are hardly aware of, and both may feel disgruntled and resentful when these are not fulfilled.

I Just Don't Know If I Can Make It

Colleen McNamara

. . . That's what I find myself saying almost every night before I fall asleep. I'm a woman alone with an infant son, trying to exist on welfare. Before the baby was born I used to find myself crying a lot because I just couldn't get the money together to buy things, like a crib and clothes, that the baby would need. I guess like any mother I wanted the best for my child, but now my tears are being shed for things much more serious. I'm 21 years old and my background was far from comfortable and stable. I was raised in a small apartment over a liquor warehouse in New York. We couldn't afford hot running water because my Mom paid the utilities and she had to think of every little way to save. She would turn the hot water heater on once a week and we would all have baths. The rest of the week we'd heat water on the stove. At night we'd all have to stay in one room to save electricity. Our food was always simple and our clothes usually made-over hand-outs.

My parents broke up when I was small because my Dad was slowly turning to drinking as a way of life. I guess it was hard for him to watch his family have to live like that even though he was working. He was a high-school dropout and an unskilled laborer, so the jobs he could find didn't pay enough to raise a family on. When Dad left, Mom started working full time as a nurse's aide at night, and by the time I was a teenager I was practically on my own. We didn't see much of her and the temptations of being on my own started getting me in trouble.

Through those years I met many a social worker and parole officer through the juvenile authorities. At 15 I had a job as a nurse's aide after school and on weekends. I've always worked and worked hard; that illusion that welfare recipients are lazy can't be proved by me.

The reason I told you about my background was to let you see that being poor and not having everything I want is not new to me. And yet the way I live now is like a constant nightmare. As I started to say earlier, I used to cry a lot before the baby was born because I couldn't get him the best of everything; now I'm happy if he's got p.j.'s to keep him warm, no matter what they look like. Now my tears are shed for a much more urgent need—food. According to the county, I'm allowed $14 worth of food stamps for two weeks—that's $7.00 a week, $1.00 a day. Last week when I got my food stamps I bought all the baby's food for the two weeks. That way when the money runs out at least the baby will have food. The other foods I bought were rice, beans, bread, catsup, potatoes, four pork chops, two quarts of milk, one box of cereal, and two cans of soup. My bill was $11.00. That means I'm left with $3.00 worth of stamps for the other thirteen days. That $3.00 will have to pay for milk, bread, and butter as they're needed. Right now my baby's only on vegetables, cereal, and formula. God only knows what I'm going to do when he starts eating meat, fruit, and fruit juice.

Please understand that I want to get back to a job as soon as I can, but it's impossible to get employment and the government cut its funds for training programs. I feel like I'm on a dead-end street. I'm cursed for being on welfare and yet the very people who condemn me won't hire me so I can get on my feet again. Is it so hard to understand why the urge to steal is becoming stronger and stronger? I receive $148 a month from welfare to pay for rent, food, clothes, transportation, telephone, and other things, such as soap, Purex, laundromat fees, deodorant, toothpaste, and toilet paper. Maybe a lot of you people take these things for granted, but when you're making a budget out of $148, there's many a time when newspaper or gift box tissue paper is used as toilet paper until the real thing can be afforded.

Many people, especially middle-class liberals, condemn poor people for being apathetic about what's happening in the country. But many of us cannot afford TV's and even a dime for the newspaper is sometimes more than we can spare. Is it any wonder that many a time we don't know what's happening in Washington and in other parts of the world? But just ask us about the things that are happening around us and we could fill a book. Ask us about that tragic battle that roars within us as we desperately try to save our faith in God while all the world is turning into a hell for us and we are being made involuntary martyrs to a country we no longer believe in. Ask us about the cops in our neighborhoods and about the schools. For God's sake, America, put down your newspapers and look around you.

Is it any wonder that the health of poor people is so bad? We can't afford balanced meals three times a day and our nerves are shot from being under so much mental strain. My body is so choked up with fear for me and my son's futures and the future of all other people like us that I can hardly breathe. And now we are burdened with the additional threat of the medical program being stopped. Many old people have already died because they were told they could no longer stay in nursing homes when the government cut their funds. They had no families and no place else to go, so they just died. If things keep up this way, soon America will have a mortality rate as high as the so-called uncivilized, underdeveloped parts of the world.

Of all the institutions in America, the institution of poverty is the only one that knows no prejudices. Poor people of all races, creeds, colors, and age groups are slowly being wasted away. I am white, but as the times get worse and worse, my existence seems to be threatened as much as any minority group, not because I'm white, but solely because I'm poor. All we want is for someone to help us help ourselves. I believe people working for change can help all of us. At least I pray you can, because you're our last hope. Otherwise, I just don't know if I can make it.

With an Eye to the Future

Phyllis Adams

Let's face it girls, every one of us has visions of someday having a beautiful home. It may be in the country, or in the city, on a hill, or in a valley, but wherever it is we do have some very definite ideas of what we want in it.

Most of us want wall to wall carpeting, Hollywood kitchens, matched cookware, crystal, and china.

These latter items we should of course choose ourselves since there is nothing more frustrating than being forced to use cookware or china which we do not like and in many cases despise, just because well meaning Aunt Mary gave it to us as an engagement or wedding gift.

There is indeed much more pleasure in choosing these things ourselves and how much more practical it is too.

The question is when is the right time to begin to accumulate our treasures.

Should we wait until after we are married and let our husbands buy them for us?—Definitely not.

There are several reasons for this. It is hard enough to make ends meet with the high cost of living today. Hubby needs a new suit—junior new shoes—the house needs painting—the car new tires, etc., etc.

Cookware? China? Better put those dreams right back on the shelf.

Supposing we could afford them after we are married. Did you ever meet a man who showed any interest in what kind of dishes his food was served on as long as they were clean?

Spend good money for nonsense like that? Perish the thought. He would rather spend his money on a new set of golf clubs, or fishing tackle, or a new rifle or lawn mower. Cookware? China? "What we have is good enough," says he. Men have very little appreciation of some of the things close to a woman's heart.

Let's try again. How about when we are engaged and about to be married? Now that sounds like a good time to start our treasure chest.

Let's face a few more facts. We have our wedding gown, bridesmaids' gifts, furniture, honeymoon plans, to mention just a few "small" items. Cookware? China? Can't afford them.

Perhaps we'll get them for shower gifts.—Wrong again.

Shower gifts average about five dollars per person. It would take an awful lot of people getting together all of the same mind to get us just one of our treasures and then it probably wouldn't be the pattern or make of cookware we want. Besides there are many other things they could get us, the choice of which wouldn't be quite so personal.

When then is the right time to start?

It is perfectly obvious that there is one time and one time only when we can be sure that we can make our dreams come true. That time is when we are single and working. We need not even be going steady or have a particular boy friend. The sooner we start the better. Our money is more or less ours to do with as we see fit. We can get the very best for just a couple of dollars per week on the installment plan. We will be establishing credit which is very important. It is a wonderful way to save money since most of us need an incentive to save money anyway.

What better incentive than a beautiful matched cookware set which it seems most girls like to start with first.

After we have learned to save each week in this manner and have established a good habit, we can then select our china and crystal.

It is a thrill to select our own treasures and see our dreams coming true.

True there are those unfortunate girls who would rather keep putting off and procrastinating, meanwhile spending all of their money on clothes, cars and other non practical items. They wind up getting married with none of the finer things of life and nothing to show for their years of work.

Most of them wish they could have the years back to do all over differently.

While we are mentioning future husbands, let's talk a little about future mother-in-laws.

It is far easier to get a husband when his mother approves of you.

Mothers are very critical of the girl their angel is going to marry. Don't ever sell short her influence on his choice either. They like to see their sons marry a practical girl who will make him a good home, rather than a clothes horse, with charge accounts in all the apparel stores in town.

So you see girls we not only insure ourselves that we will have the things we want but it helps us get a husband too.

Sometimes, unfortunately, our own mothers tell us to wait. Statistics prove that mothers who tell their daughters to wait are still waiting themselves.

Show me a mother who discourages her daughter from putting things away and I will show you a mother who does not have these things herself.

Thank goodness, mothers like this, are few and far between.

If your well meaning dad tells you to wait, you are getting first hand information on just how your own future husband would react.

The vast majority of parents, however, encourage their daughters to save their money, and realize that this is a fine way to do it. As I mentioned before, all we need is an incentive to save.

So girls get started. Don't wait another day. Choose the best now because now you can afford the best.

Some of your friends who don't believe in planning for the future will be the very ones who will envy you the most when they visit you in your beautiful home in the not too distant future.

Remember this. The difference between those who have and those who have not is planning.

Plan and do something about your future now.

Black Women in Revolt

. . . Those of us who were born and have lived in the projects all our lives are the failures of the system. We didn't get those single-family homes everyone was hustling for since 1948. Most of us black women were born from 1948 on down to the early fifties. We have seen "striving poor" black families move out and sharecropper families from the South move in, or black families without fathers. All of our families had fathers. Most of these new families didn't, or the men moved in and out and weren't the fathers of the children.

The projects always needed repairs from the beginning and we children had too much energy to be cooped up in high-rise apartments with an elevator. We wanted to get out fast, so we always took the stairs. We wanted to run, free ourselves. The pressures were bad. But we didn't know this in our heads. We just felt the urge and we acted. All the families were like this. There was always gossip, each family moving on the other, outdoing the other, the kids fighting and playing. The games were "down and dirty."

Our mothers still dream of having their own house. Many families are still struggling to get out. You see, in the beginning we knew no low-class folks were let into the projects. If you weren't married you couldn't get in. If you had a baby out of wedlock, you got put out. There's one among us who had some bitter memories about that. Later, when welfare pushed and the housing shortage for poor blacks got worse, her mother and the kids got back in. But while they were out, they lived four in one room, and they got burned out twice. In that time the mother felt forced to give one of her babies away to relatives down South. This is not an individual story. It's happened to lots of us.

Our fathers were mostly veterans of the Second World War. If they couldn't get to college, at least they got good-paying jobs as skilled factory workers, especially during the Korean War. A lot of our mothers worked, mostly in domestic service, and a few had low-paid typist jobs. Some worked in the local

Editor's note: The excerpt is from a lengthy essay written by a group of young blacks who live in a Northeastern suburban community.

hospitals as clean-up women and a very few as nurse's aides. Our fathers made
the most money, and no one ever questioned why this was. It was accepted that
our mothers worked to help save for the house. They would get paid less since
daddies were supposed to make more money. That was the American Way.
Daddies were supermen, not mommies.

Our fathers could really "rap"! They didn't fly through the sky like whitey,
but they bopped and glided along the pavements, and in the bars they were kings.
Around 1955–1956 our daddies started swilling liquor, drinking real bad and just
about making it home, on their knees. We black women children didn't know,
nor did anyone tell us, that black men were losing jobs or being offered jobs of
lower status, like in shipping or packing. This was downgrading and the beginning of one of those economic slumps you can read about in the *Wall Street
Journal* but never hear about in school. No one told us jobs had to be automated
so the factory owners could produce more cheaply. Like when some of us came
from down South, it was because machines could do our jobs for less money than
the boss paid us.

Our "pops" were "much talk and no action"! We loved them very much as
young teenage black women. We cannot make the intensity of this love for our
daddies so's you can touch it unless you have lived the way we did. As they
drank more, they beat momma more and she turned on us. Daddy now stayed
away for days and you'd see him on the corner "moving on some 'bitch.'" But
he still came home occasionally, and he brought "him some money" part of the
time. But the arguments between him and "moms" got brutal. Our momma
didn't understand that he'd lost his job because the system—capitalism—didn't
need him. She blamed the loss of the job on him. He blamed the loss of the job on
her.

We were left with half-fathers or none at all. Too many of us have spent our
teenage life looking for another daddy, and the security we learned went with
having daddies. This is our basic history—loss of security and loss of our
daddies. It made everyone of us dependent on males economically and psychologically. We can put this together now, but then there was ABSOLUTELY
NOBODY to "hip" us to what was really happening and how everything was
connected.

The fighting between our parents and between our brothers and sisters
spread and worsened. Each of us saw our own individual problems as bigger and
more important than anybody else's. We never looked back on ourselves. We
always blamed the problem on someone close to us. That's as far as we could
see. Families moved on families, and our older brothers, the favorites of the
parents, slowly began to "trip out" on "smack" (dope). Now everybody was
fighting everybody else, and none of us ever considered it had anything to do
with big capitalism and imperialism and neocolonialism. We would have laughed
at the words. They were too damn big, and we had never heard them in school.
We lived from one day to the next, with no past and no future. So fighting among
ourselves and "tripping" on a little "smokes," a little wine, was a release. We
talk about the old days now and fall out laughing. To some of us who laugh the
hardest, the memories are still too painful because we are still caught on the

system. We can still phantasize about "being somebody" or having this dress or this piece of furniture. But we know the power is in us basically because we *cannot* want those things if we really decide. Ain't nobody got the power outside of us. We have it inside! TALKING about this and the old days is a replay, like it's a way to get it out of our system because even with political consciousness, we are still trapped—and everybody is getting poorer.

There was just "no way" for our world to be broken into and made real by connecting it to the economic system we lived in, which we now know as capitalism. Each apartment was a separate world. Each individual in the family was a separate world. The very word *apartment* describes the reality of apartness. Each member of the family lived for that day or, better said, each of us lived to get to Friday when we could party and get ourself a boyfriend. We were successfully cut off from each other and the world around us.

When the world moved, it moved on us separately and we dealt with that attack separately. Because we admired that world, depended on it for all our necessities like food, clothing, water, housing, education, and the "goodies," like fancy clothes and pretty furniture—yet we were constantly "put down" by it. We were caught in a bind we couldn't get out of. Lord! How we loved "fine" clothes! But when we stole them, the clothes were taken away and sometimes we were put away. When we tried to get jobs with "big money" to buy those pretty things, we were only allowed little petty jobs with low pay. If we studied hard and got good marks so we could go to college, there was no money. Our parents were too poor.

All during the late fifties and early sixties, every move outward to join the white world was stopped cold. But the first problem was in us. We wanted that world BAD! It didn't need us or want us young black women, except as domestics, clean-up personnel in some institution, pool secretaries, waitresses, and five-and-dime store clerks. The second problem was, we didn't understand why we couldn't have it. And the third problem was, at this critical time—early sixties—no one came to patiently explain anything to us.

But now we have gone back, ourselves, to our mothers and fathers and made them tell us about their past. We've forced them to the wall many times in the last four years, making them tell us things they had learned to be ashamed of—mostly low social status. But we have put together a picture of Southern poor black women pulling together to get North. Some of the stories are exciting, like when the Ku Klux Klan attacked in North Carolina and some of the women determined to get out because the terror was too much. Others were plain and simple stories of never having enough, shacks built by the family itself on somebody else's land, no work, little income, family quarrels, and boyfriends who had already gone North leaving pregnant young women behind. Many of those babies were born and were left in the South with "granma." The young mother followed her man North, got a job and sent money home for the children. The young father had long ago just disappeared. A new man came along and there were children born here. But there was no fit place for the children to play, no one to help take care of them, and the man wanted to "play." So these children went South to be raised in the country away from the bad city.

Many of our mothers followed their older sisters up, where the first job was almost always in domestic service. They'd live together in one of the Big City slums and commute to the suburbs by bus and train. Some would sleep-in at first, save their money, get an apartment and send for other sisters, aunts, or cousins. They'd work in domestic service for years, saving their money and helping to support families, their own children down South and their nieces and nephews. Sometimes they'd save up enough to buy an old house and rent out rooms to other black women who had just come North and were domestics and wanted the privacy of their own room on their day off. This income, along with the income from renting rooms to single men doing factory work, helped to pay for the house. Most of our parents wanted to forget this past.

Our parents have always looked up and onward. This was the American Way of Life. Now here they were, living right next door, almost, to the American Dream, the rich whites. They had made it out of the South, out of the big Northern city slum into the slums of suburbia—just one more step—just one more step and they could be out of the slums entirely. So close—so damned close, and yet so far, so far away! Greedy hogs skewered to a spike, prepared for slaughter. Anytime, they could lose their jobs—twisting, turning, trying to get loose. No Way!

The word "pigs" is really a placing of our own contradictions outside of ourselves. We put the term "pigs" on the white cops who come from the same class we do, only they are white-skinned petty bourgeois. They, therefore, are more privileged. But they have the same kind of frustrations we have. They, too, are so close to the "goodies" but still so far away.

Now you take the nigger cops in our town. They all come from out of the projects, and their families look down on us still trapped inside the projects. We look down on the families around the projects who can't get in. When we were kids together, we sniggered and made fun of those just up from the South.

There is a saying kids have. "Takes one to know one!" When we started calling cops "pigs" and black-skinned cops "nigger pigs," it took a pig to know a pig. It would have been more honest of us if we had recognized that the cops and we are greedy, hungry, and eager for the "goodies" of the middle-class. We both are caught between having and not having.

In the early sixties, the projects finally blew wide open. The evening was hot. Everybody was hanging-out, grouped around the benches, sitting on the fences, laying out on the grass, sharing a bottle in the ball field. A white cop beat "the blood" to the ground, right in plain sight of everyone. Just getting his "balls off" on "the nigger" "'cause he's a nigger! Niggers are disgusting anyhow! You know how lazy they are. . . . They've got real hateful lately! . . . Besides they're scary!" Fear and anger, all knotted up together. "Hit that son-of-a-bitch!" The women moved first, covering their sons with their own bodies, screaming at the cop, cursing and moving toward him. The black man stood "stock-still"— watching, tense, rigid, unmoving.

The next day the entire project marched on City Hall. Never had there been such a spontaneous collective action. But never had a people experienced such long-lasting, razor-sharp frustration—living so near to the finer things, yet so far away from "them goodies." This reality had been building up since the early fifties. Other cities began to blow. "Burn that mother-fucker down! . . . Here, sister, take these clothes home to yo' kids! Man, gimme that bottle of gin, you know I don't dig J&B! . . . Hey, get that color TV over there! Get the kids out. The place is going up! Oh lordy me, what am I gonna do now? I ain't got no place to go!" Everybody black suffering the same contradiction, like a knife in the stomach. We had gotten to the North, made it to the Promised Land, and everything was slipping through our fingers. It was steady getting worse and there weren't no other place to go.

The anger subsided. The court case went on and on, put off and postponed, like this would tire us out. We were already empty. Our fury had spent itself. We went back "scratching for bread" and "louding" each other.

But not all of us. We younger black women hung in there for the "brother" who got his head cracked open. The white lawyer took the case for nothing. He was mad! And with the young black women's help and the pushing of the mother, they won a legal victory.

Some of the young black sisters over at the high school moved on the shit the teachers have always handed out. The brothers, too, were moving on racism. We got ourself a group going—black brothers and sisters, raised fists, blue jeans, khaki jackets, cool—we were moving. But the brothers wanted us to walk behind them. They started giving orders for us to walk between them when we went down to the Big City to liberate books on politics. They had to protect us. Where were they coming from? Black women never got no protection from nobody. We could fight as good as any man. Black brothers told us it was time to "get back" and let them lead.

Manhood was privilege—to be "somebody," at least and at last, over black women and children. Ain't that a bitch? Acting just like Mr. Whiteman over his women and children. Was this a revolution or were we exchanging one master for another? No bet! No matter how "the bloods" tried to dress this shit up in political terms, it was plain—they were playing the master and we were to play the slaves.

Play-acting didn't really make any difference, but when we graduated, we learned that women's inferiority was real and deadly. We got training jobs in the office pool. The "bloods" were on the production lines and pulling in more an hour than we were. The economic oppression for us was still as real as it had been for our black mothers. We either took those minor office jobs, or went back to "momma's" job at "Miss Anne's," or into the hospital scrubbing floors or carrying meal trays.

A very small number of us got scholarships at the local colleges. We tried our "bad-all-black-shit" there, staying to ourselves, dressing like revolutionaries. We black women were play-acting and being educated by the system. We were off the job market that was getting smaller, particularly for black women, and being allowed by the college administration to strut our "black power" shit as long as we didn't go too far. We were going to get that education and take it back to the people. Now in college we were getting the same lies the poor people were choking on in high school. They knew we were bullshitting. We had privilege and didn't want to admit it.

Those of us who got neither on-the-job-training nor a college scholarship got ourselves pregnant. We didn't really mind because it would make us dependent on men, and we liked that no matter what the political sisters said. For too many years black women had had to carry the whole load of the family without a man. Poor black women who lived outside of the projects reminded us that poor women all over the world had to keep the family going because their men were sent away when the Europeans and Americans colonized their land. Men were sent to the West as slaves, or they became migrant laborers in other parts of Africa and later Europe. When they revolted against the colonial system, they were sent to prison or killed. Thousands of Asian men became the crews of trading ships, leaving their families for years. In South Africa today, black African men are forced into the mines to pay taxes put on them by the white occupiers. They have to leave their children and their women for six months to a year. Black men ran away from the constant economic and psychological harassment in the South. South American males travelled to the big cities for work to feed their families. All poor families have had their men ripped from them by colonialism, capitalism, and imperialism.

We petty-bourgeois women, at least, did not suffer from our men being driven from the home in quite the same way. They could get low-paying jobs under capitalism. But since the middle-sixties, our men have lost jobs, gone on dope, or been sent to jail for felonies. We project women have competed like crabs in a barrel for a "blood" with a job. Not a human being, AN OBJECT and a means to get the "loot." Like our brothers, we are hooked, but not on "scag." We are hooked on the "goodies" and on men who can provide the "bread" to get the "goodies."

We were and are the most "tripped out" on clothes and furniture. Unless you've lived in a low-income project, you can't feel what it is like to have to drop everything, go downtown, and buy and buy and buy. We'd take EVERYTHING in sight if we could. If we run out of money, we come back home evil, with "an attitude," snap at anybody in a minute—our head aching with the tension, with the rage, our stomach tied in knots with fury! Goddamn it!

To see our kids the best dressed in the projects, five pairs of shoes for one child—o—o—h, that's a good feeling! But still we live in a dirty, crowded project. So near and yet so far away.

To see "our man" "bop" down the project path, every woman's head turned toward him—and he's all ours! How they envy us because he's so fine and he belongs to "this woman"! Back in the apartment, he's uptight because we spent the food money on clothes. He "gets an attitude" because we don't have supper ready and the dishes are still in the sink this morning. He says we don't care about him. "Black women ain't shit!"—so near and so far away.

"Being in love with the master and the 'goodies' makes you very empty. It drives you into fantasy and dreams. I can dream I am in this place or that place. I can't read when I'm like this. I can't concentrate. I look at TV. It romanticizes me!'' You have to have been in this predicament to know how difficult it is to come out of it with nothing waiting for you but political struggle with other women who are just like you were. They do everything not to hear you. But they know, like we knew, deep down. They just can't bear to know just yet.

Mirror, Mirror

Linda Phelps

Mirror, mirror, on the wall,
Let me be pretty, above all.

Have you ever stood in front of a mirror, looked at the blotches and irregularities of your face and yearned to be a beautiful woman? And why not? Being pretty certainly makes a girl's life easier. Your father may have held you on his knee and told you how pretty you were. Being a little lady was always a good way to please adults. If your mother was like mine, she showed you how to roll your hair and you soon learned that boys preferred you soft and giggly and pretty. Beautiful women seem to exude a magic which attracts admiration from all quarters. The gorgeous women with the flowing hair by Clairol and the gleaming white teeth by Palmolive have created an image which we carry in our brains. All women secretly desire to be beautiful. And again, why not? Don't we owe it to ourselves as self-respecting human beings to try to be as attractive as possible?

Beauty and fashion are very complex things. Human beings in all cultures have adorned themselves and covered their bodies with trinkets, bones, skins, and colors. Some cultures, especially dying ones, have made a fetish out of fashion. In other times people have condemned it: ''In that day the Lord will take away the bravery of their tinkling ornaments . . .'' What part does fashion play in American life? Should we condemn it or what?

Historically fashion has been the ideal preoccupation of those who have been dependent and oriented to the status quo. People who have been denied outlets of personal expression in society and yet who have desired a certain prominence have often turned to fashion to make their mark on the world. For example, in 15th century Germany, a great outburst of individuality and personal achievement began to break down medieval structures. Women were not allowed to participate in this movement and they took out their frustrations by producing extravagant styles of dress. Women of the Italian Renaissance, on the other hand, were nearly men's equals in education and cultural achievement and accordingly produced nothing new in fashion. If modern American culture were buried in ruins and later dug up, what would be concluded about all the pluckers, scrapers, dyes, lotions, and sprays? What would be discovered, I think, would be that some of the most highly educated women in history (for a large number at least 12 years) were being kept marginal to society and its achievements and were expressing their individuality in fashion instead.

In a certain sense, fashion gives a woman compensation for her lack of position in a society based on doing work in a recognized job or profession. She can be bizarre or creative but within conventional bounds. Fashion also supplements her identity, her inability to individualize her existence purely in her own terms. If women and wives and mothers, then they are also blondes, brunettes, broads, etc.

The major stages of a woman's life can be conceived as different problem phases in fashion and beauty. In adolescence, the young girl stands before the mirror, experimenting with different hairdos and dress, trying on this or that role to see what response she'll get. "Every smart woman keeps searching for her identity," says one hair dye ad, " . . . for a special way to shape her mouth or tilt her chin . . . a fragrance that's like her personal message to the world." How to catch the eye of a guy you're trying to attract? One is forced to do at least the minimum that all the other women are doing just to stay in the race. And the average woman spends about 2 hours a day, 1-8th of her waking hours in personal grooming. When you add the countless hours shopping, looking through magazines, discussing clothes, and worrying, probably ¼ of a woman's waking time is devoted to the complex business of making herself attractive.

Beauty is no longer merely god-given either. With the proper study and effort, any girl can be glamorous. There is no problem—sagging chin, thin dull hair, bulgy thighs—that cannot be remedied if one uses the proper exercises, lotions, or dyes. There is a trace of Horatio Alger here. Any girl—honest, hardworking, willing to invest enough time and capital—can be successful. It is the female version of the American dream; beauty is the capital a woman uses to cross class lines, to move up in the world. We must treat ourselves as a craftsman treats his raw material—anointing, coloring, plucking, waving, deodorizing, molding, restraining, concealing. "Woman makes herself," says one cosmetic consultant.

Once you've gotten your man, the next problem phase is to keep him. "There are girls at the office . . . wives must also be lovers too," goes the old song, "rush to his arms the moment he comes home to you." In addition to fending off all other women (who have equal access to the means of seduction) it is the duty of every mother to whip her daughter into shape, to develop those anxieties, patient habits, and discipline which will keep her steadfastly before her mirror throughout a lifetime. After you have gotten your daughter safely married off, the third phase is old age, or the battle to hold it off. A woman who is losing her looks is losing a big part of her capital, whether in the working world or in her husband's eyes. During this phase, her "dreams of the everyday housewife" may recall how pretty she once was, how many boyfriends she had, her past days of power and glory.

The preoccupation with fashion is not just a matter of time. Fashion also involves a whole orientation toward life. When your mother constantly fiddles with your hair, calls attention to crooked bows, soiled sashes, slips showing, you begin to become attuned to these things in yourself as well as in other women. A woman gets good at this sort of thing (this attention to detail is all part of that secret ingredient called feminine intuition). In one glance, one woman can sum up another and know what is important to know about her. A glance at the left hand tells you if she is married and thus her status. Then her dress will give you a clue about other important things: what her husband does, how her house probably looks.

Any woman who does not do her utmost to be attractive becomes an affront to the whole system. If a woman is unlucky in having fly-away hair, a tendency to put on weight, a bad complexion, or just plain bad features, she evokes the same response in every women she meets: "Why doesn't she DO something about herself?" A man who is plain or even ugly can compensate by being friendly, witty, or brainy. An ugly woman is pitied and is an affront to woman's whole image.

The pursuit of prettiness becomes the cult of femininity. It becomes the way you approach the world: you follow the rituals, play the game that becomes second-nature. Doors are opened, cigarettes lighted, men gaze at you appreciatively, you strive to please. Who are you? You are . . . WOMAN. Woman is soft, pretty, seductive, and if she tries to be other things, she will not be taken seriously. And where are the casualties of this femininity? the tall women who stoop, the flat-chested ones who cannot walk proudly, the minds that go unused, the ugly-ducklings that don't turn into swans?

Don't be mistaken. I am not in the puritan bag. Fashion is not an evil; adorning ourselves expresses part of our humanness. But in America, it is a full-time business and it is big business. It is a way of life. If you are going to play the game big, then understand what it is and where it is taking you. Don't wake up one morning when you're 35 years old, and your children don't need you anymore and look in the mirror and say:

Mirror, mirror, on the wall,
Who am I?

It Hurts to Be Alive and Obsolete:
The Ageing Woman

Zoe Moss

What, fat, forty-three, and I dare to think I'm still a person? No, I am an invisible lump. I belong in a category labelled *a priori* without interest to anyone. I am not even expected to interest myself. A middle-aged woman is comic by definition.

In this commodity culture, we are urged and coerced into defining ourselves by buying objects that demonstrate that we are, or which tell us that they will make us feel, young, affluent, fashionable. Imagine a coffee table with the bestsellers of five years ago carefully displayed. You giggle. A magazine that is old enough—say, a *New Yorker* from 1944 with the models looking healthy and almost buxom in their padded jackets—or a dress that is far enough gone not to give the impression that perhaps you had not noticed fashions had changed, can become campy and delightful. But an out-of-date woman is only embarrassing.

The mass media tell us all day and all evening long that we are inadequate, mindless, ugly, disgusting in ourselves. We must try to resemble perfect plastic objects, so that no one will notice what we really are. In ourselves we smell bad, shed dandruff, our breath has an odor, our hair stands up or falls out, we sag or stick out where we shouldn't. We can only fool people into liking us by using magic products that make us products, too.

Women, especially, are commodities. There is always a perfect plastic woman. Girls are always curling their hair or ironing it, binding their breasts or padding them. Think of the girls with straight hips and long legs skulking through the 1890's with its women defined as having breasts the size of pillows and hips like divans. Think of the Rubens woman today forever starving and dieting and crawling into rubber compression chambers that mark her flesh with livid lines and squeeze her organs into knots.

If a girl were to walk into a party in the clothes of just five or six years past, in the make-up and hairstyle of just that slight gap of time, no one would want to talk to her, no man would want to dance with her. Yet what has all that to do with even a man and a women in bed? This is not only the middle class I am talking about. I have seen hippies react the same way to somebody wearing old straight clothes.

It is a joke, but a morbid one. My daughter has a girlfriend who always laughs with her hand up to her mouth because she is persuaded her teeth are yellow, and that yellow teeth are hideous. She seems somber and never will she enjoy a natural belly laugh. Most young girls walk around with the conviction that some small part of their anatomy (nose, breasts, knees, chin) is so large or so small or so misshapen that their whole body appears to be built around that part, and all of their activities must camouflage it.

My daughter is a senior in college. She already talks about her ''youth'' with a sad nostalgia. She is worried because she is not married. That she has not met anyone that she wants to live that close to, does not seem to figure in her anxiety. Everything confirms in her a sense of time passing, that she will be left behind, unsold on the shelf. She already peers in the mirror for wrinkles and buys creams and jellies to rub into her skin. Her fear angers me but leaves me helpless. She is alienated from her body because her breasts are big and do not stand out like the breasts of store mannequins. She looks twenty-one. I look forty-three.

I want to beg her not to begin worrying, not to let in the dreadful daily gnawing already. Everyone born grows up, grows older, and ages every day until he dies. But every day in seventy thousand ways this society tells a woman that it is her sin and her guilt that she has a real living body. How can a woman respect herself when every day she stands before her mirror and accuses her face of betraying her, because every day she is, indeed, a day older.

Everything she reads, every comic strip, every song, every cartoon, every advertisement, every book and movie tells her that a woman over thirty is ugly and disgusting. She is a bag. She is to be escaped from. She is no longer an object of prestige consumption. For her to have real living sexual desires is obscene. Her touch is thought to contaminate. No man "seduces" a woman older than him: there is no conquest. It is understood she would be "glad for a touch of it." Since she would be glad, there can be no pleasure in the act. Either this society is mad or I am mad. It is considered incredible that a woman might have had experiences that are valuable or interesting and that have enriched her as a person. No, men may mature, but women just obsolesce.

All right, says the woman, don't punish me! I won't do wrong! I won't get older! Now, if a woman has at least an upper-middle-class income, no strong commitments such as a real career or a real interest in religion or art or politics; if she has a small family and hired help; if she has certain minimal genetic luck; if she has the ability to be infinitely fascinated by her own features and body, she may continue to present a youthful image. She can prolong her career as sexual object, lying about her age, rewriting her past to keep the chronology updated, and devoting herself to the cultivation of her image. Society will reward her greatly. Women in the entertainment industry are allowed to remain sexual objects (objects that are prestigeful to use or own—like Cadillacs) for much of their lives.

To be told when you have half your years still to wade through and when you don't feel inside much different than you did at twenty (you are still you!— you know that!), to be told then that you are cut off from expressing yourself sexually and often even in friendship, drives many women crazy—often literally so.

Don't tell me that it is human nature for women to cease to be attractive early. In primitive society a woman who is still useful—in that by all means far more humane definition than ours—will find a mate, whom she may share as she shares the work with his other wives. Black women are more oppressed on the job and in almost every other way in this society than white women, but at least in the ghetto men go on assuming a woman is sexual as long as she thinks so too.

Earlier mythology in which "the widow" is a big sex figure, French novels in which the first mistress is always an older woman, the Wife of Bath, all reinforce my sense that there is nothing natural about women's obsolescence.

I was divorced five years ago. Don't tell me I should have "held on to my husband." We let go with great relief. Recently he has married a woman in her late twenties. It is not surprising he should marry someone younger: most people in this society are younger than my ex-husband. In my job, most of the people I meet are younger than I am, and the same is true of people who share my interests, from skiing to resistance to the war against Vietnam.

When my daughter was little I stayed home, but luckily for me I returned to work when she entered school. I say luckily, because while I believe my ex-husband has an obligation to help our daughter, I would never accept alimony. I can get quite cold and frightened imagining what would have happened if I had stayed home until my divorce, and then, at thirty-eight, tried to find work. I used to eat sometimes at a lunchroom where the rushed and overworked waitress was in her late forties. She had to cover the whole room, and I used to leave her larger tips than I would give someone else because to watch her made me conscious of women's economic vulnerability. She was gone one day and I asked the manager at the cash register about her. "Oh, the customers didn't like her. Men come in here, they want to see a pretty face."

I have insisted on using a pseudonym in writing this article, because the cost of insisting I am not a cipher would be fatal. If I lost my job, I would have an incredible time finding another. I know I will never "get ahead." Women don't move up through the shelves of a business automatically or by keeping their mouths shut. I could be mocked into an agony of shame for writing this—but beyond that, I could so easily be let go.

I am gregarious, interested in others, and I think, intelligent. All I ask is to get to know people and to have them interested in knowing me. I doubt whether I would marry again and live that close to another individual. But I remain invisible. I think stripped down I look more attractive on some abstract scale (a bisexual Martian judging) than my ex-husband, but I am sexually and socially obsolete, and he is not. Like most healthy women my face has aged more rapidly than my body, and I look better with my clothes off. When I was young, my anxiety about myself and what was to become of me colored all my relationships with men, and I was about as sensual as a clotheshanger. I have a capacity now for taking people as they are, which I lacked at twenty; I reach orgasm in half the time and I know how to please. Yet I do not even dare show a man that I find him attractive. If I do so, he may react as if I had insulted him: with shock, with disgust. I am not even allowed to be affectionate. I am supposed to fulfill my small functions and vanish.

Often when men are attracted to me, they feel ashamed and conceal it. They act as if it were ridiculous. If they do become involved, they are still ashamed and may refuse to appear publicly with me. Their fear of mockery is enormous. There is no prestige attached to having sex with me.

Since we are all far more various sexually than we are supposed to be, often, in fact, younger men become aware of me sexually. Their response is similar to what it is when they find themselves feeling attracted to a homosexual: they turn those feelings into hostility and put me down.

Listen to me! Think what it is like to have most of your life ahead and be told you are obsolete! Think what it is like to feel attraction, desire, affection toward others, to want to tell them about yourself, to feel that assumption on which self-respect is based, that you are worth something, and that if you like someone, surely he will be pleased to know that. To be, in other words, still a living woman, and to be told every day that you are not a woman but a tired object that should disappear. That you are not a person but a joke. Well, I am a bitter joke. I am bitter and frustrated and wasted, but don't you pretend for a minute as you look at me, forty-three, fat, and looking exactly my age, that I am not as alive as you are and that I do not suffer from the category into which you are forcing me.

The Sexual Fantasies of Women

E. Barbara Hariton

Sue considers herself happily married. She enjoys sexual intercourse with her husband and usually reaches orgasm. However, just as she approaches the peak she imagines that she is tied to a table while several men caress her, touch her genitals, and have intercourse with her. It is a fleeting image; as she passes into orgasm it disappears.

Dianne too is happily married. Yet she finds sexual foreplay with her husband more exciting if she imagines herself a harem slave displaying her breasts to an adoring sheik. While having intercourse, she sometimes envisions making love in the back seat of a car or in an old-fashioned house during a group orgy. She likes to imagine being forced by one man after another. In one favorite scene she goes to a drive-in movie and is raped by a masculine figure whose face is a "blur."

Psychoanalysts, who treat many aspects of human behavior as symptoms of pathology, might conclude that Sue and Dianne were in dire need of help. Freud himself laid the grounds for just such a diagnosis by declaring that "happy people never make fantasies, only unsatisfied ones do." A disciple of Freud's, Wilhelm Reich, claimed that fantasies during intercourse were an escape mechanism, a diversionary tactic that helped people resist full orgasmic surrender. For both men, fantasies were a sign of neurosis and sexual maladjustment.

Contemporary therapists take the same attitude in working with their women patients. Their clinical reports describe sexual fantasies or daydreams as tortuous efforts to satisfy other needs through sex, as expressions of penis fear, as devices employed by women to put some psychological distance between themselves and their partners, and as mechanisms to deny responsibility for performing sex acts that otherwise would lead to intolerable guilt. Several therapists note that women are reluctant to discuss their sexual fantasies, that they seem to fear disapproval. Patients who reveal many other intimate secrets during therapy often try stubbornly to conceal these fantasies.

The disapproval these women fear is real, but it is not justified. Modern psychology supposedly liberated men and women from the moral prison of the Victorian age; actually, it replaced one set of prejudices with another. Psychology is dominated by males who find it impossible to believe that normal women might have fantasies during intercourse—and by all means not during intercourse with them. Similarly, their predecessors found it impossible to believe that normal women might have orgasms.

Sue and Dianne were not neurotic or sexually maladjusted. They were normal housewives living in an upper-class suburb of New York who participated in a study I conducted on fantasies and thoughts that occur during intercourse. The study showed that erotic fantasies are common among women, that they are not escape mechanisms, and that they often enhance sexual desire and pleasure.

To recruit women for the study, I visited class meetings of a well-attended cultural and recreational program at a town park. I also went to board meetings of PTAs, charity groups and church-affiliated women's clubs. After explaining the nature of my research, I assured the women that participants would remain anonymous. Between 30 and 60 percent of the women in the groups I approached agreed to participate, producing a sample of 141 subjects who ranged in age from 25 to 50 years.

Orgasm

I gave the women a questionnaire that focused on realistic thoughts and erotic fantasies during sexual intercourse with their husbands, nonsexual daydreams, attitudes toward sex, marital adjustment, level of anxiety, frequency and nature of orgasm, attitudes toward fantasies during intercourse, background and intelligence, and 21 personality traits. In addition, I interviewed 56 of the housewives who volunteered to talk about the questionnaire and their own fantasies.

The questionnaire listed 15 common erotic fantasies that I had gleaned from literary works, clinical reports, and my own earlier pilot study. Each woman answered every item on a scale from one to five; a minimum response (one) indicated that she never had the fantasy during intercourse with her husband, while a maximum response (five) indicated that she had the fantasy every time she had intercourse. By adding the scores on the 15 items, I obtained a measure of the general level of erotic fantasy.

I found that 65 percent of the women fantasized during intercourse with their husbands. Another 28 percent reported that they had occasional thoughts during intercourse that could be considered as fantasy. Only seven percent of the women reported that they never had any of the thoughts listed on the questionnaire.

I examined the ratings for each fantasy and compared them with answers on other parts of the questionnaire to discover the most popular themes and whether they were related to such factors as marital adjustment, personality, and general thoughts during intercourse.

Lover

Two themes were especially popular: being with another man—an old lover, a famous actor, a casual friend, and being overpowered or forced into sex by an ardent, faceless male figure. Sixty percent of the women who fantasized said that they thought of "an imaginary lover" sometimes during sexual intercourse, and 18 percent of them said they did so very often. In response to the item "I imagine that I am being overpowered or forced to surrender," 53 percent of the fantasizers reported having the fantasy sometimes and 15 percent had it very often.

One of the most important findings was that erotic fantasy did not indicate marital maladjustment. Women who had positive thoughts about their husbands during intercourse were just as likely to have erotic fantasies as those who had negative thoughts about their mates. However, the presence of such thoughts during intercourse did relate to sexual satisfaction and marital adjustment.

Women who had positive thoughts—"I think about the pleasure I am experiencing"—almost every time they had intercourse (20 percent), said they had good sexual relationships with their husbands and they usually attained orgasm. In contrast, the 16 percent who reported having negative thoughts during lovemaking—"I wish that I were not having intercourse"—almost never experienced orgasm with their husbands, and when they did, they considered it unpleasant; a number of them had extramarital affairs. The other 64 percent reported low levels of negative thoughts during intercourse, moderate levels of distracting thoughts ("I remember tasks that I must do"), and high levels of positive thoughts.

Though erotic fantasies were not related to thoughts during intercourse, they did appear to be related to personality type. When I compared answers to the fantasy items with data from the interviews and from other parts of the questionnaire, I found some interesting relationships between erotic fantasy and personality. One type of woman had varied erotic fantasies, another personality type had no fantasy, a third fantasized about other lovers and a fourth type dreamed about forced sex.

Dotty was typical of the group of women who had varied erotic fantasies during intercourse. At times she imagined herself overpowered on a beach or carried away to the desert. The passivity expressed in these fantasies did not reflect her actual role in the sex act, however, since she often was aggressive with her husband. The imaginary men in her daydreams started out as someone else, but after undressing they resembled her husband (who Dotty claimed was beautifully built). Sometimes she imagined two or more men making love to her, each touching a different part of her body. She found this kind of fantasy especially arousing and soothing. In some fantasies she pretended to be a $100-a-day call girl, in others a fabulous courtesan like Salome or a movie star like Elizabeth Taylor. Her fantasy partners were dominant men, intellectuals like William F. Buckley Jr. or physically forceful movie stars like Steve McQueen.

Women like Dotty who fantasized a great deal were impulsive, independent, and nonconformist. They showed personality characteristics usually associated with masculinity such as aggressiveness and lacked strong feminine characteristics such as affiliative and nurturing tendencies. They tended also to daydream at times other than during the sex act, and the content of these daydreams varied. Their anxiety level was higher than average, but their feelings did not focus persistently on guilt or fear as did those of more unhappy women.

These women found their fantasies sexually arousing; they were part of their general approach to lovemaking, a natural occurrence like kissing or petting. The high fantasizers had an active exploratory approach to sexuality. They reported having had premarital relations and, more often than not, extramarital experiences. They undertook these affairs in a spirit of curiosity, not as retaliation for some action by their husbands or as compensation for an unhappy marriage. (Several of these women reported that in the early days of their affairs they had relatively few fantasies. However, as the new relationships grew comfortable, fantasies appeared.)

INTERCOURSE FANTASIES

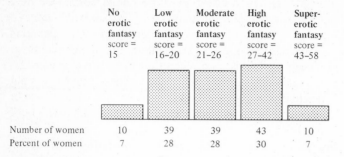

No erotic fantasy score = 15	Low erotic fantasy score = 16–20	Moderate erotic fantasy score = 21–26	High erotic fantasy score = 27–42	Super-erotic fantasy score = 43–58

Number of women	10	39	39	43	10
Percent of women	7	28	28	30	7

TEN MOST COMMON FANTASIES (IN ORDER OF THEIR FREQUENCY)

1 Thoughts of an imaginary lover enter my mind.
2 I imagine that I am being overpowered or forced to surrender.
3 I enjoy pretending that I am doing something wicked or forbidden.
4 I am in a different place like a car, motel, beach, woods, etc.
5 I relive a previous sexual experience.
6 I imagine myself delighting many men.
7 I imagine that I am observing myself or others having sex.
8 I pretend that I am another irresistibly sexy female.
9 I pretend that I struggle and resist before being aroused to surrender.
10 I daydream that I am being made love to by more than one man at a time.

Creativity

Personality traits of the women who fantasized a great deal were similar to those of creative persons, and the interviews revealed that many of these women participated in some form of creative activity. (Artistic interests also appeared, though less often, in women who had average levels of erotic fantasy, but none of the women who reported low levels of erotic fantasy were involved in an artistic pursuit.)

Elaine was one of the small group of women who reported no erotic fantasies. She was a bland, pleasant, and conservative woman in her late 40s, who had been a bookkeeper before her marriage. She was the mother of four children and had no outside interests. Although Elaine had never had psychotherapy, she felt she needed it. She was happy as a woman and against women opposing men. Elaine's upbringing was strict and sex was never discussed. Her parents were very good to her and her two sisters.

Elaine claimed that she had good communication with her husband and that they were good friends. She felt warmth and love during sex, but she rarely had orgasm. She was not often in the mood for sex, and fatigue or children's problems affected her ability to relax sexually. Elaine had few daydreams and no erotic fantasies. Women like Elaine were conciliatory, unassuming, nurturing and affiliative.

Nora belonged to the group of women who fantasized constantly about other men, places or times. She was tired of her husband but afraid to have an affair. During intercourse she fantasized about old lovers or actors like Steve

McQueen or Paul Newman, all of whom she thought daring—a quality she identified with. Sometimes she imagined a highly erotic scene in which men were lined up to make love to her while she thought, "Now you're next." She also imagined scenes from dates with boys she had known before her marriage, and sometimes she remembered an erotic scene from a pornographic magazine. Women whose fantasies resembled Nora's imaginings of other men seemed to be trying to adjust to unsatisfactory marriages; their fantasies expressed their desires to bypass their marital relationships.

Fantasizers like Nora shared some personality traits with the creative fantasizers. They were active, curious, independent, playful, impulsive, exhibitionist and nonconformist.

Mary imagined that she was in a movie theater. Two men she did not know entered and made love to her in the darkness while she passively watched the film. Her feelings were the familiar "Please! . . . Don't . . . Stop! . . . Please don't stop." She did not cooperate but wanted the men to perform more sex acts and to make her like them. The fantasies were similar to ones she had when she masturbated as a child. (She liked to imagine that a statue of Hercules, pictured on a telephone-book cover, came to life and raped her.) She enjoyed the fantasy that she could "turn on men."

Mary belonged to the fourth group: women who had recurrent fantasies of forced sex. These women invariably described their fantasies as highly erotic and claimed that they brought on orgasms. When I examined these women's answers on other parts of the questionnaire, I discovered that they frequently had multiple orgasms or intense pleasurable feelings during orgasm. Their relationships with their husbands were good. They tended to be passive during intercourse, allowing their husbands to take the lead. Their personality traits seemed to reflect this attitude; they were dependent, unobtrusive, controlled, serious, noninquisitive and conformist.

Most of the women we interviewed in this study reported overwhelmingly that their erotic fantasies were sexually arousing and pleasurable. Some used their fantasies to increase their desire if they were not ready to have intercourse or if they felt angry or distracted. Most of the time, however, fantasies appeared merely as an independent counterpoint to the sex act. One highly erotic fantasy, according to the women, was of many men touching all the erogenous parts of their bodies at once. This fantasy, which usually occurred when a woman was highly aroused, shows how imagination in pursuit of pleasure can reach beyond physical limits—in this case, the two hands and one mouth of the husband.

Helene Deutsch, the psychoanalyst, interpreted fantasies of being overcome or forced into sex as a sign that women were innately masochistic. Another psychoanalyst, Karen Horney, argued that though they were a sign of masochism, they resulted not from inborn female tendencies but from society's suppression of women.

Abraham Maslow took a different view. He noted that women high in self-esteem were the ones most likely to fantasize about submission during intercourse, while passive or masochistic women were least likely to have fantasies. The results of my study support his view. It may be that a confident woman does not let her own fantasies intimidate her, even if they seem less than idealistic. She accepts and trusts her own experiences and has little need to repress or deny them. She permits herself inexplicable images and ideas without feeling any threat to her integrity or sanity.

Aggression

It is a misnomer to label "force" fantasies masochistic. Theodor Reik says that a female masochist—a truly disturbed individual—wants to be rejected. He cited the case of a woman who imagined that she was a slave girl dancing before the Shah of Persia—as he sat indifferently playing chess. Common "force" fantasies, however, do not involve rejection or abuse. They appear in dominant and independent women, who imagine themselves desired and wooed by faceless males or groups of males while remaining unaware or unable to cooperate—unconscious, tied up, asleep, intoxicated. Though the women remain passive, they imagine themselves aroused to enjoyment by the men's efforts. In some fantasies, desirability and display are the erotic elements. The excited male watches the woman as she strips or dances before him. Perhaps as Maslow suggested, such fantasies are images of emotional processes that, in animals, link sexuality, aggression, dominance and display.

The finding that erotic fantasies are fleeting and partial suggests that they may be vestiges of fantasies experienced earlier in greater depth and detail. The women in my study related their erotic fantasies to masturbation fantasies and to daydreams stimulated by reading and by watching movies. Many women imagined being "taken" in cars, hallways, movie balconies, or subways. Such images appear to be left over from adolescent sexual daydreams; they do not reflect actual events. A young girl who spends much of her time daydreaming about sex may permanently condition these thoughts to erotic feelings. Images resurface during marriage and add to the realistic excitement. The evidence suggests that material for erotic fantasies develops early and that a lifetime of psychosexual development unfolds in these fantasies during mature sexual intercourse. Three factors probably contribute to a woman's tendency to fantasize during intercourse:

1   A capacity to respond with imagery to her own body's sensations and to environmental experiences (that is, having the personality style of a fantasizer).
2   The ability to allow herself to experience sexuality during childhood and adolescence in a primitive fashion without censuring or rationalizing the experience (for example, being able to play doctor).
3   A strong sexual need throughout the developmental years.

That primitive images cling to sexuality certainly is not a new discovery. Freud made it a basic element in his theory of human development. He stressed, however, that the ultimate achievement of maturity and emotional health would be an unambivalent, tender relationship between the sexes, capped by mutual orgasm. Supposedly, we should outgrow our need for fantasies. Psychoanalysts, however, seem to have underestimated the importance of primitive emotions, which may serve as a source of creative inspiration, motivation and ecstasy. Therese Benedek discovered that efforts to cure a patient of erotic fantasies often destroy the patient's ability to have an orgasm, and Nathaniel Ross observed that many anxious and irrational persons enjoy sex and attain orgasm, while many so-called genitally mature persons have dull sex lives.

My study suggests new ways to view some aspects of female sexuality. A woman making love experiences more than an idealistic, interpersonal exchange or a tender, mature, unambivalent relationship with her husband. In stressing the interpersonal aspects of sexuality, we should not overlook the individual facets. During intercourse, a woman experiences herself, her own sexuality, her husband's sexuality, and her desire for him. Childhood feelings, adolescent day-dreams, biological inheritance and social conditioning interact. A truly tender and trusting relationship between marital partners would permit the free release of primitive images and allow a woman to experience both her desire for her husband and the desires that drew her to him long before they met.

The Socialized Penis

Jack Litewka

This is, to a certain degree, a personal story. I felt the need to make it public because I have sensed for a long time, and now see more clearly every day, the disaster of sexuality in its present forms. Some women have been struggling with this reality. They have attempted to expose the male/female myth in the hope of creating a healthier reality. But most men have been (at best) silent or (at worst) dishonest—and often ignorant and defensive. This essay is an attempt to help men begin talking among themselves and hopefully with women.

The people who should have initiated the dialogue are psychoanalysts and psychiatrists: the psycho-healers. But they have failed us. And themselves. By and large, they have concentrated their energies on helping people adapt to the realities of the existing social system rather than examining the foundations of that system. But, like the rest of us, these people are damaged. And being damaged, they are incapable of dealing with their own experience. Have you seen much written or spoken about masturbation? I haven't. The psycho-healers, most of whom are men, always talk about the phenomenon of masturbation as if it was "other," "out there." Have you ever heard a psycho-healer say, "When I masturbate(d). . ."? Of course not. They are incapable or terrified of dealing with their own experience. So I am attempting to deal with mine, with those of men I know, in an effort to help us begin to deal more honestly with one aspect of male socialization.

Like the psycho-healers, like everyone, I am also damaged. I may be incapable of asking the right questions. I know I'm not able now to supply the "answers" that are needed. Desperately needed. But I'm going to try, and I hope that other men will also begin trying. Through persistence and honesty and perhaps by accident, we'll end up asking the right questions and be better able to answer them.

I'm very grateful to a few close friends, male and female, who are involved in this struggle and who have given me support and encouragement and criticism and chunks of their own lives in the writing of this essay. I'm also very happy that the Women's Movement exists and that many women are committed to undoing the damage done to all of us. I am not going to re-discuss what women writers have already explored. The sexual socialization of men in this century is what I want to deal with. More specifically, socialized sexual response. Still more specifically, the socialized penis. My penis, not just those of other men out there.

I was raised in America and learned—as did many other boys in my childhood and men I know now—to perform sexually on desire or request. This perfor-mance I think can be considered the norm, an ability that most males wanted to develop or maintain. The males who didn't conform to this norm usually felt incomplete, unskilled, or unmanly. And this insufficiency often resulted in self-damning fear and anxiety, while other "healthy" males who automatically or easily conformed to the norm just cruised along, dropping anchor in this or that port when entertainment's hunger urged.

I think I am typical of most American males when I say that getting aroused, getting an erection, was not a major problem in adolescence. If there was a major problem, it was in not knowing what to do, or not being allowed to do anything, with an erection. So you had to learn how to hide it or deal with the embarrass-ment of its discovery.

I don't know when I began to be annoyed with the way women and men relate. Like most men, I think, I only dealt with a relationship when I had experienced enough and was troubled enough to look back at a previous relation-ship. But by the time one seriously begins to examine male/female relationships, it is usually too late. Because one has already been thoroughly socialized. So instead of dealing with male/female relationships, one is incapable of examining them, or refuses to examine them, or represses what one knows, or stands under it intellectually and laughs at the absurdity. Or tragedy.

In the last year and a half, something happened to me on three separate occasions that made me decide to seriously analyze the way I had been sexually socialized. I now understand that the incidents occurred because I was already grappling with the origins of my sexuality.

Incident 1   A woman I liked (and who liked me—"love" may be a mythic word so it is not being used, especially since it has nothing to do with erection) and I were in bed together for the first time. We talked and hugged and played. To my surprise and dismay, I didn't get an erection. At least not at the propitious moment (I did have erections now and then throughout the night). And I didn't know why. Maybe I was just too tired or had been fucking and masturbating too much (though that had never been a problem before). But it didn't disturb me too much because the woman was supportive and we both knew there would be other nights. So we rolled together, smelled each other, heard our breathing, and had a lovely night despite absence of coitus.

In the following year, I had a few relationships and my penis was its old arrogant self, so that one night seemed an unexplained oddity and was pretty much forgotten. My sexual life had the same sexual dynamic as my previous sexual history, so things were back to normal. But then came round two.

Incident 2 Similar in all respects to Incident 1. No erection at the right time. Again, I did have erections now and then throughout the night. Again, I didn't know why. But I knew it wasn't from being too tired or fucking or masturbating too much, since I hadn't slept with a woman in about a month and since I had spent the past week on vacation just reading, resting, doing odd jobs—not masturbating—and enjoying the absence of tension. Again, it wasn't a hassle because the woman knew me and I knew her and we both knew people the other had slept with, so it was chalked off as a freak with neither of us to blame. We touched along the whole length of our bodies and discussed basketball, politics, and our social/sexual histories. She fell asleep. I couldn't, my brain gnawing at me, having scary thoughts about a present (temporary) or impending impotency, and resolving to do something—but not knowing what.

Simplistically, I made an assumption: it had to be me or the woman I was with. But since it had happened with two different women, I figured it was me (though there might have been similarities between the women and the situations). But since I had performed sexually in a normal way many times in the year between these incidents, I assumed that it had to be something about these particular women in combination with me.

My immediate concern was my own fright. The "no erection at the right time" syndrome had happened to me twice. I was scared, very scared. Images of impotence hung in the air and wouldn't disappear. So I got in touch with an old love who I still spend a loving night or two with every five or six months and with whom I had always had good sexual chemistry. We got together two nights later and history prevailed: my penis had its timing back and I performed like the stud I was always meant to be. Which was a tremendous relief.

But I still had no answer to my question: why didn't I get an erection at the right time on two different occasions when I was with women I wanted to be with and who wanted to be with me, when there was mutual attraction and social/political/intellectual compatibility? I had a few clues, a few hunches, a few theories. But at best they were very partial answers. So I started to do a lot of thinking and isolated myself from old loves and potential new ones. I decided to read a lot of 19th-century porno literature, hoping that there might be repeated patterns (and there were) of male/female sexual activities that I could learn something from. (I realize now that this was a cop-out, a refusal or inability to look at my self, my own sexual experience; and that to look at "other" sexuality, to learn from second-hand experience, was a safer path and one of less resistance. And for that reason, too, it may actually have been the only way I could start the examination.) I also read a lot of feminist writings, and continued to have many and long talks with a few close friends, all of whom are intensely involved with the liberation of people. I learned much during this time (a lot of which I already knew but couldn't make cohere), not all of which lends itself to this essay. But it all fed into an increasingly less diffuse puzzle.

Incident 3   This occasion was similar in almost all respects to Incidents 1 and 2, occurring about 18 months after the first incident and 6 months after the second. Between the second and third incidents, my sexual life had again been normal (for me).

This time I wasn't as frightened because I had already begun to figure out what the fuck was going on and had the reassurance that I was determined enough to maybe, just maybe, see it through to solution. Again, the woman was supportive and someone who I had gone through many things with over the years: this was just going to be another thing that we would have to deal with. Also, there was some hope because perceptions were beginning to clump together.

It became increasingly clear to me that in order to find answers to my emerging questions, I would have to go back and retrace the steps that were parts of my sexual history. Simultaneously, I was thinking that if my socialized sexuality was in any way similar to that of other men, then my formulations wouldn't be idiosyncratic to my experience. And as clues found me, I remembered old talks with young male friends and checked them against recent talks with adult male friends. It seemed that we had all gone through a basically similar process (with countless variations). Even those males who had not conformed to the norm, who didn't perform sexually according to the book, were affected by the norm process (sometimes resulting in a devastating social and sexual isolation). So I thought it would be worth the effort to construct a norm, however flawed, to determine what shape that image took. And to see if that image could teach.

The Initiation of a Young Male: In looking back on my sexual experiences and those of male friends, a very definite and sequential pattern was evident. I'm talking about actual (overt) sexual events, not subliminal or imagined or representational sexual experiences. I'm thinking of adolescent times in adolescent terms when males begin to experiment and develop their knowledge and expertise. I'm thinking about things you did sequentially as you got older. With a few total exceptions and an odd irregularity or two (like fucking a "whore" before you'd kissed a "girl") among the many men I have known and talked with, the sequence runs roughly as follows.

You kiss a girl. You kiss a girl a number of times. You kiss a girl continuously (make-out). You kiss a girl continuously and get your tongue into the act. All through this process you learn to use your hands to round out the orchestration, at first with simple clumsy chords and later with complex harmonies (with the woman, of course, being the instrument made to respond to the musician). You, as a young male, are told (or figure out) what sensitive spots you should seek, and learn more as the young female (hopefully) responds to your hands. First you just hug and grasp. Then you make little circles on her shoulders with your fingers. Then you go for the back of the neck, and run your fingers through her hair (music, please), and then over her face and throat. Then the outer ear (lobes especially). And middle ear. Then lower back (at which point your tongue might cover the ear as a stand-in for the absent hand). Then the tender sides of the waist above the (maybe-not-yet) hip bones. Then the belly. And after, the upper belly and the rib cage. Here let us take a deep breath before the great leap upward to the breast, which is a bold act broken into a number of ritualistic steps. First the hand over one breast, with blouse and bra between your hand and the female's flesh. This is a move that took special courage (balls?) and was very exciting for it seemed a new level of sensuality (which it was for the female, but for the male? no, only a new level of expectation). Then came a kind of figure-eight roving over the chest from one breast to the other (if your position allowed—how many right-handed lovers out there?). Then a sneaking between buttons (later unbuttoned) so your hand is on the breast with only the bra separating you from flesh. (Or if this procedure was too uncouth or too visible to others in the dusky room or impossible because of a a no-button sweater, you worked underneath the garment from a fleshy belly right up to the bra.) Then, by means of gradually developed finger dexterity, you begin to attack the flesh of the breast itself, working down from the top of the bra into the cup. And if you hadn't yet picked up any signs of female complicity in your previous experience, it was often clear here. If she sat and breathed normally, your fingers didn't stand a chance (bras were worn very tightly in my junior high school so that nipples were always pointing up at your eyes). If she wanted to be helpful, she would deeply exhale and move her shoulder forward so there was space between the bra and the breast. (Women's cooperation during all these events is an interesting topic and really should be written about by a woman.) And here came the rainbow's gold—the assault on the nipple. While a kiss was exciting, and cupping a breast breath-taking, the conquest of the nipple was transcendent. Partly because it was the only part of a female's anatomy that we have dealt with so far that isn't normally seen or even partly exposed. Also because you knew that when this was achieved, the girl really liked you, and that getting the bra unhooked and off would not be far away. Maybe as soon as next week. When older, the same night. And you also sensed that you were getting closer to the core of sexuality (excuse the geographically mixed metaphor). Then began the assault on the crotch, in steps similar to those of the battle of the breast. You caressed her hip, worked around to her ass, pulled her close to announce (if it hadn't already been discovered) the existence of your penis and give it some pleasurable friction (and provide the girls with a topic of gossip later? if you were erect). Then you worked down to the side of her leg. Then the front of her thigh. Then with a deep breath, and microscopic steps, you slowly progressed toward the vaginal entrance (how many of you had imagined the entrance 4 inches higher than you found it to be?). Now here there are many variables: was it at a swim party when she only had on the bottom part of a two-piece suit, or was she wearing jeans, or did she have a skirt on? Whatever the case, you usually ended up rubbing her crotch through cloth and then worked down from her belly toward her crotch, getting your hand (as one variation of the phrase goes) in her pants. Then you sort of played around above or on top of her slit and eventually got a finger in it, and by accident or design (depending on your previous intelligence briefings) found the "magic button." And soon (usually), all hell broke loose, and more than ever before, you didn't quite know what to do with yourself if fucking wasn't yet in the script.

And that pretty much covers the pre-coital scenario. Except it was described in a semi-humorous manner and, as a male, many of these events were terrifying. You, most often, had to take the first step. And you could be rejected. Refused. Denied. Cold and flat. And that could hurt. Hurt bad. In your own eyes and in your male friends' eyes. Being scared to try and therefore not trying could just as easily become the subject of psychological self-punishment and social ostracism. So there was always this elementary duality: while apparently the aggressor and conqueror, you were captive to a judgment by the female who would accept or reject you.

Also important to remember is how these events were reported to/discussed with male friends after the party or date. Or gone over in your own mind, again and again, detail by detail. How every step along the initiation route was stimulating and could/did cause an erection (remember the 4-hour erections and blue balls?). How we compared notes, made tactical suggestions, commented on important signs—heavier breathing, torso writhing, aggressive hands, a more daring tongue, involvement of teeth, goose bumps, erected nipples, and when menstruation occurred or was expected to occur. Which girls like what, since in those days "relationships" were short-lived and you never knew which female you might be with another time. And if you were ever in doubt as to what came next in the scenario, your friends informed you of the specifics of the next escalation. And sometimes, if that wasn't possible, the female you were with (embarrassingly enough) let you know in any one of a number of subtle (or not-so-subtle) ways what was next on the agenda.

There were, in retrospect, many funny occasions that cropped up in this initiation process. I don't really need to talk about them because you probably have your own to tell. What stuns me now is that origins of the tragedy of sex emerge clearly from that process of socialized sexuality.

Three elements seem to reappear constantly in every step of the development of male sexual stimulus and response: Objectification, Fixation, and Conquest. (Idealization is a romantic concept that is both bible and aspirin for the three basic elements and tends to obfuscate them.) In any given situation, the order of occurrence and importance of these elements varies, but I believe the order given corresponds to the chronological reality (most of the time) and is more easily discussed.

Objectification   From a very young age, males are taught by everyone to objectify females (except Mom?). They generalize the female, in an almost platonic sense. This generalized woman is a concept, a lump sum, a thing, an object, a non-individualized category. The female is always "other." Against this backdrop males begin, when society allows, overtly to exercise bits of their sexuality.

Males learn to objectify through a process of "definition." We identify, and have identified for us, many female attributes. It starts simply: girls have long hair, wear ribbons in it, have on dresses, and like pink and yellow things. And, of course, they play with dolls. Then comes a sexual understanding: females have no penis, bear children, have breasts, thinner waists, and hips that swell. Until we realize the vagina's existence, we think females are missing their penis and in its absence is a void (are they incomplete?). As we accrue this knowledge, the female social role has already been defined everywhere for us. If we play hospital, the little girls are, of course, the nurses and we, of course, the doctors. It it's time for exercise at school, they play hopscotch while we play football. When it's time to learn practical living skills, they sew and bake while we use tools and build. They are easily recognized as different. There's them and there's us. And who'd want to do a silly girl's thing anyhow?

Fixation   Part of male sexual initiation is learning to fixate on portions of the female's anatomy: at first, breasts, and later, that hidden unknown quantity, the vagina. Somewhere, in some deep cavern in our brain, before we consciously know about sexuality, it must register on us that we never see males touching the female chest or lower belly. And in movies, on TV, in advertisements, where else can we look when the camera's eye focuses on breasts? So our eye is trained and we fixate. Emotionally, too. We learn that if we do that, we will eventually get pleasure and have fun. And be men. Be seen as male. Be reacted to as male.

Because of the way we are socialized, erection follows fixation or occurs in a situation in which fixation plays a role. We observe this coincidence. We learn we can *will* an erection without a woman being near us. And since it is pleasurable (and, at first, astounding), since it gives us assurance that we are male, we create erections out of our imagination, by merely objectifying a female of our choice, fixating on the parts of her body that excite, and usually manipulating that body (see Conquest, below). By denying this process, by repressing our desire and fantasy, we avoid embarrassing erections in public, which is vital since we are always "seeing" breasts and vaginas, hundreds of them, which have the potential of putting us into gear. So we exercise control over our penis while often saying that our penis has a mind of its own—all of which is true.

Conquest   To conquer is a highly valued skill in our society. We are taught to alter the enemy into nothingness, to convert the bear into a stuffed head and rug, to gain power and rule. It's very much either/or: you're a winner or a loser, a good guy or a bad guy, someone who's made it or hasn't. Male initiation rites and activities always require trophies (e.g., sports) and the more numerous and advanced your "awards," the more of a man you are. In sexual matters, the male conquers when he succeeds in reducing the female from a being into a thing and achieves some level or form of sexual gratification—a kiss, or your hand on her breast, or intercourse, depending on your age, sexual advancement, and surrounding social norms. Conquest logically (ahem) follows Objectification and Fixation. I mean, after all, what the hell's the sense of objectifying and fixating if you're not going to get off your ass and do a little conquering? And when we do conquer, what is the trophy? In the old days it might have been a lock of hair or a garter strap. A ring can also announce your achievement. But always, your own knowledge of what transpired is your reward—being pleased with yourself and being able to say to yourself, "I am a man." And if others have knowledge of your conquest, your knowing that they know is as great an award as any.

That, in brief, is the Objectification/Fixation/Conquest dynamic. The implications and ramifications of these elements of socialized sexual responses are staggering and too numerous to attempt to list and discuss here. But let me offer one implication (as an example) that seems realistic to me: that male sexual responses have little (or nothing) to do with the specific female we are with at any given moment. Any number of lips or breasts or vaginas would do—as long as we can objectify, fixate, and conquer, an erection and (provided there is some form of penile friction) ejaculation will occur.

If this example rubs you the wrong way, think about the existence and effectiveness of pornography, both verbal and photographic. What pornography does is create a fertile environment that makes it "natural" for the imagination to objectify, fixate on, and conquer a verbally or photographically depicted female. So without even a female being present in the flesh, the penis grows. Now you may say that the female *is* present, that is, in the male mind. And I'd agree, but the female is not physically there. So in a certain sense, most males become a self-contained sexual system—not homo- or heterosexual, but self-sexual.

This shouldn't surprise anyone: it's based in our physiology and it's based in society's denial of sexual gratification. But, on conscious and unconscious levels, this is threateningly close to homosexuality. Because having a penis and getting erections is equivalent to maleness and ego, it seems that what's important to us as males is the male genitalia, and that might appear suspect to the puritan heterosexual mind-set.

How then do we draw the line between our own penis and all those other penises which are virtually identical to our own? The answer: we do to our penis what we do to females. We objectify it, fixate on it, and conquer it. In that way we "thingify" our penis, make it "other," so that we can talk about "it" and apologize for "its" behavior and laugh at "it" as if it were a child on the rambunctious side whom we can't control. So we have confirmed "its" separateness from us. We can even give our penis a name, like John Thomas or Peter, which states positively to the world that our penis is its own man. (And therefore we are not responsible for its actions?)

Because our penis is central to our own sense of ego and manhood, it is natural that anything that causes erections (with the resulting pleasure and power and self-identification) is to be used. Objectification/Fixation/Conquest of females allows us to function this way. Because we have been socialized to respond that way. So we *do* function that way (nothing succeeds like success, etc.).

Now there is a new female before us. Without really knowing her, without really knowing (or caring?) what she thinks or feels, we "like" her. Because she is female. Because she is "other" and with her you will be your self—a male in a potential relationship that re-establishes, affirms, proves your manhood. Which means that at the moment of meeting, we have already objectified the female.

And for our maleness, this is a necessary first step which permits us to fixate and hopefully go on to conquer so that our climax can strengthen our ego and sense of maleness. When you hear a man "complain" that he's slept with his wife "hundreds of times, and each time I have to seduce her as if she was a virgin," you observe a woman who has learned her lessons too well and a man who loves responding to them (though I don't mean this to be an example of a typical relationship). Seduction, in its crudest sense and crassest form, is nothing more than Fixation and Conquest made possible because the male has already made a generalized object out of a specific female. (Listen to the language: cunt, tits, pussy, boobs, snatch, jugs . . .) This is the procedure males follow to get their sexual machinery into gear (with many personal idiosyncrasies, which is why prostitutes keep careful notes on the likes and dislikes of their clientele). Again, pornography and its effectiveness is telling us that we needn't have a real, living, breathing female with us to respond sexually. What is needed for a good old healthy erection to occur is the opportunity to objectify, fixate, and conquer.

Well, now we have some clues as to how our penis gets socialized and what it responds to, and there are endless questions to ask. But my first question is: What happened to me on those three occasions when I didn't get it up at the proper time?

Tell me how this sounds. My relationship to the woman and the woman's relationship to me was similar in all three instances. They were women I knew very well. They were people I liked very much. Liked because they were decent, liked because they were loving, liked because they were involved in the struggle (at great risk and cost) to make this world a better place. But with them, though I find them very attractive, I didn't automatically play stud the way I had been socialized to do. Because I knew them as whole beings, I couldn't objectify them, and consequently couldn't fixate on (though I tried) or conquer them. And they didn't put pressure on me to do that (and as women can, and do, for a variety of reasons). So, I didn't play my role and they didn't play theirs. No roles; no seduction, no Objectification/Fixation/Conquest—ergo, no erection (except at those odd, non-propitious times when I was probably unconsciously fixating on a part of their body or fantasizing and got the penis into gear).

We spent, I think, very intimate and sensuous moments together. And since those evenings, we've talked about what happened. And about this essay (each of the women has read it). And we'll spend other evenings together, trying to learn about the damage, the terrible damage, that has been done to all of us. And stopping its continuance. And trying to undo as much of it as we can. Well, that's one possible explanation for the "no erection at the right time" mystery. And I come off looking pretty good. Looking pretty damn egalitarian. At least I did until I talked to a friend who, given the same information, had an entirely different interpretation of what happened. Her version follows.

I have, to a certain degree, re-socialized myself and become liberated because I was able to accept these women on all levels as equals. Except for one level: I was not capable of accepting females as sexual equals. I held onto this last bastion of male supremacy with a death-grip. I was willing to deal with these women on a human (rather than male-to-female) basis, except in relating to them sexually, where I still had to deal with them on an objectify, fixate, and conquer basis. But since I couldn't objectify them, I rejected these women rather than give up my last heirloom of maleness. I totally refused to allow them to sexually stimulate or arouse me. By preventing my penis from getting into gear, I ironically preserved my male superiority in the situation. This is because the women, who also need to be re-socialized, would not understand that my lack of erection was a result of fearing that I was going to lose touch with the last remnant of male socialization. They could not understand that I was in fact forestalling my own liberation because I lacked the courage or the knowledge necessary for the last step. What the women would feel is that I have rejected them, since they knew other women stimulated me sexually. They would feel that there is something wrong with them, some way in which they are lacking, if they can't arouse me. So in refusing to allow myself to be stimulated by them, I have in fact turned the tables and made them feel inadequate in relation to me. In making them feel inadequate, I made them doubt the very thing in themselves that I was doubting in myself—sexuality. And while they are pretty liberated, it is the area of their own sexuality which they still have to deal with more.

Well, there's another explanation for the syndrome. And I don't come off looking so good. In fact, I look rather bad. Even desperate. It's an interpretation that is fairly consistent and contains energy. When I first heard it, it really threw me, which gives some credence to its validity. Then I thought, although my friend's interpretation is interesting, I really think mine is more accurate. But that may be male equivocation. Also, I'm not sure that the two interpretations are mutually exclusive (to explain that would take another essay). But the important points to remember are that we still have much to learn and that there are alternatives to avoiding, fearing, and ignoring present sexual realities. If we nurture our blindness and cheer our resistance to change, the damage will continue and worsen.

Some of you may be thinking that because all three instances dealt with the first night of a relationship, the analyses are invalid. And some of you may be thinking that even if a relationship begins in a classical sex-role way, the couple can still grow beyond the male/female roles that they embodied when they first met. I agree, but with major qualifications. I have seen relationships that never grow beyond where they began. No comment necessary. I have also seen relationships that have grown, but I think we have to ask: What is the nature of that growth? What do they grow from? I think those are important questions because when the shit hits the fan in a relationship, friends of the couple will often say things like: "After all those years . . . ."; "It's hard for me to believe . . . ."; "Of all the couples we knew, they seemed . . . ."; "It came out of nowhere . . . ."; "I just can't understand . . . ." Was the couple's break-up really "unexpected"? There are surprises, I think, only if certain basic questions were never asked, existing realities not examined, and alternatives not explored.

The terrifying (to me) evidence is that we males never are dealing with the whole female being at the beginning of a relationship. We have been socialized, on behalf of our penis, to divide a woman's body up. The vernacular of males is usually a dead give-away and varies from slightly crude to incredibly crude. Phrases like "I'm an ass man" or "a breast man" or "a cunt man" or "a leg man" are common self-perceptions and self-descriptions. The street jargon of males watching females stroll by is similar: "Would I like to get my hands on those tits" or "Look at that beaver [cunt]" or "I could suck those sweet nipples for days." The refined professor in the yard gazing at a coed amongst the grass and trees might offer up "a veritable Diana with alabaster orbs" in a non-iambic mode. But the phenomenon is the same. Fixation. That is how we see. We objectify (generalize) the woman and then we fixate on a physical characteristic. And even later in a relationship, when to varying degrees we do deal with the whole female person, very often we snap back into our original sex roles (as if sleeping together for the first time?). We do it because that is how we have been socialized to act and respond. We do it because it is the path of least resistance. We do it. It is the only way we know.

During the past year I have tried to call up and reabsorb conversations I have had with various males over the years concerning females. I've also spent a lot of time talking to all kinds of males, working class and professional, young single males and males who are "happily married and have three lovely children." When sexual fantasies were discussed, I found that there are very similar fantasies among most males.

The fantasy is revealing. "The ideal turn-on would be two or three women at once, who are lesbians, and who are of different racial/cultural origins." Why is this the super dream? Simple: it allows for magnified Objectification, Fixation, and Conquest. Two or three women are more than one. Lesbians are by definition the most difficult conquest, so they are potentially the greatest trophy, the strongest vitamin for building healthy egos and solid definitions of self as powerful male. Differing racial/cultural origins add exotic uniqueness and make one a universal image of manhood. And this, remember, is the common fantasy of what are normally regarded as sexually healthy, well-adjusted males.

So, while many relationships do grow beyond the initial sex-role encounters, I think it becomes increasingly clear that the growth is upon a diseased foundation. And as a result, there are built-in limitations (and too often, built-in tragedies) in relationships as we know them—which means perhaps all relationships we have seen, known, or been personally involved in. And that is why we can no longer feign surprise when a relationship we consider good and mature begins to crumble and the old sex roles come exploding off the blocks like sprint champions. It happens in many forms, depending on the cultural/educational/economic backgrounds of the people involved. But it does happen. Has happened. Will continue to happen—if left unexamined.

I've spoken to a number of friends about this essay and asked them to read it and offer criticisms. They did. Some were nervous, some astounded, some calm, some just smiled. But most of them agreed with the general thrust of the argument (there were disagreements over specifics). And we talked for many hours about sexuality. But our discussions didn't have an immediate or visible effect on our existing realities. Because we have all been thoroughly socialized. We are all trained actors. Character actors. Method actors. And no method actor with 20 years or more experience is going to lose his skill, forget or confuse his role, miss the lines at the right time, unless the script is re-written or eliminated, and sets changed, and the desires and expectations of the cast, stage hands, directors and audience re-socialized.

I want to ask people to do that, but I can't. Because I don't know what that kind of re-socialization entails. I have some vague ideas, but at this point I'm struggling. I can't offer any simple answers. Obviously, there are many risks involved. Some of my male and female friends, who are pretty open and enlightened people, have said that they would rather keep things the way they are if trying to change them is going to cause doubt, pain, and an awful lot of work. I suspect that those conditions will have to be a step in the transition (although easier than we think); men and women are going to have to be prepared for rough times and be ready to deal with them. But when I look around me and see the alternatives to taking risks and living with uncertainty, those alternatives are so unpalatable that the need to change becomes a command. Even though it's not going to be a rose garden. At least for a while. . . .

Facing Up to Breast Cancer
Susan G. Radner

Finding a lump in one's breast is a possibility that terrifies women. In spite of all the TV programs and ads from the American Cancer Society, as well as the self-help courses offered in many colleges, many women do not examine their breasts regularly, or acknowledge what they find. I put off as long as I could the recognition that there was something not quite normal about my right breast, telling myself the usual evasions: it didn't feel like the lump I had touched in the demonstration dummy from the American Cancer Society; my breasts were just lumpy; besides, I had to finish school and get my grades in. Only after the semester was over and the lump had not gone away did I make an appointment with my doctor.

A standard medical procedure seems to be to watch the lump for a while, to see if any changes occur. But if the lump is a malignant tumor, this procedure is extremely risky, for the tumor can be watched from a localized cancer to a spreading one. The first doctor I consulted wanted me to return in four weeks. After I looked startled, he asked if I was overly concerned about it. When I said, rather reluctantly, "Well, yes," he changed the interval to two weeks. I decided to seek another opinion, this time from a breast surgeon. By a simple medical procedure, aspiration, he was able to determine that my lump was a tumor and not a harmless cyst. Since it was a tumor, the next step had to be a biopsy, and arrangements were made to have me admitted to the hospital. In other words, if a lump is not a cyst it is a tumor—either benign or malignant. And if it is a malignant tumor, long-term survival depends on catching it early, before the cancer has spread to the lymph nodes and circulation system. If her doctor wants to watch her lump for a while, a woman should consult another doctor. (It should be noted that the results of a mammogram (X-ray of the breast) are not always conclusive. While a mammogram can spot small cancers, a negative mammogram is not proof that there is no malignancy. Such proved to be the fact in my case.)

Waiting to be admitted to the hospital, I had too much time for fantasies about what would happen. I didn't allow myself to think about the possibility of dying, but losing my breast seemed almost as bad. Even though I had never been particularly hung up on my breasts, they were part of me, and I associated them with making love and being feminine. Having grown to maturity in the fifties, I had always been aware that I was inadequate by the standards of the day. My breasts were small (I had difficulty squeezing them into a bra) and one was much smaller than the other. I had worn a padded bra through most of my high school years, and my decision to wear a natural bra was an act of defiance and an assertion of my identity. I took to the bra-lessness of the seventies as my revenge on the big-breasted women of the fifties. So I had always been aware of my breasts, and I could not visualize what I would look like without one, and without my chest muscles as well. I knew that the breast would be missing, and I would have scars, and I would look somehow hideous, the word I kept repeating, but I had no image for what this hideousness would look like. And, of course, I was sure that no one could possibly love me like that.

I emphasize these fantasies because I think that these kinds of attitudes are what cause so many women to die of breast cancer, the largest killer of women aged thirty-five to fifty. A woman cannot help being raised in our culture, and she becomes a victim of her conditioning. This culture conspires to keep women breast-conscious. Women in bathing suits have been selling products for as long as Coca-Cola has existed. Erotic or pornographic magazines correlate breasts with sexual arousal and gratification, both for men and women. As the dancer says in *Chorus Line,* "tits and ass" are how women are judged. So a woman picks up the messages: (large, beautiful) breasts are a sign of femininity; she had better do as well as she can with the breasts that she has; to "improve" herself she can buy a bikini, an uplift bra, a well-cut dress. With these aids she learns to accept herself, even if she doesn't look like the pictures in *Playboy.* When she has reached the point of saying, "Well, that's the way I look," it is very difficult to imagine herself without even this minimal standard of acceptability. It is not surprising, therefore, that when she finds a lump she ignores it as long as she can, and thinks that losing a breast is the worst fate that can happen to her. No one has ever told her that she will be the same person with or without her breast, and if they do now, she doesn't believe them. She has internalized the images.

This process may be a miniature of the overall adjustment women make to their bodies. Women's bodies have always been considered the property of the whole culture, to be painted, photographed, touched, in varying degrees of dress or undress. A (middle-class) adolescent female becomes totally absorbed in her body—her hair, her face, as well as her breasts and her "figure." She knows that her appearance will be the currency which will purchase her status in her adult life. As she pores over the magazines or sees pictures of women on TV, she compares herself to these images. Since the aim of the media is to get her to buy products, she purchases those which she thinks will best help her to look like the images communicated to her. In other words, she tries to adjust to her body by molding it into an acceptable image. Since not until quite recently, with the enactment of Title IX legislation, were girls encouraged to participate in athletics, women did not really know their bodies very well. The adjustment made was totally superficial—using pimple cream or makeup, losing or gaining weight—without any real understanding of how their bodies worked and of what they were capable. So, while a woman picks up messages that her body is very important to her, that she must watch and tend it, she really does not know much about it. This explains, perhaps, why so many adult women do not feel very comfortable with their bodies, and see themselves as graceless and clumsy. And it is at least a partial explanation of why women (at least until recently) take the aging process so hard. A woman sees the body she has been taking such good care of slipping away from her. In spite of all her efforts, the gray hairs come in, the laugh lines turn into wrinkles, and her waist thickens. These events all signal the end of her desirability. Losing a breast can be seen as the final blow, happening, as it does, usually, after age thirty-five. (I was thirty-seven.) Just when a woman thinks she has come to terms with her body, and when it is beginning to slouch into middle-age, it is dramatically altered, and altered in such a way as to put her permanently out of the physical-attractiveness competition. The accompanying feelings of self-loathing and disgust are inevitable.

But looked at from a realistic perspective, a mastectomy, even a radical mastectomy, is not the worst thing that can happen to a woman. Seen in the context of other amputations, which it very rarely is, losing a breast is not nearly so bad as losing an arm or leg. Faced with the possibility of death, losing a breast is a small price to pay. Life can and does continue as before. The corset industry has created "life-like" prostheses, so that cosmetically a woman can continue to look attractive. In fact, I found that for the first time in my life, I looked balanced equally on both sides. I can continue to do all the activities I had done previously, from playing tennis to making love. My husband, as promised, continued to love me, and our marriage, now that the terror of my possibly dying was over, may have actually been strengthened. So the problem is not the reality of mastectomy but the fantasies around it. These fantasies are potentially lethal for women. They are the creation of a culture which treats women's bodies as commodities and which sets arbitrary definitions of femininity. Women are kept ignorant and insecure about their bodies. Until these issues are confronted, women will continue to die of breast cancer.

SUGGESTIONS FOR FURTHER READING: Part I

The following is a list of anthologies that contain a wide variety of readings on the women's movement. Most or all of these volumes contain comprehensive bibliographies that can be used to supplement the suggested readings mentioned in this book.

Gornick, Vivian, and Barbara K. Moran (eds.): *Women in Sexist Society,* Signet, New York, 1972.

Hammer, Signe (ed.): *Women Body and Culture,* Harper, New York, 1975.

Liberation Now! Dell, New York, 1971.

Miller, Jean Baker (ed.): *Psychoanalysis and Women,* Penguin Books, Baltimore, 1973.

Morgan, Robin (ed.): *Sisterhood Is Powerful,* Vintage Books, New York, 1970.

Reiter, Rayna R. (ed.): *Toward an Anthropology of Women,* Monthly Review Press, New York, 1975.

Rosaldo, Michelle Zimbalist, and Louise Lamphere (eds.): *Woman Culture and Society,* Stanford University Press, Stanford, Calif., 1974.

Roszak, Betty, and Theodore Roszak (eds.): *Masculine/Feminine,* Harper, New York, 1969.

Salper, Roberta (ed.): *Female Liberation,* Knopf, New York, 1972.

Stacey, Judith, Susan Bereaud, and Joan Daniels (eds.): *And Jill Came Tumbling After: Sexism in American Education,* Dell, New York, 1974.

Part II

Alternative Feminist Frameworks

THE ROOTS OF OPPRESSION

It is a general law that naturally dominant elements and naturally dominated elements exist . . . the rule of free man over the slave is one type of domination; that of man over woman is another.

Aristotle

God almighty made the women and the Rockefeller gang of thieves made the ladies.

Mother Jones

Talk not to us of chivalry, that died long ago. . . . In social life, true, a man in love will jump to pick up a glove or bouquet for a silly girl of sixteen, whilst at home he will permit his aged mother to carry pails of water and armfuls of wood, or permit his wife to lug a twenty-pound baby, hour after hour, without ever offering to relieve her.

Elizabeth Cady Stanton, 1855

I know it's old-fashioned, but I do feel that women just are inferior to men—in almost every way. So women should concentrate on being just that—women—and leave the rest to men. I'm sure everybody would be a lot happier.

Janet Pearce
"Pet of the Month," *Penthouse,* December 1969

For me, women are only amusing, a hobby. No one spends too much time on a hobby.

Henry Kissinger
In an interview with Oriana Fallaci, 1973

For if the phrase biology is destiny has any meaning for a woman right now it has to be the urgent project of woman reclaiming herself, her own biology in her own image, and this is why the lesbian is the revolutionary feminist and every other feminist is a woman who wants a better deal from her old man.

Jill Johnston

Feminism is the theory and lesbianism is the practice.

Ti-Grace Atkinson

THE ROOTS OF OPPRESSION

Part I of this book showed that both women and men in our society are dissatisfied with central areas of their lives. In the late 1960s, the women's movement forcefully articulated these problems, making many people aware for the first time that their misery was generally shared. This realization led to a recognition that women's problems were not due to individual failures to cope, but that rather they were rooted in the structure of the existing society. It followed that the resolution of women's problems required changes in that society. Part II of this anthology presents several attempts by feminists to state in the most general terms the kinds of social changes that are required.

Most of the theories we shall present here contain some speculation about the historical origins of women's oppression. That is to say, they attempt to uncover its *historical* roots. A reader encountering such speculations for the first time may well wonder why contemporary feminists devote so much energy to an enterprise whose conclusions can never be more than tentative and which may not appear directly relevant to the situation of women and men today.

Perhaps the easiest way to explain the feminists' interest in the historical origins of women's oppression is to remind the reader how much easier it is to understand a friend when one knows her past, and especially when one learns the circumstances in which she grew up. Seemingly irrational quirks or preferences may become quite intelligible when seen in the context of the person's past life. In the same way, present social phenomena are likely to become more intelligible when viewed as the unfolding of the past.

To uncover the historical origins of women's oppression is not, of course, to assume that those causes are still effective in perpetuating that oppression. Nor is it to assume that they are not. One task of a theory is to determine the relevance of "origins" to the present-day situation. To the extent that the original causes are still operative, a discovery of the historical roots can show us where to focus our energy in order to change the situation. If those original causes are not relevant to the contemporary situation, or to the extent that they are not, a theory which demonstrates this fact can refute an old explanation for women's oppression.

This latter point brings out the fact that talk of roots or origins should not be understood only in a historical way. "The roots of women's oppression" may also refer to those conditions, biological or social, which are the most important in continuing women's subordination today. That is to say, to uncover the root causes of women's oppression, in this nonhistorical sense, is to discover not only which biological facts or which social institutions operate to limit women's choices but also which facts or institutions must be changed in order to effect a significant and permanent increase in women's capacity to choose. Obviously, to do this requires a comprehensive analysis of the relations between our biology and our major social institutions. Such an analysis will have to indicate specific changes that must be made (see Part III), and its truth will be tested, in large part, by the effectiveness of the changes that it indicates.

CONSERVATISM

The conservative view of women's situation in society is not feminist, because it denies that women are oppressed. It is included in this volume because, despite a decade of activity by the contemporary women's movement, antifeminism is still alive if not entirely well. Further, the presuppositions of the conservative reasoning are used not only to justify sexism but also to rationalize other kinds of social inequality, such as racism and poverty. Hence, if we can figure out what is wrong with conservative antifeminism, we will have the basic theoretical tools to refute other arguments used to defend social inequality.

As we define *conservatism,* it rests on the view that human nature is essentially the same in all times and in all places. This does not mean that everybody is equal in talents and abilities: as we shall see, conservatives are more likely than not to deny this. But it does claim that human interests, desires, abilities, and needs are determined by innate factors rather than by an individual's own efforts, by the situation in which he or she finds himself or herself, or by some combination of both.

There are many different conservative theories of human nature. Our book gives two examples. Freud claims that there are universal psychological differences between the sexes, and he sees these as a response to girls' and boys' discoveries of the physiological differences between them. Hence his oft-quoted remark that anatomy is destiny. Although some aspects of Freud's views were radical for his time, we can see how they also served to justify keeping women in their traditional place. Goldberg, too, argues for universal psychological differences between the sexes, but he claims that at least one main difference results from the fact that the male child's brain receives far greater stimulation from the male hormone, testosterone. According to Goldberg, this results in greater aggression on the part of the male child— aggression which he believes results in universal male dominance.

For both the authors represented in this section, psychological differences between the sexes result, directly or indirectly, from human biology. Hence, these differences are seen as both natural and unchangeable. All these claims have been challenged by feminists. Marxists and some liberals, in different ways, have attacked the conservative belief in the biological determination of psychological differences between the sexes; radical feminists have disputed the view that biological differences are unchangeable. These criticisms will be explained shortly. In addition, many feminists have criticized the conservative assumption that what is natural is right. They point out that there are a number of meanings of the term "natural," but that none of them implies that what is natural should be free from human intervention. For instance, disease may be natural, but that does not mean that it should go untreated. The reader interested in further exploration of the concept of the natural, as applied to human activities and institutions, is referred to the material cited at the end of Part II.

LIBERALISM

Liberal philosophy has its origins in the "social contract" theories of the sixteenth and seventeenth centuries, but the oppression of women did not attract much attention from liberal thinkers until the publication, in 1792, of Mary Wollstonecraft's *A Vindication of the Rights of Women.* At that time, the possession of rationality was considered the proper basis for imputing rights, and Wollstonecraft argued, to the chagrin of many, that women's rights should be equal to those of men on the grounds that women were equal possessors of the capacity to reason. She believed that the apparent inferiority of women's intellects was due to women's inferior education.

Wollstonecraft's theme has been continued by liberal feminists, such as Taylor and Mill in the nineteenth century, right up to the present day. The stress is always on equality of opportunity. Thus Taylor and Mill argue that women's legal rights should be the same as those of men and that women should receive the same educational opportunities. Modern feminists, such as Betty Friedan and Gloria Steinem, who protest against contemporary sexist discrimination, are making essentially the same point.

It should be noted that the liberal does not launch a thoroughgoing critique of the conservative theory of human nature. That is to say, liberals are not committed to denying that there may be innate inequalities between persons in general and between women and men in particular. What they point out is that the current inequality in the opportunities and education available to women and to men suggests very strongly that psychological differences may be learned rather than inherited.

It should also be noted that liberals do not criticize *as such* social inequalities in wealth, position, and power. What they do criticize is their distribution on the grounds of some inherited and not obviously relevant characteristic such as family, race, or sex. Liberals believe that each individual should be able to rise in society as far as her or his talents permit, unhindered by restraints of law or custom. The proper reward for the exercise of an individual's talents should be determined by the demand for such talents in a market economy. All these presumptions, of course, are challenged by Marxists.

For the liberal, then, the roots of women's oppression lie in our lack of equal civil rights and educational opportunities. There is no attempt at historical speculation as to why such a lack should exist. Since the roots are so easily visible, women's oppression can be tackled directly by an attack on sexist discrimination. When this discrimination has been eliminated, women will have been liberated.

TRADITIONAL MARXISM

Contrary to the conservative, the Marxist rejects explicitly the notion of an essential and biologically determined human nature. Marx saw that, throughout the course of history, human beings in different places and in different times have had recourse to many different techniques in order to feed, clothe, shelter, and reproduce themselves. These different techniques of survival have required many different forms of social organization and hence have shaped many different kinds of social relations between persons. For the Marxist, what persons are like—their motivations, interests, and abilities, and even their needs—is very largely a function of the form of society in which they live and of their place in that society. Yet, insofar as human beings create forms of social organization, persons are not seen as totally passive beings at the mercy of their environment; rather, as they create their society, they are the ultimate and active creators of their own nature.

In addition to rejecting the biologism of conservatives, Marxists reject the liberal's belief that it is possible for people to have genuine equality of opportunity for the development of their potential while they remain within a class society where the many produce the wealth but the wealth and power end up in the hands of a few. In such a society, the pursuit of profit by the ruling class determines all aspects of life—the conditions under which people work and the education they receive, for example—and even the quality of personal relations is shaped by the profit motive, which Marxists see as degrading human existence.

From this brief sketch of Marxist theory, it is plain that the Marxist will locate the origins of women's oppression not in biology but rather in a particular system of social organization. In fact, the traditional Marxist sees women's oppression as originating with the introduction of private property. Private ownership of the means of production by relatively few persons, and those all male, instituted a class system. Contemporary corporate capitalism and imperialism are but the latest phase of this development and the root cause of most of the inequality and misery in the world today.

Marxists claim that recognizing the irreconcilable conflict between economic classes is the most important key to understanding social change. It follows that they view sexism as a secondary phenomenon, a symptom of a more fundamental form of oppression. In the traditional Marxist analysis, the main precondition for women's liberation is a socialist revolution whereby the means of production become once again the property of society as a whole. Once this has happened, traditional Marxists believe, prejudice against women will disappear.

RADICAL FEMINISM

Radical feminism is the least developed and systematic of the theories with which we shall deal. Several different views have been labeled "radical feminist," either by their inventors or by others. We shall attempt to indicate what we see as common to all radical feminist theories.

In our view, what distinguishes radical feminism from all other feminist theories is its insistence that the oppression of women is fundamental. This claim can be interpreted in several different ways. It may mean:

1 That women were, historically, the first oppressed group
2 That women's oppression is the most widespread, existing in virtually every known society
3 That women's oppression is the deepest in that it is the hardest to eradicate and cannot be removed by other social changes such as the abolition of class society

4 That women's oppression causes the most suffering to its victims, qualitatively as well as quantitatively, although this suffering may often go unrecognized because of the sexist prejudices of both the oppressors and the victims

5 That women's oppression, as Firestone claims, provides a conceptual model for understanding all other forms of oppression

Different radical feminists emphasize different aspects of the fundamental nature of women's oppression, but all agree on at least the first three claims listed above. There is less radical feminist agreement on the causes of women's oppression. For Firestone (excerpted here), women's oppression originates in our biological child-bearing function; other radical feminists suggest that it may be a result of the alleged genetic male tendency toward aggression; still other radical feminists leave it causally unexplained. We shall see later in the book that this failure to agree on the root causes of women's oppression leads to some divergence in the recommendations for social change which are made by radical feminists.

Shulamith Firestone's *The Dialectic of Sex* contains what is probably the classical radical feminist account of the roots of women's oppression. Firestone believes that these roots are ultimately biological, grounded in the fact (if it is one) that women's child-bearing function made them dependent on men for physical survival. She infers that women's liberation requires no less than a biological revolution, one which would permit the extrauterine reproduction of children and hence would eliminate the physical dependence of women on men. It is at this point that the radical feminist challenges the conservative on his own ground: women's subordination may indeed be biologically grounded, but biology itself can be changed by technology.

Most of the rest of Firestone's book consists of a detailed demonstration of the radical feminist claim that oppression on the basis of sex provides the conceptual model for understanding other forms of oppression, such as racism and class society. Firestone also outlines her recommendations for the future of work, sexuality, the family, and child rearing. Her book is provocative and full of insights and is heartily recommended to the reader.

Charlotte Bunch's account of the roots of women's oppression is less overtly biological than Firestone's; hence, she does not see women's liberation as requiring a biological revolution. However, Bunch does believe both that women's subjugation was the first form of women's oppression and that it remains the deepest. Since women are oppressed primarily by sexism and only secondarily by racism and class society, Bunch argues that our struggles must be directed first of all against sexism. And she believes that in order to do this, we must become lesbian. In Bunch's article, we see our first clear application of the feminist insight that the personal is political: for Bunch, lesbianism is not merely a personal preference but a political decision made within the context of a political struggle.

SOCIALIST FEMINISM

Socialist feminist theory begins with a basic acceptance of the historical materialist approach that was begun by Marx and Engels. It argues, however, that the traditional Marxist analysis needs to be enriched if it is to be thoroughly adequate for understanding the multifaceted nature of women's oppression. By placing an emphasis on understanding the cultural institutions (the family, heterosexual intercourse, etc.)

that play a major role in oppressing women, this theory incorporates the central radical feminist insights; by insisting on analyzing these institutions within the context of class society, socialist feminism continues to employ a fundamentally Marxist method.

Because of their insistence on the importance of a class analysis, socialist feminists reject the assumption made by many earlier feminists that women all have much the same problems and are oppressed in essentially similar ways. Although there are indeed ways in which all women are oppressed, notably by being viewed as sexual objects, this assumption ignores the particular problems of working-class and third-world women. For example, liberal feminists began a much needed struggle over the right of women to obtain safe and legal abortions, but for a long time the women's movement remained oblivious to the plight of third-world women, who were and are struggling against compulsory sterilization and for the right to conceive and bear children without the fear of poverty and degradation. Thus socialist feminists recommend that we should study the problems faced by women in different classes and from different racial groups, and they urge us to analyze those problems by reference to both class oppression and male privilege.

In discussing the historical roots of women's oppression, socialist feminists tend to try to repair some of the difficulties with Engels's account. Some even argue that sexism began prior to and thus independently of class society. Gayle Rubin gives a fascinating account of the origins of women's oppression as rooted in the institution of kinship. By enforcing exogamy and using women in interfamilial exchange, this institution created and consolidated extrafamilial ties. The cost, however, was the sexual repression of both girls and boys, the imposition of a norm of heterosexuality, and the social creation of a passive feminine nature. Rubin sees Freudian theory as a description of this process. It correctly perceives girls' and boys' reaction to their own anatomy, but points out that they are discovering this anatomy in a social context which is already sexist.

It follows from Rubin's account that liberation for women would require a society which was not only classless but also genderless, a society in which the biological fact of sex received no social recognition (except, presumably, for reproductive purposes). In explaining why such a change is necessary, Rubin's work may well provide the theoretical underpinning for much contemporary socialist-feminist practice. It is interesting that Juliet Mitchell, in *Psycho-Analysis and Feminism,* produces an account of the historical origins of women's oppression which is quite similar to Rubin's.

Whether or not they ultimately accept anything like this account of the historical origins of women's oppression, all socialist feminists agree that sexism is at least as fundamental as economic oppression. And in their analyses of the contemporary situation, they all emphasize how capitalism and sexism reinforce each other. The piece reprinted from Juliet Mitchell's *Woman's Estate* (also highly recommended) is a revision of her classic paper "Women: The Longest Revolution," which was first published in 1966 and which began a whole new tradition of attempts to understand the contemporary position of women in terms of Marxist categories. Unlike radical feminism, these attempts refuse to treat economic oppression as secondary; unlike traditional Marxism, they refuse to treat sexist oppression as secondary. Their aim is to create a theory which demonstrates the inseparability of these two forms of oppression and the consequent need to struggle simultaneously against both.

CONSERVATISM: Sexism as Natural Inequality

Femininity
Sigmund Freud

. . . In conformity with its peculiar nature, psycho-analysis does not try to describe what a woman is—that would be a task it could scarcely perform—but sets about enquiring how she comes into being, how a woman develops out of a child with a bisexual disposition. . . .

. . . A little girl is as a rule less aggressive, defiant and self-sufficient; she seems to have a greater need for being shown affection and on that account to be more dependent and pliant. It is probably only as a result of this pliancy that she can be taught more easily and quicker to control her excretions: urine and faeces are the first gifts that children make to those who look after them, and controlling them is the first concession to which the instinctual life of children can be induced. One gets an impression, too, that little girls are more intelligent and livelier than boys of the same age; they go out more to meet the external world and at the same time form stronger object-cathexes. I cannot say whether this lead in development has been confirmed by exact observations, but in any case there is no question that girls cannot be described as intellectually backward. These sexual differences are not, however, of great consequence: they can be outweighed by individual variations. For our immediate purposes they can be disregarded.

Both sexes seem to pass through the early phases of libidinal development in the same manner. It might have been expected that in girls there would already have been some lag in aggressiveness in the sadistic-anal phase, but such is not the case. Analysis of children's play has shown our women analysts that the aggressive impulses of little girls leave nothing to be desired in the way of abundance and violence. With their entry into the phallic phase the differences between the sexes are completely eclipsed by their agreements. We are now obliged to recognize that the little girl is a little man. In boys, as we know, this phase is marked by the fact that they have learnt how to derive pleasurable sensations from their small penis and connect its excited state with their ideas of sexual intercourse. Little girls do the same thing with their still smaller clitoris. It seems that with them all their masturbatory acts are carried out on this penis-equivalent, and that the truly feminine vagina is still undiscovered by both sexes. It is true that there are a few isolated reports of early vaginal sensations as well, but it could not be easy to distinguish these from sensations in the anus or vestibulum; in any case they cannot play a great part. We are entitled to keep to our view that in the phallic phase of girls the clitoris is the leading erotogenic zone. But it is not, of course, going to remain so. With the change to femininity the clitoris should wholly or in part hand over its sensitivity, and at the same time its importance, to the vagina. This would be one of the two tasks which a woman has to perform in the course of her development, whereas the more fortunate man has only to continue at the time of his sexual maturity the activity that he has previously carried out at the period of the early efflorescence of his sexuality.

We shall return to the part played by the clitoris; let us now turn to the second task with which a girl's development is burdened. A boy's mother is the first object of his love, and she remains so too during the formation of his Oedipus complex and, in essence, all through his life. For a girl too her first object must be her mother (and the figures of wet-nurses and foster-mothers that merge into her). The first object-cathexes occur in attachment to the satisfaction of the major and simple vital needs, and the circumstances of the care of children are the same for both sexes. But in the Oedipus situation the girl's father has become her love-object, and we expect that in the normal course of development she will find her way from this paternal object to her final choice of an object. In the course of time, therefore, a girl has to change her erotogenic zone and her object—both of which a boy retains. The question then arises of how this happens: in particular, how does a girl pass from her mother to an attachment to her father? or, in other words, how does she pass from her masculine phase to the feminine one to which she is biologically destined? . . .

. . . All these factors—the slights, the disappointments in love, the jealousy, the seduction followed by prohibition—are, after all, also in operation in the relation of a *boy* to his mother and are yet unable to alienate him from the maternal object. Unless we can find something that is specific for girls and is not present or not in the same way present in boys, we shall not have explained the termination of the attachment of girls to their mother.

I believe we have found this specific factor, and indeed where we expected to find it, even though in a surprising form. Where we expected to find it, I say, for it lies in the castration complex. After all, the anatomical distinction [between the sexes] must express itself in psychical consequences. It was, however, a surprise to learn from analyses that girls hold their mother responsible for their lack of a penis and do not forgive her for their being thus put at a disadvantage.

As you hear, then, we ascribe a castration complex to women as well. And for good reasons, though its content cannot be the same as with boys. In the latter the castration complex arises after they have learnt from the sight of the female genitals that the organ which they value so highly need not necessarily accompany the body. At this the boy recalls to mind the threats he brought on himself by his doings with that organ, he begins to give credence to them and falls under the influence of fear of castration, which will be the most powerful motive force in his subsequent development. The castration complex of girls is also started by the sight of the genitals of the other sex. They at once notice the difference and, it must be admitted, its significance too. They feel seriously wronged, often declare that they want to "have something like it too," and fall a victim to "envy for the penis," which will leave ineradicable traces on their development and the formation of their character and which will not be surmounted in even the most favourable cases without a severe expenditure of psychical energy. The girl's recognition of the fact of her being without a penis does not by any means imply that she submits to the fact easily. On the contrary, she continues to hold on for a long time to the wish to get something like it herself and she believes in that possibility for improbably long years; and analysis can show that, at a period when knowledge of reality has long since rejected the fulfilment of the wish as unattainable, it persists in the unconscious and retains a considerable cathexis of energy. The wish to get the longed-for penis eventually in spite of everything may contribute to the motives that drive a mature woman to analysis, and what she may reasonably expect from analysis—a capacity, for instance, to carry on an intellectual profession—may often be recognized as a sublimated modification of this repressed wish.

One cannot very well doubt the importance of envy for the penis. You may take it as an instance of male injustice if I assert that envy and jealousy play an even greater part in the mental life of women than of men. It is not that I think these characteristics are absent in men or that I think they have no other roots in women than envy for the penis; but I am inclined to attribute their greater amount in women to this latter influence. . . .

The discovery that she is castrated is a turning-point in a girl's growth. Three possible lines of development start from it: one leads to sexual inhibition or to neurosis, the second to change of character in the sense of a masculinity complex, the third, finally, to normal femininity. We have learnt a fair amount, though not everything, about all three.

The essential content of the first is as follows: the little girl has hitherto lived in a masculine way, has been able to get pleasure by the excitation of her clitoris and has brought this activity into relation with her sexual wishes directed towards her mother, which are often active ones; now, owing to the influence of her penis-envy, she loses her enjoyment in her phallic sexuality. Her self-love is mortified by the comparison with the boy's far superior equipment and in consequence she renounces her masturbatory satisfaction from her clitoris, repudiates her love for her mother and at the same time not infrequently represses a good part of her sexual trends in general. No doubt her turning away from her mother does not occur all at once, for to begin with the girl regards her castration as an individual misfortune, and only gradually extends it to other females and finally to her mother as well. Her love was directed to her *phallic* mother; with the discovery that her mother is castrated it becomes possible to drop her as an object, so that the motives for hostility, which have long been accumulating, gain the upper hand. This means, therefore, that as a result of the discovery of women's lack of a penis they are debased in value for girls just as they are for boys and later perhaps for men.

You all know the immense aetiological importance attributed by our neurotic patients to their masturbation. They make it responsible for all their troubles and we have the greatest difficulty in persuading them that they are mistaken. In fact, however, we ought to admit to them that they are right, for masturbation is the executive agent of infantile sexuality, from the faulty development of which they are indeed suffering. But what neurotics mostly blame is the masturbation of the period of puberty; they have mostly forgotten that of early infancy, which is what is really in question. . . . From the development of girls, which is what my present lecture is concerned with, I can give you the example of a child herself trying to get free from masturbating. She does not always succeed in this. If envy for the penis has provoked a powerful impulse against clitoridal masturbation but this nevertheless refuses to give way, a violent struggle for liberation ensues in which the girl, as it were, herself takes over the role of her deposed mother and gives expression to her entire dissatisfaction with her inferior clitoris in her efforts against obtaining satisfaction from it. Many years later, when her masturbatory activity has long since been suppressed, an interest still persists which we must interpret as a defence against a temptation that is still dreaded. It manifests itself in the emergence of sympathy for those to whom similar difficulties are attributed, it plays a part as a motive in contracting a marriage and, indeed, it may determine the choice of a husband or lover. Disposing of early infantile masturbation is truly no easy or indifferent business.

Along with the abandonment of clitoridal masturbation a certain amount of activity is renounced. Passivity now has the upper hand, and the girl's turning to her father is accomplished principally with the help of passive instinctual impulses. You can see that a wave of development like this, which clears the phallic activity out of the way, smooths the ground for femininity. If too much is not lost in the course of it through repression, this femininity may turn out to be normal. The wish with which the girl turns to her father is no doubt originally the wish for the penis which her mother has refused her and which she now expects from her father. The feminine situation is only established, however, if the wish for a penis is replaced by one for a baby, if, that is, a baby takes the place of a penis in accordance with an ancient symbolic equivalence. It has not escaped us that the girl has wished for a baby earlier, in the undisturbed phallic phase: that, of course, was the meaning of her playing with dolls. But that play was not in fact an expression of her femininity; it served as an identification with her mother with the intention of substituting activity for passivity. *She* was playing the part of her mother and the doll was herself: now she could do with the baby everything that her mother used to do with her. Not until the emergence of the wish for a penis does the doll-baby become a baby from the girl's father, and thereafter the aim of the most powerful feminine wish. Her happiness is great if later on this wish for a baby finds fulfilment in reality, and quite especially so if the baby is a little boy who brings the longed-for penis with him. Often enough in her combined picture of "a baby from her father" the emphasis is laid on the baby and her father left unstressed. In this way the ancient masculine wish for the possession of a penis is still faintly visible through the femininity now achieved. But perhaps we ought rather to recognize this wish for a penis as being *par excellence* a feminine one.

With the transference of the wish for a penis-baby on to her father, the girl has entered the situation of the Oedipus complex. Her hostility to her mother, which did not need to be freshly created, is now greatly intensified, for she becomes the girl's rival, who receives from her father everything that she desires from him. For a long time the girl's Oedipus complex concealed her pre-Oedipus attachment to her mother from our view, though it is nevertheless so important and leaves such lasting fixations behind it. For girls the Oedipus situation is the outcome of a long and difficult development; it is a kind of preliminary solution, a position of rest which is not soon abandoned, especially as the beginning of the latency period is not far distant. And we are now struck by a difference between the two sexes, which is probably momentous, in regard to the relation of the Oedipus complex to the castration complex. In a boy the Oedipus complex, in which he desires his mother and would like to get rid of his father as being a rival, develops naturally from the phase of his phallic sexuality. The threat of castration compels him, however, to give up that attitude. Under the impression of the danger of losing his penis, the Oedipus complex is abandoned, repressed and, in the most normal cases, entirely destroyed, and a severe super-ego is set up as its heir. What happens with a girl is almost the opposite. The castration complex prepares for the Oedipus complex instead of destroying it; the girl is driven out of her attachment to her mother through the influence of her envy for the penis and she enters the Oedipus situation as though into a haven of refuge. In the absence of fear of castration the chief motive is lacking which leads boys to surmount the Oedipus complex. Girls remain in it for an indeterminate length of time; they demolish it late and, even so, incompletely. In these circumstances the formation of the super-ego must suffer; it cannot attain the strength and independence which give it its cultural significance, and feminists are not pleased when we point out to them the effects of this factor upon the average feminine character.

To go back a little. We mentioned as the second possible reaction to the discovery of female castration the development of a powerful masculinity complex. By this we mean that the girl refuses, as it were, to recognize the unwelcome fact and, defiantly rebellious, even exaggerates her previous masculinity, clings to her clitoridal activity and takes refuge in an identification with her phallic mother or her father. What can it be that decides in favour of this outcome? We can only suppose that it is a constitutional factor, a greater amount of activity, such as is ordinarily characteristic of a male. However that may be, the essence of this process is that at this point in development the wave of passivity is avoided which opens the way to the turn towards femininity. The extreme achievement of such a masculinity complex would appear to be the influencing of the choice of an object in the sense of manifest homosexuality. Analytic experience teaches us, to be sure, that female homosexuality is seldom or never a direct continuation of infantile masculinity. Even for a girl of this kind it seems necessary that she should take her father as an object for some time and enter the Oedipus situation. But afterwards, as a result of her inevitable disappointments from her father, she is driven to regress into her early masculinity complex. The significance of these disappointments must not be exaggerated; a girl who is destined to become feminine is not spared them, though they do not have the same effect. The predominance of the constitutional factor seems indisputable; but the two phases in the development of female homosexuality are well mirrored in the practices of homosexuals, who play the parts of mother and baby with each other as often and as clearly as those of husband and wife.

What I have been telling you here may be described as the prehistory of women. It is a product of the very last few years and may have been of interest to you as an example of detailed analytic work. . . .

It is not my intention to pursue the further behaviour of femininity through puberty to the period of maturity. Our knowledge, moreover, would be insufficient for the purpose. But I will bring a few features together in what follows. Taking its prehistory as a starting-point, I will only emphasize here that the development of femininity remains exposed to disturbance by the residual phenomena of the early masculine period. Regressions to the fixations of the pre-Oedipus phases very frequently occur; in the course of some women's lives there is a repeated alternation between periods in which masculinity or femininity gains the upper hand. Some portion of what we men call "the enigma of women" may perhaps be derived from this expression of bisexuality in women's lives. But another question seems to have become ripe for judgement in the course of these researches. We have called the motive force of sexual life "the libido." Sexual life is dominated by the polarity of masculine-feminine; thus the notion suggests itself of considering the relation of the libido to this antithesis. It would not be surprising if it were to turn out that each sexuality had its own special libido appropriated to it, so that one sort of libido would pursue the aims of a masculine sexual life and another sort those of a feminine one. But nothing of the kind is true. There is only one libido, which serves both the masculine and the feminine sexual functions. To it itself we cannot assign any sex; if, following the conventional equation of activity and masculinity, we are inclined to describe it as masculine, we must not forget that it also covers trends with a passive aim. Nevertheless the juxtaposition "feminine libido" is without any justification. Furthermore, it is our impression that more constraint has been applied to the libido when it is pressed into the service of the feminine function, and that—to speak teleologically—Nature takes less careful account of its [that function's] demands than in the case of masculinity. And the reason for this may lie— thinking once again teleologically—in the fact that the accomplishment of the aim of biology has been entrusted to the aggressiveness of men and has been made to some extent independent of women's consent.

The sexual frigidity of women, the frequency of which appears to confirm this disregard, is a phenomenon that is still insufficiently understood. Sometimes it is psychogenic and in that case accessible to influence; but in other cases it suggests the hypothesis of its being constitutionally determined and even of there being a contributory anatomical factor.

I have promised to tell you of a few more psychical peculiarities of mature femininity, as we come across them in analytic observation. We do not lay claim to more than an average validity for these assertions; nor is it always easy to distinguish what should be ascribed to the influence of the sexual function and what to social breeding. Thus, we attribute a larger amount of narcissism to femininity, which also affects women's choice of object, so that to be loved is a stronger need for them than to love. The effect of penis-envy has a share, further, in the physical vanity of women, since they are bound to value their charms more highly as a late compensation for their original sexual inferiority. Shame, which is considered to be a feminine characteristic *par excellence* but is far more a matter of convention than might be supposed, has as its purpose, we believe, concealment of genital deficiency. We are not forgetting that at a later time shame takes on other functions. It seems that women have made few contributions to the discoveries and inventions in the history of civilization; there is, however, one technique which they may have invented—that of plaiting and weaving. If that is so, we should be tempted to guess the unconscious motive for the achievement. Nature herself would seem to have given the model which this achievement imitates by causing the growth at maturity of the pubic hair that conceals the genitals. The step that remained to be taken lay in making the threads adhere to one another, while on the body they stick into the skin and are only matted together. If you reject this idea as fantastic and regard my belief in the influence of lack of a penis on the configuration of femininity as an *idée fixe,* I am of course defenceless.

The determinants of women's choice of an object are often made unrecognizable by social conditions. Where the choice is able to show itself freely, it is often made in accordance with the narcissistic ideal of the man whom the girl had wished to become. If the girl has remained in her attachment to her father—that is, in the Oedipus complex—her choice is made according to the paternal type. Since, when she turned from her mother to her father, the hostility of her ambivalent relation remained with her mother, a choice of this kind should guarantee a happy marriage. But very often the outcome is of a kind that presents a general threat to such a settlement of the conflict due to ambivalence. The hostility that has been left behind follows in the train of the positive attachment and spreads over on to the new object. The woman's husband, who to begin with inherited from her father, becomes after a time her mother's heir as well. So it may easily happen that the second half of a woman's life may be filled by the struggle against her husband, just as the shorter first half was filled by her rebellion against her mother. When this reaction has been lived through, a second marriage may easily turn out very much more satisfying. Another alteration in a woman's nature, for which lovers are unprepared, may occur in a marriage after the first child is born. Under the influence of a woman's becoming a mother herself, an identification with her own mother may be revived, against which she had striven up till the time of her marriage, and this may attract all the available libido to itself, so that the compulsion to repeat reproduces an unhappy marriage between her parents. The difference in a mother's reaction to the birth of a son or a daughter shows that the old factor of lack of a penis has even now not lost its strength. A mother is only brought unlimited satisfaction by her relation to a son; this is altogether the most perfect, the most free from ambivalence of all human relationships. A mother can transfer to her son the ambition which she has been obliged to suppress in herself, and she can expect from him the satisfaction of all that has been left over in her of her masculinity complex. Even a marriage is not made secure until the wife has succeeded in making her husband her child as well and in acting as a mother to him.

A woman's identification with her mother allows us to distinguish two strata: the pre-Oedipus one which rests on her affectionate attachment to her mother and takes her as a model, and the later one from the Oedipus complex which seeks to get rid of her mother and take her place with her father. We are no doubt justified in saying that much of both of them is left over for the future and that neither of them is adequately surmounted in the course of development. But the phase of the affectionate pre-Oedipus attachment is the decisive one for a woman's future: during it preparations are made for the acquisition of the characteristics with which she will later fulfil her role in the sexual function and perform her invaluable social tasks. It is in this identification too that she acquires her attractiveness to a man, whose Oedipus attachment to his mother it kindles into passion. How often it happens, however, that it is only his son who obtains what he himself aspired to! One gets an impression that a man's love and a woman's are a phase apart psychologically.

The fact that women must be regarded as having little sense of justice is no doubt related to the predominance of envy in their mental life; for the demand for justice is a modification of envy and lays down the condition subject to which one can put envy aside. We also regard women as weaker in their social interests and as having less capacity for sublimating their instincts than men. The former is no doubt derived from the dissocial quality which unquestionably characterizes all sexual relations. Lovers find sufficiency in each other, and families too resist inclusion in more comprehensive associations. The aptitude for sublimation is subject to the greatest individual variations. On the other hand I cannot help mentioning an impression that we are constantly receiving during analytic practice. A man of about thirty strikes us as a youthful, somewhat unformed individual, whom we expect to make powerful use of the possibilities for development opened up to him by analysis. A woman of the same age, however, often frightens us by her psychical rigidity and unchangeability. Her libido has taken up final positions and seems incapable of exchanging them for others. There are no paths open to further development; it is as though the whole process had already run its course and remains thenceforward insusceptible to influence—as though, indeed, the difficult development to femininity had exhausted the possibilities of the person concerned. . . .

The Inevitability of Patriarchy

Steven Goldberg

If Male Aggression Were the Only Difference . . .

. . . *Aggression is the only sexual difference that we can explain with direct (as opposed to convincing, but hypothetical) biological evidence.* . . .

Therefore, *we are assuming throughout this chapter that there are no differences between men and women except in the hormonal system that renders the man more aggressive.* This alone would explain patriarchy, male dominance, and male attainment of high-status roles; for the male hormonal system gives men an insuperable "head start" toward attaining those roles which any society associates with leadership or high status as long as the roles are not ones that males are biologically incapable of filling.

Aggression and Attainment

In other words, I believe that in the past we have been looking in the wrong direction for the answer to the question of why every society rewards male roles with higher status than it does female roles (even when the male tasks in one society are the female tasks in another). While it is true that men are always in the positions of authority from which status tends to be defined, male roles are not given high status primarily *because* men fill these roles; men fill these roles because their biological aggression "advantage" can be manifested *in any non-child related area rewarded by high status in any society*. (Again: the line of reasoning used in this book demonstrates only that the biological factors we discuss would make the social institutions we discuss inevitable and does not preclude the existence of other forces also leading in the same direction; there may be a biologically based tendency for women to prefer male leadership, but there need not be for male attainment of leadership and high-status roles to be inevitable.) As we shall see, this aggression "advantage" can be most manifested and can most enable men to reap status rewards *not* in those relatively homogeneous, collectivist primitive societies in which both male and female must play similar economic roles if the society is to survive or in the monarchy (which guarantees an occasional female leader); this biological factor will be given freest play in the complex, relatively individualistic, bureaucratic, democratic society which, of necessity, must emphasize organizational authority and in which social mobility is relatively free of traditional barriers to advancement. There were more female heads of state in the first two-thirds of the sixteenth century than in the first two-thirds of the twentieth.

The mechanisms involved here are easily seen if we examine any roles that males have attained by channeling their aggression toward such attainment. We will assume for now that equivalent women could *perform* the tasks of roles as well as men if they could attain the roles. Here we can speak of the corporation president, the union leader, the governor, the chairman of an association, or any other role or position for which aggression is a precondition for attainment. Now the environmentalist and the feminist will say that the fact that all such roles are nearly always filled by men is attributable not to male aggression but to the fact that women have not been allowed to enter the competitive race to attain these positions, that they have been told that these positions are in male areas, and that girls are socialized away from competing with boys in general. Women *are* socialized in this way, but again we must ask why. If innate male aggression has nothing to do with male attainment of positions of authority and status in the political, academic, scientific, or financial spheres, if aggression has nothing to do with the reasons why *every* society socializes girls away from those areas which are given high status and away from competition in general, then why is it never the *girls* in any society who are socialized toward these areas, why is it never the nonbiological roles played by women that have high status, why is it always boys who are told to compete, and why do women never "force" men into the low-status, nonmaternal roles that women play in every society?

These questions pose no problem if we acknowledge a male aggression that enables men to attain any nonbiological role given high status by any society. For one need merely consider the result of a society's *not* socializing women away from competitions with men, from its *not* directing girls toward roles women are more capable of playing than are men or roles with status low enough that men will not strive for them. No doubt some women would be aggressive enough to succeed in competitions with men and there would be considerably more women in high-status positions than there are now. But most women would lose in such competitive struggles with men (because men have the aggression advantage) and so most women would be forced to live adult lives as failures in areas in which the society had *wanted them to succeed*. It is women, far more than men, who would never allow a situation in which girls were socialized in such a way that the vast majority of them were doomed to adult lifetimes of failure to live up to their own expectations. . . .

Socialization's Conformation to Biological Reality

Socialization is the process by which society prepares children for adulthood. The way in which its goals conform to the reality of biology is seen quite clearly when we consider the method in which testosterone generates male aggression (testosterone's serially developing nature). Preadolescent boys and girls have roughly equal testosterone levels, yet young boys are far more aggressive than young girls. Eva Figes has used this observation to dismiss incorrectly the possibility of a hormone-aggression association.[1] Now it is quite probable that the boy is more aggressive than the girl for a purely biological reason. We have seen that it is simplistic to speak simply in terms of hormone levels and that there is evidence of male-female differences in the behavior of infants shortly after birth (when differential socialization is not a plausible explanation of such differences). The fetal alteration of the boy's brain by the testosterone that was generated by his testes has probably left him far more sensitive to the aggression-related properties of the testosterone that is present during boyhood than the girl, who did not receive such alteration. But let us for the moment assume that this is not the case. This does not at all reduce the importance of the hormonal factor. For even if the boy is more aggressive than the girl only because the society allows him to be, the boy's socialization still flows from society's acknowledging biological reality. Let us consider what would happen if girls have the same innate aggression as boys and if a society did not socialize girls away from aggressive competitions. Perhaps half of the third-grade baseball team would be female. As many girls as boys would frame their expectations in masculine values and girls would develop not their feminine abilities but their masculine ones. During adolescence, however, the same assertion of the male chromosomal program that causes the boys to grow beards raises their testosterone level, and their potential for aggression, to a level far above that of the adolescent woman. If society did not teach young girls that beating boys at competitions was unfeminine (behavior inappropriate for a woman), if it did not socialize them away from the political and economic areas in which aggression leads to attainment, these girls would grow into adulthood with self-images based not on

[1]Eva Figes, *Patriarchal Attitudes* (Greenwich, Conn.: Fawcett World, 1971), p. 8.

succeeding in areas for which biology has left them better prepared than men, but on competitions that most women could not win. If women did not develop feminine qualities as girls (assuming that such qualities do not spring automatically from female biology) then they would be forced to deal with the world in the aggressive terms of men. They would lose every source of power their feminine abilities now give them and they would gain nothing. . . .

Discrimination of a Sort

If one is convinced that sexual biology gives the male an advantage in aggression, competitiveness, and dominance, but he does not believe that it engenders in men and women different propensities, cognitive aptitudes, and modes of perception, and if he considers it discrimination when male aggression leads to attainment of position even when aggression is not relevant to the task to be performed, then the unavoidable conclusion is that discrimination so defined is unavoidable. Even if one is convinced from the discussion in the following sections that the differing biological substrates that underlie the mental apparatus of men and women *do* engender different propensities, cognitive aptitudes, and modes of perception, he will probably agree that the relevance of this to male attainment of male roles is small when compared to the importance of male biological aggression to attainment. Innate tendencies to specific aptitudes *would* indicate that at any given level of competence there will be more men than women or vice versa (depending on the qualities relevant to the task) and that the very best will, in all probability, come from the sex whose potentials are relevant to the task. Nonetheless, drastic sexual differences in occupational and authority roles reflect male aggression and society's acknowledgment of it far more than they do differences in aptitudes, yet they are still inevitable.

In addition, even if artificial means were used to place large numbers of women in authority positions, it is doubtful that stability could be maintained. Even in our present male bureaucracies problems arise whenever a subordinate is more aggressive than his superior and, if the more aggressive executive is not allowed to rise in the bureaucracy, delicate psychological adjustments must be made. Such adjustments are also necessary when a male bureaucrat has a female superior. When such situations are rare exceptions adjustments can be made without any great instability occurring, particularly if the woman in the superior position complements her aggression with sensitivity and femininity. It would seem likely, however, that if women shared equally in power at each level of the bureaucracy, chaos would result for two reasons. Even if we consider the bureaucracy as a closed system, the excess of male aggression would soon manifest itself either in men moving quickly up the hierarchy or in a male refusal to acknowledge female authority. But a bureaucracy is not a closed system, and the discrepancy between male dominance in private life and bureaucratic female dominance (from the point of view of the male whose superior is a woman) would soon engender chaos. Consider that even the present minute minority of women in high authority positions expend enormous amounts of energy trying *not* to project the commanding authority that is seen as the mark of a good male executive. It is true that the manner in which aggression is manifested will be affected by the values of the society in general and the nature of the field of competition in particular; aggression in an academic environment is camouflaged far more than in the executive arena. While a desire for control and power and a single-mindedness of purpose are no doubt relevant, here aggression is not easily defined. One might inject the theoretical argument that women could attain positions of authority and leadership by countering the male's advantage in aggression with feminine abilities. Perhaps, but the equivalents of the executive positions in every area of suprafamilial life in every society have been attained by men, and there seems no reason to believe that, suddenly, feminine means will be capable of neutralizing male aggression in these areas. And, in any case, an emphasis on feminine abilities is hardly what the feminists desire. All of this can be seen in a considerably more optimistic light, from the point of view of most women, if one considers that the biological abilities possessed only by women are complemented by biologically generated propensities directing women to roles that can be filled only by women. But it is still the same picture.

Fifty-one Percent of the Vote

Likewise, one who predicates political action on a belief that a society is oppressive until half of the positions of authority are filled by women faces the insuperable task of overcoming a male dominance that has forced every political and economic system to conform to it and that may be maintained as much by the refusal of women to elect widespread female leadership as by male aggression and ability. No doubt an exceptional configuration of factors will someday result in a woman's being elected president, but if one considers a society "sexist" until it no longer associates authority primarily with men and until a woman leader is no longer an exception, then he must resign himself to the certainty that all societies will be "sexist" forever. Feminists make much of the fact that women constitute a slight majority of voters but in doing so make the assumption that it is possible to convince the women who constitute this majority to elect equal female leadership. This is a dubious assumption since the members of a society will inevitably associate authority with males if patriarchy and male dominance are biologically inevitable. It would be even more dubious if there is an innate tendency for women to favor men who "take the lead." However, proceeding from this assumption and assuming that the feminists were success-ful, it is a sure bet that democracy—which obviously is not biologically inevitable (not patriarchy, which is)—would be eliminated as large numbers of males battled for the relatively small numbers of positions of power from which the rules that govern the battle are made. In any real society, of course, women can have the crucial effect of mobilizing political power to achieve particular goals and of electing those men who are motivated by relatively more life-sustaining values than other men just as mothers have the crucial effect of coloring and humanizing the values of future male leaders.

"Oppression"

All of this indicates that the theoretical model that conceives of male success in attaining positions of status, authority, and leadership as *oppression* of the female is incorrect if only because it sees male aggressive energies as *directed toward* females and sees the institutional mechanisms that flow from the fact of male aggression as *directed toward* "oppressing" women. In reality these male energies are directed toward attainment of desired positions and toward succeeding in whatever areas a particular society considers important. The fact that women lose out in these competitions, so that the sex-role expectations of a society would have to become different for men and women even if they were not different for other reasons, is an inevitable byproduct of the reality of the male's aggression advantage and not the cause, purpose, or primary function of it. In other words, men who attain the more desired roles and positions do so because they channel their aggression advantage toward such attainment; whether the losers in such competitions are other men or women is important only in that— because so few women succeed in these competitions—the society will attach different expectations to men and women (making it more difficult for the exceptional, aggressive, woman to attain such positions even when her aggression is equal to that of the average man). Perhaps one could at least begin to defend a model that stressed "oppression" if he dealt only with male dominance in dyadic relationships; here male energies are directed toward the female, but to call that which is inevitable "oppression" would seem to confuse more than clarify and, if one feels that male dominance is "oppressive," this model offers an illusory hope of change where there is no possibility of change. Male dominance is the emotional resolution (felt by both the man and the woman) of the difference between a man and a woman in the biological factors relevant to aggression; male authority in dyadic relationships, and the socialization of boys and girls toward this male authority, is societal conformation to this biological difference and a result of society's attempting to most smoothly and effectively utilize this difference. Note that all that I say in this paragraph—indeed, in this book—accepts the feminist assumption that women do not follow their own biologically generated imperatives, which are eternally different from those of men. I do this in an attempt to show the inadequacy of the feminist model and not because it is less than ludicrous to suppose that women do not hear their own drummer. This book does not pretend to explain female behavior, but merely to show that women would have to behave as they do if they were nothing more than less aggressive men. If one reversed the feminist model he could view the desire of the vast majority of women to have children as oppressing men by succeeding in an area in which men are doomed by their biology to fail. Such a theoretical model leaves much to be desired.

LIBERALISM: Sexism as Legal Inequality

The Subjection of Women
John Stuart Mill

The object of this Essay is to explain as clearly as I am able, the grounds of an opinion which I have held from the very earliest period when I had formed any opinions at all on social or political matters, and which, instead of being weakened or modified, has been constantly growing stronger by the progress of reflection and the experience of life: That the principle which regulates the existing social relations between the two sexes—the legal subordination of one sex to the other—is wrong in itself, and now one of the chief hindrances to human improvement; and that it ought to be replaced by a principle of perfect equality, admitting no power or privilege on the one side, nor disability on the other.

The very words necessary to express the task I have undertaken, show how arduous it is. But it would be a mistake to suppose that the difficulty of the case must lie in the insufficiency or obscurity of the grounds of reason on which my conviction rests. The difficulty is that which exists in all cases in which there is a mass of feeling to be contended against. So long as an opinion is strongly rooted in the feelings, it gains rather than loses in stability by having a preponderating weight of argument against it. For if it were accepted as a result of argument, the refutation of the argument might shake the solidity of the conviction; but when it rests solely on feeling, the worse it fares in argumentative contest, the more persuaded its adherents are that their feeling must have some deeper ground, which the arguments do not reach; and while the feeling remains, it is always throwing up fresh intrenchments of argument to repair any breach made in the old. And there are so many causes tending to make the feelings connected with this subject the most intense and most deeply-rooted of all those which gather round and protect old institutions and customs, that we need not wonder to find them as yet less undermined and loosened than any of the rest by the progress of the great modern spiritual and social transition; nor suppose that the barbarisms to which men cling longest must be less barbarisms than those which they earlier shake off. . . .

. . . In the first place, the opinion in favour of the present system, which entirely subordinates the weaker sex to the stronger, rests upon theory only; for there never has been trial made of any other: so that experience, in the sense in which it is vulgarly opposed to theory, cannot be pretended to have pronounced any verdict. And in the second place, the adoption of this system of inequality never was the result of deliberation, or forethought, or any social ideas, or any notion whatever of what conduced to the benefit of humanity or the good order of society. It arose simply from the fact that from the very earliest twilight of human society, every woman (owing to the value attached to her by men, combined with her inferiority in muscular strength) was found in a state of bondage to some man. Laws and systems of polity always begin by recognising the relations they find already existing between individuals. They convert what was a mere physical fact into a legal right, give it the sanction of society, and principally aim at the substitution of public and organized means of asserting and protecting these rights, instead of the irregular and lawless conflict of physical strength. Those who had already been compelled to obedience became in this manner legally bound to it. Slavery, from being a mere affair of force between the master and the slave, became regularized and a matter of compact among the masters, who, binding themselves to one another for common protection, guaranteed by their collective strength the private possessions of each, including his slaves. In early times, the great majority of the male sex were slaves, as well as the whole of the female. And many ages elapsed, some of them ages of high cultivation, before any thinker was bold enough to question the rightfulness, and the absolute social necessity, either of the one slavery or of the other. . . .

If people are mostly so little aware how completely, during the greater part of the duration of our species, the law of force was the avowed rule of general conduct, any other being only a special and exceptional consequence of peculiar ties—and from how very recent a date it is that the affairs of society in general have been even pretended to be regulated according to any moral law; as little do people remember or consider, how institutions and customs which never had any ground but the law of force, last on into ages and states of general opinion which never would have permitted their first establishment. Less than forty years ago, Englishmen might still by law hold human beings in bondage as saleable property: within the present century they might kidnap them and carry them off, and work them literally to death. This absolutely extreme case of the law of force, condemned by those who can tolerate almost every other form of arbitrary power, and which, of all others, presents features the most revolting to the feelings of all who look at it from an impartial position, was the law of civilized and Christian England within the memory of persons now living: and in one half of Anglo-Saxon America three or four years ago, not only did slavery exist, but the slave trade, and the breeding of slaves expressly for it, was a general practice between slave states. Yet not only was there a greater strength of sentiment against it, but, in England at least, a less amount either of feeling or of interest in favour of it, than of any other of the customary abuses of force: for its motive was the love of gain, unmixed and undisguised; and those who profited by it were a very small numerical fraction of the country, while the natural feeling of all who were not personally interested in it, was unmitigated abhorrence. So extreme an instance makes it almost superfluous to refer to any other: but consider the long duration of absolute monarchy. In England at present it is the almost universal conviction that military despotism is a case of the law of force, having no other origin or justification. Yet in all the great nations of Europe except England it either still exists, or has only just ceased to exist, and has even now a strong party favourable to it in all ranks of the people, especially among persons of station and consequence. Such is the power of an established system, even when far from universal; when not only in almost every period of history there have been great and well-known examples of the contrary system, but these have almost invariably been afforded by the most illustrious and most prosperous communities. In this case, too, the possessor of the undue power, the person directly interested in it, is only one person, while those who are subject to it and suffer from it are literally all the rest. The yoke is naturally and necessarily humiliating to all persons, except the one who is on the throne, together with, at most, the one who expects to succeed to it. How different are these cases from that of the power of men over women! I am not now prejudging the question of its justifiableness. I am showing how vastly more permanent it could not but be, even if not justifiable, than these other dominations which have nevertheless lasted down to our own time. Whatever gratification of pride there is in the possession of power, and whatever personal interest in its exercise, is in this case not confined to a limited class, but common to the whole male sex. Instead of being, to most of its supporters, a thing desirable chiefly in the abstract, or, like the political ends usually contended for by factions, of little private importance to any but the leaders; it comes home to the person and hearth of every male head of a family, and of every one who looks forward to being so. The clodhopper exercises, or is to exercise, his share of the power equally with the highest nobleman. And the case is that in which the desire of power is the strongest: for every one who desires power, desires it most over those who are nearest to him, with whom his life is passed, with whom he has most concerns in common, and in whom any independence of his authority is oftenest likely to interfere with his individual preferences. If, in the other cases specified, power manifestly grounded only on force, and having so much less to support them, are so slowly and with so much difficulty got rid of, much more must it be so with this, even if it rests on no better foundation than those. We must consider, too, that the possessors of the power have facilities in this case, greater than in any other, to prevent any uprising against it. Every one of the subjects lives under the very eye, and almost, it may be said, in the hands, of one of the masters—in closer intimacy with him than with any of her fellow-subjects; with no means of combining against him, no power of even locally overmastering him, and, on the other hand, with the strongest motives for seeking his favour and avoiding to give him offence. In struggles for political emancipation, everybody knows how often its champions are bought off by bribes, or daunted by terrors. In the case of women, each individual of the subject-class is in a chronic state of bribery and intimidation combined. In setting up the standard of resistance, a large number of the leaders, and still more of the followers, must make an almost complete sacrifice of the pleasures or the alleviations of their own individual lot. If ever any system of privilege and enforced subjection had its yoke tightly riveted on the necks of those who are kept down by it, this has. . . .

All causes, social and natural, combine to make it unlikely that women should be collectively rebellious to the power of men. They are so far in a position different from all other subject classes, that their masters require something more from them than actual service. Men do not want solely the obedience of women, they want their sentiments. All men, except the most brutish, desire to have, in the woman most nearly connected with them, not a forced slave but a willing one, not a slave merely, but a favourite. They have therefore put everything in practice to enslave their minds. The masters of all other slaves rely, for maintaining obedience, on fear; either fear of themselves, or religious fears. The masters of women wanted more than simple obedience, and they turned the whole force of education to effect their purpose. All women are brought up from the very earliest years in the belief that their ideal of character is the very opposite to that of men; not self-will, and government by self-control, but submission, and yielding to the control of others. All the moralities tell them that it is the duty of women, and all the current sentimentalities that it is their nature, to live for others; to make complete abnegation of themselves, and to have no life but in their affections. And by their affections are meant the only ones they are allowed to have—those to the men with whom they are connected, or to the children who constitute an additional and indefeasible tie between them and a man. When we put together three things—first, the natural attraction between opposite sexes; secondly, the wife's entire dependence on the husband, every privilege or pleasure she has being either his gift, or depending entirely on his will; and lastly, that the principal object of human pursuit, consideration, and all objects of social ambition, can in general be sought or obtained by her only through him, it would be a miracle if the object of being attractive to men had not become the polar star of feminine education and formation of character. And, this great means of influence over the minds of women having been acquired, an instinct of selfishness made men avail themselves of it to the utmost as a means of holding women in subjection, by representing to them meekness, submissiveness, and resignation of all individual will into the hands of a man, as an essential part of sexual attractiveness. Can it be doubted that any of the other yokes which mankind have succeeded in breaking, would have subsisted till now if the same means had existed, and had been as sedulously used, to bow down their minds to it? If it had been made the object of the life of every young plebeian to find personal favour in the eyes of some patrician, of every young serf with some seigneur; if domestication with him, and a share of his personal affections, had been held out as the prize which they all should look out for, the most gifted and aspiring being able to reckon on the most desirable prizes; and if, when this prize had been obtained, they had been shut out by a wall of brass from all interests not centering in him, all feelings and desires but those which he shared or inculcated; would not serfs and seigneurs, plebeians and patricians, have been as broadly distinguished at this day as men and women are? and would not all but a thinker here and there, have believed the distinction to be a fundamental and unalterable fact in human nature?

The preceding considerations are amply sufficient to show that custom, however universal it may be, affords in this case no presumption, and ought not to create any prejudice, in favour of the arrangements which place women in social and political subjection to men. But I may go farther, and maintain that the course of history, and the tendencies of progressive human society, afford not only no presumption in favour of this system of inequality of rights, but a strong one against it; and that, so far as the whole course of human improvement up to this time, the whole stream of modern tendencies, warrants any inference on the subject, it is, that this relic of the past is discordant with the future, and must necessarily disappear.

For, what is the peculiar character of the modern world—the difference which chiefly distinguishes modern institutions, modern social ideas, modern life itself, from those of times long past? It is, that human beings are no longer born to their place in life, and chained down by an inexorable bond to the place they are born to, but are free to employ their faculties, and such favourable chances as offer, to achieve the lot which may appear to them most desirable. Human society of old was constituted on a very different principle. All were born to a fixed social position, and were mostly kept in it by law, or interdicted from any means by which they could emerge from it. As some men are born white and others black, so some were born slaves and others freemen and citizens; some were born patricians, others plebeians; some were born feudal nobles, others commoners and *roturiers*. A slave or serf could never make himself free, nor, except by the will of his master, become so. In most European countries it was not till towards the close of the middle ages, and as a consequence of the growth of regal power, that commoners could be ennobled. Even among nobles, the eldest son was born the exclusive heir to the paternal possessions, and a long time elapsed before it was fully established that the father could disinherit him. Among the industrious classes, only those who were born members of a guild, or were admitted into it by its members, could lawfully practise their calling within its local limits; and nobody could practise any calling deemed important, in any but the legal manner—by processes authoritatively prescribed. Manufacturers have stood in the pillory for presuming to carry on their business by new and improved methods. In modern Europe, and most in those parts of it which have participated most largely in all other modern improvements, diametrically opposite doctrines now prevail. Law and government do not undertake to prescribe by whom any social or industrial operation shall or shall not be conducted, or what modes of conducting them shall be lawful. These things are left to the unfettered choice of individuals. Even the laws which required that workmen should serve an apprenticeship, have in this country been repealed: there being ample assurance that in all cases in which an apprenticeship is necessary, its necessity will suffice to enforce it. The old theory was, that the least possible should be left to the choice of the individual agent; that all he had to do should, as far as practicable, be laid down for him by superior wisdom. Left to himself he was sure to go wrong, The modern conviction, the fruit of a thousand years of experience, is, that things in which the individual is the person directly interested, never go right but as they are left to his own discretion; and that any regulation of them by authority, except to protect the rights of others, is sure to be mischievous. This conclusion, slowly arrived at, and not adopted until almost every possible application of the contrary theory had been made with disastrous result, now (in the industrial department) prevails universally in the most advanced countries, almost universally in all that have pretensions to any sort of advancement. It is not that all processes are supposed to be equally good, or all persons to be equally qualified for everything; but that freedom of individual choice is now known to be the only thing which procures the adoption of the best processes, and throws each operation into the hands of those who are best qualified for it. Nobody thinks it necessary to make a law that only a strong-armed man shall be a blacksmith. Freedom and competition suffice to make blacksmiths strong-armed men, because the weak-armed can earn more by engaging in occupations for which they are more fit. In consonance with this doctrine, it is felt to be an overstepping of the proper bounds of authority to fix beforehand, on some general presumption, that certain persons are not fit to do certain things. It is now thoroughly known and admitted that if some such presumptions exist, no such presumption is infallible. Even if it be well grounded in a majority of cases, which it is very likely not to be, there will be a minority of exceptional cases in which it does not hold: and in those it is both an injustice to the individuals, and a detriment to society, to place barriers in the way of their using their faculties for their own benefit and for that of others. In the cases, on the other hand, in which the unfitness is real, the ordinary motives of human conduct will on the whole suffice to prevent the incompetent person from making, or from persisting in, the attempt.

If this general principle of social and economical science is not true; if individuals, with such help as they can derive from the opinion of those who know them, are not better judges than the law and the government, of their own capacities and vocation; the world cannot too soon abandon this principle, and return to the old system of regulations and disabilities. But if the principle is true, we ought to act as if we believed it, and not to ordain that to be born a girl instead of a boy, any more than to be born black instead of white, or a commoner instead of a nobleman, shall decide the person's position through all life—shall interdict people from all the more elevated social positions, and from all, except a few, respectable occupations. Even were we to admit the utmost that is ever pretended as to the superior fitness of men for all the functions now reserved to them, the same argument applies which forbids a legal qualification for members of Parliament. If only once in a dozen years the conditions of eligibility exclude a fit person, there is a real loss, while the exclusion of thousands of unfit persons is no gain; for if the constitution of the electoral body disposes them to choose unfit persons, there are always plenty of such persons to choose from. In all things of any difficulty and importance, those who can do them well are fewer than the need, even with the most unrestricted latitude of choice: and any limitation of the field of selection deprives society of some chances of being served by the competent, without ever saving it from the incompetent.

At present, in the more improved countries, the disabilities of women are the only case, save one, in which laws and institutions take persons at their birth, and ordain that they shall never in all their lives be allowed to compete for certain things. . . .

The social subordination of women thus stands out an isolated fact in modern social institutions; a solitary breach of what has become their fundamental law; a single relic of an old world of thought and practice exploded in everything else, but retained in the one thing of most universal interest. . . .

The least that can be demanded is, that the question should not be considered as prejudged by existing fact and existing opinion, but open to discussion on its merits, as a question of justice and expediency: the decision on this, as on any of the other social arrangements of mankind, depending on what an enlightened estimate of tendencies and consequences may show to be most advantageous to humanity in general, without distinction of sex. And the discussion must be a real discussion, descending to foundations, and not resting satisfied with vague and general assertions. It will not do, for instance, to assert in general terms, that the experience of mankind has pronounced in favour of the existing system. Experience cannot possibly have decided between two courses, so long as there has only been experience of one. If it be said that the doctrine of the equality of the sexes rests only on theory, it must be remembered that the contrary doctrine also has only theory to rest upon. All that is proved in its favour by direct experience, is that mankind have been able to exist under it, and to attain the degree of improvement and prosperity which we now see; but whether that prosperity has been attained sooner, or is now greater, than it would have been under the other system, experience does not say. On the other hand, experience does say, that every step in improvement has been so invariably accompanied by a step made in raising the social position of women, that historians and philosophers have been led to adopt their elevation or debasement as on the whole the surest test and most correct measure of the civilization of a people or an age. Through all the progressive period of human history, the condition of women has been approaching nearer to equality with men. This does not of itself prove that the assimilation must go on to complete equality; but it assuredly affords some presumption that such is the case.

Neither does it avail anything to say that the *nature* of the two sexes adapts them to their present functions and position, and renders these appropriate to them. Standing on the ground of common sense and the constitution of the human mind, I deny that any one knows, or can know, the nature of the two sexes, as long as they have only been seen in their present relation to one another. If men had ever been found in society without women, or women without men, or if there had been a society of men and women in which the women were not under the control of the men, something might have been positively known about the mental and moral differences which may be inherent in the nature of each. What is now called the nature of women is an eminently artificial thing—the result of forced repression in some directions, unnatural stimulation in others. It may be asserted without scruple, that no other class of dependents have had their character so entirely distorted from its natural proportions by their relation with their masters; for, if conquered and slave races have been, in some respects, more forcibly repressed, whatever in them has not been crushed down by an iron heel has generally been let alone, and if left with any liberty of development, it has developed itself according to its own laws; but in the case of women, a hot-house and stove cultivation has always been carried on of some of the capabilities of their nature, for the benefit and pleasure of their masters. . . .

Hence, in regard to that most difficult question, what are the natural differences between the two sexes—a subject on which it is impossible in the present state of society to obtain complete and correct knowledge—while almost everybody dogmatizes upon it, almost all neglect and make light of the only means by which any partial insight can be obtained into it. This is, an analytic study of the most important department of psychology, the laws of the influence of circumstances on character. For, however great and apparently ineradicable the moral and intellectual differences between men and women might be, the evidence of their being natural differences could only be negative. Those only could be inferred to be natural which could not possibly be artificial—the residuum, after deducting every characteristic of either sex which can admit of being explained from education or external circumstances. The profoundest knowledge of the laws of the formation of character is indispensable to entitle any one to affirm even that there is any difference, much more what the difference is, between the two sexes considered as moral and rational beings; and since no one, as yet, has that knowledge, (for there is hardly any subject which, in proportion to its importance, has been so little studied), no one is thus far entitled to any positive opinion on the subject. Conjectures are all that can at present be made; conjectures more or less probable, according as more or less authorized by such knowledge as we yet have of the laws of psychology, as applied to the formation of character.

Even the preliminary knowledge, what the differences between the sexes now are, apart from all questions as to how they are made what they are, is still in the crudest and most incomplete state. . . .

One thing we may be certain of—that what is contrary to women's nature to do, they never will be made to do by simply giving their nature free play. The anxiety of mankind to interfere in behalf of nature, for fear lest nature should not succeed in effecting its purpose, is an altogether unnecessary solicitude. What women by nature cannot do, it is quite superfluous to forbid them from doing. What they can do, but not so well as the men who are their competitors, competition suffices to exclude them from; since nobody asks for protective duties and bounties in favour of women; it is only asked that the present bounties and protective duties in favour of men should be recalled. If women have a greater natural inclination for some things than for others, there is no need of laws or social inculcation to make the majority of them do the former in preference to the latter. Whatever women's services are most wanted for, the free play of competition will hold out the strongest inducements to them to undertake. And, as the words imply, they are most wanted for the things for which they are most fit; by the apportionment of which to them, the collective faculties of the two sexes can be applied on the whole with the greatest sum of valuable result.

The general opinion of men is supposed to be, that the natural vocation of a woman is that of a wife and mother. I say, is supposed to be, because, judging from acts—from the whole of the present constitution of society—one might infer that their opinion was the direct contrary. They might be supposed to think that the alleged natural vocation of women was of all things the most repugnant to their nature; insomuch that if they are free to do anything else—if any other means of living, or occupation of their time and faculties, is open, which has any chance of appearing desirable to them—there will not be enough of them who will be willing to accept the condition said to be natural to them. If this is the real opinion of men in general, it would be well that it should be spoken out. I should like to hear somebody openly enunciating the doctrine (it is already implied in much that is written on the subject)—"It is necessary to society that women should marry and produce children. They will not do so unless they are compelled. Therefore it is necessary to compel them." The merits of the case would then be clearly defined. It would be exactly that of the slaveholders of South Carolina and Louisiana. "It is necessary that cotton and sugar should be grown. White men cannot produce them. Negroes will not, for any wages which we choose to give. *Ergo* they must be compelled." An illustration still closer to the point is that of impressment. Sailors must absolutely be had to defend the country. It often happens that they will not voluntarily enlist. Therefore there must be the power of forcing them. How often has this logic been used! and, but for one flaw in it, without doubt it would have been successful up to this day. But it is open to the retort—First pay the sailors the honest value of their labour. When you have made it as well worth their while to serve you, as to work for other employers, you will have no more difficulty than others have in obtaining their services. To this there is no logical answer except "I will not": and as people are now not only ashamed, but are not desirous, to rob the labourer of his hire, impressment is no longer advocated. Those who attempt to force women into marriage by closing all other doors against them, lay themselves open to a similar retort. If they mean what they say, their opinion must evidently be, that men do not render the married condition so desirable to women, as to induce them to accept it for its own recommendations. It is not a sign of one's thinking the boon one offers very attractive, when one allows only Hobson's choice, "that or none." And here, I believe, is the clue to the feelings of those men, who have a real antipathy to the equal freedom of women. I believe they are afraid, not lest women should be unwilling to marry, for I do not think that any one in reality has that apprehension; but lest they should insist that marriage should be on equal conditions; lest all women of spirit and capacity should prefer doing almost anything else, not in their own eyes degrading, rather than marry, when marrying is giving themselves a master, and a master too of all their earthly possessions. And truly, if this consequence were necessarily incident to marriage, I think that the apprehension would be very well founded. I agree in thinking it probable that few women, capable of anything else, would, unless under an irresistible *entrainement,* rendering them for the time insensible to anything but itself, choose such a lot, when any other means were open to them of filling a conventionally honourable place in life: and if men are determined that the law of marriage shall be a law of despotism, they are quite right, in point of mere policy, in leaving to women only Hobson's choice. But, in that case, all that has been done in the modern world to relax the chain on the minds of women, has been a mistake, They never should have been allowed to receive a literary education. Women who read, much more women who write, are, in the existing constitution of things, a contradiction and a disturbing element: and it was wrong to bring women up with any acquirements but those of an odalisque, or of a domestic servant.

National Organization for Women (NOW)
Bill of Rights

I   Equal Rights Constitutional Amendment
II   Enforce Law Banning Sex Discrimination in Employment
III   Maternity Leave Rights in Employment and in Social Security Benefits
IV   Tax Deduction for Home and Child Care Expenses for Working Parents
V   Child Care Centers
VI   Equal and Unsegregated Education
VII   Equal Job Training Opportunities and Allowances for Women in Poverty
VIII The Right of Women to Control Their Reproductive Lives

WE DEMAND:

I   That the United States Congress immediately pass the Equal Rights Amendment to the Constitution to provide that "Equality of rights under the law shall not be denied or abridged by the United States or by any State on account of sex," and that such then be immediately ratified by the several States.

II   That equal employment opportunity be guaranteed to all women, as well as men, by insisting that the Equal Employment Opportunity Commission enforces the prohibitions against sex discrimination in employment under Title VII of the Civil Rights Act of 1964 with the same vigor as it enforces the prohibitions against racial discrimination.

III   That women be protected by law to ensure their rights to return to their jobs within a reasonable time after childbirth without loss of seniority or other accrued benefits, and be paid maternity leave as a form of social security and/or employee benefit.

IV   Immediate revision of tax laws to permit the deduction of home and child care expenses for working parents.

V   That child care facilities be established by law on the same basis as parks, libraries, and public schools, adequate to the needs of children from the pre-school years through adolescence, as a community resource to be used by all citizens from all income levels.

VI   That the right of women to be educated to their full potential equally with men be secured by Federal and State Legislation, eliminating all discrimination and segregation by sex, written and unwritten, at all levels of education, including colleges, graduate and professional schools, loans and fellowships, and Federal and State training programs such as the Job Corps.

VII   The right of women in poverty to secure job training, housing, and family allowances on equal terms with men, but without prejudice to a parent's right to remain at home to care for his or her children; revision of welfare legislation and poverty programs which deny women dignity, privacy and self-respect.

VIII   The right of women to control their own reproductive lives by removing from penal codes laws limiting access to contraceptive information and devices and laws governing abortion.

TRADITIONAL MARXISM: Sexism as a Result of the Class System

The Origin of the Family, Private Property, and the State

Friedrich Engels

. . . According to the materialistic conception, the determining factor in history is, in the final instance, the production and reproduction of immediate life. This, again, is of a twofold character: on the one side, the production of the means of existence, of food, clothing and shelter and the tools necessary for that production; on the other side, the production of human beings themselves, the propagation of the species. The social organization under which the people of a particular historical epoch and a particular country live is determined by both kinds of production: by the stage of development of labor on the one hand and of the family on the other. The lower the development of labor and the more limited the amount of its products, and consequently, the more limited also the wealth of the society, the more the social order is found to be dominated by kinship groups. However, within this structure of society based on kinship groups the productivity of labor increasingly develops, and with it private property and exchange, differences of wealth, the possibility of utilizing the labor power of others, and hence the basis of class antagonisms: new social elements, which in the course of generations strive to adapt the old social order to the new conditions, until at last their incompatibility brings about a complete upheaval. In the collision of the newly developed social classes, the old society founded on kinship groups is broken up. In its place appears a new society, with its control centered in the state, the subordinate units of which are no longer kinship associations, but local associations; a society in which the system of the family is completely dominated by the system of property, and in which there now freely develop those class antagonisms and class struggles that have hitherto formed the content of all *written* history. . . .

Morgan was the first person with expert knowledge to attempt to introduce a definite order into the history of primitive man; so long as no important additional material makes changes necessary, his classification will undoubtedly remain in force.

Of the three main epochs—savagery, barbarism, and civilization—he is concerned, of course, only with the first two and the transition to the third. . . .

Reconstructing thus the past history of the family, Morgan, in agreement with most of his colleagues, arrives at a primitive stage when unrestricted sexual freedom prevailed within the tribe, every woman belonging equally to every man and every man to every woman. . . .

According to Morgan, from this primitive state of promiscuous intercourse there developed, probably very early:

1 The Consanguine Family, the First Stage of the Family

Here the marriage groups are separated according to generations: all the grandfathers and grandmothers within the limits of the family are all husbands and wives of one another; so are also their children, the fathers and mothers; the latter's children will form a third circle of common husbands and wives; and their children, the great-grandchildren of the first group, will form a fourth. In this form of marriage, therefore, only ancestors and progeny, and parents and children, are excluded from the rights and duties (as we should say) of marriage with one another. Brothers and sisters, male and female cousins of the first, second, and more remote degrees, are all brothers and sisters of one another, and *precisely for that reason* they are all husbands and wives of one another. At this stage the relationship of brother and sister also includes as a matter of course the practice of sexual intercourse with one another. In its typical form, such a family would consist of the descendants of a single pair, the descendants of these descendants in each generation being again brothers and sisters, and therefore husbands and wives, of one another. . . .

2 The Punaluan Family

If the first advance in organization consisted in the exclusion of parents and children from sexual intercourse with one another, the second was the exclusion of sister and brother. On account of the greater nearness of age, this second advance was infinitely more important, but also more difficult, than the first. It was effected gradually, beginning probably with the exclusion from sexual intercourse of one's own brothers and sisters (children of the same mother) first in isolated cases and then by degrees as a general rule (even in this century exceptions were found in Hawaii), and ending with the prohibition of marriage even between collateral brothers and sisters, or, as we should say, between first, second, and third cousins. It affords, says Morgan, "a good illustration of the operation of the principle of natural selection." There can be no question that the tribes among whom inbreeding was restricted by this advance were bound to develop more quickly and more fully than those among whom marriage between brothers and sisters remained the rule and the law. How powerfully the influence of this advance made itself felt is seen in the institution which arose directly out of it and went far beyond it—the gens, which forms the basis of the social order of most, if not all, barbarian peoples of the earth and from which in Greece and Rome we step directly into civilization.

After a few generations at most, every original family was bound to split up. The practice of living together in a primitive communistic household which prevailed without exception till late in the middle stage of barbarism set a limit, varying with the conditions but fairly definite in each locality, to the maximum size of the family community. As soon as the conception arose that sexual intercourse between children of the same mother was wrong, it was bound to exert its influence when the old households split up and new ones were founded (though these did not necessarily coincide with the family group). One or more lines of sisters would form the nucleus of the one household and their own brothers the nucleus of the other. It must have been in some such manner as this that the form which Morgan calls the punaluan family originated out of the consanguine family. According to the Hawaiian custom, a number of sisters, natural or collateral (first, second or more remote cousins) were the common wives of their common husbands, from among whom, however, their own brothers were excluded. These husbands now no longer called themselves brothers, for they were no longer necessarily brothers, but *punalua*—that is, intimate companion, or partner. Similarly, a line of natural or collateral brothers had a number of women, *not* their sisters, as common wives, and these wives called one another *punalua*. This was the classic form of family structure [*Familienformation*], in which later a number of variations was possible, but whose essential feature was the mutually common possession of husbands and wives within a definite family circle, from which, however, the brothers of the wives—first one's own and later also collateral—and conversely also the sisters of the husbands, were excluded. . . .

In all forms of group family, it is uncertain who is the father of a child; but it is certain who its mother is. Though she calls *all* the children of the whole family her children and has a mother's duties toward them, she nevertheless knows her own children from the others. It is therefore clear that in so far as group marriage prevails, descent can only be proved on the *mother's* side and that therefore only the *female* line is recognized. And this is in fact the case among all peoples in the period of savagery or in the lower stage of barbarism. . . .

3 The Pairing Family

A certain amount of pairing, for a longer or shorter period, already occurred in group marriage or even earlier; the man had a chief wife among his many wives (one can hardly yet speak of a favorite wife), and for her he was the most important among her husbands. This fact has contributed considerably to the confusion of the missionaries, who have regarded group marriage sometimes as promiscuous community of wives, sometimes as unbridled adultery. But these customary pairings were bound to grow more stable as the gens developed and the classes of "brothers" and "sisters" between whom marriage was impossible became more numerous. The impulse given by the gens to the prevention of marriage between blood relatives extended still further. Thus among the Iroquois and most of the other Indians at the lower stage of barbarism, we find that marriage is prohibited between *all* relatives enumerated in their system—which includes several hundred degrees of kinship. The increasing complication of these prohibitions made group marriages more and more impossible; they were displaced by the *pairing family*. In this stage, one man lives with one woman, but the relationship is such that polygamy and occasional infidelity remain the right of the men, even though for economic reasons polygamy is rare, while from the woman the strictest fidelity is generally demanded throughout the time she lives with the man and adultery on her part is cruelly punished. The marriage tie can, however, be easily dissolved by either partner; after separation, the children still belong as before to the mother alone. . . .

Thus the history of the family in primitive times consists in the progressive narrowing of the circle, originally embracing the whole tribe, within which the two sexes have a common conjugal relation. The continuous exclusion, first of nearer, then of more and more remote relatives, and at last even of relatives by marriage, ends by making any kind of group marriage practically impossible. Finally, there remains only the single, still loosely linked pair, the molecule with whose dissolution marriage itself ceases. This in itself shows what a small part individual sex love, in the modern sense of the word, played in the rise of monogamy. Yet stronger proof is afforded by the practice of all peoples at this stage of development. Whereas in the earlier forms of the family, men never lacked women but, on the contrary, had too many rather than too few, women had now become scarce and highly sought after. Hence it is with the pairing marriage that there begins the capture and purchase of women—widespread *symptoms,* but no more than symptoms, of the much deeper change that had occurred. . . .

The pairing family, itself too weak and unstable to make an independent household necessary or even desirable, in no wise destroys the communistic household inherited from earlier times. Communistic housekeeping, however, means the supremacy of women in the house; just as the exclusive recognition of the female parent, owing to the impossibility of recognizing the male parent with certainty, means that the women—the mothers—are held in high respect. One of the most absurd notions taken over from 18th century enlightenment is that in the beginning of society woman was the slave of man. Among all savages and all barbarians of the lower and middle stages, and to a certain extent of the upper stage also, the position of women is not only free, but honorable. As to what it still is in the pairing marriage, let us hear the evidence of Ashur Wright, for many years missionary among the Iroquois Senecas:

> As to their family system, when occupying the old long houses [communistic households comprising several families], it is probable that some one clan [gens] predominated, the women taking in husbands, however, from the other clans [gentes]. . . . Usually, the female portion ruled the house. . . . The stores were in common; but woe to the luckless husband or lover who was too shiftless to do his share of the providing. No matter how many children, or whatever goods he might have in the house, he might at any time be ordered to pick up his blanket and budge; and after such orders it would not be healthful for him to attempt to disobey. The house would be too hot for him; and . . . he must retreat to his own clan [gens]; or, as was often done, go and start a new matrimonial alliance in some other. The women were the great power among the clans [gentes], as everywhere else. They did not hesitate, when occasion required, "to knock off the horns," as it was technically called, from the head of a chief, and send him back to the ranks of the warriors [Morgan, 1963: 464 *fn*].

The communistic household, in which most or all of the women belong to one and the same gens, while the men come from various gentes, is the material foundation of that supremacy of the women which was general in primitive times, and which it is Bachofen's third great merit to have discovered. The reports of travelers and missionaries, I may add, to the effect that women among savages and barbarians are overburdened with work in no way contradict what has been said. The division of labor between the two sexes is determined by quite other causes than by the position of woman in society. Among peoples where the women have to work far harder than we think suitable, there is often much more real respect for women than among our Europeans. The lady of civilization, surrounded by false homage and estranged from all real work, has an infinitely lower social position than the hard-working woman of barbarism, who was regarded among her people as a real lady (lady, *frowa, Frau*—mistress) and who was also a lady in character. . . .

The first beginnings of the pairing family appear on the dividing line between savagery and barbarism; they are generally to be found already at the upper stage of savagery, but occasionally not until the lower stage of barbarism. The pairing family is the form characteristic of barbarism, as group marriage is characteristic of savagery and monogamy of civilization. To develop it further, to strict monogamy, other causes were required than those we have found active hitherto. In the single pair the group was already reduced to its final unit, its two-atom molecule: one man and one woman. Natural selection, with its progressive exclusions from the marriage community, had accomplished its task; there was nothing more for it to do in this direction. Unless new, *social* forces came into play, there was no reason why a new form of family should arise from the single pair. But these new forces did come into play.

We now leave America, the classic soil of the pairing family. No sign allows us to conclude that a higher form of family developed here or that there was ever permanent monogamy anywhere in America prior to its discovery and conquest. But not so in the Old World.

Here the domestication of animals and the breeding of herds had developed a hitherto unsuspected source of wealth and created entirely new social relations. Up to the lower stage of barbarism, permanent wealth had consisted almost solely of house, clothing, crude ornaments and the tools for obtaining and preparing food—boat, weapons, and domestic utensils of the simplest kind. Food had to be won afresh day by day. Now, with their herds of horses, camels, asses, cattle, sheep, goats, and pigs, the advancing pastoral peoples—the Semites on the Euphrates and the Tigris, and the Aryans in the Indian country of the Five Streams (Punjab), in the Ganges region, and in the steppes then much more abundantly watered by the Oxus and the Jaxartes—had acquired property which only needed supervision and the rudest care to reproduce itself in steadily increasing quantities and to supply the most abundant food in the form of milk and meat. All former means of procuring food now receded into the background; hunting, formerly a necessity, now became a luxury.

But to whom did this new wealth belong? Originally to the gens, without a doubt. Private property in herds must have already started at an early period, however. Is it difficult to say whether the author of the so-called first book of

Moses regarded the patriarch Abraham as the owner of his herds in his own right as head of a family community or by right of his position as actual hereditary head of a gens. What is certain is that we must not think of him as a property owner in the modern sense of the word. And it is also certain that at the threshold of authentic history we already find the herds everywhere separately owned by heads of families, as are the artistic products of barbarism (metal implements, luxury articles and, finally, the human cattle—the slaves).

For now slavery had also been invented. To the barbarian of the lower stage, a slave was valueless. Hence the treatment of defected enemies by the American Indians was quite different from that at a higher stage. The men were killed or adopted as brothers into the tribe of the victors; the women were taken as wives or otherwise adopted with their surviving children. At this stage human labor power still does not produce any considerable surplus over and above its maintenance costs. That was no longer the case after the introduction of cattle breeding, metalworking, weaving and, lastly, agriculture. Just as the wives whom it had formerly been so easy to obtain had now acquired an exchange value and were bought, so also with labor power, particularly since the herds had definitely become family possessions. The family did not multiply so rapidly as the cattle. More people were needed to look after them; for this purpose use could be made of the enemies captured in war, who could also be bred just as easily as the cattle themselves.

Once it had passed into the private possession of families and there rapidly begun to augment, this wealth dealt a severe blow to the society founded on pairing marriage and the matriarchal gens. Pairing marriage had brought a new element into the family. By the side of the natural mother of the child it placed its natural and attested father with a better warrant of paternity, probably, than that of many a "father" today. According to the division of labor within the family at that time, it was the man's part to obtain food and the instruments of labor necessary for the purpose. He therefore also owned the instruments of labor, and in the event of husband and wife separating, he took them with him, just as she retained her household goods. Therefore, according to the social custom of the time, the man was also the owner of the new source of subsistence, the cattle, and later of the new instruments of labor, the slaves. But according to the custom of the same society, his children could not inherit from him. For as regards inheritance, the position was as follows:

At first, according to mother right—so long, therefore, as descent was reckoned only in the female line—and according to the original custom of inheritance within the gens, the gentile relatives inherited from a deceased fellow member of their gens. His property had to remain within the gens. His effects being insignificant, they probably always passed in practice to his nearest gentile relations—that is, to his blood relations on the mother's side. The children of the dead man, however, did not belong to his gens, but to that of their mother; it was from her that they inherited, at first conjointly with her other blood-relations, later perhaps with rights of priority; they could not inherit from their father because they did not belong to his gens within which his property had to remain. When the owner of the herds died, therefore, his herds would go first to his brothers and sisters and to his sister's children, or to the issue of his mother's sisters. But his own children were disinherited.

Thus on the one hand, in proportion as wealth increased it made the man's position in the family more important than the woman's, and on the other hand created an impulse to exploit this strengthened position in order to overthrow, in favor of his children, the traditional order of inheritance. This, however, was impossible so long as descent was reckoned according to mother right. Mother right, therefore, had to be overthrown, and overthrown it was. This was by no means so difficult as it looks to us today. For this revolution—one of the most decisive ever experienced by humanity—could take place without disturbing a single one of the living members of a gens. All could remain as they were. A simple decree sufficed that in the future the offspring of the male members should remain within the gens, but that of the female should be excluded by being transferred to the gens of their father. The reckoning of descent in the female line and the matriarchal law of inheritance were thereby overthrown, and the male line of descent and the paternal law of inheritance were substituted for them. As to how and when this revolution took place among civilized peoples, we have no knowledge. It falls entirely within prehistoric times. But that it *did* take place is more than sufficiently proved by the abundant traces of mother right which have been collected. . . .

The overthrow of mother right was the *world historical defeat of the female sex.* The man took command in the home also; the woman was degraded and reduced to servitude; she became the slave of his lust and a mere instrument for the production of children. This degraded position of the woman, especially conspicuous among the Greeks of the heroic and still more of the classical age, has gradually been palliated and glossed over, and sometimes clothed in a milder form; in no sense has it been abolished.

The establishment of the exclusive supremacy of the man shows its effects first in the patriarchal family, which now emerges as an intermediate form. Its essential characteristic is not polygyny, of which more later, but "the organization of a number of persons, bond and free, into a family under paternal power for the purpose of holding lands and for the care of flocks and herds. . . . (In the Semitic form) the chiefs, at least, lived in polygamy. . . . Those held to servitude and those employed as servants lived in the marriage relation" [Morgan, 1963: 474].

Its essential features are the incorporation of unfree persons and paternal power; hence the perfect type of this form of family is the Roman. The original meaning of the word "family" *(familia)* is not that compound of sentimentality and domestic strife which forms the ideal of the present-day philistine; among the Romans it did not at first even refer to the married pair and their children but only to the slaves. *Famulus* means domestic slave, and *familia* is the total number of slaves belonging to one man. As late as the time of Gaius, the *familia, id est patrimonium* (family, that is, the patrimony, the inheritance) was bequeathed by will. The term was invented by the Romans to denote a new social organism whose head ruled over wife and children and a number of slaves, and was invested under Roman paternal power with rights of life and death over them all.

This term, therefore, is no older than the ironclad family system of the Latin tribes, which came in after field agriculture and after legalized servitude, as well as after the separation of the Greeks and Latins [Morgan, 1963: 478].

Marx adds:

The modern family contains in germ not only slavery (*servitus*) but also serfdom, since from the beginning it is related to agricultural services. It contains *in miniature* all the contradictions which later extend throughout society and its state.

Such a form of family shows the transition of the pairing family to monogamy. In order to make certain of the wife's fidelity and therefore of the paternity of the children, she is delivered over unconditionally into the power of the husband; if he kills her, he is only exercising his rights. . . .

4   The Monogamous Family

It develops out of the pairing family, as previously shown, in the transitional period between the upper and middle stages of barbarism; its decisive victory is one of the signs that civilization is beginning. It is based on the supremacy of the man, the express purpose being to produce children of undisputed paternity; such paternity is demanded because these children are later to come into their father's property as his natural heirs. It is distinguished from pairing marriage by the much greater strength of the marriage tie, which can no longer be dissolved at either partner's wish. As a rule, it is now only the man who can dissolve it and put away his wife. The right of conjugal infidelity also remains secured to him, at any rate by custom (the *Code Napoléon* explicitly accords it to the husband as long as he does not bring his concubine into the house), and as social life develops he exercises his right more and more; should the wife recall the old form of sexual life and attempt to revive it, she is punished more severely than ever. . . .

. . . It is the existence of slavery side by side with monogamy, the presence of young, beautiful slaves belonging unreservedly to the *man*, that stamps monogamy from the very beginning with its specific character of monogamy *for the woman only*, but not for the man. And that is the character it still has today. . . .

This is the origin of monogamy as far as we can trace it back among the most civilized and highly developed people of antiquity. It was not in any way the fruit of individual sex love, with which it had nothing whatever to do; marriages remained as before marriages of convenience. It was the first form of the family to be based not on natural but on economic conditions—on the victory of private property over primitive, natural communal property. The Greeks themselves put the matter quite frankly: the sole exclusive aims of monogamous marriage were to make the man supreme in the family and to propagate, as the future heirs to his wealth, children indisputably his own. Otherwise, marriage was a burden, a duty which had to be performed whether one liked it or not to gods, state, and one's ancestors. In Athens the law exacted from the man not only marriage but also the performance of a minimum of so-called conjugal duties.

Thus when monogamous marriage first makes its appearance in history, it is not as the reconciliation of man and woman, still less as the highest form of such a reconciliation. Quite the contrary monogamous marriage comes on the scene as the subjugation of the one sex by the other; it announces a struggle between the sexes unknown throughout the whole previous prehistoric period. In an old unpublished manuscript written by Marx and myself in 1846, I find the words: "The first division of labor is that between man and woman for the propagation of children." And today I can add: The first class opposition that appears in history coincides with the development of the antagonism between man and woman in monogamous marriage, and the first class oppression coincides with that of the female sex by the male. Monogamous marriage was a great historical step forward; nevertheless, together with slavery and private wealth, it opens the period that has lasted until today in which every step forward is also relatively a step backward, in which prosperity and development for some is won through the misery and frustration of others. It is the cellular form of civilized society in which the nature of the oppositions and contradictions fully active in that society can be already studied. . . .

. . . With the rise of the inequality of property—already at the upper stage of barbarism, therefore—wage labor appears sporadically side by side with slave labor, and at the same time, as its necessary correlate, the professional prostitution of free women side by side with the forced surrender of the slave. Thus the heritage which group marriage has bequeathed to civilization is double-edged, just as everything civilization brings forth is double-edged, double-tongued, divided against itself, contradictory: here monogamy, there hetaerism with its most extreme form, prostitution. For hetaerism is as much a social institution as any other; it continues the old sexual freedom—to the advantage of the men. Actually, not merely tolerated but gaily practiced by the ruling classes particularly, it is condemned in words. But in reality this condemnation never falls on the men concerned, but only on the women; they are despised and outcast in order that the unconditional supremacy of men over the female sex may be once more proclaimed as a fundamental law of society. . . .

Thus, wherever the monogamous family remains true to its historical origin and clearly reveals the antagonism between the man and the woman expressed in the man's exclusive supremacy, it exhibits in miniature the same oppositions and contradictions as those in which society has been moving, without power to resolve or overcome them, ever since it split into classes at the beginning of civilization. . . .

Our jurists, of course, find that progress in legislation is leaving women with no further ground of complaint. Modern civilized systems of law increasingly acknowledge first, that for a marriage to be legal it must be a contract freely entered into by both partners and secondly, that also in the married state both partners must stand on a common footing of equal rights and duties. If both these demands are consistently carried out, say the jurists, women have all they can ask.

This typically legalist method of argument is exactly the same as that which the radical republican bourgeois uses to put the proletarian in his place. The labor contract is to be freely entered into by both partners. But it is considered to have been freely entered into as soon as the law makes both parties equal on *paper*. The power conferred on the one party by the difference of class position, the pressure thereby brought to bear on the other party—the real economic position of both—that is not the law's business. Again, for the duration of the labor contract, both parties are to have equal rights in so far as one or the other does not expressly surrender them. That economic relations compel the worker to surrender even the last semblance of equal rights—here again, that is no concern of the law.

In regard to marriage, the law, even the most advanced, is fully satisfied as soon as the partners have formally recorded that they are entering into the marriage of their own free consent. What goes on in real life behind the juridical scenes, how this free consent comes about—that is not the business of the law and the jurist. And yet the most elementary comparative jurisprudence should show the jurist what this free consent really amounts to. In the countries where an obligatory share of the paternal inheritance is secured to the children by law and they cannot therefore be disinherited—in Germany, in the countries with French law and elsewhere—the children are obliged to obtain their parents' consent to their marriage. In the countries with English law, where parental consent to a marriage is not legally required, the parents on their side have full freedom in the testamentary disposal of their property and can disinherit their children at their pleasure. It is obvious that in spite and precisely because of this fact freedom of marriage among the classes with something to inherit is in reality not a whit greater in England and America than it is in France and Germany.

As regards the legal equality of husband and wife in marriage, the position is no better. The legal inequality of the two partners bequeathed to us from earlier social conditions is not the cause but the effect of the economic oppression of the woman. In the old communistic household, which comprised many couples and their children, the task entrusted to the women of managing the household was as much a public, a socially necessary industry as the procuring of food by the men. With the patriarchal family and still more with the single monogamous family, a change came. Household management lost its public character. It no longer concerned society. It became a *private service;* the wife became the head servant, excluded from all participation in social production. Not until the coming of modern large-scale industry was the road to social production opened to her again—and then only to the proletarian wife. But it was opened in such a manner that, if she carries out her duties in the private service of her family, she remains excluded from public production and unable to earn; and if she wants to take part in public production and earn independently, she cannot carry out family duties. And the wife's position in the factory is the position of women in all branches of business, right up to medicine and the law. The modern individual family is founded on the open or concealed domestic slavery of the wife, and modern society is a mass composed of these individual families as its molecules.

In the great majority of cases today, at least in the possessing classes, the husband is obliged to earn a living and support his family, and that in itself gives him a position of supremacy without any need for special legal titles and privileges. Within the family he is the bourgeois, and the wife represents the proletariat. In the industrial world, the specific character of the economic oppression burdening the proletariat is visible in all its sharpness only when all special legal privileges of the capitalist class have been abolished and complete legal equality of both classes established. The democratic republic does not do away with the opposition of the two classes; on the contrary, it provides the clear field on which the fight can be fought out. And in the same way, the peculiar character of the supremacy of the husband over the wife in the modern family, the necessity of creating real social equality between them and the way to do it, will only be seen in the clear light of day when both possess legally complete equality of rights. Then it will be plain that the first condition for the liberation of the wife is to bring the whole female sex back into public industry, and that this in turn demands that the characteristic of the monogamous family as the economic unit of society be abolished.

Women:
Caste, Class or Oppressed Sex?

Evelyn Reed

The new stage in the struggle for women's liberation already stands on a higher ideological level than did the feminist movement of the last century. Many of the participants today respect the Marxist analysis of capitalism and subscribe to Engels's classic explanation of the origins of women's oppression. It came about through the development of class society, founded upon the family, private property, and the state.

But there still remain considerable misunderstandings and misinterpretations of Marxist positions, which have led some women who consider themselves radicals or socialists to go off course and become theoretically disoriented. Influenced by the myth that women have always been handicapped by their childbearing functions, they tend to attribute the roots of women's oppression, at least in part, to biological sexual differences. In actuality its causes are exclusively historical and social in character.

Some of these theorists maintain that women constitute a special class or caste. Such definitions are not only alien to the views of Marxism but lead to the false conclusion that it is not the capitalist system but men who are the prime enemy of women. I propose to challenge this contention.

The findings of the Marxist method, which have laid the groundwork for explaining the genesis of woman's degradation, can be summed up in the following propositions:

First, women were not always the oppressed or "second" sex. Anthropology, or the study of prehistory, tells us the contrary. Throughout primitive society, which was the epoch of tribal collectivism, women were the equals of men and recognized by man as such.

Second, the downfall of women coincided with the breakup of the matriarchal clan commune and its replacement by class-divided society with its institutions of the patriarchal family, private property and state power.

The key factors which brought about this reversal in woman's social status came out of the transition from a hunting and food-gathering economy to a far higher mode of production based upon agriculture, stock raising and urban crafts. The primitive division of labor between the sexes was replaced by a more complex social division of labor. The greater efficiency of labor gave rise to a sizable surplus product, which led first to differentiations and then to deepgoing divisions among the various segments of society.

By virtue of the directing roles played by men in large-scale agriculture, irrigation and construction projects, as well as in stock raising, this surplus wealth was gradually appropriated by a hierarchy of men as their private property. This, in turn, required the institution of marriage and the family to fix the legal ownership and inheritance of a man's property. Through monogamous marriage the wife was brought under the complete control of her husband who was thereby assured of legitimate sons to inherit his wealth.

As men took over most of the activities of social production, and with the rise of the family institution, women became relegated to the home to serve their husbands and families. The state apparatus came into existence to fortify and legalize the institutions of private property, male dominion and the father-family, which later were sanctified by religion.

This, briefly, is the Marxist approach to the origins of woman's oppression. Her subordination did not come about through any biological deficiency as a sex. It was the result of the revolutionary social changes which destroyed the equalitarian society of the matriarchal gens or clan and replaced it with a patriarchal class society which, from its birth, was stamped with discriminations and inequalities of many kinds, including the inequality of the sexes. The growth of this inherently oppressive type of socioeconomic organization was responsible for the historic downfall of women.

But the downfall of women cannot be fully understood, nor can a correct social and political solution be worked out for their liberation, without seeing what happened at the same time to men. It is too often overlooked that the patriarchal class system which crushed the matriarchy and its communal social relations also shattered its male counterpart, the fratriarchy—or tribal brotherhood of men. Woman's overthrow went hand in hand with the subjugation of the mass of toiling men to the master class of men.

The import of these developments can be more clearly seen if we examine the basic character of the tribal structure which Morgan, Engels and others described as a system of "primitive communism." The clan commune was both a sisterhood of women and a brotherhood of men. The sisterhood of women, which was the essence of the matriarchy, denoted its collectivist character. The women worked together as a community of sisters; their social labors largely sustained the whole community. They also raised their children in common. An individual mother did not draw distinctions between her own and her clan sisters' progeny, and the children in turn regarded all the older sisters as their mutual mothers. In other words, communal production and communal possessions were accompanied by communal child-raising.

The male counterpart of this sisterhood was the brotherhood, which was molded in the same communal pattern as the sisterhood. Each clan or phratry of clans comprising the tribe was regarded as a "brotherhood" from the male standpoint just as it was viewed as a "sisterhood" or "motherhood" from the female standpoint. In this matriarchal-brotherhood the adults of both sexes not only produced the necessities of life together but also provided for and protected the children of the community. These features made the sisterhood and brotherhood a system of "primitive communism."

Thus, before the family that had the individual father standing at its head came into existence, the functions of fatherhood were a *social,* and not a *family* function of men. More than this, the earliest men who performed the services of fatherhood were not the mates or "husbands" of the clan sisters but rather their clan brothers. This was not simply because the processes of physiological paternity were unknown in ancient society. More decisively, this fact was irrelevant in a society founded upon collectivist relations of production and communal child-raising.

However odd it may seem to people today, who are so accustomed to the family form of child-raising, it was perfectly natural in the primitive commune for the clan brothers, or "mothers' brothers," to perform the paternal functions for their sisters' children that were later taken over by the individual father for his wife's children.

The first change in this sister-brother clan system came with the growing tendency for pairing couples, or "pairing families" as Morgan and Engels called them, to live together in the same community and household. However, this simple cohabitation did not substantially alter the former collectivist relations or the productive role of the women in the community. The sexual division of labor which had formerly been allotted between clan sisters and brothers became gradually transformed into a sexual division of labor between husbands and wives.

But so long as collectivist relations prevailed and women continued to participate in social production, the original equality between the sexes more or less persisted. The whole community continued to sustain the pairing units, just as each individual member of these units made his and her contribution to the labor activities.

Consequently, the pairing family, which appeared at the dawn of the family system, differed radically from the nuclear family of our times. In our ruthless competitive capitalist system every tiny family must sink or swim through its own efforts—it cannot count on assistance from outside sources. The wife is dependent upon the husband while the children must look to the parents for their subsistence, even if the wage earners who support them are stricken by unemployment, sickness or death. In the period of the pairing family, however, there was no such system of dependency upon "family economics," since the whole community took care of each individual's basic needs from the cradle to the grave.

This was the material basis for the absence, in the primitive commune, of those social oppressions and family antagonisms with which we are so familiar.

It is sometimes said or implied that male domination has always existed and that women have always been brutally treated by men. Contrariwise, it is also widely believed that the relations between the sexes in matriarchal society were merely the reverse of our own—with women dominating men. Neither of these propositions is borne out by the anthropological evidence.

It is not my intention to glorify the epoch of savagery nor advocate a romantic return to some past "golden age." An economy founded upon hunting and food-gathering is the lowliest stage in human development, and its living conditions were rude, crude and harsh. Nevertheless, we must recognize that male and female relations in that kind of society were fundamentally different from ours.

Under the clan system of the sisterhood of women and the brotherhood of men there was no more possibility for one sex to dominate the other than there was for one class to exploit another. Women occupied the most eminent position because they were the chief producers of the necessities of life as well as the procreators of new life. But this did not make them the oppressors of men. Their communal society excluded class, racial or sexual tyranny.

As Engels pointed out, with the rise of private property, monogamous marriage and the patriarchal family, new social forces came into play in both society at large and the family setup which destroyed the rights exercised by earliest womankind. From simple cohabitation of pairing couples there arose the rigidly fixed, legal system of monogamous marriage. This brought the wife and children under the complete control of the husband and father who gave the family his name and determined their conditions of life and destiny.

Women, who had once lived and worked together as a community of sisters and raised their children in common, now became dispersed as wives of individual men serving their lords and masters in individual households. The former equalitarian sexual division of labor between the men and women of the commune gave way to a family division of labor in which the woman was more and more removed from social production to serve as a household drudge for husband, home and family. Thus women, once "governesses" of society, were degraded under the class formations to become the governess of a man's children and his chief housemaid.

This abasement of women has been a permanent feature of all three stages of class society, from slavery through feudalism to capitalism. So long as women led or participated in the productive work of the whole community, they commanded respect and esteem. But once they were dismembered into separate family units and occupied a servile position in home and family, they lost their prestige along with their influence and power.

Is it any wonder that such social changes should bring about intense and long-enduring antagonism between the sexes? As Engels says:

> Monogamy then does by no means enter history as a reconciliation of man and wife, and still less as the highest form of marriage. On the contrary, it enters as the subjugation of one sex by the other, as the proclamation of an antagonism between the sexes unknown in all preceding history. . . . The first class antagonism appearing in history coincides with the development of the antagonism of man and wife in monogamy, and the first class oppression with that of the female by the male sex *(Origin of the Family, Private Property, and the State)*.

Here it is necessary to note a distinction between two degrees of women's oppression in monogamous family life under the system of private property. In the productive farm family of the preindustrial age, women held a higher status and were accorded more respect than they receive in the consumer family of our own city life, the nuclear family.

So long as agriculture and craft industry remained dominant in the economy, the farm family, which was a large or "extended" family, remained a viable productive unit. All its members had vital functions to perform according to sex and age. The women in the family helped cultivate the ground and engaged in home industries as well as bearing children, while the children and older folks produced their share according to ability.

This changed with the rise of industrial and monopoly capitalism and the nuclear family. Once masses of men were dispossessed from the land and small businesses to become wage earners in factories, they had nothing but their labor power to sell to the capitalist bosses for their means of subsistence. The wives of these wage earners, ousted from their former productive farm and homecraft labors, became utterly dependent upon their husbands for the support of themselves and their children. As men became dependent upon their bosses, the wives became more dependent upon their husbands.

By degrees, therefore, as women were stripped of their economic self-dependence, they fell ever lower in social esteem. At the beginning of class society they had been removed from *social* production and social leadership to become farm-family producers, working through their husbands for home and family. But with the displacement of the productive farm family by the nuclear family of industrial city life, they were driven from their last foothold on solid ground.

Women were then given two dismal alternatives. They could either seek a husband as provider and be penned up thereafter as housewives in city tenements or apartments to raise the next generation of wage slaves. Or the poorest and most unfortunate could go as marginal workers into the mills and factories (along with the children) and be sweated as the most downtrodden and underpaid section of the labor force.

Over the past generations women wage workers have conducted their own labor struggles or fought along with men for improvements in their wages and working conditions. But women as dependent housewives have had no such means of social struggle. They could only resort to complaints or wrangles with husband and children over the miseries of their lives. The friction between the sexes became deeper and sharper with the abject dependency of women and their subservience to men.

Despite the hypocritical homage paid to womankind as the "sacred mother" and devoted homemaker, the *worth* of women sank to its lowest point under capitalism. Since housewives do not produce commodities for the market nor create any surplus value for the profiteers, they are not central to the operations of capitalism. Only three justifications for their existence remain under this system: as breeders, as household janitors, and as buyers of consumer goods for the family.

While wealthy women can hire servants to do the dull chores for them, poor women are riveted to an endless grind for their whole lives. Their condition of servitude is compounded when they are obliged to take an outside job to help sustain the family. Shouldering two responsibilities instead of one, they are the "doubly oppressed."

Even middle-class housewives in the Western world, despite their economic advantages, are victimized by capitalism. The isolated, monotonous, trivial circumstances of their lives lead them to "living through" their children—a relationship which fosters many of the neuroses that afflict family life today. Seeking to allay their boredom, they can be played upon and preyed upon by the profiteers in the consumer goods fields. This exploitation of women as consumers is part and parcel of a system that grew up in the first place for the exploitation of men as producers.

The capitalists have ample reason for glorifying the nuclear family. Its petty household is a goldmine for all sorts of hucksters from real estate agents to the manufacturers of detergents and cosmetics. Just as automobiles are produced for individual use instead of developing adequate mass transportation, so the big corporations can make more money by selling small homes on private lots to be equipped with individual washing machines, refrigerators, and other such items. They find this more profitable than building large-scale housing at low rentals or developing community services and child-care centers.

In the second place, the isolation of women, each enclosed in a private home and tied to the same kitchen and nursery chores, hinders them from banding together and becoming a strong social force or a serious political threat to the Establishment,

What is the most instructive lesson to be drawn from this highly condensed survey of the long imprisonment of womankind in the home and family of class society—which stands in such marked contrast to their stronger, more independent position in preclass society? It shows that the inferior status of the female sex is not the result of their biological makeup or the fact that they are the childbearers. Childbearing was no handicap in the primitive commune; it *became* a handicap, above all, in the nuclear family of our times. Poor women are torn apart by the conflicting obligations of taking care of their children at home while at the same time working outside to help sustain the family. Women, then, have been condemned to their oppressed status by the same social forces and relations which have brought about the oppression of one class by another, one race by another, and one nation by another. It is the capitalist system—the ultimate stage in the development of class society—which is the fundamental source of the degradation and oppression of women.

Some women in the liberation movement dispute these fundamental theses of Marxism. They say that the female sex represents a separate caste or class. Ti-Grace Atkinson, for example, takes the position that women are a separate *class:* Roxanne Dunbar says that they comprise a separate *caste*. Let us examine these two theoretical positions and the conclusions that flow from them.

First, are women a caste? The caste hierarchy came first in history and was the prototype and predecessor of the class system. It arose after the breakup of the tribal commune with the emergence of the first marked differentiations of segments of society according to the new divisions of labor and social functions. Membership in a superior or inferior station was established by being born into that caste.

It is important to note, however, that the caste system was also inherently and at birth a class system. Furthermore, while the caste system reached its fullest development only in certain regions of the world, such as India, the class system evolved far beyond it to become a world system, which engulfed the caste system.

This can be clearly seen in India itself, where each of the four chief castes— the Brahmans or priests, the soldiers, the farmers and merchants, and the laborers, along with the "out-castes" or pariahs—had their appropriate places in an exploitative society. In India today, where the ancient caste system survives in decadent forms, capitalist relations and power prevail over all the inherited precapitalist institutions, including the caste relics.

However, those regions of the world which advanced fastest and farthest on the road to civilization bypassed or overleaped the caste system altogether. Western civilization, which started with ancient Greece and Rome, developed from slavery through feudalism to the maturest stage of class society, capitalism.

Neither in the caste system nor the class system—nor in their combinations—have women comprised a separate caste or class. Women themselves have been separated into the various castes and classes which made up these social formations.

The fact that women occupy an inferior status as a *sex* does not *ipso facto* make women either an inferior caste or class. Even in ancient India women belonged to different castes, just as they belong to different classes in contemporary capitalist society. In the one case their social status was determined by birth into a caste; in the other it is determined by their own or their husband's wealth. But the two can be fused—for women as for men. Both sexes can belong to a superior caste and possess superior wealth, power and status.

What, then, does Roxanne Dunbar want to convey when she refers to all women (regardless of class) as comprising a separate caste? And what consequences for action does she draw from this characterization? The exact content of both her premise and her conclusions are not clear to me, and perhaps to many others. They therefore deserve closer examination.

Speaking in a loose and popular way, it is possible to refer to women as an inferior "caste"—as is sometimes done when they are also called "slaves" or "serfs"—when the intent is merely to indicate that they occupy the subordinate position in male-dominated society. The use of the term "caste" would then only expose the impoverishment of our language, which has no special word to indicate womankind as the oppressed sex. But more than this seems to be involved, if we judge from the paper by Roxanne Dunbar dated February 1970 which supersedes her previous positions on this question.

In that document she says that her characterization of women as an exploited caste is nothing new; that Marx and Engels likewise "analyzed the position of the female sex in just such a way." This is simply not the case. Neither Marx in *Capital,* nor Engels in *The Origin of the Family, Private Property, and the State,* nor in any writings by noted Marxists from Lenin to Luxemburg on this matter, has woman been defined by virtue of her sex as a "caste." Therefore this is not a mere verbal squabble over the misuse of a term, It is a distinct departure from Marxism, although presented in the name of Marxism.

I would like clarification from Roxanne Dunbar on the conclusions she draws from her theory. For, if all women belong to an inferior caste, and all men belong to the superior caste, it would consistently follow that the central axis of a struggle for liberation would be a "caste war" of all women against all men to bring about the liberation of women. This conclusion would seem to be confirmed by her statement that "we live under an international caste system. . . ."

This assertion is equally non-Marxist. What Marxists say is that we live under an international *class* system. And they further state that it will require not a caste war, but a *class struggle*—of all the oppressed, male and female alike—to consummate women's liberation along with the liberation of all the oppressed masses. Does Roxanne Dunbar agree or disagree with this viewpoint on the paramount role of the class struggle?

Her confusion points up the necessity for using precise language in a scientific exposition. However downtrodden women are under capitalism, they are not chattel slaves any more than they are feudal serfs or members of an inferior caste. The social categories of slave, serf and caste refer to stages and features of past history and do not correctly define the position of women in our society.

If we are to be precise and scientific, women should be defined as an "oppressed *sex.*"

Turning to the other position, it is even more incorrect to characterize women as a special "class." In Marxist sociology a class is defined in two interrelated ways: by the role it plays in the processes of production and by the stake it has in the ownership of property. Thus the capitalists are the major power in our society because they own the means of production and thereby control the state and direct the economy. The wage workers who create the wealth own nothing but their labor power, which they have to sell to the bosses to stay alive.

Where do women stand in relation to these polar class forces? They belong to all strata of the social pyramid. The few at the top are part of the plutocratic class; more among us belong to the middle class; most of us belong to the proletarian layers of the population. There is an enormous spread from the few wealthy women of the Rockefeller, Morgan and Ford families to the millions of poor women who subsist on welfare dole. *In short, women, like men, are a multiclass sex.*

This is not an attempt to divide women from one another but simply to recognize the actual divisions that exist. The notion that all women as a sex have more in common than do members of the same class with one another is false. Upper-class women are not simply bedmates of their wealthy husbands. As a rule they have more compelling ties which bind them together. They are economic, social and political bedmates, united in defense of private property, profiteering, militarism, racism—and the exploitation of other women.

To be sure, there can be individual exceptions to this rule, especially among young women today. We remember that Mrs. Frank Leslie, for example, left a $2 million bequest to further the cause of women's suffrage, and other upper-class women have devoted their means to secure civil rights for our sex. But it is quite another matter to expect any large number of wealthy women to endorse or support a revolutionary struggle which threatens their capitalist interests and privileges. Most of them scorn the liberation movement, saying openly or implicitly, "What do we need to be liberated from?"

Is it really necessary to stress this point? Tens of thousands of women went to the Washington antiwar demonstrations in November 1969 and again in May 1970. Did they have more in common with the militant men marching beside them on that life-and-death issue—or with Mrs. Nixon, her daughters, and the wife of the attorney general, Mrs. Mitchell, who peered uneasily out of her window and saw the specter of another Russian Revolution in those protesting masses? Will the wives of bankers, generals, corporation lawyers, and big industrialists be firmer allies of women fighting for liberation than working-class men, black and white, who are fighting for theirs? Won't there be both men and women on both sides of the class struggle? If not, is the struggle to be directed against men as a sex rather than against the capitalist system?

It is true that all forms of class society have been male-dominated and that men are trained from the cradle on to be chauvinistic. But it is not true that men as such represent the main enemy of women. This crosses out the multitudes of downtrodden, exploited men who are themselves oppressed by the main enemy of women, which is the capitalist system. These men likewise have a stake in the liberation struggle of the women; they can and will become our allies.

Although the struggle against male chauvinism is an essential part of the tasks that women must carry out through their liberation movement, it is incorrect to make that the central issue. This tends to conceal or overlook the role of the ruling powers who not only breed and benefit from all forms of discrimination and oppression but are also responsible for breeding and sustaining male chauvinism. Let us remember that male supremacy did not exist in the primitive commune, founded upon sisterhood and brotherhood. Sexism, like racism, has its roots in the private property system.

A false theoretical position easily leads to a false strategy in the struggle for women's liberation. Such is the case with a segment of the Redstockings who state in their *Manifesto* that "women are an oppressed *class.*" If all women compose a class then all men must form a counterclass—the oppressor class. What conclusion flows from this premise? That there are no men in the oppressed class? Where does this leave the millions of oppressed white working men who, like the oppressed blacks, Chicanos and other minorities, are exploited by the monopolists? Don't they have a central place in the struggle for social revolution? At what point and under what banner do these oppressed peoples of all races and both sexes join together for common action against their common enemy? To oppose women as a class against men as a class can only result in a diversion of the real class struggle.

Isn't there a suggestion of this same line in Roxanne Dunbar's assertion that female liberation is the basis for social revolution? This is far from Marxist strategy since it turns the real situation on its head. Marxists say that social revolution is the basis for full female liberation—just as it is the basis for the liberation of the whole working class. In the last analysis the real allies of women's liberation are all those forces which are impelled for their own reasons to struggle against and throw off the shackles of the imperialist masters.

The underlying source of women's oppression, which is capitalism, cannot be abolished by women alone, nor by a coalition of women drawn from all classes. It will require a worldwide struggle for socialism by the working masses, female and male alike, together with every other section of the oppressed, to overthrow the power of capitalism, which is centered today in the United States.

In conclusion, we must ask, what are the connections between the struggle for women's liberation and the struggle for socialism?

First, even though the full goal of women's liberation cannot be achieved short of the socialist revolution, this does not mean that the struggle to secure reforms must be postponed until then. It is imperative for Marxist women to fight shoulder to shoulder with all our embattled sisters in organized actions for specific objectives from now on. This has been our policy ever since the new phase of the women's liberation movement surfaced a year or so ago, and even before.

The women's movement begins, like other movements for liberation, by putting forward elementary demands. These are: equal opportunities with men in education and jobs; equal pay for equal work; free abortions on demand; and child-care centers financed by the government but controlled by the community. Mobilizing women behind these issues not only gives us the possibility of securing some improvements but also exposes, curbs and modifies the worst aspects of our subordination in this society.

Second, why do women have to lead their own struggles for liberation, even though in the end the combined anticapitalist offensive of the whole working class will be required for the victory of the socialist revolution? The reason is that no segment of society which has been subjected to oppression, whether it consists of Third World people or of women, can delegate the leadership and promotion of their fight for freedom to other forces—even though other forces can act as their allies. We reject the attitude of some political tendencies that say they are Marxists but refuse to acknowledge that women have to lead and organize their own independent struggle for emancipation, just as they cannot understand why blacks must do the same.

The maxim of the Irish revolutionists—"who would be free themselves must strike the blow"—fully applies to the cause of women's liberation. Women must themselves strike the blows to gain their freedom. And this holds true after the anticapitalist revolution triumphs as well as before.

In the course of our struggle, and as part of it, we will reeducate men who have been brainwashed into believing that women are naturally the inferior sex due to some flaws in their biological makeup. Men will have to learn that, in the hierarchy of oppressions created by capitalism, their chauvinism and dominance is another weapon in the hands of the master class for maintaining its rule. The exploited worker, confronted by the even worse plight of his dependent housewife, cannot be complacent about it—he must be made to see the source of the oppressive power that has degraded them both.

Finally, to say that women form a separate caste or class must logically lead to extremely pessimistic conclusions with regard to the antagonism between the sexes in contrast with the revolutionary optimism of the Marxists. For unless the two sexes are to be totally separated, or the men liquidated, it would seem that they will have to remain forever at war with each other.

As Marxists we have a more realistic and hopeful message. We deny that women's inferiority was predestined by her biological makeup or has always existed. Far from being eternal, woman's subjugation and the bitter hostility between the sexes are no more than a few thousand years old. They were produced by the drastic social changes which brought the family, private property and the state into existence.

This view of history points up the necessity for a no less thoroughgoing revolution in socioeconomic relations to uproot the causes of inequality and achieve full emancipation for our sex. This is the purpose and promise of the socialist program, and this is what we are fighting for.

RADICAL FEMINISM: Sexism as the
Fundamental Inequality

The Dialectic of Sex

Shulamith Firestone

Sex class is so deep as to be invisible. Or it may appear as a superficial inequality, one that can be solved by merely a few reforms, or perhaps by the full integration of women into the labor force. But the reaction of the common man, woman, and child—"*That? Why you can't change *that!* You must be out of your mind!*"—is the closest to the truth. We are talking about something every bit as deep as that. This gut reaction—the assumption that, even when they don't know it, feminists are talking about changing a fundamental biological condition—is an honest one. That so profound a change cannot be easily fit into traditional categories of thought, e.g., "political," is not because these categories do not apply but because they are not big enough: radical feminism bursts through them. If there were another word more all-embracing than *revolution* we would use it.

Until a certain level of evolution had been reached and technology had achieved its present sophistication, to question fundamental biological conditions was insanity. Why should a woman give up her precious seat in the cattle car for a bloody struggle she could not hope to win? But, for the first time in some countries, the preconditions for feminist revolution exist—indeed, the situation is beginning to *demand* such a revolution.

The first women are fleeing the massacre, and, shaking and tottering, are beginning to find each other. Their first move is a careful joint observation, to resensitize a fractured consciousness. This is painful: No matter how many levels of consciousness one reaches, the problem always goes deeper. It is everywhere. The division yin and yang pervades all culture, history, economics, nature itself; modern Western versions of sex discrimination are only the most recent layer. To so heighten one's sensitivity to sexism presents problems far worse than the black militant's new awareness of racism: Feminists have to question, not just all of *Western* culture, but the organization of culture itself, and further, even the very organization of nature. Many women give up in despair: if *that's* how deep it goes they don't want to know. Others continue strengthening and enlarging the movement, their painful sensitivity to female oppression existing for a purpose: eventually to eliminate it.

Before we can act to change a situation, however, we must know how it has arisen and evolved, and through what institutions it now operates. Engels' "[We must] examine the historic succession of events from which the antagonism has sprung in order to discover in the conditions thus created the means of ending the conflict." For feminist revolution we shall need an analysis of the dynamics of sex war as comprehensive as the Marx-Engels analysis of class antagonism was for the economic revolution. More comprehensive. For we are dealing with a larger problem, with an oppression that goes back beyond recorded history to the animal kingdom itself.

In creating such an analysis we can learn a lot from Marx and Engels: Not their literal opinions about women—about the condition of women as an oppressed class they know next to nothing, recognizing it only where it overlaps with economics—but rather their analytic *method*.

Marx and Engels outdid their socialist forerunners in that they developed a method of analysis which was both *dialectical* and *materialist*. The first in centuries to view history dialectically, they saw the world as process, a natural flux of action and reaction, of opposites yet inseparable and interpenetrating. Because they were able to perceive history as movie rather than as snapshot, they attempted to avoid falling into the stagnant "metaphysical" view that had trapped so many other great minds. (This sort of analysis itself may be a product of the sex division.) They combined this view of the dynamic interplay of historical forces with a materialist one, that is, they attempted for the first time to put historical and cultural change on a real basis, to trace the development of economic classes to organic causes. By understanding thoroughly the mechanics of history, they hoped to show men how to master it.

Socialist thinkers prior to Marx and Engels, such as Fourier, Owen, and Bebel, had been able to do no more than moralize about existing social inequalities, positing an ideal world where class privilege and exploitation should not exist—in the same way that early feminist thinkers posited a world where male privilege and exploitation ought not exist—by mere virtue of good will. In both cases, because the early thinkers did not really understand how the social injustice had evolved, maintained itself, or could be eliminated, their ideas existed in a cultural vacuum, utopian. Marx and Engels, on the other hand, attempted a scientific approach to history. They traced the class conflict to its real economic origins, projecting an economic solution based on objective economic preconditions already present: the seizure by the proletariat of the means of production would lead to a communism in which government had withered away, no longer needed to repress the lower class for the sake of the higher. In the classless society the interests of every individual would be synonymous with those of the larger society.

But the doctrine of historical materialism, much as it was a brilliant advance over previous historical analysis, was not the complete answer, as later events bore out. For though Marx and Engels grounded their theory in reality, it was only a *partial* reality. Here is Engels' strictly economic definition of historical materialism from *Socialism: Utopian or Scientific:*

> Historical materialism is that view of the course of history which seeks the *ultimate* cause and the great moving power of all historical events in the economic development of society, in the changes of the modes of production and exchange, in the consequent division of society into distinct classes, and in the struggles of these classes against one another. (Italics mine)

Further, he claims:

> . . . that all past history with the exception of the primitive stages was the history of class struggles; that these warring classes of society are always the products of the modes of production and exchange—in a word, of the economic conditions of their time; that the *economic* structure of society always furnishes the real basis, starting from which we can alone work out the *ultimate* explanation of the whole superstructure of juridical and political institutions as well as of the religious, philosophical, and other ideas of a given historical period. (Italics mine)

It would be a mistake to attempt to explain the oppression of women according to this strictly economic interpretation. The class analysis is a beautiful piece of work, but limited: although correct in a linear sense, it does not go deep enough. There is a whole sexual substratum of the historical dialectic that Engels at times dimly perceives, but because he can see sexuality only through an economic filter, reducing everything to that, he is unable to evaluate in its own right.

Engels did observe that the original division of labor was between man and woman for the purposes of child-breeding; that within the family the husband was the owner, the wife the means of production, the children the labor; and that reproduction of the human species was an important economic system distinct from the means of production.

But Engels has been given too much credit for these scattered recognitions of the oppression of women as a class. In fact he acknowledged the sexual class system only where it overlapped and illuminated his economic construct. Engels didn't do so well even in this respect. But Marx was worse: There is a growing recognition of Marx's bias against women (a cultural bias shared by Freud as well as all men of culture), dangerous if one attempts to squeeze feminism into an orthodox Marxist framework—freezing what were only incidental insights of Marx and Engels about sex class into dogma. Instead, we must enlarge historical materialism to *include* the strictly Marxian, in the same way that the physics of relativity did not invalidate Newtonian physics so much as it drew a circle around it, limiting its application—but only through comparison—to a smaller sphere. For an economic diagnosis traced to ownership of the means of production, even of the means of *re*production, does not explain everything. There is a level of reality that does not stem directly from economics.

The assumption that, beneath economics, reality is psychosexual is often rejected as ahistorical by those who accept a dialectical materialist view of history because it seems to land us back where Marx began: groping through a fog of utopian hypotheses, philosophical systems that might be right, that might be wrong (there is no way to tell), systems that explain concrete historical developments by *a priori* categories of thought; historical materialism, however, attempted to explain "knowing" by "being" and not vice versa.

But there is still an untried third alternative: We can attempt to develop a materialist view of history based on sex itself. . . .

. . . Let us first try to develop an analysis in which biology itself—procreation—is at the origin of the dualism. The immediate assumption of the layman that the unequal division of the sexes is "natural" may be well-founded. We need not immediately look beyond this. Unlike economic class, sex class sprang directly from a biological reality: men and women were created different, and not equally privileged. Although, as De Beauvoir points out, this difference of itself did not necessitate the development of a class system—the domination of one group by another—the reproductive *functions* of these differences did. The biological family is an inherently unequal power distribution. The need for power leading to the development of classes arises from the psychosexual formation of each individual according to this basic imbalance, rather than, as Freud, Norman O. Brown, and others have, once again overshooting their mark, postulated, some irreducible conflict of Life against Death, Eros vs. Thanatos.

The *biological family*—the basic reproductive unit of male/female/infant, in whatever form of social organization—is characterized by these fundamental—if not immutable—facts:

1 That women throughout history before the advent of birth control were at the continual mercy of their biology—menstruation, menopause, and "female ills," constant painful childbirth, wetnursing and care of infants, all of which made them dependent on males (whether brother, father, husband, lover, or clan, government, community-at-large) for physical survival.

2 That human infants take an even longer time to grow up than animals, and thus are helpless and, for some short period at least, dependent on adults for physical survival.

3 That a basic mother/child interdependency has existed in some form in every society, past or present, and thus has shaped the psychology of every mature female and every infant.

4 That the natural reproductive difference between the sexes led directly to the first division of labor at the origins of class, as well as furnishing the paradigm of caste (discrimination based on biological characteristics).

These biological contingencies of the human family cannot be covered over with anthropological sophistries. Anyone observing animals mating, reproducing, and caring for their young will have a hard time accepting the "cultural relativity" line. For no matter how many tribes in Oceania you can find where the connection of the father to fertility is not known, no matter how many matrilineages, no matter how many cases of sex-role reversal, male housewifery, or even empathic labor pains, these facts prove only one thing: the amazing *flexibility* of human nature. But human nature is adaptable *to* something, it is, yes, determined by its environmental conditions. And the biological family that we have described has existed everywhere throughout time. Even in matriarchies where woman's fertility is worshipped, and the father's role is unknown or unimportant, if perhaps not on the genetic father, there is still some dependence of the female and the infant on the male. And though it is true that the nuclear family is only a recent development, one which, as I shall attempt to show, only intensifies the psychological penalties of the biological family, though it is true that throughout history there have been many variations on this biological family, the contingencies I have described existed in all of them, causing specific psychosexual distortions in the human personality.

But to grant that the sexual imbalance of power is biologically based is not to lose our case. We are no longer just animals. And the Kingdom of Nature does not reign absolute. As Simone de Beauvoir herself admits:

> The theory of historical materialism has brought to light some important truths. Humanity is not an animal species, it is a historical reality. Human society is an antiphysis—in a sense it is against nature; it does not passively submit to the presence of nature but rather takes over the control of nature on its own behalf. This arrogation is not an inward, subjective operation; it is accomplished objectively in practical action.

Thus, the "natural" is not necessarily a "human" value. Humanity has begun to outgrow nature: we can no longer justify the maintenance of a discriminatory sex class system on grounds of its origins in Nature. Indeed, for pragmatic reasons alone it is beginning to look as if we *must* get rid of it.

The problem becomes political, demanding more than a comprehensive historical analysis, when one realizes that, though man is increasingly capable of freeing himself from the biological conditions that created his tyranny over women and children, he has little reason to want to give this tyranny up. As Engels said, in the context of economic revolution:

> It is the law of division of labor that lies at the basis of the division into classes [Note that this division itself grew out of a fundamental biological division]. But this does not prevent the ruling class, once having the upper hand, from consolidating its power at the expense of the working class, from turning its social leadership into an intensified exploitation of the masses.

Though the sex class system may have originated in fundamental biological conditions, this does not guarantee once the biological basis of their oppression has been swept away that women and children will be freed. On the contrary, the new technology, especially fertility control, may be used against them to reinforce the entrenched system of exploitation.

So that just as to assure elimination of economic classes requires the revolt of the underclass (the proletariat) and, in a temporary dictatorship, their seizure of the means of *production,* so to assure the elimination of sexual classes requires the revolt of the underclass (women) and the seizure of control of *reproduction:* not only the full restoration to women of ownership of their own bodies, but also their (temporary) seizure of control of human fertility—the new population biology as well as all the social institutions of childbearing and childrearing. And just as the end goal of socialist revolution was not only the elimination of the economic class *privilege* but of the economic class *distinction* itself, so the end goal of feminist revolution must be, unlike that of the first feminist movement, not just the elimination of male *privilege* but of the sex *distinction* itself: genital differences between human beings would no longer matter culturally. (A reversion to an unobstructed *pansexuality*—Freud's "polymorphous perversity"—would probably supersede hetero/homo/bi-sexuality.) The reproduction of the species by one sex for the benefit of both would be replaced by (at least the option of) artificial reproduction: children would be born to both sexes equally, or independently of either, however one chooses to look at it; the dependence of the child on the mother (and vice versa) would give way to a greatly shortened dependence on a small group of others in general, and any remaining inferiority to adults in physical strength would be compensated for culturally. The division of labor would be ended by the elimination of labor altogether (cybernation). The tyranny of the biological family would be broken.

And with it the psychology of power. As Engels claimed for strictly socialist revolution:

> The existence of not simply this or that ruling class but of any ruling class at all [will have] become an obsolete anachronism.

That socialism has never come near achieving this predicated goal is not only the result of unfulfilled or misfired economic preconditions, but also because the Marxian analysis itself was insufficient: it did not dig deep enough to the psychosexual roots of class. Marx was onto something more profound than he knew when he observed that the family contained within itself in embryo all the antagonisms that later develop on a wide scale within the society and the state. For unless revolution uproots the basic social organization, the biological family—the vinculum through which the psychology of power can always be smuggled—the tapeworm of exploitation will never be annihilated. We shall need a sexual revolution much larger than—inclusive of—a socialist one to truly eradicate all class systems. . . .

Lesbians in Revolt

Charlotte Bunch

The development of Lesbian-Feminist politics as the basis for the liberation of women is our top priority; this article outlines our present ideas. In our society which defines all people and institutions for the benefit of the rich, white male, the Lesbian is in revolt. In revolt because she defines herself in terms of women and rejects the male definitions of how she should feel, act, look, and live. To be a Lesbian is to love oneself, woman, in a culture that denegrates and despises women. The Lesbian rejects male sexual/political domination; she defies his world, his social organization, his ideology, and his definition of her as inferior.

Lesbianism puts women first while the society declares the male supreme. Lesbianism threatens male supremacy at its core. When politically conscious and organized, it is central to destroying our sexist, racist, capitalist, imperialist system.

Male society defines Lesbianism as a sexual act, which reflects men's limited view of women: they think of us only in terms of sex. They also say Lesbians are not real women, so a real woman is one who gets fucked by men. We say that a Lesbian is a woman whose sense of self and energies, including sexual energies, center around women—she is woman identified. The woman-identified-woman commits herself to other women for political, emotional, physical, and economic support. Women are important to her. She is important to herself. Our society demands that commitment from women be reserved for men.

The Lesbian, woman-identified-woman, commits herself to women not only as an alternative to oppressive male/female relationships but primarily because she *loves* women. Whether consciously or not, by her actions, the Lesbian has recognized that giving support and love to men over women perpetuates the system that oppresses her. If women do not make a commitment to each other, which includes sexual love, we deny ourselves the love and value traditionally given to men. We accept our second class status. When women do give primary energies to other women, then it is possible to concentrate fully on building a movement for our liberation.

Woman-identified Lesbianism is, then, more than a sexual preference, it is a political choice. It is political because relationships between men and women are essentially political, they involve power and dominance. Since the Lesbian actively rejects that relationship and chooses women, she defies the established political system.

Of course, not all Lesbians are consciously woman-identified, nor are all committed to finding common solutions to the oppression they suffer as women and Lesbians. Being a Lesbian is part of challenging male supremacy, but not the end. For the Lesbian or heterosexual woman, there is no individual solution to oppression.

The Lesbian may think that she is free since she escapes the personal oppression of the individual male/female relationship. But to the society she is still a woman, or worse, a visible Lesbian. On the street, at the job, in the schools, she is treated as an inferior and is at the mercy of men's power and whims. (I've never heard of a rapist who stopped because his victim was a Lesbian.) This society hates women who love women, and so, the Lesbian, who escapes male dominance in her private home, receives it doubly at the hands of male society; she is harassed, outcast, and shuttled to the bottom. Lesbians must become feminists and fight against woman oppression, just as feminists must become Lesbians if they hope to end male supremacy.

U.S. society encourages individual solutions, apolitical attitudes, and reformism to keep us from political revolt and out of power. Men who rule, and male leftists who seek to rule, try to depoliticize sex and the relations between men and women in order to prevent us from acting to end our oppression and challenging their power. As the question of homosexuality has become public, reformists define it as a private question of who you sleep with in order to sidetrack our understanding of the politics of sex. For the Lesbian-Feminist, it is not private; it is a political matter of oppression, domination, and power. Reformists offer solutions which make no basic changes in the system that oppresses us, solutions which keep power in the hands of the oppressor. The only way oppressed people end their oppression is by seizing power: People whose rule depends on the subordination of others do not voluntarily stop oppressing others. Our subordination is the basis of male power.

Sexism Is the Root of All Oppression

The first division of labor, in pre-history, was based on sex: men hunted, women built the villages, took care of children, and farmed. Women collectively controlled the land, language, culture, and the communities. Men were able to conquer women with the weapons that they developed for hunting when it became clear that women were leading a more stable, peaceful, and desirable existence. We do not know exactly how this conquest took place, but it is clear that the original imperialism was male over female: the male claiming the female body and her service as his territory (or property).

Having secured the domination of women, men continued this pattern of suppressing people, now on the basis of tribe, race, and class. Although there have been numerous battles over class, race, and nation during the past 3000 years, none has brought the liberation of women. While these other forms of oppression must be ended, there is no reason to believe that our liberation will come with the smashing of capitalism, racism, or imperialism today. Women will be free only when we concentrate on fighting male supremacy.

Our war against male supremacy does, however, involve attacking the latter day dominations based on class, race, and nation. As Lesbians who are outcasts from every group, it would be suicidal to perpetuate these man-made divisions among ourselves. We have no heterosexual privileges, and when we publicly assert our Lesbianism, those of us who had them lose many of our class and race privileges. Most of our privileges as women are granted to us by our relationships to men (fathers, husbands, boyfriends) whom we now reject. This does not mean that there is no racism or class chauvinism within us, but we must destroy these divisive remnants of privileged behavior among ourselves as the first step toward their destruction in the society. Race, class, and national oppressions come from men, serve ruling class white men's interests, and have no place in a woman-identified revolution.

Lesbianism Is the Basic Threat to Male Supremacy

Lesbianism is a threat to the ideological, political, personal, and economic basis of male supremacy. The Lesbian threatens the ideology of male supremacy by destroying the lie about female inferiority, weakness, passivity, and by denying women's "innate" need for men. Lesbians literally do not need men (even for procreation if the science of cloning is developed).

The Lesbian's independence and refusal to support one man undermines the personal power that men exercise over women. Our rejection of heterosexual sex challenges male domination in its most individual and common form. We offer all women something better than submission to personal oppression. We offer the beginning of the end of collective and individual male supremacy. Since men of all races and classes depend on female support and submission for practical tasks and feeling superior, our refusal to submit will force some to examine their sexist behavior, to break down their own destructive privileges over other humans, and to fight against those privileges in other men. They will have to build new selves that do not depend on oppressing women and learn to live in social structures that do not give them power over anyone.

Heterosexuality separates women from each other; it makes women define themselves through men; it forces women to compete against each other for men and the privilege which comes through men and their social standing. Heterosexual society offers women a few privileges as compensation if they give up their freedom: for example, mothers are respected and "honored," wives or lovers are socially accepted and given some economic and emotional security, a woman gets physical protection on the street when she stays with her man, etc. The privileges give heterosexual women a personal and political stake in maintaining the status quo.

The Lesbian receives none of these heterosexual privileges or compensations since she does not accept the male demands on her. She has little vested interest in maintaining the present political system since all of its institutions—church, state, media, health, schools—work to keep her down. If she understands her oppression, she has nothing to gain by supporting white rich male America and much to gain from fighting to change it. She is less prone to accept reformist solutions to women's oppression.

Economics is a crucial part of woman oppression, but our analysis of the relationship between capitalism and sexism is not complete. We know that Marxist economic theory does not sufficiently consider the role of women or Lesbians, and we are presently working on this area.

However, as a beginning, some of the ways that Lesbians threaten the economic system are clear: In this country, women work for men in order to survive, on the job and in the home. The Lesbian rejects this division of labor at its roots; she refuses to be a man's property, to submit to the unpaid labor system of housework and childcare. She rejects the nuclear family as the basic unit of production and consumption in capitalist society.

The Lesbian is also a threat on the job because she is not the passive/part-time woman worker that capitalism counts on to do boring work and be part of a surplus labor pool. Her identity and economic support do not come through men, so her job is crucial and she cares about job conditions, wages, promotion, and status. Capitalism cannot absorb large numbers of women demanding stable employment, decent salaries, and refusing to accept their traditional job exploitation. We do not understand yet the total effect that this increased job dissatisfaction will have. It is, however, clear that as women become more intent upon taking control of their lives, they will seek more control over their jobs, thus increasing the strains on capitalism and enhancing the power of women to change the economic system.

Lesbians Must Form Our Own Movement to Fight Male Supremacy

Feminist-Lesbianism, as the most basic threat to male supremacy, picks up part of the Women's Liberation analysis of sexism and gives it force and direction. Women's Liberation lacks direction now because it has failed to understand the importance of heterosexuality in maintaining male supremacy and because it has failed to face class and race as real differences in women's behavior and political needs. As long as straight women see Lesbianism as a bedroom issue, they hold back the development of politics and strategies which would put an end to male supremacy and they give men an excuse for not dealing with their sexism.

Being a Lesbian means ending identification with, allegiance to, dependence on, and support of heterosexuality. It means ending your personal stake in the male world so that you join women, individually and collectively, in the struggle to end your oppression. Lesbianism is the key to liberation and only women who cut their ties to male privilege can be trusted to remain serious in the struggle against male dominance. Those who remain tied to men, individually or in political theory, cannot always put women first. It is not that heterosexual women are evil or do not care about women. It is because the very essence, definition, and nature of heterosexuality is men first. Every woman has experienced that desolation when her sister puts her man first in the final crunch: heterosexuality demands that she do so. As long as women still benefit from heterosexuality, receive its privileges and security, they will at some point have to betray their sisters, especially Lesbian sisters who do not receive those benefits.

Women in women's liberation have understood the importance of having meetings and other events for women only. It has been clear that dealing with men divides us and saps our energies and that it is not the job of the oppressed to explain our oppression to the oppressor. Women also have seen that collectively, men will not deal with their sexism until they are forced to do so. Yet, many of these same women continue to have primary relationships with men individually and do not understand why Lesbians find this oppressive. Lesbians cannot grow politically or personally in a situation which denies the basis of our politics: that Lesbianism is political, that heterosexuality is crucial to maintaining male supremacy.

Lesbians must form our own political movement in order to grow. Changes which will have more than token effects on our lives will be led by woman-identified Lesbians who understand the nature of our oppression and are therefore in a position to end it.

SOCIALIST FEMINISM: The Interdependence of Gender and Class

A View of Socialist Feminism

Charlotte Perkins Gilman Chapter of the New American Movement

We believe that socialist feminism is essential to the struggle for the liberation of all women and the destruction of capitalism. We derive roots, strength, and direction from the feminist movement and from the socialist movement. Yet we believe that neither approach alone can achieve our goals for economic justice and a society where all women and men are equal. Socialist feminism provides a synthesis of both movements, while providing its unique perspective, vision, strategies, and contributions to theory.

As Feminists

As feminists, we see sexism as a primary focus; we fight against all forms and facets of sexism. We attack the inferior economic and legal status of women. We oppose the sexual division of labor, in which men and women have different responsibilities for home and family and unequal work divisions in the outside work place. We struggle for control of reproduction: for the freedom to choose contraception, abortion, or sterilization when we want them, but never to have any imposed, as they are on many poor and minority women. We challenge societal definitions of "femininity" and "masculinity" and seek freedom to define ourselves as we wish. We see "personal" issues as aspects of ourselves and society that are basic to change—sexuality, life-style, and family.

As Socialists

As socialists, we see ourselves involved in the historic struggle of working people against a system which creates poverty in the midst of wealth; alienating work in a technological society; divisions between black and white, male and female, workers in this country and abroad: capitalism. All people who struggle against capitalism and for a socialist society must work together to challenge that system and its institutions.

The Tension

There remains a tension between socialism and feminism. Each regards its own particular focus as primary, and the other as secondary. Socialists insist on their unifying analysis, yet feminists can point to past failures of the left to address either the oppression women face, or the sexism within the left itself.

We insist on a socialist-feminist movement because:

1   Sexism has a life of its own. It has existed throughout human history, under every economic system.

2 Capitalism determines the particular forms of sexism in a capitalist society. The subjugation of women contributes to capitalists' domination of society.

Any movement which fails to deal with *both* of these fundamental realities cannot succeed. Thus, we believe socialist-feminism is the necessary approach for both feminists and socialists.

Why Socialist Feminism?

The demands of feminism cannot be met by capitalist society. In order to achieve such goals as the elimination of sex roles, free 24-hour day care, and women's control over their own bodies, women must not only struggle to build a strong women's movement, but must work along with other oppressed groups. Socialist feminism moves beyond an attempt to create equality of women within the system to a struggle for equality within a new system that is not dependent on male domination or any exploitation of one group by another. This results in seeing feminism within a larger revolutionary context. For example, when we organize for day care, we challenge the power structure and economic system that are responsible for the present inadequacies. We expose the priorities and interests of those people who are determining and carrying out the current policies. We explore the implications of socialized child care, and its effect on working women and men.

Why Feminist Socialism?

Even though women are divided by class society, we are all united by our oppression as women. Just as women cannot achieve their full liberation except under socialism, so socialism cannot truly succeed unless all people are free from exploitation, manipulation, and prejudice.

Feminism provides the key to the cultural dimension of any successful revolutionary movement. Traditional socialist politics has focused on the public realms of "politics," goods production outside the home, and material needs. But feminism has taught us that the personal *is* political; that production in the "private" world of the home, while invisible under capitalism, is economically and socially critical; and that our culture, as well as our economic system, gives some people power over other people's lives. Any movement which ignores these learnings will surely fail, for it warps its vision and cuts itself off from the strength and knowledge of the female half of the working class. The fight against sexism reinforces the essential recognition that what is important is not just redistribution of goods, but a change in authority, control, and ideas.

Sexism's roots are deep; we must struggle not only against the institutions that maintain it, but against our own roles and attitudes. Feminism brings to the movement an attention to relationships *within* the movement, to the nature and functions of leadership, and to the importance of working collectively.

Women's pain and anger are real. When the broad interests of women and the interests of the working class seem to conflict, it is our task to clarify the interrelationships of those movements and seek programs that speak to all women's needs from a class perspective. Socialists committed to working for a society that is against all forms of oppression and exploitation must join in the struggle against sexism and together with other oppressed people fight for a new social and economic order.

Woman's Estate
Juliet Mitchell

Radical feminism attempts to solve the problem of analysing the oppression of women by making it *the* problem. The largest, first and foremost. While such a theory remains descriptive of the experience, it *does* nevertheless stress the magnitude of the problem. What we need is a theory that is at once large enough and yet is capable of being specific. We have to see *why* women have always been oppressed, and *how* they are oppressed now, and how differently elsewhere. As radical feminists demand, we must dedicate ourselves to a theory of the oppression of all women and yet, at the same time, not lose sight of the historical specificity in the general statement. We should ask the feminist questions, but try to come up with some Marxist answers.

The situation of women is different from that of any other oppressed social group: they are half of the human species. In some ways they are exploited and oppressed like, and along with, other exploited classes or oppressed groups—the working-class, Blacks, etc. . . . Until there is a revolution in production, the labour situation will prescribe women's situation within the world of men. But women are offered a universe of their own: the family. Women are exploited at work, and relegated to the home: the two positions compound their oppression. Their subservience in production is obscured by their assumed dominance in their own world—the family. What is the family? And what are the actual functions that a woman fulfils within it? Like woman herself, the family appears as a natural object, but is actually a cultural creation. There is nothing inevitable about the form or role of the family, any more than there is about the character or role of women. It is the function of ideology to present these given social types as aspects of Nature itself. Both can be exalted, paradoxically, as ideals. The "true" woman and the "true" family are images of peace and plenty: in actuality they may both be sites of violence and despair. The apparently natural condition can be made to appear more attractive than the arduous advance of human beings towards culture. But what Marx wrote about the bourgeois myths of the Golden Ancient World describes precisely women's realm.

> . . . in one way the child-like world of the ancients appears to be superior; and this is
> so, insofar as we seek for closed shape, form and established limitation. The ancients

provide a narrow satisfaction, whereas the modern world leaves us unsatisfied, or, where it appears to be satisfied with itself, is *vulgar* and *mean*.[1]

The ideology of "woman" presents her as an undifferentiated whole—"a woman," alike the world over, eternally the same. Likewise the "concept" of the family is of a unit that endures across time and space, there have always been families. . . . Within its supposed permanent structure, eternal woman finds her place. So the notion goes. . . . Any analysis of woman, and of the family, must uncoil this ideological concept of their permanence and of their unification into a monolithic whole, mother and child, a woman's place . . . her natural destiny. Theoretical analysis and revolutionary action must destructure and destroy the inevitability of this combination.

Past socialist theory has failed to differentiate woman's condition into its separate structures, which together form a complex—not a simple—unity. To do this will mean rejecting the idea that woman's condition can be deduced derivatively from the economy (Engels), or equated symbolically with society (early Marx). Rather, it must be seen as a *specific* structure, which is a unity of different elements. The variations of woman's condition throughout history will be the result of different combinations of these elements—we will thus have not a linear narrative of economic development (De Beauvoir) for the elements will be combined in different ways at different times. In a complex totality each independent sector has its own autonomous reality though each is ultimately, but only ultimately, determined by the economic factor. This complex totality means that no contradiction in society is ever simple. As each sector can move at a different pace, the synthesis of the different time-scales in the total structure means that sometimes contradictions cancel each other out, and sometimes they reinforce one another. Because the unity of woman's condition at any time is in this way the product of several structures, moving at different paces, it is always "overdetermined."[2]

The key structures of woman's situation can be listed as follows: Production, Reproduction, Sexuality and the Socialization of Children. The concrete combination of these produce the "complex unity" of her position; but each separate structure may have reached a different "moment" at any given historical time. Each then must be examined separately in order to see what the present unity is, and how it might be changed. The notes that follow do not pretend to give a historical account of each sector. They are only concerned with some general reflections on the different roles of women and some of their interconnections.

[1]Karl Marx: *Pre-Capitalist Economic Formations,* ed. Hobsbawm, Lawrence & Wishart, 1964, p. 85.

[2]See Louis Althusser: "Contradiction and Overdetermination," in *For Marx,* Allen Lane, London, 1970. To describe the movement of this complexity, as I have mentioned above, Althusser uses the Freudian term "overdetermination." The phrase *"unité de rupture"* (mentioned below) refers to the moment when the contradictions so reinforce one another as to coalesce into the conditions for a revolutionary change.

1   PRODUCTION

The biological differentiation of the sexes into male and female and the division
of labour that is based on this have *seemed,* throughout history, an interlocked
necessity. Anatomically smaller and weaker, woman's physiology and her psy-
chobiological metabolism appear to render her a less useful member of a workforce. It is always stressed how, particularly in the early stages of social
development, man's physical superiority gave him the means of conquest over
nature which was denied to women. Once woman was accorded the menial tasks
involved in maintenance while man undertook conquest and creation, she
became an aspect of the things preserved: private property and children. Marx,
Engels, Bebel, De Beauvoir—the major socialist writers on the subject—link the
confirmation and continuation of woman's oppression after the establishment of
her physical inferiority for hard manual work with the advent of private property.
But woman's physical weakness has never prevented her from performing work
as such (quite apart from bringing up children)—only specific types of work, in
specific societies. In Primitive, Ancient, Oriental, Medieval and Capitalist societies, the *volume* of work performed by women has always been considerable (it
has usually been much more than this). It is only its form that is in question.
Domestic labour, even today, is enormous if quantified in terms of productive
labour.[3] It has been calculated in Sweden, that 2,340 million hours a year are
spent by women in housework compared with 1,290 million hours in industry.
The Chase Manhattan Bank estimated a woman's overall working week averaged 99.6 hours. In any case women's physique alone has never permanently or
even predominantly relegated them to menial domestic chores. In many peasant
societies, women have worked in the fields as much as, or more than, men.

Physical Weakness and Coercion

The assumption behind most socialist analyses is that the crucial factor starting
the whole development of feminine subordination was women's lesser capacity
for demanding physical work. But, in fact, this is a major oversimplification.
Even in these terms, historically it has been woman's lesser capacity for violence
as well as for work, that has determined her subordination. In most societies
woman has not only been less able than man to perform arduous kinds of work,
she has also been less able to fight. Man not only has the strength to assert
himself against nature, but also against his fellows. *Social coercion* has inter-
played with the straightforward division of labour, based on biological capacity,
to a much greater extent than is generally admitted. Women have been *forced* to

---

[3]Apologists who make out that housework, though time-consuming, is light and relatively
enjoyable, are refusing to acknowledge the dull and degrading routine it entails. Lenin commented
crisply: "You all know that even when women have full rights, they still remain factually downtrodden because all housework is left to them. In most cases housework is the most unproductive, the
most barbarous and the most arduous work a woman can do. It is exceptionally petty and does not
include anything that would in any way promote the development of the woman." (*Collected Works,*
vol. XXX, p. 43.)

do "women's work." Of course, this force may not be actualized as direct aggression. In primitive societies women's lesser physical suitability for the hunt is assumed to be evident. In agricultural societies where women's inferiority is socially instituted, they are given the arduous task of tilling and cultivation. For this coercion is necessary. In developed civilizations, and more complex societies, woman's physical deficiencies again become relevant. Women are thought to be of no use either for war or in the construction of cities. But with early industrialization, coercion once more becomes important. As Marx wrote: "insofar as machinery dispenses with muscular power, it becomes a means of employing labourers of slight muscular strength, and those whose bodily development is incomplete, but whose limbs are all the more supple. The labour of women and children was, therefore, the first thing sought for by capitalists who used machinery."[4]

René Dumont points out that in many zones of tropical Africa today men are often idle, while women are forced to work all day. "The African woman experiences a three-fold servitude: through forced marriage; through her dowry and polygamy, which increases the leisure time of men and simultaneously their social prestige; and finally through the very unequal division of labour"[5] (This exploitation has no "natural" source whatever. Women may perform their "heavy" duties in contemporary African peasant societies, not for fear of physical reprisal by their men, but because these duties are "customary" and built into the role structures of the society. A further point is that coercion implies a different relationship from coercer to coerced than does exploitation. It is political rather than economic. In describing coercion Marx said that the master treated the slave or serf as the "inorganic and natural condition of its own reproduction." That is to say, labour itself becomes like other natural things—cattle or soil:

> The original conditions of production appear as natural prerequisites, *natural conditions of the existence of the producer,* just as his living body, however reproduced and developed by him, is not originally established by himself, but appears as his *prerequisite.*[6]

This is pre-eminently woman's condition. For far from woman's *physical* weakness removing her from productive work, her *social* weakness has in these cases evidently made her the major slave of it.

This truth, elementary though it may seem, has nevertheless been constantly ignored by socialist writers on the subject, with the result that there is an unfounded optimism in their predictions of the future. For, if it is just the biological incapacity for the hardest physical work which has determined the subordination of women, then the prospect of an advanced machine technology,

---

[4]Karl Marx: *Capital,* I, p. 394.
[5]René Dumont: *L'Afrique Noire est Mal Partie,* 1962, p. 210.
[6]Karl Marx: *Precapitalist Economic Formations,* op. cit., p. 87.

abolishing the need for strenuous physical exertion, would seem to promise, therefore, the liberation of women. For a moment industrialization itself thus seems to herald women's liberation. Engels, for instance, wrote:

> The first premise for the emancipation of women is the reintroduction of the entire female sex into public industry. . . . And this has become possible only as a result of modern large-scale industry, which not only permits of the participation of women in production in large numbers, but actually calls for it and, moreover, strives to convert private domestic work also into a public industry.[7]

What Marx said of early industrialism is no less, but also *no more* true of an automated society:

> . . . it is obvious that the fact of the collective working group being composed of individuals of both sexes and all ages, must necessarily, *under suitable conditions,* become a source of human development; although in its spontaneously developed, brutal, capitalist form, where the labourer exists for the process of production, and not the process of production for the labourer, that fact is a pestiferous source of corruption and slavery.[8]

Industrial labour and automated technology both promise the preconditions for women's liberation alongside man's—but no more than the preconditions. It is only too obvious that the advent of industrialization has not so far freed women in this sense, either in the West or in the East. De Beauvoir hoped that automation would make a decisive, qualitative difference by abolishing altogether the physical differential between the sexes. But any reliance on this in itself accords an independent role to technique which history does not justify. Under capitalism, automation could possibly lead to an ever-growing structural unemployment which would expel women (along with immigrants)—the latest and least integrated recruits to the labour force and ideologically the most expendable for a bourgeois society—from production after only a brief interlude in it. Technology is mediated by the total structure, and it is this which will determine woman's future in work relations. It is the relationship between the social forces and technology that Firestone's "ecological" revolution ultimately ignores.

Physical deficiency is not now, any more than in the past, a sufficient explanation of woman's relegation to inferior status. Coercion has been ameliorated to an ideology shared by both sexes. Commenting on the results of her questionnaire of working women, Viola Klein notes: "There is no trace of feminine egalitarianism—militant or otherwise—in any of the women's answers to the questionnaire; nor is it even implicitly assumed that women have a 'Right to Work.'"[9] Denied, or refusing, a role in *production,* woman does not even

---

[7]Friedrich Engels: op. cit., II, pp. 233, 311.
[8]Karl Marx: *Capital,* I, p. 394.
[9]Viola Klein: "Working Wives," *Institute of Personnel Management Occasional Papers,* no. 15, 1960, p. 13.

create the preconditions of her liberation. But even her presence in the work force does not erode her oppression in the family.

2 THE REPRODUCTION OF CHILDREN

Women's absence from the critical sector of production historically, of course, has been caused not just by their assumed physical weakness in a context of coercion—but also by their role in reproduction. Maternity necessitates withdrawals from work, but this is not a decisive phenomenon. It is rather women's role in reproduction which has become, in capitalist society at least, the spiritual "complement" of men's role in production. Bearing children, bringing them up, and maintaining the home—these form the core of woman's natural vocation, in this ideology. This belief has attained great force because of the seeming universality of the family as a human institution. There is little doubt that Marxist analyses have underplayed the fundamental problems posed here. The complete failure to give any operative content to the slogan of "abolition" of the family is striking evidence of this (as well as of the vacuity of the notion).

The biological function of maternity is a universal, atemporal fact, and as such has seemed to escape the categories of Marxist historical analysis. However, from it is made to follow the so-called stability and omnipresence of the family, if in very different forms.[10] Once this is accepted, women's social subordination—however emphasized as an honourable, but different role (cf. the equal-but-"separate" ideologies of Southern racists)—can be seen to follow inevitably as an *insurmountable* bio-historical fact. The causal chain then goes: maternity, family, absence from production and public life, sexual inequality.

The lynch-pin in this line of argument is the idea of the family. The notion that "family" and "society" are virtually co-extensive or that an advanced society not founded on the nuclear family is now inconceivable, despite revolutionary posturings to the contrary, is still widespread. It can only be seriously discussed by asking just what the family is—or rather what women's role in the family is. Once this is done, the problem appears in quite a new light. For it is obvious that woman's role in the family—primitive, feudal or bourgeois—partakes of three quite different structures: reproduction, sexuality, and the socialization of children. These are historically, not intrinsically, related to each other in the present modern family. We can easily see that they needn't be. For instance, biological parentage is not necessarily identical with social parentage (adoption). Thus it is essential to discuss not the family as an unanalysed entity, but the separate *structures* which today compose it but which tomorrow may be decomposed into a new pattern.

As I have said, reproduction is seen as an apparently constant atemporal phenomenon—part of biology rather than history. In fact this is an illusion. What is true is that the "mode of reproduction" does not vary with the "mode of

---

[10]Philippe Ariès in *Centuries of Childhood,* 1962, shows that though the family may in some form always have existed it was often submerged under more forceful structures. In fact according to Ariès it has only acquired its present significance with the advent of industrialization.

production''; it can remain effectively the same through a number of different modes of production. For it has been defined till now by its uncontrollable, natural character and to this extent has been an unmodified biological fact. As long as reproduction remained a natural phenomenon, of course, women were effectively doomed to social exploitation. In any sense, they were not "masters" of a large part of their lives. They had no choice as to whether or how often they gave birth to children (apart from precarious methods of contraception or repeated dangerous abortions); their existence was essentially subject to biological processes outside their control.

Contraception

Contraception which was finally invented as a rational technique only in the nineteenth century was thus an innovation of world-historic importance. It is only just now beginning to show what immense consequences it could have, in the form of the Pill. For what it means is that at last the mode of reproduction potentially could be transformed. Once child-bearing becomes totally voluntary (how much so is it in the West, even today?) its significance is fundamentally different. It need no longer be the sole or ultimate vocation of woman; it becomes one option among others.

History is the development of man's transformation of nature, and thereby of himself—of human nature—in different modes of production. Today there are the technical possibilities for the transformation and "humanization" of the most natural part of human culture. This is what a change in the mode of reproduction could mean.

We are far from this state of affairs yet. In Italy the sale of contraceptives remains illegal. In many countries it is difficult to get reliable means. The oral contraceptive is still the privilege of a moneyed minority in a few western countries. Even here the progress has been realized in a typically conservative and exploitative form. It is made only for women, who are thus "guinea-pigs" in a venture which involves both sexes.

The fact of overwhelming importance is that easily available contraception threatens to dissociate sexual from reproductive experience—which all contemporary ideology tries to make inseparable, as the *raison d'être* of the family.

Reproduction and Production

At present, reproduction in our society is often a kind of sad mimicry of production. Work in a capitalist society is an alienation of labour in the making of a social product which is confiscated by capital. But it can still sometimes be a real act of creation, purposive and responsible, even in the conditions of the worst exploitation. Maternity is often a caricature of this. The biological product—the child—is treated as if it were a solid product. Parenthood becomes a kind of substitute for work, an activity in which the child is seen as an object created by the mother, in the same way as a commodity is created by a worker. Naturally, the child does not literally escape, but the mother's alienation can be much worse than of the worker whose product is appropriated by the boss. The child as an autonomous person, inevitably threatens the activity which claims to create it continually merely as a *possession* of the parent. Possessions are felt as extensions of the self. The child as a possession is supremely this. Anything the child does is therefore a threat to the mother herself, who has renounced her autonomy through this misconception of her reproductive role. There are few more precarious ventures on which to base a life.

Furthermore even if the woman has emotional control over her child, legally and economically both she and it are subject to the father. The social cult of maternity is matched by the real socio-economic powerlessness of the mother. The psychological and practical benefits men receive from this are obvious. The converse of woman's quest for creation in the child is man's retreat from his work into the family: "When we come home, we lay aside our mask and drop our tools, and are no longer lawyers, sailors, soldiers, statesmen, clergymen, but only men. We fall again into our most human relations, which, after all, are the whole of what belongs to us as we are ourselves."[11]

Unlike her non-productive status, her capacity for maternity *is* a definition of woman. But it is only a physiological definition. Yet so long as it is allowed to remain a substitute for action and creativity, and the home an area of relaxation for men, woman will remain confined to the species, to her universal and natural condition.

3 SEXUALITY

Sexuality has traditionally been the most tabooed dimension of women's situation. The meaning of sexual freedom and its connection with women's freedom is a subject which few socialist writers have cared to broach. "Socialist morality" in the Soviet Union for a long time debarred serious discussion of the subject within the world communist movement. Marx himself—in this respect somewhat less liberal than Engels—early in his life expressed traditional views on the matter:

> . . . the sanctification of the sexual instinct through exclusivity, the checking of instinct by laws, the moral beauty which makes nature's commandment ideal in the form of an emotional bond—(this is) the spiritual essence of marriage.[12]

Yet it is obvious that throughout history women have been appropriated as sexual objects, as much as progenitors or producers. Indeed, the sexual relationship can be assimilated to the statute of possession much more easily and completely than the productive or reproductive relationship. Contemporary sexual vocabulary bears eloquent witness to this—it is a comprehensive lexicon of reification—"bird, fruit, chick . . ." Later Marx was well aware of this: "*Marriage* . . . is incontestably a form of *exclusive private property*."[13] But neither he nor his successors ever tried seriously to envisage the implications of

---

[11]J. A. Froude: *Nemesis of Faith*, 1849, p. 103.
[12]Karl Marx: "Chapitre de Mariage," *Oeuvres Complètes*, ed. Molitor, *Oeuvres Philosophiques*, I, p. 25.
[13]Karl Marx: *Private Property and Communism*, op. cit., p. 153.

this for socialism, or even for a structural analysis of women's conditions. Communism, Marx stressed in the same passage, would not mean mere "communalization" of women as common property. Beyond this, he never ventured.

Some historical considerations are in order here. For if socialists have said nothing, the gap has been filled by liberal ideologues. Fairly recently, in his book, *Eros Denied,* Wayland Young argues that western civilization has been uniquely repressive sexually, and, in a plea for greater sexual freedom today, compares it at some length with oriental and ancient societies. It is striking, however, that his book makes no reference whatever to women's status in these different societies, or to the different forms of marriage-contract prevalent in them. This makes the whole argument a purely formal exercise—an obverse of socialist discussions of women's position which ignore the problem of sexual freedom and its meanings. For while it is true that certain oriental or ancient (and indeed primitive) cultures were much less puritanical than western societies, it is absurd to regard this as a kind of "transposable value" which can be abstracted from its social structure. In effect, in many of these societies sexual openness was accompanied by a form of polygamous exploitation which made it, in practice, an expression simply of masculine domination. Since art was the province of man, too, this freedom finds a natural and often powerful expression in art—which is often quoted as if it were evidence of the total quality of human relationships in the society. Nothing could be more misleading. What is necessary, rather than this naïve, hortatory core of historical example, is some account of the co-variation between the degrees of sexual liberty and openness, and the position and dignity of women in different societies. . . .

Sexuality and the Position of Women: Today

The situation today is defined by a new contradiction. Once formal conjugal equality (monogamy) is established, sexual freedom as such—which under polygamous conditions was usually a form of exploitation—becomes, conversely, a possible force for liberation. It then means, simply, the freedom of both sexes to transcend the limits of present sexual institutions.

Historically, then, there has been a dialectical movement in which sexual expression was "sacrificed" in an epoch of more-or-less puritan repression, which nevertheless produced a greater parity of sexual roles and in turn creates the precondition for a genuine sexual liberation, in the dual sense of equality *and* freedom—whose unity defines socialism.

The current wave of sexual liberalization, in the present context, *could* become conducive to the greater general freedom of women. Equally, it could presage new forms of oppression. The puritan-bourgeois creation of "counterpart" (not equal) has produced the *precondition* for emancipation. But it gave statutory legal equality to the sexes at the cost of greatly intensified repression. Subsequently—like private property itself—it has become a brake on the further development of a free sexuality. Capitalist market relations have historically been a precondition of socialism; bourgeois marital relations (contrary to the denunciation of the *Communist Manifesto*) may equally be a precondition of women's liberation.

4 SOCIALIZATION OF CHILDREN

Woman's biological "destiny" as mother becomes a cultural vocation in her role as socializer of children. In bringing up children, woman achieves her main social definition. Her suitability for socialization springs from her physiological condition: her ability to produce milk and occasional relative inability to undertake strenuous work loads. It should be said at the outset that suitability is not inevitability. Several anthropologists make this clear. Lévi-Strauss writes:

> In every human group, women give birth to children and take care of them, and men rather have as their speciality hunting and warlike activities. Even there, though, we have ambiguous cases: of course, men never give birth to babies, but in many societies . . . they are made to act as if they did.[14]

Evans-Pritchard's description of the Nuer tribe depicts just such a situation. Margaret Mead comments on the element of wish-fulfilment in the assumption of a *natural* correlation of femininity and nurturance:

> We have assumed that because it is convenient for a mother to wish to care for her child, this is a trait with which women have been more generously endowed by a careful teleological process of evolution. We have assumed that because men have hunted, an activity requiring enterprise, bravery and initiative, they have been endowed with these useful attitudes as part of their sex-temperament.[15]

However, the cultural allocation of roles in bringing up children—and the limits of its variability—is not the essential problem for consideration. What is much more important is to analyse the nature of the socialization process itself and its requirements.

The sociologist, Talcott Parsons, in his detailed analysis claims that it is essential for the child to have two "parents," one who plays an "expressive" role, and one who plays an "instrumental" role.[16] The nuclear family revolves around the two axes of generational hierarchy (parents and children), and of the two parental roles (mother-expressive and father-instrumental). The role division derives from the mother's ability and the father's inability to breast-feed. In all groups, Parsons and his colleagues assert, even in those primitive tribes where the father appears to nurture the child (such as those discussed by Evans-Pritchard and Mead), the male plays the instrumental role *in relation* to the wife-mother. At one stage the mother plays an instrumental and expressive

---

[14]Claude Lévi-Strauss: "The Family," in *Man, Culture and Society,* ed. H. L. Shapiro, 1956, p. 274.

[15]Margaret Mead: "Sex and Temperament," in *The Family and The Sexual Revolution,* op. cit., pp. 207–8.

[16]Talcott Parsons and Robert F. Bales: *Family, Socialization and Interaction Process,* 1956, p. 47. "The area of instrumental function concerns relations of the system to its situation outside the system . . . and 'instrumentally' establishing the desired relations to *external* goal-objects. The expressive area concerns the 'internal' affairs of the system, the maintenance of integrative relations between the members, and regulation of the patterns and tension levels of its component units."

role *vis-à-vis* her infant: this is in the very first years when she is the source of approval and disapproval as well as of love and care. However, after this, the father, or male substitute (in matrilineal societies the mother's brother) takes over. In a modern industrial society two types of role are clearly important: the adult role in the family of procreation, and the adult occupational role in outside work. The function of the family as such reflects the function of the women within it; it is primarily expressive. The person playing the integrated-adaptive-expressive role cannot be off all the time on instrumental-occupational errands— hence there is a built-in inhibition of the woman's work outside the home. Parsons's analysis makes clear the exact role of the maternal socializer in contemporary American society.[17] It fails to go on to state that other aspects and modes of socialization are conceivable. What is valuable in Parsons' work is simply his insistence on the central importance of socialization as a process which is constitutive of any society (no Marxist has provided a comparable analysis). His general conclusion is that:

> It seems to be without serious qualification the opinion of competent personality psychologists that, though personalities differ greatly in their degrees of rigidity, certain broad fundamental patterns of "character" are laid down in childhood (so far as they are not genetically inherited) and are not radically changed by adult experience. The exact degree to which this is the case or the exact age levels at which plasticity becomes greatly diminished, are not at issue here. The important thing is the fact of childhood character formation and its relative stability after that.[18]

Infancy

This seems indisputable: one of the great revolutions of modern psychology has been the discovery of the decisive specific weight of infancy in the course of an individual life—a psychic time disproportionately greater than the chronological time. Freud began the revolution with his work on infantile sexuality; Melanie Klein radicalized it with her work on the first year of the infant's life. The result is that today we know far more than ever before how delicate and precarious a process the passage from birth to childhood is for everyone. It would seem that the fate of the adult personality can be largely decided in the initial months of life. The preconditions for the later stability and integration demand an extraordinary degree of care and intelligence on the part of the adult who is socializing the child, as well as a persistence through time of the same person.

These undoubted advances in the scientific understanding of childhood have been widely used as an argument to reassert women's quintessential maternal function, at a time when the traditional family has seemed increasingly eroded.

---

[17] One of Parsons' main theoretical innovations is his contention that what the child strives to internalize will vary with the content of the reciprocal role relationships in which he is a participant. R. D. Laing, in *Family and Individual Structure,* 1966, contends that a child may internalize an entire system—i.e., "the family."

[18] Talcott Parsons: *The Social System,* 1952, p. 227. There is no doubt that the Women's Liberation Movement, with its practical and theoretical stress on the importance of child-care, has accorded the subject the seriousness it needs. See, for instance, "Women's Liberation: Notes on Child-Care" produced by the Women's Centre, 36 West 22nd St., New York.

The psychologist, Bowlby, studying evacuee children in the Second World War, declared: "essential for mental health is that the infant and young child should experience a warm, intimate, and continuous relationship with his mother,"[19] setting a trend which has become cumulative since. The emphasis of familial ideology has shifted from a cult of the biological ordeal of maternity (the pain which makes the child precious, etc.) to a celebration of mother-care as a social act. This can reach ludicrous extremes:

> For the mother, breast-feeding becomes a complement to the act of creation. It gives her a heightened sense of fulfilment and allows her to participate in a relationship as close to perfection as any that a woman can hope to achieve. . . . The simple fact of giving birth, however, does not of itself fulfil this need and longing. . . . Motherliness is a way of life. It enables a woman to express her total self with the tender feelings, the protective attitudes, the encompassing love of the motherly woman.[20]

The tautologies, the mystifications, the sheer absurdities point to the gap between reality and ideology.

Family Patterns

This ideology corresponds in dislocated form to a real change in the pattern of the family. As the family has become smaller, each child has become more important; the actual *act* of reproduction occupies less and less time, and the socializing and nurturance process increase commensurately in significance. Contemporary society is obsessed by the physical, moral and sexual problems of childhood and adolescence. Ultimate responsibility for these is placed on the mother. Thus the mother's reproductive role has retreated as her socializing role has increased. In the 1890s in England a mother spent fifteen years in a state of pregnancy and lactation: in the 1960s she spent an average of four years. Compulsory schooling from the age of five, of course, reduces the maternal function very greatly after the initial vulnerable years.

The present situation is then one in which the qualitative importance of socialization during the early years of the child's life has acquired a much greater significance than in the past—while the quantitative amount of a mother's life spent either in gestation or child-rearing has greatly diminished. It follows that socialization cannot simply be elevated to the woman's new maternal vocation. Used as a mystique, it becomes an instrument of oppression. Moreover, there is no inherent reason why the biological and social mother should coincide. The process of socialization is, in itself, invariable—but the person of the socializer can vary. Observers of collective methods of child-rearing in the kibbutzim in Israel note that the child who is reared by a trained nurse (though normally maternally breast-fed) does not suffer the back-wash of typical parental anxieties

---

[19]John Bowlby, cit. Bruno Bettelheim: "Does Communal Education Work? The Case of the Kibbutz," in *The Family and the Sexual Revolution*, op. cit., p. 295. These evacuee war children were probably suffering from more than mother-loss, e.g. bombings and air-raids?

[20]Betty Ann Countrywoman: *Redbook*, June, 1960, cit. Betty Friedan: *The Feminine Mystique*, Penguin, 1965, p. 51.

and thus may positively gain by the system. This possibility should not be fetishized in its turn (Jean Baby, speaking of the post-four-year-old child, goes so far as to say that "complete separation appears indispensable to guarantee the liberty of the child as well as the mother."[21]) But what it does reveal is the viability of plural forms of socialization—neither necessarily tied to the nuclear family, nor to the biological parent, or rather to *one* of the biological parents— the mother.

CONCLUSION

The lesson of these reflections is that the liberation of women can only be achieved if *all four* structures in which they are integrated are transformed— Production, Reproduction, Sexuality and Socialization. A modification of any of them can be offset by a reinforcement of another (as increased socialization has made up for decreased reproduction). This means that a mere permutation of the form of exploitation is achieved. . . .

Probably it is only in the highly developed societies of the West that an authentic liberation of women can be envisaged today. But for this to occur, there must be a transformation of *all* the structures into which they are inte- grated, and all the contradictions must coalesce, to explode—a *unité de rupture*. A revolutionary movement must base its analysis on the uneven development of each structure, and attack the weakest link in the combination. This may then become the point of departure for a general transformation. What is the situation of the different structures today? What is the concrete situation of the women in each of the positions in which they are inserted?

The Traffic in Women[1]

Gayle Rubin

The literature on women—both feminist and anti-feminist—is a long rumination on the question of the nature and genesis of women's oppression and social subordination. The question is not a trivial one, since the answers given it determine our visions of the future, and our evaluation of whether or not it is realistic to hope for a sexually egalitarian society. More importantly, the analysis

[21]Jean Baby: *Un Monde Meilleur,* Maspero, 1964, p. 99.
[1]Acknowledgments are an inadequate expression of how much this paper, like most, is the product of many minds. They are also necessary to free others of the responsibility for what is ultimately a personal vision of a collective conversation. I want to free and thank the following persons: Tom Anderson and Arlene Gorelick, with whom I co-authored the paper from which this one evolved; Rayna Reiter, Larry Shields, Ray Kelly, Peggy White, Norma Diamond, Randy Reiter, Frederick Wyatt, Anne Locksley, Juliet Mitchell, and Susan Harding, for countless conversations and ideas; Marshall Sahlins, for the revelation of anthropology; Lynn Eden, for sardonic editing; the members of Women's Studies 340/004, for my initiation into teaching; Sally Brenner, for heroic typing; Susan Lowes, for incredible patience; and Emma Goldman, for the title.

of the causes of women's oppression forms the basis for any assessment of just what would have to be changed in order to achieve a society without gender hierarchy. Thus, if innate male aggression and dominance are at the root of female oppression, then the feminist program would logically require either the extermination of the offending sex, or else a eugenics project to modify its character. If sexism is a by-product of capitalism's relentless appetite for profit, then sexism would wither away in the advent of a successful socialist revolution. If the world historical defeat of women occurred at the hands of an armed patriarchal revolt, then it is time for Amazon guerrillas to start training in the Adirondacks. . . .

Marx once asked: "What is a Negro slave? A man of the black race. The one explanation is as good as the other. A Negro is a Negro. He only becomes a slave in certain relations. A cotton spinning jenny is a machine for spinning cotton. It becomes *capital* only in certain relations. Torn from these relationships it is no more capital than gold in itself is money or sugar is the price of sugar" (Marx, 1971b:28). One might paraphrase: What is a domesticated woman? A female of the species. The one explanation is as good as the other. A woman is a woman. She only becomes a domestic, a wife, a chattel, a playboy bunny, a prostitute, or a human dictaphone in certain relations. Torn from these relationships, she is no more the helpmate of man than gold in itself is money . . . etc. What then are these relationships by which a female becomes an oppressed woman? The place to begin to unravel the system of relationships by which women become the prey of men is in the overlapping works of Claude Lévi-Strauss and Sigmund Freud. The domestication of women, under other names, is discussed at length in both of their *oeuvres*. In reading through these works, one begins to have a sense of a systematic social apparatus which takes up females as raw materials and fashions domesticated women as products. Neither Freud nor Lévi-Strauss sees his work in this light, and certainly neither turns a critical glance upon the processes he describes. Their analyses and descriptions must be read, therefore, in something like the way in which Marx read the classical political economists who preceded him (on this, see Althusser and Balibar, 1970:11-69). Freud and Lévi-Strauss are in some sense analogous to Ricardo and Smith: They see neither the implications of what they are saying, nor the implicit critique which their work can generate when subjected to a feminist eye. Nevertheless, they provide conceptual tools with which one can build descriptions of the part of social life which is the locus of the oppression of women, of sexual minorities, and of certain aspects of human personality within individuals. I call that part of social life the "sex/gender system," for lack of a more elegant term. As a preliminary definition, a "sex/gender system" is the set of arrangements by which a society transforms biological sexuality into products of human activity, and in which these transformed sexual needs are satisfied.

The purpose of this essay is to arrive at a more fully developed definition of the sex/gender system, by way of a somewhat idiosyncratic and exegetical reading of Lévi-Strauss and Freud. . . .

Other names have been proposed for the sex/gender system. The most common alternatives are "mode of reproduction" and "patriarchy." It may be foolish to quibble about terms, but both of these can lead to confusion. All three proposals have been made in order to introduce a distinction between "economic" systems and "sexual" systems, and to indicate that sexual systems have a certain autonomy and cannot always be explained in terms of economic forces. "Mode of reproduction," for instance, has been proposed in opposition to the more familiar "mode of production." But this terminology links the "economy" to production, and the sexual system to "reproduction." It reduces the richness of either system, since "productions" and "reproductions" take place in both. Every mode of production involves reproduction—of tools, labor, and social relations. We cannot relegate all of the multi-faceted aspects of social reproduction to the sex system. Replacement of machinery is an example of reproduction in the economy. On the other hand, we cannot limit the sex system to "reproduction" in either the social or biological sense of the term. A sex/gender system is not simply the reproductive moment of a "mode of production." The formation of gender identity is an example of production in the realm of the sexual system. And a sex/gender system involves more than the "relations of procreation," reproduction in the biological sense.

The term "patriarchy" was introduced to distinguish the forces maintaining sexism from other social forces, such as capitalism. But the use of "patriarchy" obscures other distinctions. Its use in analogous to using capitalism to refer to all modes of production, whereas the usefulness of the term "capitalism" lies precisely in that it distinguishes between the different systems by which societies are provisioned and organized. Any society will have some system of "political economy." Such a system may be egalitarian or socialist. It may be class stratified, in which case the oppressed class may consist of serfs, peasants, or slaves. The oppressed class may consist of wage laborers, in which case the system is properly labeled "capitalist." The power of the term lies in its implication that, in fact, there are alternatives to capitalism.

Similarly, any society will have some systematic ways to deal with sex, gender, and babies. Such a system may be sexually egalitarian, at least in theory, or it may be "gender stratified," as seems to be the case for most or all of the known examples. But it is important—even in the face of a depressing history— to maintain a distinction between the human capacity and necessity to create a sexual world, and the empirically oppressive ways in which sexual worlds have been organized. Patriarchy subsumes both meanings into the same term. Sex/gender system, on the other hand, is a neutral term which refers to the domain and indicates that oppression is not inevitable in that domain, but is the product of the specific social relations which organize it.

Finally, there are gender-stratified systems which are not adequately described as patriarchal. Many New Guinea societies (Enga, Maring, Bena Bena, Huli, Melpa, Kuma, Gahuku-Gama, Fore, Marind Anim, ad nauseum; see Berndt, 1962; Langness, 1967; Rappaport, 1975; Read, 1952; Meggitt, 1970; Glasse, 1971; Strathern, 1972; Reay, 1959, Van Baal, 1966; Lindenbaum, 1973) are viciously oppressive to women. But the power of males in these groups is not founded on their roles as fathers or patriarchs, but on their collective adult maleness, embodied in secret cults, men's houses, warfare, exchange networks, ritual knowledge, and various initiation procedures. Patriarchy is a specific form of male dominance, and the use of the term ought to be confined to the Old Testament-type pastoral nomads from whom the term comes, or groups like them. Abraham was a Patriarch—one old man whose absolute power over wives, children, herds, and dependents was an aspect of the institution of fatherhood, as defined in the social group in which he lived.

Whichever term we use, what is important is to develop concepts to adequately describe the social organization of sexuality and the reproduction of the conventions of sex and gender. We need to pursue the project Engels abandoned when he located the subordination of women in a development within the mode of production.[2] To do this, we can imitate Engels in his method rather than in his results. Engels approached the task of analyzing the "second aspect of material life" by way of an examination of a theory of kinship systems. Kinship systems are and do many things. But they are made up of, and reproduce, concrete forms of socially organized sexuality. Kinship systems are observable and empirical forms of sex/gender systems.

Kinship
(On the Part Played by Sexuality in the Transition
from Ape to "Man")

To an anthropologist, a kinship system is not a list of biological relatives. It is a system of categories and statuses which often contradict actual genetic relationships. There are dozens of examples in which socially defined kinship statuses take precedence over biology. The Nuer custom of "woman marriage" is a case in point. The Nuer define the status of fatherhood as belonging to the person in whose name cattle bridewealth is given for the mother. Thus, a woman can be married to another woman, and be husband to the wife and father of her children, despite the fact that she is not the inseminator (Evans-Pritchard, 1951:107-09).

In pre-state societies, kinship is the idiom of social interaction, organizing economic, political, and ceremonial, as well as sexual, activity. One's duties, responsibilities, and privileges vis-à-vis others are defined in terms of mutual kinship or lack thereof. The exchange of goods and services, production and distribution, hostility and solidarity, ritual and ceremony, all take place within the organizational structure of kinship. The ubiquity and adaptive effectiveness of kinship has led many anthropologists to consider its invention, along with the invention of language, to have been the developments which decisively marked the discontinuity between semi-human hominids and human beings (Sahlins, 1960; Livingstone, 1969; Lévi-Strauss, 1969). . . .

In taking up Engels' project of extracting a theory of sex oppression from the study of kinship, we have the advantage of the maturation of ethnology since

[2]Engels thought that men acquired wealth in the form of herds and, wanting to pass this wealth to their own children, overthrew "mother right" in favor of patrilineal inheritance. "The overthrow of mother right was the *world historical defeat of the female sex*. The man took command in the home also; the woman was degraded and reduced to servitude; she became the slave of his lust and a mere instrument for the production of children" (Engels, 1972:120-21; italics in original). As has been often pointed out, women do not necessarily have significant social authority in societies practicing matrilineal inheritance (Schneider and Gough, 1962).

the nineteenth century. We also have the advantage of a peculiar and particularly appropriate book, Lévi-Strauss' *The Elementary Structures of Kinship*. This is the boldest twentieth-century version of the nineteenth-century project to understand human marriage. It is a book in which kinship is explicitly conceived of as an imposition of cultural organization upon the facts of biological procreation. It is permeated with an awareness of the importance of sexuality in human society. It is a description of society which does not assume an abstract, genderless human subject. On the contrary, the human subject in Lévi-Strauss's work is always either male or female, and the divergent social destinies of the two sexes can therefore be traced. Since Lévi-Strauss sees the essence of kinship systems to lie in an exchange of women between men, he constructs an implicit theory of sex oppression. . . .

. . . It was Mauss who first theorized as to the significance of one of the most striking features of primitive societies: the extent to which giving, receiving, and reciprocating gifts dominates social intercourse. In such societies, all sorts of things circulate in exchange—food, spells, rituals, words, names, ornaments, tools, and powers.

> Your own mother, your own sister, your own pigs, your own yams that you have piled up, you may not eat. Other people's mothers, other people's sisters, other people's pigs, other people's yams that they have piled up, you may eat. (Arapesh, cited in Lévi-Strauss, 1969:27)

In a typical gift transaction, neither party gains anything. In the Trobriand Islands, each household maintains a garden of yams and each household eats yams. But the yams a household grows and the yams it eats are not the same. At harvest time, a man sends the yams he has cultivated to the household of his sister; the household in which he lives is provisioned by his wife's brother (Malinowski, 1929). Since such a procedure appears to be a useless one from the point of view of accumulation or trade, its logic has been sought elsewhere. Mauss proposed that the significance of gift giving is that it expresses, affirms, or creates a social link between the partners of an exchange. Gift giving confers upon its participants a special relationship of trust, solidarity, and mutual aid. One can solicit a friendly relationship in the offer of a gift; acceptance implies a willingness to return a gift and a confirmation of the relationship. Gift exchange may also be the idiom of competition and rivalry. There are many examples in which one person humiliates another by giving more than can be reciprocated. Some political systems, such as the Big Man systems of highland New Guinea, are based on exchange which is unequal on the material plane. An aspiring Big Man wants to give away more goods than can be reciprocated. He gets his return in political prestige.

Although both Mauss and Lévi-Strauss emphasize the solidary aspects of gift exchange, the other purposes served by gift giving only strengthen the point that it is an ubiquitous means of social commerce. Mauss proposed that gifts were the threads of social discourse, the means by which such societies were held together in the absence of specialized governmental institutions. "The gift is the primitive way of achieving the peace that in civil society is secured by the state. . . . Composing society, the gift was the liberation of culture" (Sahlins, 1972:169, 175).

Lévi-Strauss adds to the theory of primitive reciprocity the idea that marriages are a most basic form of gift exchange, in which it is women who are the most precious of gifts. He argues that the incest taboo should best be understood as a mechanism to insure that such exchanges take place between families and between groups. Since the existence of incest taboos is universal, but the content of their prohibitions variable, they cannot be explained as having the aim of preventing the occurrence of genetically close matings. Rather, the incest taboo imposes the social aim of exogamy and alliance upon the biological events of sex and procreation. The incest taboo divides the universe of sexual choice into categories of permitted and prohibited sexual partners. Specifically, by forbidding unions within a group it enjoins marital exchange between groups.

> The prohibition on the sexual use of a daughter or a sister compels them to be given in marriage to another man, and at the same time it establishes a right to the daughter or sister of this other man. . . . The woman whom one does not take is, for that very reason, offered up. (Lévi-Strauss, 1969:51)

> The prohibition of incest is less a rule prohibiting marriage with the mother, sister, or daughter, than a rule obliging the mother, sister, or daughter to be given to others. It is the supreme rule of the gift. . . . (Ibid.:481)

The result of a gift of women is more profound than the result of other gift transactions, because the relationship thus established is not just one of reciprocity, but one of kinship. The exchange partners have become affines, and their descendents will be related by blood: "Two people may meet in friendship and exchange gifts and yet quarrel and fight in later times, but intermarriage connects them in a permanent manner" (Best, cited in Lévi-Strauss, 1969:481). . . .

. . . The exchange of women does not necessarily imply that women are objectified, in the modern sense, since objects in the primitive world are imbued with highly personal qualities. But it does imply a distinction between gift and giver. If women are the gifts, then it is men who are the exchange partners. And it is the partners, not the presents, upon whom reciprocal exchange confers its quasi-mystical power of social linkage. The relations of such a system are such that women are in no position to realize the benefits of their own circulation. As long as the relations specify that men exchange women, it is men who are the beneficiaries of the product of such exchanges—social organization.

> The total relationship of exchange which constitutes marriage is not established between a man and a woman, but between two groups of men, and the woman figures only as one of the objects in the exchange, not as one of the partners. . . . This remains true even when the girl's feelings are taken into consideration, as, moreover, is usually the case. In acquiescing to the proposed union, she precipitates or allows

the exchange to take place, she cannot alter its nature. . . . (Lévi-Strauss in ibid.:115)[3]

To enter into a gift exchange as a partner, one must have something to give. If women are for men to dispose of, they are in no position to give themselves away.

"What woman," mused a young Northern Melpa man, "is ever strong enough to get up and say, 'Let us make *moka,* let us find wives and pigs, let us give our daughters to men, let us wage war, let us kill our enemies!' No indeed not! . . . they are little rubbish things who stay at home simply, don't you see?" (Strathern, 1972:161)

What women indeed! The Melpa women of whom the young man spoke can't get wives, they *are* wives, and what they get are husbands, an entirely different matter. The Melpa women can't give their daughters to men, because they do not have the same rights in their daughters that their male kin have, rights of bestowal (although *not* of ownership).

The "exchange of women" is a seductive and powerful concept. It is attractive in that it places the oppression of women within social systems, rather than in biology. Moreover, it suggests that we look for the ultimate locus of women's oppression within the traffic in women, rather than within the traffic in merchandise. It is certainly not difficult to find ethnographic and historical examples of trafficking in women. Women are given in marriage, taken in battle, exchanged for favors, sent as tribute, traded, bought, and sold. Far from being confined to the "primitive" world, these practices seem only to become more pronounced and commercialized in more "civilized" societies. Men are of course also trafficked—but as slaves, hustlers, athletic stars, serfs, or as some other catastrophic social status, rather than as men. Women are transacted as slaves, serfs, and prostitutes, but also simply as women. And if men have been sexual subjects—exchangers—and women sexual semi-objects—gifts—for much of human history, then many customs, clichés, and personality traits seem to make a great deal of sense (among others, the curious custom by which a father gives away the bride).

The "exchange of women" is also a problematic concept. Since Lévi-Strauss argues that the incest taboo and the results of its application constitute the origin of culture, it can be deduced that the world historical defeat of women occurred with the origin of culture, and is a prerequisite of culture. If his analysis is adopted in its pure form, the feminist program must include a task even more onerous than the extermination of men; it must attempt to get rid of culture and substitute some entirely new phenomena on the face of the earth. However, it would be a dubious proposition at best to argue that if there were no exchange of

[3]This analysis of society as based on bonds between men by means of women makes the separatist responses of the women's movement thoroughly intelligible. Separatism can be seen as a mutation in social structure, as an attempt to form social groups based on unmediated bonds between women. It can also be seen as a radical denial of men's "rights" in women, and as a claim by women of rights in themselves.

women there would be no culture, if for no other reason than that culture is, by definition, inventive. It is even debatable that "exchange of women" adequately describes all of the empirical evidence of kinship systems. Some cultures, such as the Lele and the Luma, exchange women explicitly and overtly. In other cultures, the exchange of women can be inferred. In some—particularly those hunters and gatherers excluded from Lévi-Strauss's sample—the efficacy of the concept becomes altogether questionable. What are we to make of a concept which seems so useful and yet so difficult?

The "exchange of women" is neither a definition of culture nor a system in and of itself. The concept is an acute, but condensed, apprehension of certain aspects of the social relations of sex and gender. A kinship system is an imposition of social ends upon a part of the natural world. It is therefore "production" in the most general sense of the term: a molding, a transformation of objects (in this case, people) to and by a subjective purpose (for this sense of production, see Marx, 1971a:80–99). It has its own relations of production, distribution, and exchange, which include certain "property" forms in people. These forms are not exclusive, private property rights, but rather different sorts of rights that various people have in other people. Marriage transactions—the gifts and material which circulate in the ceremonies marking a marriage—are a rich source of data for determining exactly who has which rights in whom. It is not difficult to deduce from such transactions that in most cases women's rights are considerably more residual than those of men.

Kinship systems do not merely exchange women. They exchange sexual access, genealogical statuses, lineage names and ancestors, rights and *people*—men, women, and children—in concrete systems of social relationships. These relationships always include certain rights for men, others for women. "Exchange of women" is a shorthand for expressing that the social relations of a kinship system specify that men have certain rights in their female kin, and that women do not have the same rights either to themselves or to their male kin. In this sense, the exchange of women is a profound perception of a system in which women do not have full rights to themselves. The exchange of women becomes an obfuscation if it is seen as a cultural necessity, and when it is used as the single tool with which an analysis of a particular kinship system is approached.

If Lévi-Strauss is correct in seeing the exchange of women as a fundamental principle of kinship, the subordination of women can be seen as a product of the relationships by which sex and gender are organized and produced. The economic oppression of women is derivative and secondary. But there is an "economics" of sex and gender, and what we need is a political economy of sexual systems. We need to study each society to determine the exact mechanisms by which particular conventions of sexuality are produced and maintained. The "exchange of women" is an initial step toward building an arsenal of concepts with which sexual systems can be described.

Deeper into the Labyrinth

. . . Although every society has some sort of division of tasks by sex, the assignment of any particular task to one sex or the other varies enormously. In some groups, agriculture is the work of women, in others, the work of men. Women carry the heavy burdens in some societies, men in others. There are even examples of female hunters and warriors, and of men performing child-care tasks. Lévi-Strauss concludes from a survey of the division of labor by sex that it is not a biological specialization, but must have some other purpose. This purpose, he argues, is to insure the union of men and women by making the smallest viable economic unit contain at least one man and one woman.

> The very fact that it [the sexual division of labor] varies endlessly according to the society selected for consideration shows that . . . it is the mere fact of its existence which is mysteriously required, the form under which it comes to exist being utterly irrelevant, at least from the point of view of any natural necessity . . . the sexual division of labor is nothing else than a device to institute a reciprocal state of dependency between the sexes. (Lévi-Strauss, 1971:347-48)

The division of labor by sex can therefore be seen as a "taboo": a taboo against the sameness of men and women, a taboo dividing the sexes into two mutually exclusive categories, a taboo which exacerbates the biological differences between the sexes and thereby *creates* gender. The division of labor can also be seen as a taboo against sexual arrangements other than those containing at least one man and one woman, thereby enjoining heterosexual marriage. . . .

Gender is a socially imposed division of the sexes. It is a product of the social relations of sexuality. Kinship systems rest upon marriage. They therefore transform males and females into "men" and "women," each an incomplete half which can only find wholeness when united with the other. Men and women are, of course, different. But they are not as different as day and night, earth and sky, yin and yang, life and death. In fact, from the standpoint of nature, men and women are closer to each other than either is to anything else—for instance, mountains, kangaroos, or coconut palms. The idea that men and women are more different from one another than either is from anything else must come from somewhere other than nature. Furthermore, although there is an average difference between males and females on a variety of traits, the range of variation of those traits shows considerable overlap. There will always be some women who are taller than some men, for instance, even though men are on the average taller than women. But the idea that men and women are two mutually exclusive categories must arise out of something other than a nonexistent "natural" opposition. Far from being an expression of natural differences, exclusive gender identity is the suppression of natural similarities. It requires repression: in men, of whatever is the local version of "feminine" traits; in women, of the local definition of "masculine" traits. The division of the sexes has the effect of repressing some of the personality characteristics of virtually everyone, men and women. The same social system which oppresses women in its relations of exchange, oppresses everyone in its insistence upon a rigid division of personality.

Furthermore, individuals are engendered in order that marriage be guaranteed. Lévi-Strauss comes dangerously close to saying that heterosexuality is an instituted process. If biological and hormonal imperatives were as overwhelming as popular mythology would have them, it would hardly be necessary to insure heterosexual unions by means of economic interdependency. Moreover, the incest taboo presupposes a prior, less articulate taboo on homosexuality. A prohibition against *some* heterosexual unions assumes a taboo against *non*-heterosexual unions. Gender is not only an identification with one sex; it also entails that sexual desire be directed toward the other sex. The sexual division of labor is implicated in both aspects of gender—male and female it creates them, and it creates them heterosexual. The suppression of the homosexual component of human sexuality, and by corollary, the oppression of homosexuals, is therefore a product of the same system whose rules and relations oppress women. . . .

One last generality could be predicted as a consequence of the exchange of women under a system in which rights to women are held by men. What would happen if our hypothetical woman not only refused the man to whom she was promised, but asked for a woman instead? If a single refusal were disruptive, a double refusal would be insurrectionary. If each woman is promised to some man, neither has a right to dispose of herself. If two women managed to extricate themselves from the debt nexus, two other women would have to be found to replace them. As long as men have rights in women which women do not have in themselves, it would be sensible to expect that homosexuality in women would be subject to more suppression than in men.

In summary, some basic generalities about the organization of human sexuality can be derived from an exegesis of Lévi-Strauss's theories of kinship. These are the incest taboo, obligatory heterosexuality, and an asymmetric division of the sexes. The asymmetry of gender—the difference between exchanger and exchanged—entails the constraint of female sexuality. Concrete kinship systems will have more specific conventions, and these conventions vary a great deal. While particular socio-sexual systems vary, each one is specific, and individuals within it will have to conform to a finite set of possibilities. Each new generation must learn and become its sexual destiny, each person must be encoded with its appropriate status within the system. . . .

Anthropology, and descriptions of kinship systems, do not explain the mechanisms by which children are engraved with the conventions of sex and gender. Psychoanalysis, on the other hand, is a theory about the reproduction of kinship. Psychoanalysis describes the residue left within individuals by their confrontation with the rules and regulations of sexuality of the societies to which they are born. . . .

. . . Psychoanalysis provides a description of the mechanisms by which the sexes are divided and deformed, of how bisexual, androgynous infants are transformed into boys and girls. Psychoanalysis is a feminist theory *manqué*.

The Oedipus Hex

. . . It is in explaining the acquisition of "femininity" that Freud employs the concepts of penis envy and castration which have infuriated feminists since he first introduced them. The girl turns from the mother and represses the "masculine" elements of her libido as a result of her recognition that she is castrated.

She compares her tiny clitoris to the larger penis, and in the face of its evident superior ability to satisfy the mother, falls prey to penis envy and a sense of inferiority. She gives up her struggle for the mother and assumes a passive feminine position vis-à-vis the father. Freud's account can be read as claiming that femininity is a consequence of the anatomical differences between the sexes. He has therefore been accused of biological determinism. Nevertheless, even in his most anatomically stated versions of the female castration complex, the "inferiority" of the woman's genitals is a product of the situational context: the girl feels less "equipped" to possess and satisfy the mother. If the pre-Oedipal lesbian were not confronted by the heterosexuality of the mother, she might draw different conclusions about the relative status of her genitals. . . .

Kinship, Lacan, and the Phallus

Lacan suggests that psychoanalysis is the study of the traces left in the psyches of individuals as a result of their conscription into systems of kinship. . . . Kinship is the culturalization of biological sexuality on the societal level; psycho-analysis describes the transformation of the biological sexuality of individuals as they are enculturated. . . .

The Oedipal complex is an apparatus for the production of sexual personal-ity. It is a truism to say that societies will inculcate in their young the character traits appropriate to carrying on the business of society. For instance, E. P. Thompson (1963) speaks of the transformation of the personality structure of the English working class, as artisans were changed into good industrial workers. Just as the social forms of labor demand certain kinds of personality, the social forms of sex and gender demand certain kinds of people. In the most general terms, the Oedipal complex is a machine which fashions the appropriate forms of sexual individuals (see also the discussion of different forms of "historical individuality" in Althusser and Balibar, 1970:112, 251-53).

In the Lacanian theory of psychoanalysis, it is the kin terms that indicate a structure of relationships which will determine the role of any individual or object within the Oedipal drama. For instance, Lacan makes a distinction between the "function of the father" and a particular father who embodies this function. In the same way, he makes a radical distinction between the penis and the "phallus," between organ and information. The phallus is a set of meanings conferred upon the penis. . . .

In Freud's terminology, the Oedipal complex presents two alternatives to a child: to have a penis or to be castrated. In contrast, the Lacanian theory of the castration complex leaves behind all reference to anatomical reality. . . . The alternative presented to the child may be rephrased as an alternative between having, or not having, the phallus. Castration is not having the (symbolic) phallus. Castration is not a real "lack," but a meaning conferred upon the genitals of a woman. . . . The phallus is, as it were, a distinctive feature differentiating "castrated" and "noncastrated." The presence or absence of the phallus carries the differences between two sexual statuses, "man" and "woman" (see Jakobson and Halle, 1971, on distinctive features). Since these are not equal, the phallus also carries a meaning of the dominance of men over women, and it may be inferred that "penis envy" is a recognition thereof. Moreover, as long as men have rights in women which women do not have in themselves, the phallus also carries the meaning of the difference between "exchanger" and "exchanged," gift and giver. . . .

Oedipus Revisited

. . . Freud's theory of femininity has been subjected to feminist critique since it was first published. To the extent that it is a rationalization of female subordination, this critique has been justified. To the extent that it is a description of a process which subordinates women, this critique is a mistake. As a description of how phallic culture domesticates women, and the effects in women of their domestication, psychoanalytic theory has no parallel (see also Mitchell, 1971 and 1974; Lasch, 1974). And since psychoanalysis is a theory of gender, dismissing it would be suicidal for a political movement dedicated to eradicating gender hierarchy (or gender itself). We cannot dismantle something that we underestimate or do not understand. The oppression of women is deep; equal pay, equal work, and all of the female politicians in the world will not extirpate the roots of sexism. Lévi-Strauss and Freud elucidate what would otherwise be poorly perceived parts of the deep structures of sex oppression. They serve as reminders of the intractability and magnitude of what we fight, and their analyses provide preliminary charts of the social machinery we must rearrange.

Women Unite to Off the Oedipal Residue of Culture

The precision of the fit between Freud and Lévi-Strauss is striking. Kinship systems require a division of the sexes. The Oedipal phase divides the sexes. Kinship systems include sets of rules governing sexuality. The Oedipal crisis is the assimilation of these rules and taboos. Compulsory heterosexuality is the product of kinship. The Oedipal phase constitutes heterosexual desire. Kinship rests on a radical difference between the rights of men and women. The Oedipal complex confers male rights upon the boy, and forces the girl to accommodate herself to her lesser rights.

This fit between Lévi-Strauss and Freud is by implication an argument that our sex/gender system is still organized by the principles outlined by Lévi-Strauss, despite the entirely nonmodern character of his data base. The more recent data on which Freud bases his theories testifies to the endurance of these sexual structures. If my reading of Freud and Lévi-Strauss is accurate, it suggests that the feminist movement must attempt to resolve the Oedipal crisis of culture by reorganizing the domain of sex and gender in such a way that each individual's Oedipal experience would be less destructive. The dimensions of such a task are difficult to imagine, but at least certain conditions would have to be met.

Several elements of the Oedipal crisis would have to be altered in order that the phase not have such disastrous effects on the young female ego. The Oedipal phase institutes a contradiction in the girl by placing irreconcilable demands upon her. On the one hand, the girl's love for the mother is induced by the mother's job of child care. The girl is then forced to abandon this love because of the female sex role—to belong to a man. If the sexual division of labor were such that adults of both sexes cared for children equally, primary object choice would be bisexual. If heterosexuality were not obligatory, this early love would not have to be suppressed, and the penis would not be overvalued. If the sexual property system were reorganized in such a way that men did not have overriding rights in women (if there was no exchange of women) and if there were no gender, the entire Oedipal drama would be a relic. In short, feminism must call for a revolution in kinship.

The organization of sex and gender once had functions other than itself—it organized society. Now, it only organizes and reproduces itself. The kinds of relationships of sexuality established in the dim human past still dominate our sexual lives, our ideas about men and women, and the ways we raise our children. But they lack the functional load they once carried. One of the most conspicuous features of kinship is that it has been systematically stripped of its functions—political, economic, educational, and organizational. It has been reduced to its barest bones—*sex and gender.*

Human sexual life will always be subject to convention and human intervention. It will never be completely "natural," if only because our species is social, cultural, and articulate. The wild profusion of infantile sexuality will always be tamed. The confrontation between immature and helpless infants and the developed social life of their elders will probably always leave some residue of disturbance. But the mechanisms and aims of this process need not be largely independent of conscious choice. Cultural evolution provides us with the opportunity to seize control of the means of sexuality, reproduction, and socialization, and to make conscious decisions to liberate human sexual life from the archaic relationships which deform it. Ultimately, a thoroughgoing feminist revolution would liberate more than women. It would liberate forms of sexual expression, and it would liberate human personality from the straightjacket of gender. . . .

The Political Economy of Sex

It would be nice to be able to conclude here with the implications for feminism and gay liberation of the overlap between Freud and Lévi-Strauss. But I must suggest, tentatively, a next step on the agenda: a Marxian analysis of sex/gender systems. Sex/gender systems are not ahistorical emanations of the human mind; they are products of historical human activity.

We need, for instance, an analysis of the evolution of sexual exchange along the lines of Marx's discussion in *Capital* of the evolution of money and commodities. There is an economics and a politics to sex/gender systems which is obscured by the concept of "exchange of women." . . .

In short, there are other questions to ask of a marriage system than whether or not it exchanges women. Is the woman traded for a woman, or is there an equivalent? Is this equivalent only for women, or can it be turned into something else? If it can be turned into something else, is it turned into political power or wealth? On the other hand, can bridewealth be obtained only in marital exchange, or can it be obtained from elsewhere? Can women be accumulated through amassing wealth? Can wealth be accumulated by disposing of women? Is a marriage system part of a system of stratification?

These last questions point to another task for a political economy of sex. Kinship and marriage are always parts of total social systems, and are always tied into economic and political arrangements. . . .

. . . Sexual systems cannot, in the final analysis, be understood in complete isolation. A full-bodied analysis of women in a single society, or throughout history, must take *everything* into account: the evolution of commodity forms in women, systems of land tenure, political arrangements, subsistence technology, etc. Equally important, economic and political analyses are incomplete if they do not consider women, marriage, and sexuality. . . .

This sort of endeavor is, in the final analysis, exactly what Engels tried to do in his effort to weave a coherent analysis of so many of the diverse aspects of social life. He tried to relate men and women, town and country, kinship and state, forms of property, systems of land tenure, convertibility of wealth, forms of exchange, the technology of food production, and forms of trade, to name a few, into a systematic historical account. Eventually, someone will have to write a new version of *The Origin of the Family, Private Property, and the State,* recognizing the mutual interdependence of sexuality, economics, and politics without underestimating the full significance of each in human society.

SUGGESTIONS FOR FURTHER READING: Part II

This selected bibliography does not include those important works from which excerpts appear already in this book. The reader is reminded that in Part III of this book the feminist theories are applied to specific problems. Hence, the suggestions for further reading which are given at the end of the sections on work, the family, and sexuality also constitute further readings in feminist theory.

Bunch, Charlotte, and Nancy Myron: *Class and Feminism,* Diana Press, Baltimore, 1974.
de Beauvoir, Simone: *The Second Sex,* Knopf, New York, 1953.
Koedt, Anne, Ellen Levine, and Anita Rapone: *Radical Feminism,* Quadrangle/The New York Times Book Company, 1973.
Lenin, V. I.: *The Emancipation of Women,* International Publishers, New York, 1934.
Millett, Kate: *Sexual Politics,* Avon Books, New York, 1971.
Wollstonecraft, Mary: *A Vindication of the Rights of Woman,* 1792.

The following are discussions (both academic and popular) which focus specifically on the concept of women's nature and its political implications.

Broverman, Inge K., et al.: "Sex Role Stereotypes and Clinical Judgements of Mental Health," *Journal of Consulting and Clinical Psychology,* vol. 34, no. 1, February 1970.

Chesler, Phyllis: *Women and Madness,* Doubleday, New York, 1972.

Mead, Margaret: *Sex and Temperament in Three Savage Societies,* Apollo, New York, 1967.

Pierce, Christine: "Natural Law, Language, and Women," in Vivian Gornick and Barbara K. Moran (eds.), *Women in Sexist Society,* Basic Books, New York, 1971.

Trebilcot, Joyce: "Sex Roles: The Argument from Nature," *Ethics,* vol. 85, pp. 249–255, 1975.

Weisstein, Naomi: *Kinder, Kuche, Kirche as Scientific Law: Psychology Constructs the Female,* New England Free Press, Boston, 1968. Reprinted in a revised version in many feminist anthologies.

Women: A Journal of Liberation. Volume 1, number 1 is devoted to the topic "Inherent Nature or Cultural Conditioning" and contains several interesting articles, including "Training the Woman to Know Her Place: The Power of a Nonconscious Ideology," by Sandra L. and Daryl J. Bem.

Part III

Practice: The Implications
of the Theories

FILLING IN THE FRAMEWORKS:
WORK

There is no career more exciting or exacting for a woman than marriage to a great man.

Mrs. Georgina Battiscombe
In her biography of Mrs. Gladstone

By middle age, when men are at their best, a devoted woman worker is apt to degenerate into fussiness or worse.

Margaret Pickel, 1946

We must start with the realization that, as much as women want to be good scientists or engineers, they want first and foremost to be womanly companions for men.

Bruno Bettelheim

But no one can evade the fact, that in taking up a masculine calling, studying, and working in a man's way, woman is doing something not wholly in agreement with, if not directly injurious to, her feminine nature.

Carl Jung

True women's liberation does not lie in a formalistic or material equality with the other sex, but in the recognition of that specific in the feminine personality—the ability of a woman to be a mother.

Pope Paul VI

As we saw in Part I, women tend to be paid considerably less than men for doing the same work. We are systematically excluded from certain professions and trades and systematically tracked into others. The work we are encouraged to perform in society at large tends to be an extension of the tasks we are expected to perform within the home and family. Women are heavily represented in the service areas, social work, nursing, primary school teaching, etc., and systematically excluded from other kinds of work. It is now notorious that opportunities for women and men to receive education and to acquire various skills differ markedly. From an early age girl children and boy children are encouraged to develop different physical and mental capacities and to form markedly different expectations about their future options.

The ways we explain and evaluate the sexual division of labor will differ dramatically depending upon the particular theoretical framework we use to organize and evaluate social reality. For example, while the existence of a sexual division of labor will be seen as problematic according to most frameworks, at least one, the conservative, will fail to identify the division as a problem at all.

CONSERVATISM

As we have seen, the conservative tends to view human beings as possessing fundamentally innate and unchangeable capacities. It is not surprising, then, to find that conservatism regards the pronounced sexual division of labor in contemporary society as the natural expression of the biological differences between women and men. Conservatives point to differences in physiology, hormonal balance, and genetic composition as suiting women and men for different tasks. Some crude versions of conservative theory actually claim that women (unlike men) are biologically suited to perform repetitive detailed labor for long periods of time. Others argue that women alone are suited to caring for young children because they are naturally patient and passive and thus can cope with the isolation of the individual household and the constant demands of infants and small children.

Other more sophisticated versions of conservative theory, like the one offered by Tiger and Fox, propose a seemingly less mechanistic account of the relation between biology and sex roles. In the selection included here they emphasize different "emotional, intellectual and social skills and enthusiasm" as the basis for what they maintain is a virtually universal division of labor according to gender.

What is crucial about the conservative theory is that it treats the sexual division of labor as essentially natural and usually goes on to equate the perpetuation of this "natural" division with a just and good state of affairs. It gives little if any consideration to the role of socialization in maintaining the sexual division of labor and tends to ignore anthropological evidence citing societies in which heavy manual labor is routinely the responsibility of women rather than of men. In fact, it ignores our own recent experience in the United States, where during World War II thousands of women were mobilized to take over jobs in heavy industry vacated by men who went off to fight.

LIBERALISM

The liberal theorist is less concerned with the origins of the sexual division of labor than with bringing about the equitable treatment of all members of society in the present. This is understandable when we remind ourselves that liberalism grew up as a theory to press for the legal and social rights of the rising bourgeoisie against a feudal order which apportioned rights on the basis of birth and inherited position. Liberalism argues for the equal opportunity of all human beings to acquire education and training commensurate with their ability and the opportunity to use that training to achieve whatever place in the society the individual is able. Thus liberalism maintains, not that all individuals can attain the same achievement or fulfillment, but rather that gender in itself is no more a proper criterion for determining what opportunities an individual should have than was nobility of birth. Given equal opportunity, different individuals will prove themselves suited to different jobs and careers, and the removal of discrimination in the area of employment will permit all individuals to fulfill themselves to the greatest extent.

Appeals to individual self-fulfillment and distributive justice are not the only arguments that the liberal uses in defending the distribution of jobs through a competition in which each individual has an equal opportunity. This method of job distribution is also claimed to maximize each individual's contribution to society as a whole. Hence we find in liberal feminist writings, from Mary Wollstonecraft and J. S. Mill right up to the present time, constant references to the general advantages which are supposed to accrue to society through the fuller utilization of women's talents. It is interesting to note that these liberal feminist arguments are merely applications of Adam Smith's classic belief that when each individual pursues her or his own economic self-interest, the "invisible hand" of Providence, working through a market economy, will coordinate these selfish strivings so that the net consequences are to the benefit of all.

In the contemporary period, liberal feminists, especially the National Organization for Women, have been the moving force behind the campaign to pass the Equal Rights Amendment (the ERA). Focusing on discrimination in employment as a major problem facing women today, the liberal feminist seeks to obtain legal equality for women in the areas of employment and business. A parallel struggle is also being carried out within the labor union movement, where female workers find that a predominantly male union leadership is often unconcerned with the particular problems of women, who lack seniority and job security within the trades and who are excluded entirely from many trade unions. Patricia Cayo Sexton writes on the composition and goals of the founding convention of the Coalition of Labor Union Women (CLUW).

TRADITIONAL MARXISM

Traditional Marxism opposes the discrimination that keeps some women out of the industrial labor force entirely and relegates others to the lowest ranks of the force. However, it does not believe that this discrimination can be entirely eliminated as long as capitalism persists. This, it says, is because the existence of a group of poorly paid workers who can be marshalled in and out of the workforce at will is crucial if the capitalist is to maintain and increase profits. Profits depend on having workers produce considerably more value than is returned to them in the form of their wages. We call this "surplus value." The capitalist wishes to extract as much labor as possible from workers while keeping their wages as low as possible. Because of competition between workers for jobs, low wages paid to women and third-world workers keep the average wage of all workers down. In addition, the existence of a pool of nonemployed but potential workers means that all employed workers know that others are available to take their jobs if their productivity falls, and bosses are quick to point this out. For these reasons, the traditional Marxist argues that sexism

in the form of discrimination against women workers is not accidental but a necessary aspect of capitalism. The way to struggle against sexism, according to this
interpretation, is to struggle against capitalism. The Marxist urges that women
become part of the industrial labor force so that as members of the working class
they can struggle with men to overthrow the system of private property and class
domination, which, it is felt, is at the root of women's oppression. The reader is urged
to review the concluding pages of Engels's discussion in Part II of this volume for the
classic statement of this position.

In this section Margaret Benston provides a contemporary version of Engels's
analysis of the relation between woman's work and her status in society. In particular, Benston asks whether women's labor occupies a unique position within the
economy at large. She concludes that, for the most part, women, even those who
work outside the home, are given exclusive responsibility for housework, which
under our system of commodity production is not considered "real" work. She
concludes that housework must be industrialized in order to be recognized as
significant, and women must be integrated into public labor if the basis for their
oppression is to be removed. To this end, the traditional Marxist believes that
obtaining legal equality for women will not liberate us but that it is a preliminary step
to exposing the differences in power and wealth that predominate in class society
and rob all working people of dignity and freedom.

Many Marxists support the ERA because they agree with Engels that it is
important to expose the inadequacy of establishing mere legal equality. Passage of
the ERA will help people realize that women will not have genuine equality as long as
they are economically dependent on men. Other Marxists oppose the ERA on the
grounds that it will bring little if any relief to working-class women. They see it as a
threat to the gains made in protective legislation by all workers and fear that bosses
will use it as an excuse to remove rules mandating rest periods, prohibiting manda-
tory night work, etc., many of which were originally instituted to permit women equal
access to jobs. In addition, they fear that emphasis on the ERA will delude women
into defining equality in legalistic terms so that feminists will mistakenly hail the
passage of the ERA as a kind of ultimate victory without recognizing that a formal
end to discrimination will leave untouched the inequalities in wealth and power that
have the fundamental determining effect on people's lives.

RADICAL FEMINISM

It is more than accidental that so few radical feminists have concerned themselves
with the specific situation of women at the work place. They acknowledge the
discrimination that women workers face in contemporary society, but, unlike the
Marxists, they place no special emphasis on this aspect of women's oppression.
Work is merely one of the many areas which reflect the deeper biological/psychologi-
cal antagonisms which lie at the root of women's situation. Some radical feminists
accept the need for a class analysis and others reject it; but since all radical feminists
see a sexual division as underlying their problem and as even more basic than the
class division of society, they believe that the struggle against oppression is not to be
carried out in the work place or by focusing on women as workers. They feel we must
direct our attention to the totality of cultural institutions and relations that define
women's subordinate status.

Insofar as radical feminists do concern themselves with women and work, they
are likely to take a position similar to the one Jennifer Woodul elaborates in her

article included in this section. Woodul sees feminist businesses as an important way for women to gain actual power in the world. To this end the radical feminist maintains that it is important for women to learn every aspect of business life and to find ways to create new kinds of structures and new forms of organization that will permit women to work together in ways which are not exploitative. Preliminary efforts in this area include the establishment of feminist banks, credit unions, gynecological and abortion clinics, restaurants, bookshops, etc.

On the surface there would appear to be considerable similarity in the response that liberal feminists and radical feminists make to the discrimination experienced by women in the work world. Both wish to organize aspects of economic life so that women may hold positions of power. The significant difference in their reactions is that liberals see power for women in society as it exists as being an end in itself. Radical feminists, on the other hand, view the achievement of power for women in the existing system as being merely the way to enable women to force significant changes in that system.

SOCIALIST FEMINISM

The socialist feminist is concerned as much with women's work in the home as with women's work in the industrial labor force. In the labor force women's generally inferior status assures the capitalist of obtaining the most labor for the least pay. Because women are taught to consider their roles as wives and mothers as primary, we accept lower-rank jobs at disproportionately low wages and can be marshalled in and out of the workforce according to the needs of the capitalists.

Socialist feminist theory rejects the dichotomy between home/family and work place that is maintained by virtually every other theory. Instead it argues that domestic work is indeed work. Different socialist theories have offered different kinds of analyses of the nature of women's work in the home, focusing at times on women's role in reproducing labor power, at other times on women's role in facilitating the consumption of commodities (cooking macaroni so that it becomes edible), at other times on our responsibility for providing emotional support to men; but all socialist feminist theories maintain that understanding the nature of domestic labor and its role in maintaining the exploitation of the class society as a whole is a crucial task for feminist thinkers. Further examination of socialist feminist views on domestic work appears in our discussion of the socialist feminist analysis of the family.

Because they conceive the relationship between so-called "public" and "private" labor as so intimate and so crucial for capitalism, some socialist feminists maintain that challenging women's domestic functions and liberating us from them will in itself strike a significant blow against the class system. Along these lines a demand for wages for housework grew up within the women's movement in Italy. The demand spread rapidly because of its immediate appeal. Giuliana Pompei, a spokesperson for the movement, argues that this demand will win recognition for women's invisible labor in the home because it will give it status as real work while not subjecting women to the alienating and debilitating aspects of factory labor. Carole Lopate argues that the wages-for-housework demand is poorly conceived because it would leave unchanged the relations in the home and the tasks that are defined by the needs and in the interests of capitalism. The whole institution of the nuclear family as a private sphere operating to buttress the capitalist system needs to be reevaluated.

CONSERVATISM

Give and Take

Lionel Tiger and Robin Fox

One thing that every system has to take into account is the sexual division of labor. We have maintained elsewhere in this book that the degree and nature of the participation of men and women in the economy is very different. We suggested that this goes back to the evolution of the hunting animal, where male and female were assigned radically different tasks, each essential to the success and survival of the group, and that therefore they were subjected to very different kinds of selection pressure. We can come to the same conclusions about economic as political division of labor, but the details differ insofar as women are of necessity deeply involved in the economy at the same time that they are shut out completely from any political activity. But it can be predicted that in each case men will want to keep them from controlling the system, and women will be unlikely to make effective inroads on any scale into the centers of economic power. The roots of this dilemma are deep in our history. Women did not hunt.

Some of the physical differences between males and females, which are related to different roles during our formative evolution, have already been discussed, but it is necessary here to note some of them briefly in order to root behavior directly in its biological context. These differences are first of all based on clear reproductive distinctions. Female reproductive physiology places simple structural limits on what women can do. They must have wider pelvises than men, because the birth canal must accommodate the infant's large head; therefore they use more energy in locomotion, because their hips swing wider from side to side. In addition, the fat deposits on their buttocks are heavy and use up precious energy. Accordingly, women cannot run as quickly or for as long as men. Of course, there is a normal curve of variation here as elsewhere, and some women will run faster than some men; the curve of variations of the male and female will overlap, but the curves are nonetheless real and significant. This is true also of the ability to throw objects such as balls and spears—a matter obviously relevant to a hunting animal. Furthermore, females adapt less readily than males to changes in temperature—a considerable hazard in hot environments. We now know that there are predictable and disruptive effects on female performance that depend on their menstrual cycles; and it remains an abiding index of male callousness to female realities that rarely are these normal and foreseeable stimuli considered in arranging work and even domestic schedules. (This can become positively inequitable when females are engaged in crucial tests of various kinds. For example, some reports indicate that females achieve some fourteen-percent-lower grades on examination during the premenstrual days, when they are at a considerable disadvantage. Depending on the nature of the examination in question, a woman may be affected for her entire career because she could not demonstrate the ability she normally has. Conversely, if she were to confront this examination at mid-cycle, her performance might be better than usual. In another milieu, the first female Russian astronaut has argued that while women could do the tasks men do, it was still necessary to take the menstrual cycle into account in managing the routines of space flight.)

There is a series of other differences of this kind that could be described, but it is clearly more relevant today to focus less upon explicitly physical features of work performance than upon those involving emotional, intellectual, and social skills and enthusiasm. There are, after all, relatively few jobs in industrial societies that demand strength of arm and speed of foot so greedily that females could not meet the needs. Women can and do drive huge trucks and airplanes, operate elaborate machines, and physically cope with the air-conditioned cabins and power-assisted controls of huge cranes and earth movers. There is very little justification for assuming that any job that men now do women could not do too. And vice versa: aside from bearing and suckling children, there is no characteristically women's work that some husky baritone copilot could not do. Our ideas about equality and the right to widespread social participation of men and women all urge us overwhelmingly in the direction of a society in which male and female roles are more or less interchangeable and in which no particular cachet or stigma attaches to men doing what was once women's work, or the other way around.

But the reality falls far short of the ideal. The potentialities are felt only weakly in what actually still goes on. One of the few general rules about human cultures that anthropologists can safely affirm is that in all known societies a distinction is made between "women's work" and "men's work." The inconsistencies in attitudes are plentiful and comical from one society to another; in one place, men will carry water and women will plant yams, while ten villages away the inhabitants will defend with high intensity the obviously correct proposition that women must carry water and men plant yams. So the first point is that even where the distinctions are not especially reasonable or defensible, they are inevitably made. The next general feature of this division of labor by sex is that some jobs are widely thought to be the rightful provinces of males, and others of females. Hunting, the manufacture of weapons, and the construction of boats are almost universally thought to be male, while such tasks as grinding seeds and gathering nuts are reckoned females' work nearly everywhere. This follows understandably from the hunting past.

But what is not easily understandable is the extraordinary persistence of the division of labor by sex in societies with different forms and levels of industrialization, different climates, different histories, and varying notions about the good man, the good woman, and the good life. This must be explained.

We have already indicated how persistent male-female differences both baffled ideologists and violated the laws of chance. There is no particular reason why females must be part of formal politics. But women must work, and they must be part of the economy, any economy. Of course, in broad terms, they always are, to the extent that they do housework, prepare food, mind and socialize children, and attend to the clothing of their family. That this is not regarded as work in the sense that factory labor is, is a conceit of economic analysis, and part, besides, of a general devaluation of intimate (as opposed to public) activity—a devaluation that applies to the do-it-yourself man who contributes nothing to the Gross National Product when he builds himself a bookshelf but pushes it up two hundred dollars when he buys one from a shop. Women have to be in on the economy. But a basic element of the biogrammar here seems to be that they have to be in on only specially defined terms: there appears to be a tendency to define some work as female and some as male, and to maintain the distinction whatever the content and whatever the cost. This is the same principle of male-bond-female-exclusion that, in politics, so rudely circumscribed the female role. In economic matters, since females cannot be excluded totally, at least they can be segregated into some set specific activities.

But does it go deeper even than this? We argued that the central arena of politics was male because of differences in male and female potentials for successful large-scale competitive bonding. Insofar as the central arena of economic life demands similar organization, we would expect males to dominate it. Where business and industry, or the organization of production consumption and exchange, generally demand cohort activity, it will be male cohorts who will be in evidence. Where control is involved, men will work together and women will be excluded or allowed in only if they agree to play male roles in a male fashion. Women usually lend themselves to this strategy by agreeing that it is not specific female skills that they bring to their roles as executives, and that in simply filling male positions they are substitute males. This attitude strictly delimits female behavior in business.

It also accounts for the pressures against overt sexuality on the job. Seductive arts are disruptive of male cohesion. The outlaw band or the board of directors assumes that they are not part of its normal routines, and women who want seriously to play the power game must leave their false eyelashes at home.

This may seem a facetious point, but it is a point that underlies a very serious truth. False eyelashes are supplements to female courtship-display behavior. They enhance the "recognition flutter" and coy covering of the dilating pupils in courtship exchanges. As such they are part of the apparatus that aids in promoting and cementing the courtship bond. This is a male-female bond and operates in the arena of sexual competition and eventual mating. It is outside of and inimical to the male-made bond that operates in the politicoeconomic arena for purpose of cohort formation and maintenance in the pursuit of effective defense and predation. This is a point difficult, of course, to prove, yet it seems clear enough: that one serious if tragicomic reason for the difficulty females experience in male work groups is not that males dislike females but rather that the force of their enthusiasm for females can disrupt the work and endanger the integrity of groups of men.

We needn't waste sympathy on men harassed by such enthusiasm for women that they reject them as colleagues and force them into occupational ghettos so the precious male mystique will remain undisturbed. Our suggestion is that it is not malice alone, and not prejudice only, and not just cultural lag and individual fear that stimulate an obvious antifemale inequity. The same pattern emerges both in countries that devalue women and in countries that eagerly support them. The opportunities for women in the economy of the United States have declined over the past sixty years, though the number of women with advanced and technical education has increased enormously. The Israeli experience, both in and out of the kibbutz, is even more discouraging to those who looked to their ideology about sexual equality to produce radical social change. And in Russia itself, the first and most important revolutionary society, the position of women has not been improved in any sense commensurate with either the expressed idealism of the community or its willingness to try relatively egalitarian socioeconomic forms and approaches to the ownership and control of wealth.

So it cannot be a conspiracy of men against women that once swept the world that now—so apparently securely—sets limits to the range of female options to enter the powerful macrostructures of economic life. The evidence against conspiracy comes from too heterogeneous a set of places: females are obviously able to do the tasks men can—that is, when they are given the opportunity; males are unlikely to have deliberately thought up ways of maintaining women in their homes for domestic and sexual convenience and then brainwashed them to accept such an exploitative situation—if exploitative it is. Perhaps, as with some of the other bonds, we are dealing here with a regularity of the biogrammar that has to do with ancient forms of survival that mark us still today. That the thrilling and elaborate innovations of our technology seem to have relatively little effect on the work relationships of men and women attests either to the unimportance of technology—which is foolish—or to the importance of the biogrammar. Though puritans and Calvinists will shrink at the thought, it may be true that social relationships are more important than work encounters, and the apparent rigidity of the sexual division of labor represents both men and women "voting with their feet" for the notion that difference does not necessarily connote inferiority or superiority, and that the division of labor is not necessarily the squalid display of human invidiousness that, for example, racism undoubtedly is. The sexual division of labor has no racial home. The analogy is faulty because sex differences are important biologically and tangible behaviorally, whereas racial ones are unimportant biologically and meaningless behaviorally. The bad analogy confuses policy even more than it confuses people: to avoid the consequences of racism, it is imperative that all people be treated equally, but to avoid the features of the sexual division of labor that many men and women find undesirable, it may be necessary to treat men and women differently and not deny their real biologies in the name of theoretical equities. . . .

LIBERALISM

In Support of the ERA

Maureen Reagan

Equality of rights under the law shall not be denied or abridged by the United States or by any State on account of sex.

Strange how these 24 words, which could do so much for all of us, have managed to frighten many people in our country.

The proposed 27th Amendment to the Constitution, when ratified, will guarantee total equality for women in every state in the Union. ERA will ensure an examination of the codes of law in all 50 states and call for a strict prohibition of discrimination based on sex.

With all the benefits awaiting womankind—to say nothing of mankind— why all the fuss and the furor over ratification? Why the battle? Why are some women uninformed, misinformed or downright uninterested?

For the last year I have been speaking all over the country for the Equal Rights Amendment. I have seen women in doubt and listened to women who fear the possibilities of equality. They imagine themselves sharing washrooms with the opposite sex, supporting their families singlehanded, seeing their daughters drafted into the military and forced onto a battlefield—all this if the Equal Rights Amendment becomes law. To dislodge these misconceptions, I would like to get at the truths—just what the ERA represents, what women stand to gain.

The basic principle of the Equal Rights Amendment is that if a law restricts women's rights, that law no longer will be valid; if it protects women, that protection will be extended to men. ERA concerns legal attitudes, not personal relationships. Who opens the door, who takes out the garbage, who brings home the pay check, are not legal concerns. ERA does not mean that women who wish to be homemakers will be legally forced into the job market. If a couple decide that the husband will work outside the home and the wife will work within it, that is a private matter, between the two of them. The ERA ensures only that if a woman chooses to work outside her home and finds a job, her pay will be equal to that of a man holding a similar job.

This concept of equal rights is not a new one. For 200 years America's women have struggled for the rights that would be accorded them under ERA—equality in all areas of life, financial, legal and social. Abigail Adams was one of the earliest advocates. On May 7, 1776, she sent her now-celebrated letter to her husband John, hard at work in Philadelphia helping to draft the Declaration of Independence:

"In the new code of laws which I suppose it will be necessary for you to make," she wrote, "I desire that you would remember the ladies and be more generous and favorable to them than your ancestors. Remember that all men would be tyrants if they could. If particular attention is not paid to the ladies, we are determined to foment a rebellion and will not hold ourselves bound by any laws in which we have no voice or representation.''

But Adams replied, ''Depend on it, we know better than to repeal our masculine systems.'' And indeed, after stating its purpose, the Declaration of Independence goes on to say; ''We hold these truths to be self-evident, that all *men* are created equal . . .'' (italics mine).

But that did not end women's fight for equality. Throughout the 19th century, women activists complained openly of their lack of franchise and worked diligently for suffrage. Essayist Fanny Fern heard a woman comment that the vote was totally unimportant to womanhood and was prompted to remark, ''I feel pity in this glorious year of our Lord, 1869, that she should still prefer going back to the Dark Ages.'' Writer Margaret Fuller said it earlier and even more succinctly in 1845: ''We would have every arbitrary barrier thrown down, we would have every path laid open to woman as freely as to man.''

Elizabeth Blackwell, the first woman graduate of a medical school; Victoria Woodhull, the first woman candidate for President; Elizabeth Cady Stanton and Susan B. Anthony, political activists—these were only a few of the thousands of women who worked unceasingly for equal opportunity.

With the ratification of the 19th Amendment, in 1920, women finally won the vote—but not full equality under the law. An equal-rights amendment would bring about that equality. But in spite of Congressional passage of ERA in 1972, until four more states join the 34 that have already ratified it the amendment cannot become law.

How would the Federal ERA affect state law? ERA would go into effect nationwide two years after its ratification, giving each state time to determine which of its laws restricts rights, which must be amended and which must be repealed. Here in California, we have been working on an examination of our codes since ratifying the proposed 27th Amendment in 1972. To demonstrate the complexities of the task: The legislature passed a credit law for women, proving by the mere necessity for such legislation that discrimination against women in credit transactions did exist.

But it immediately became apparent that this new bill did not deal with the particular problems of married women. When buying property, for example, a couple often were forced to omit the working wife's earnings from the credit application—consequently, from a practical standpoint, reducing the amount of money they could expect to borrow. Why? Because the bank, unhindered by a law against discrimination, would not accept a wife's income as security for a loan. What if she became pregnant and stopped working? bank officials reasoned.

This is truly an interference in the couple's private life, plus an assumption that they cannot be trusted to manage their financial affairs sensibly. Such interference is not possible under ERA. California now has a separate credit law just for married women. A piecemeal approach, admittedly—but without an equal rights amendment for 200 years, we have to keep adding and changing laws to make up for past legislative inequities.

In a re-examination of California's rape laws, the legislature passed a reform bill stating that a woman's prior sex life—except for her relations, if any, with the male defendant in a case—was inadmissible as evidence against her. It was fascinating to hear the debate in which some of the most liberal members spoke against the reform, because, they argued, if a woman's prior sex life was ruled out, the rights of the defendant might be in jeopardy!

It's bad enough that in most cities in this country, women do not feel safe if they walk on the streets at night. They shouldn't have to fear abuse by our legal system as well. Yet in 35 or our 50 states a woman must prove she resisted rape, often by showing bruises and lacerations incurred at danger to her life. In Nebraska she has to prove she resisted until "overcome by fear."

If you happen to work, either by choice or by necessity, you should be aware of some rather arbitrary employment laws. For example, in some states an employer has to pay a woman overtime after she's put in 40 hours of work a week, whereas the employer has to pay a man overtime only after 48 hours. This would seem to be beneficial to women. What it really means, however, is that an employer can get eight hours' more work out of a man than a woman before paying overtime rates. If both a woman and a man are applying for the same job, who is the better candidate from the viewpoint of the employer? Obviously the man is—yet in this case the law exploits him too.

The most blatant discrimination against women still occurs in credit. A woman who has worked before and during her marriage and who has maintained a high joint credit rating with her husband for years suddenly may find herself deprived of credit if her husband loses his job. What if she were to stop working? asks the bank. Who would make the payments? asks the department store. In the eyes of these creditors she has become a bad credit risk. This would not be possible under ERA.

After a divorce action a woman may find that her high credit rating is no longer hers. Often a company with whom she and her husband had joint credit simply assumes it was the husband who paid the bills each month, and thus the high credit rating automatically belongs to him. This assumption would not be legal under ERA.

What about widows? At a time when a woman is in emotional shock, often when her family income is sharply diminished, when she is faced with responsibilities for which she may not be prepared, she should be able to begin putting together the pieces of her life under legal protection, not legal manipulation and intimidation.

But in some states her credit is cut off until her husband's estate is finally settled. And in some community-property states, because of archaic inheritance laws, a widow loses control of her own property until the entire estate has gone through probate. It may take years before the court makes sure of the legitimacy of the will and the executor assesses the value of the property, sees that the taxes are paid and distributes the monies according to the will. So she waits. When a wife dies, on the other hand, the husband retains control of his share of the property through the whole probate process. Such inequity in state law would be eliminated with the passage of the Federal ERA.

Until we ratify the 27th Amendment and include women as equal citizens under our Federal Constitution, the original intent of the Women's Movement as defined since Abigail Adams will not have been accomplished. Until all women realize the importance of this political action, it will not occur.

Ask yourself these questions: Should a woman keep her own credit rating when she marries or divorces? Should she have equal access to higher education? Should women receive equal pay for equal work, be promoted to positions of responsibility in business and be able to pursue careers regardless of their marital status?

If you answered these questions affirmatively, do they still strike you as the hysterical utterances of a small group of unfeminine women? Or are they questions you've been asking yourself for some time?

These are the issues at stake with the Equal Rights Amendment. The amendment would require changes in the basic legal, social and economic attitudes we have been conditioned to accept for centuries. To my mind, we should not delay action; we are not the same people we were 200 years ago. Would those who oppose ratification of the ERA have been opposed to abolishing slavery because it meant change? Isn't equality in this nation what we hold most dear, the very foundation of our existence?

The idea that you can't legislate social attitudes is quite correct, but legislation can stop the cycle of social conditioning from which these attitudes flow.

Equalizing sports activities in our schools, both in hours and dollars spent, will instill in young girls the same healthy, competitive spirit and sense of self-esteem that, we are told, such athletic programs are building in young boys.

Equalizing scholarships to higher education will afford deserving women an education they presently are denied. How is it that almost any football aspirant can find a college or university scholarship but a woman athlete of Olympic quality is neglected?

Government and industrial use of generic employment titles such as police officer, fire fighter, council member, advertising executive, copy writer, makeup artist, maintenance engineer, will go a long way toward changing misconceptions in children's minds. Both men and women can be fire fighters. Only a man can be a fire*man*.

Young women graduating from high school and college today are taking advantage of newly opened opportunities in law, medicine, law enforcement and the military. Some aspire to the more traditional careers for women such as teaching and nursing. Others will seek a good and lasting marriage within the home environment. But whatever they choose, it will be their choice, and deserving of the respect and recognition accorded any profession.

If the brave women who pioneered America had known that their role in the Western Expansion would go down in some history books as the story of "the men [who] came West with their cattle and their women," would they have stopped short of fomenting Abigail's rebellion? Would they have demanded their equal right to recognition?

We owe those women a victorious conclusion to this long political struggle.

We owe it to ourselves.

Workers (Female) Arise!
On Founding the Coalition of
Labor Union Women

Patricia Cayo Sexton

*Girls, you must take this matter to heart seriously now, for you have established a union,
and for the first time in woman's history in the United States, you are placed, and by your
own efforts, on a level with men, as far as possible, to obtain wages for your labor. . . .
Keep at it now, girls, and you will achieve full and plenteous success.*

Susan B. Anthony
At the founding of the Women's Typographical Union No. 1, 1868

Women workers are equal to men at least in a quantitative sense. Well, almost.
There are nearly as many women as men in the work force—about 43 percent of
the total. When my mother was 20 years old, in 1920, women came to only 20
percent of the work force. Today, about half of all women between 18 and 65,
including those with children, are working. The more education a woman has,
the more likely she is to work, probably because she can get a better job and will
earn enough to finance child and home care. Women are no longer marginal to
the work force; they are in the middle of it, at least in numbers.

The biggest change among workers has been in the number of married
women who work. In grandmother's time only the spinsters worked or the
widow woman who took in washing. Now married women form by far the largest
group of women who work. In 1971 married women comprised 60 percent of
working women, followed by single women (22 percent of the total), widowed
women (8 percent), divorced women (6 percent), and separated women (5
percent). Only about a third of all working women (35 percent) have husbands
who earn $7,000 and over. Thus, two out of three women work because they
have to. This need makes most women workers centrally concerned with economic issues.

Mothers are also doing it—working. While the number of women workers
more than doubled since the early 1940s, the number of working mothers
increased eight times! Half of all wives who worked in 1972 had children under
18. Even more striking, 28 percent of working wives had children under age six.
While the increase of working mothers was about 11 percent between 1960 and
1972, the rise was 75 percent among mothers with children under age three—and
only 2 percent of these children were in day-care centers. (In 1972 there were 5.6
million children under six who had working mothers, but only 905,000 day-care
slots.)

Full-time, year-round women workers earn little than half of what males
earn ($5,593 to $9,399 for males in 1971). This vast discrepancy has less to do
with unequal pay for equal work, an issue that has been settled on most industrial
jobs, than with upgrading, promotion, hiring, and the *kinds* of jobs women

perform. While the occupations of men are quite diversified, women are much more likely to be clerical workers than anything else. More than one woman in three is a clerical worker. Only one woman in six is a blue-collar worker and those who are, work as "operatives" rather than "craftsmen." Indeed, the only large occupational group women have not cracked is that of "craftsmen." More women are farm workers (501,000) than craftsmen (360,000). Yet more men work in crafts than in any other occupational group (over 10 million). Except for elite jobs, the skilled trades remain the major male fortress.

About twice as many men as women are managers and administrators, the best-paying occupational group. About the same proportion of women as men are in "professional and technical occupations." As of now, the best opportunities for women are in these professional and technical jobs. More of these jobs are open to them, and women make a higher proportion of the average male salary (69 percent) than in other occupations. Also, two of the major hurdles to the upgrading of women are not present here: requirements of physical strength and the need to "boss" other employees.

The profile of the average woman worker has changed considerably. In the 1920s it was that of a young (average age 28), single, factory worker or clerk. Now it is that of an older (38) married woman working in a variety of jobs. If employment holds up, the participation of women in the labor force will contine to increase. Women will have smaller families, more time, more educational and job opportunities. There will also be more jobs they can do. They may even become craftsmen, as new technologies develop and as the performance of many jobs requires less physical strength.

For the great mass of women workers, economic upgrading can come through three main routes: (1) unionization; (2) upgrading and promotion on the jobs; (3) training for other jobs, in professional and technical occupations.

CLUW

To see what progress women workers were making along these routes, I attended the March 1974 founding convention of CLUW (the Coalition of Labor Union Women) in Chicago. It was probably the largest labor convention ever held, in all history. And almost nobody there but us women. While conventions (like fads) come and go, the significance of this one may long linger on.

About 600 delegates were expected when the meeting was planned a year earlier. But a few months before the gathering, registrations rose to 1,500. The arrangements committee was in shock. There was no place to seat, let alone sleep, so many people.

On the convention's opening morning the convenors (torn between joy and terror) announced that 2,100 delegates had registered. By afternoon, the figure had risen to over 3,200! Even the UAW, whose conventions are probably bigger than any other union's, draws only 2,500 tops. . . .

Setting the Tone

Opening the convention, beautiful and black Addie Wyatt, director of women's activities for the Amalgamated Meat Cutters, said:

People ask, "Why are union women getting it together?" I say, "Women every-where else are doing it. It's time we did it." People ask, "Why can't the union resolve the problems?" I say, "We *are* the union. We are going to stay in the family and we are going to make our union responsive to our needs. This is not divisive of our union. We've given so much and settled for so little."

Women work for the same reasons as men. They have to. Even when we disagree here, we don't have to be disagreeable. Don't *dis*respect each other. Women have been disrespected long enough. Let's not do it to each other.

Olga Madar, CLUW's new president, said, "The women's movement gave an impetus to our moving ahead." She praised the Women's Equity Action League, NOW, and the National Women's Political Caucus. Actually the rela-tionship of the Coalition to the women's movement is more that of siblings than of child and parent. Both have the same origins. I believe those origins are less in ideas and movements than in economics and technology. Ideas are always around. They need something to germinate in, if they are to grow. That life-giving medium has been: (1) the relatively full employment of the last 20 years; (2) a technology that makes jobs easier for women to perform—as well as a method of birth control enabling people to regulate family size. The civil rights movement has passed on its inspiration. It has also passed on to women inclusion in the Civil Rights Act. It was almost a footnote to the law, but to women it has made all the difference. The civil rights movement too was born of an economy that could offer opportunity in industrial jobs (and education) to blacks.

I don't wish to deny people with ideas due credit for creating social movements. But our words are mainly transmitters. The main power comes out of the movement of economic and technological history. It is not impossible for women to get a fair or equal share when there is a scramble for scarce jobs and goods, but it is far easier to get that share (or at least some of it) when jobs and goods are in abundant supply.

The CLUW women, because they are unionists, understand this very well. Their brief resolution on legislation began: "The major concerns of women workers which require legislation are: *the economy as it relates to their liveli-hood;* the health and safety of themselves and their families; child care; equal rights" (my italics). Specifically, their first concern was raising and spreading the coverage of the minimum wage, an economic issue. Their concern was full employment.

There was no debate at the convention about birth control, abortion, marriage and the family. Most people regarded these issues as marginal and/or divisive. There was no expressed hostility to the women's liberation movement. A "gay caucus" advertised a meeting, which irritated some women, but there was no discussion of gay issues aside from a roundly defeated effort to link gay job rights onto women's job rights.

The goals of the convention were to adopt a statement of purpose and an organizational structure. The adopted purposes were: (1) organizing unorganized women; (2) affirmative action in the work place; (3) political action and legisla-tion; (4) participation of women within their unions.

It was the last that got the biggest audience response: ". . . to inspire and educate union women to . . . strengthen their participation, to encourage their leadership and their movement into policy-making roles within their own unions." As these women go into battle with employers and legislators, they naturally also want to put their own house in order. They want to move out of "women's work" in their own unions and into policy-making positions.

A hopeful aspect is that many union men support this goal. Indeed, many women I talked to said they came to the convention because a male union officer asked them to go. Of course, there is a long, hard road from going to a women's convention to membership on a local executive board. Too often "participation" means doing the flunky work, cooking and cleaning up, while men are paid to sit around and make decisions. . . .

Upgrading

I asked women at the convention what they considered the most important issues for them on the job. Many said "equal pay." What they usually meant was not "equal pay for equal work," since most unionized jobs have that, but an equal chance to get a better job. They are concerned about upgrading, entry into male-dominated job classifications, and promotions.

A social worker from Illinois said, for example, that guards in their state mental hospital are paid much more than matrons. Both do much the same work except that guards have a few assignments that put them in a different, and higher-paying, classification. Many women talked about the "separate seniority lists" in their shops that kept them from moving into departments where the jobs and pay were better.

Several auto workers from Indiana said they were most concerned about "upgrading." In their plant (which makes compact transmissions with manual shifts, a good item these days), they recently had the first woman upgrader in 30 years. (In auto, an upgrader is an employee with seniority who moves up into a skilled trade, taking longer to reach journeyman status than the apprentice but making "the rate of the job" rather than the apprentice reduced rate.) They were quick to add: "It's the company's fault, not the union's." Two things were important in the new upgrading of women. The company hadn't hired women in 29 years; now they are hiring women. Also, the law helped. The company began upgrading women after charges had been filed with the EEOC (Equal Employment Opportunities Commission). Then, too, some work classifications have been reserved for males. Tool and gage inspection, for instance, a good job but regarded as a "family man's job," was given out on the basis of seniority, of which men had more. Now women are moving into these classifications. Sometimes women can leap across classification barriers simply by applying. One young woman (Doris Vanderhoogen of UAW Local 264 in West Allis, Wisconsin) became a foundry worker this way. She and a friend were desperate for a job that paid a living wage. They looked through the yellow pages for plant listings. When they came to "foundries," they said, "That's it. Those are male jobs so they must pay well." They called around and finally made an appointment to see the president of Federal Malleable. They persuaded him to hire them in the foundry.

> They called it "Bob's Follies." They said we would never last, that we couldn't take the heat and the dirt. When we walked in there, we were scared to death. At first there was some resentment from the men, but when they learned we weren't a threat, it was OK. We get on fine. There are 12 women now and 150 men. We do everything the men do except the actual pouring of the iron. The company will put women there too.

The good wages she makes? A base of $3.92 an hour, open to incentive pay up to $5.80 an hour. She has worked there almost two years. "They consider us like one of the guys. They hardly notice. I don't know if we should be proud of that or not."

She is a grinder. Castings come to her covered with large burrs and she grinds them until they are smooth. Women are oven tenders (baking the cores), shell-machine operators, furnace operators, everything.

> Most people look at me like I was crazy. You have to earn a living wage now. The working conditions are livable. Even if you don't look so good when you get off work, you accomplish something. It's going into something that women have never done before. It's pioneering.
>
> [She insisted, though I didn't ask:] I'm very proud to belong to the UAW. We get complete backing for equal pay and rights. The local president is fantastic. He backs us one hundred percent. We get help from all the staff. We have a very active Women's Advisory Council to the union in our region, and we get a lot of female participation. We counsel our own women, we carry on community action programs, and we branch out into other areas. CLUW is going to be one of the best things that ever happened to us.

An IAM woman (Machinist) from St. Paul, Minnesota, Lodge 1313, a local of 2,300 people, said, "A lot of the problems are the women's own fault. Women sit back, especially the young ones. Why don't they come to meetings?" She is the financial secretary of her lodge and has been for many years.

> I broke the ice. When I came in the men were nice but cold. It's different now. I joke with them and they joke with me. One financial secretary came to me and said, "You know, it's not that I didn't like you, but when you first came on this job I said to myself, 'If she can do this job, what is going to happen to my job?' "

She is Polish, single, and feels there is no discrimination either in the IAM or the plant. Women work on all jobs, she says, but they are not active in the union. She feels that Polish men find it harder to accept the change in women's jobs.

Her point of view is not uncommon among women who have been able to make it *alone* into men's work. . . .

TRADITIONAL MARXISM

Women and Society
V. I. Lenin

Capitalism combines formal equality with economic and, consequently, social inequality. This is one of the principal distinguishing features of capitalism, one that is mendaciously screened by the supporters of the bourgeoisie, the liberals, and that is not understood by the petty-bourgeois democrats. Out of this distinguishing feature of capitalism, by the way, the necessity arises, while fighting resolutely for economic equality, openly to recognize capitalist inequality and, under certain conditions, even to include this open recognition of inequality as a basis for the proletarian state organization (the Soviet constitution).

But capitalism *cannot* be consistent even with regard to formal equality (equality before the law, ''equality'' between the well-fed and the hungry, between the property-owner and the propertyless). And one of the most flagrant manifestations of this inconsistency is the *inferior position* of woman compared with man. Not a single bourgeois state, not even the most progressive, republican democratic state, has brought about complete equality of rights.

But the Soviet Republic of Russia promptly wiped out, *without any exception,* every trace of inequality in the legal status of woman, and secured her complete equality in its laws.

It is said that the level of culture is best characterized by the legal status of woman. There is a grain of profound truth in this saying. From this point of view, only the dictatorship of the proletariat, only the socialist state, could achieve and did achieve a higher level of culture.

Therefore, the foundation (and consolidation) of the first Soviet Republic— and alongside and in connection with this, the Communist International— inevitably lends a new, unparalleled, powerful impetus to the working women's movement.

For, when we speak of those who, under capitalism, were directly or indirectly, wholly or partially oppressed, it is precisely the Soviet system, and the Soviet system only, that secures democracy. This is clearly demonstrated by the position of the working class and the poor peasants. It is clearly demonstrated by the position of women.

But the Soviet system represents the final decisive conflict for the *abolition of classes,* for economic and social equality. *For us,* democracy, even democracy for those who were oppressed under capitalism, including democracy for the oppressed sex, *is inadequate.*

The working women's movement has for its object the fight for the economic and social, and not merely formal, equality of woman. The main task is to draw the women into socially productive labor, extricate them from ''domestic

slavery,'' free them of their stultifying and humiliating resignation to the perpetual and exclusive atmosphere of the kitchen and nursery.

It is a long struggle, requiring a radical remaking both of social technique
and of customs. But this struggle will end with the complete triumph of
communism.

The Political Economy of
Women's Liberation

Margaret Benston

The position of women rests, as everything in our complex society, on an economic base.

Eleanor Marx and Edward Aveling

The "woman question" is generally ignored in analyses of the class structure of
society. This is so because, on the one hand, classes are generally defined by
their relation to the means of production and, on the other hand, women are not
supposed to have any unique relation to the means of production. The category
seems instead to cut across all classes; one speaks of working-class women,
middle-class women, etc. The status of women is clearly inferior to that of men,[1]
but analysis of this condition usually falls into discussing socialization, psychology, interpersonal relations, or the role of marriage as a social institution.[2] Are
these, however, the primary factors? In arguing that the roots of the secondary
status of women are in fact economic, it can be shown that women as a group do
indeed have a definite relation to the means of production and that this is
different from that of men. The personal and psychological factors then follow
from this special relation to production, and a change in the latter will be a
necessary (but not sufficient) condition for changing the former.[3] If this special
relation of women to production is accepted, the analysis of the situation of
women fits naturally into a class analysis of society.

The starting point for discussion of classes in a capitalist society is the
distinction between those who own the means of production and those who sell
their labor power for a wage. As Ernest Mandel says:

> The proletarian condition is, in a nutshell, the lack of access to the means of
> production or means of subsistence which, in a society of generalized commodity

---

[1]Marlene Dixon, "Secondary Social Status of Women." (Available from US. Voice of
Women's Liberation Movement, 1940 Bissell, Chicago, Illinois 60614.)

[2]The biological argument is, of course, the first one used, but it is not usually taken seriously by
socialist writers. Margaret Mead's *Sex and Temperament* is an early statement of the importance of
culture instead of biology.

[3]This applies to the group or category as a whole. Women as individuals can and do free
themselves from their socialization to a great degree (and they can even come to terms with the
economic situation in favorable cases), but the majority of women have no chance to do so.

production, forces the proletarian to sell his labor power. In exchange for this labor power he receives a wage which then enables him to acquire the means of consumption necessary for satisfying his own needs and those of his family.

This is the structural definition of wage earner, the proletarian. From it necessarily flows a certain relationship to his work, to the products of his work, and to his overall situation in society, which can be summarized by the catchword alienation. But there does not follow from this structural definition any necessary conclusions as to the level of his consumption . . . the extent of his needs, or the degree to which he can satisfy them.[4]

We lack a corresponding structural definition of women. What is needed first is not a complete examination of the symptoms of the secondary status of women, but instead a statement of the material conditions in capitalist (and other) societies which define the group "women." Upon these conditions are built the specific superstructures which we know. An interesting passage from Mandel points the way to such a definition:

The commodity . . . is a product created to be exchanged on the market, as opposed to one which has been made for direct consumption. *Every commodity must have both a use-value and an exchange-value.*

It must have a use-value or else nobody would buy it. . . . A commodity without a use-value to anyone would consequently be unsalable, would constitute useless production, would have no exchange-value precisely because it had no use-value.

On the other hand, every product which has use-value does not necessarily have exchange-value. It has an exchange-value only to the extent that the society itself, in which the commodity is produced, is founded on exchange, is a society where exchange is a common practice. . . .

In capitalist society, commodity production, the production of exchange-values, has reached its greatest development. It is the first society in human history where the major part of production consists of commodities. It is not true, however, that all production under capitalism is commodity production. Two classes of products still remain simple use-value.

The first group consists of all things produced by the peasantry for its own consumption, everything directly consumed on the farms where it is produced. . . .

The second group of products in capitalist society which are not commodities but remain simple use-value consists of all things produced in the home. Despite the fact that considerable human labor goes into this type of household production, it still remains a production of use-values and not of commodities. Every time a soup is made or a button sewn on a garment, it constitutes production, but it is not production for the market.

The appearance of commodity production and its subsequent regularization and generalization have radically transformed the way men labor and how they organize society.[5]

---

[4]Ernest Mandel, "Workers Under Neocapitalism," paper delivered at Simon Fraser University. (Available through the Department of Political Science, Sociology and Anthropology, Simon Fraser University, Burnaby, B.C., Canada.)

[5]Ernest Mandel, *An Introduction to Marxist Economic Theory* (New York: Merit Publishers, 1967), pp. 10-11.

What Mandel may not have noticed is that his last paragraph is precisely correct. The appearance of commodity production has indeed transformed the way that *men* labor. As he points out, most household labor in capitalist society (and in the existing socialist societies, for that matter) remains in the premarket stage. This is the work which is reserved for women and it is in this fact that we can find the basis for a definition of women.

In sheer quantity, household labor, including child care, constitutes a huge amount of socially necessary production. Nevertheless, in a society based on commodity production, it is not usually considered "real work" since it is outside of trade and the market place. It is pre-capitalist in a very real sense. This assignment of household work as the function of a special category "women" means that this group *does* stand in a different relation to production than the group "men." We will tentatively define women, then, as that group of people who are responsible for the production of simple use-values in those activities associated with the home and family.

Since men carry no responsibility for such production, the difference between the two groups lies here. Notice that women are not excluded from commodity production. Their participation in wage labor occurs but, as a group, they have no structural responsibility in this area and such participation is ordinarily regarded as transient. Men, on the other hand, are responsible for commodity production; they are not, in principle, given any role in household labor. For example, when they do participate in household production, it is regarded as more than simply exceptional; it is demoralizing, emasculating, even harmful to health. (A story on the front page of the *Vancouver Sun* in January 1969 reported that men in Britain were having their health endangered because they had to do too much housework!)

The material basis for the inferior status of women is to be found in just this definition of women. In a society in which money determines value, women are a group who work outside the money economy. Their work is not worth money, is therefore valueless, is therefore not even real work. And women themselves, who do this valueless work, can hardly be expected to be worth as much as men, who work for money. In structural terms, the closest thing to the condition of women is the condition of others who are or were also outside of commodity production, i.e., serfs and peasants.

In her recent paper on women, Juliet Mitchell introduces the subject as follows: "In advanced industrial society, women's work is only marginal to the total economy. Yet it is through work that man changes natural conditions and thereby produces society. Until there is a revolution in production, the labor situation will prescribe women's situation within the world of men."[6] The statement of the marginality of women's work is an unanalyzed recognition that the work women do is *different* from the work that men do. Such work is not marginal, however; it is just not wage labor and so is not counted. She even says later in the same article, "Domestic labor, even today, is enormous if quantified in terms of productive labor." She gives some figures to illustrate: In Sweden,

[6]Juliet Mitchell, "Women: The Longest Revolution," *New Left Review,* December 1966.

2,340 million hours a year are spent by women in housework compared with 1,290 million hours spent by women in industry. And the Chase Manhattan Bank estimates a woman's overall work week at 99.6 hours.

However, Mitchell gives little emphasis to the basic economic factors (in fact she condemns most Marxists for being "overly economist") and moves on hastily to superstructural factors, because she notices that "the advent of industrialization has not so far freed women." What she fails to see is that no society has thus far industrialized housework. Engels points out that the "first premise for the emancipation of women is the reintroduction of the entire female sex into public industry. . . . And this has become possible not only as a result of modern large-scale industry, which not only permits the participation of women in production in large numbers, but actually calls for it and, moreover, strives to convert private domestic work also into a public industry."[7] And later in the same passage: "Here we see already that the emancipation of women and their equality with men are impossible and must remain so as long as women are excluded from socially productive work and restricted to housework, which is private." What Mitchell has not taken into account is that the problem is not simply one of getting women into *existing* industrial production but the more complex one of converting private production of household work into public production.

For most North Americans, domestic work as "public production" brings immediate images of Brave New World or of a vast institution—a cross between a home for orphans and an army barracks—where we would all be forced to live. For this reason, it is probably just as well to outline here, schematically and simplistically, the nature of industrialization.

A pre-industrial production unit is one in which production is small-scale and reduplicative; i.e., there are a great number of little units, each complete and just like all the others. Ordinarily such production units are in some way kin-based and they are multi-purpose, fulfilling religious, recreational, educational, and sexual functions along with the economic function. In such a situation, desirable attributes of an individual, those which give prestige, are judged by more than purely economic criteria: for example, among approved character traits are proper behavior to kin or readiness to fulfill obligations.

Such production is originally not for exchange. But if exchange of commodities becomes important enough, then increased efficiency of production becomes necessary. Such efficiency is provided by the transition to industrialized production which involves the elimination of the kin-based production unit. A large-scale, non-reduplicative production unit is substituted which has only one function, the economic one, and where prestige or status is attained by economic skills. Production is rationalized, made vastly more efficient, and becomes more

---

[7]Frederick Engels, *Origin of the Family, Private Property and the State* (Moscow: Progress Publishers, 1968), Chapter IX, p. 158. The anthropological evidence known to Engels indicated primitive woman's dominance over man. Modern anthropology disputes this dominance but provides evidence for a more nearly equal position of women in the matrilineal societies used by Engels as examples. The arguments in this work of Engels do not require the former dominance of women but merely their former equality, and so the conclusions remain unchanged.

and more public—part of an integrated social network. An enormous expansion of man's productive potential takes place. Under capitalism such social productive forces are utilized almost exclusively for private profit. These can be thought of as *capitalized* forms of production.

If we apply the above to housework and child rearing, it is evident that each family, each household, constitutes an individual production unit, a pre-industrial entity, in the same way that peasant farmers or cottage weavers constitute pre-industrial production units. The main features are clear, with the reduplicative, kin-based, private nature of the work being the most important. (It is interesting to notice the other features: the multipurpose functions of the family, the fact that desirable attributes for women do not center on economic prowess, etc.) The rationalization of production effected by a transition to large-scale production has not taken place in this area.

Industrialization is, in itself, a great force for human good; exploitation and dehumanization go with capitalism and not necessarily with industrialization. To advocate the conversion of private domestic labor into a public industry under capitalism is quite a different thing from advocating such conversion in a socialist society. In the latter case the forces of production would operate for human welfare, not private profit, and the result should be liberation, not dehumanization. In this case we can speak of *socialized* forms of production.

These definitions are not meant to be technical but rather to differentiate between two important aspects of industrialization. Thus the fear of the barracks-like result of introducing housekeeping into the public economy is most realistic under capitalism. With socialized production and the removal of the profit motive and its attendant alienated labor, there is no reason why, *in an industrialized society,* industrialization of housework should not result in better production, i.e., better food, more comfortable surroundings, more intelligent and loving child-care, etc., than in the present nuclear family.

The argument is often advanced that, under neocapitalism, the work in the home has been much reduced. Even if this is true, it is not structurally relevant. Except for the very rich, who can hire someone to do it, there is for most women, an irreducible minimum of necessary labor involved in caring for home, husband, and children. For a married woman without children this irreducible minimum of work probably takes fifteen to twenty hours a week; for a woman with small children the minimum is probably seventy or eighty hours a week.[8] (There is some resistance to regarding child-rearing as a job. That labor is involved, i.e., the production of use-value, can be clearly seen when exchange-value is also involved—when the work is done by baby sitters, nurses, child-care centers, or teachers. An economist has already pointed out the paradox that if a man marries his housekeeper, he reduces the national income, since the money he gives her is no longer counted as wages.) The reduction of housework to the minimums given

_____

[8]Such figures can easily be estimated. For example, a married woman without children is expected each week to cook and wash up (10 hours), clean house (4 hours), do laundry (1 hour), and shop for food (1 hour). The figures are *minimum* times required each week for such work. The total, 16 hours, is probably unrealistically low; even so, it is close to half of a regular work week. A mother with young children must spend at least six or seven days a week working close to 12 hours.

is also expensive; for low-income families more labor is required. In any case, household work remains structurally the same—a matter of private production.

One function of the family, the one taught to us in school and the one which is popularly accepted, is the satisfaction of emotional needs: the needs for closeness, community, and warm secure relationships. This society provides few other ways of satisfying such needs; for example, work relationships or friendships are not expected to be nearly as important as a man-woman-with-children relationship. Even other ties of kinship are increasingly secondary. This function of the family is important in stabilizing it so that it can fulfill the second, purely economic, function discussed above. The wage-earner, the husband-father, whose earnings support himself, also "pays for" the labor done by the mother-wife and supports the children. The wages of a man buy the labor of two people. The crucial importance of this second function of the family can be seen when the family unit breaks down in divorce. The continuation of the economic function is the major concern where children are involved; the man must continue to pay for the labor of the woman. His wage is very often insufficient to enable him to support a second family. In this case his emotional needs are sacrificed to the necessity to support his ex-wife and children. That is, when there is a conflict the economic function of the family very often takes precedence over the emotional one. And this is a society which teaches that the major function of the family is the satisfaction of emotional needs.[9]

As an economic unit, the nuclear family is a valuable stabilizing force in capitalist society. Since the production which is done in the home is paid for by the husband-father's earnings, his ability to withhold his labor from the market is much reduced. Even his flexibility in changing jobs is limited. The woman, denied an active place in the market, has little control over the conditions that govern her life. Her economic dependence is reflected in emotional dependence, passivity, and other "typical" female personality traits. She is conservative, fearful, supportive of the status quo.

Furthermore, the structure of this family is such that it is an ideal consumption unit. But this fact, which is widely noted in Women's Liberation literature, should not be taken to mean that this is its primary function. If the above analysis is correct, the family should be seen primarily as a production unit for housework and child-rearing. *Everyone* in capitalist society is a consumer; the structure of the family simply means that it is particularly well suited to encourage consumption. Women in particular *are* good consumers; this follows naturally from their responsibility for matters in the home. Also, the inferior status of women, their general lack of a strong sense of worth and identity, make them more exploitable than men and hence better consumers.

The history of women in the industrialized sector of the economy has depended simply on the labor needs of that sector. Women function as a massive reserve army of labor. When labor is scarce (early industrialization, the two world wars, etc.) then women form an important part of the labor force. When there is less demand for labor (as now under neocapitalism) women become a

---

[9]For evidence of such teaching, see any high school text on the family.

surplus labor force—but one for which their husbands and not society are economically responsible. The "cult of the home" makes its reappearance during times of labor surplus and is used to channel women out of the market economy. This is relatively easy since the pervading ideology ensures that no one, man or woman, takes women's participation in the labor force very seriously. Women's real work, we are taught, is in the home; this holds whether or not they are married, single, or the heads of households.

At all times household work is the responsibility of women. When they are working outside the home they must somehow manage to get both outside job and housework done (or they supervise a substitute for the housework). Women, particularly married women with children, who work outside the home simply do two jobs; their participation in the labor force is only allowed if they continue to fulfill their first responsibility in the home. This is particularly evident in countries like Russia and those in Eastern Europe where expanded opportunities for women in the labor force have not brought about a corresponding expansion in their liberty. Equal access to jobs outside the home, while one of the preconditions for women's liberation, will not in itself be sufficient to give equality for women; as long as work in the home remains a matter of private production and is the responsibility of women, they will simply carry a double work-load.

A second prerequisite for women's liberation which follows from the above analysis is the conversion of the work now done in the home as private production into work to be done in the public economy.[10] To be more specific, this means that child-rearing should no longer be the responsibility solely of the parents. Society must begin to take responsibility for children; the economic dependence of women and children on the husband-father must be ended. The other work that goes on in the home must also be changed—communal eating places and laundries for example. When such work is moved into the public sector, then the material basis for discrimination against women will be gone.

These are only preconditions. The idea of the inferior status of women is deeply rooted in the society and will take a great deal of effort to eradicate. But once the structures which produce and support that idea are changed then, and only then, can we hope to make progress. It is possible, for example, that a change to communal eating places would simply mean that women are moved from a home kitchen to a communal one. This *would* be an advance, to be sure, particularly in a socialist society where work would not have the inherently exploitative nature it does now. Once women are freed from private production in the home, it will probably be very difficult to maintain for any long period of time a rigid definition of jobs by sex. This illustrates the interrelation between the two preconditions given above: true equality in job opportunity is probably impossible without freedom from housework, and the industrialization of housework is unlikely unless women are leaving the home for jobs.

The changes in production necessary to get women out of the home might seem to be, in theory, possible under capitalism. One of the sources of women's

---

[10]This is stated clearly by early Marxist writers besides Engels. Relevant quotes from Engels have been given in the text. . . .

liberation movements may be the fact that alternative capitalized forms of home production now exist. Day care is available, even if inadequate and perhaps expensive; convenience foods, home delivery of meals, and take-out meals are widespread; laundries and cleaners offer bulk rates. However, cost usually prohibits a complete dependence on such facilities, and they are not available everywhere, even in North America. These should probably then be regarded as embryonic forms rather than completed structures. However, they clearly stand as alternatives to the present system of getting such work done. Particularly in North America, where the growth of "service industries" is important in maintaining the growth of the economy, the contradictions between these alternatives and the need to keep women in the home will grow.

The need to keep women in the home arises from two major aspects of the present system. First, the amount of unpaid labor performed by women is very large and very profitable to those who own the means of production. To pay women for their work, even at minimum wage scales, would imply a massive redistribution of wealth. At present, the support of a family is a hidden tax on the wage earner—his wage buys the labor power of two people. And second, there is the problem of whether the economy can expand enough to put all women to work as a part of the normally employed labor force. The war economy has been adequate to draw women partially into the economy but not adequate to establish a need for all or most of them. If it is argued that the jobs created by the industrialization of housework will create this need, then one can counter by pointing to (1) the strong economic forces operating for the status quo and against capitalization discussed above, and (2) the fact that the present service industries, which somewhat counter these forces, have not been able to keep up with the growth of the labor force as presently constituted. The present trends in the service industries simply create "underemployment" in the home; they do not create new jobs for women. So long as this situation exists, women remain a very convenient and elastic part of the industrial reserve army. Their incorporation into the labor force on terms of equality—which would create pressure for capitalization of housework—is possible only with an economic expansion so far achieved by neocapitalism only under conditions of full-scale war mobilization.

In addition, such structural changes imply the complete breakdown of the present nuclear family. The stabilizing consuming functions of the family, plus the ability of the cult of the home to keep women out of the labor market, serve neocapitalism too well to be easily dispensed with. And, on a less fundamental level, even if these necessary changes in the nature of household production were achieved under capitalism it would have the unpleasant consequence of including *all* human relations in the cash nexus. The atomization and isolation of people in Western society is already sufficiently advanced to make it doubtful if such complete psychic isolation could be tolerated. It is likely in fact that one of the major negative emotional responses to women's liberation movements may be exactly such a fear. If this is the case, then possible alternatives—cooperatives, the kibbutz, etc.—can be cited to show that psychic needs for community and warmth can in fact be better satisfied if other structures are substituted for the nuclear family.

At best the change to capitalization of housework would only give women the same limited freedom given most men in capitalist society. This does not mean, however, that women should wait to demand freedom from discrimination. There *is* a material basis for women's status; we are not merely discriminated against, we are exploited. At present, our unpaid labor in the home is necessary if the entire system is to function. Pressure created by women who challenge their role will reduce the effectiveness of this exploitation. In addition, such challenges will impede the functioning of the family and may make the channeling of women out of the labor force less effective. All of these will hopefully make quicker the transition to a society in which the necessary structural changes in production can actually be made. That such a transition will require a revolution I have no doubt; our task is to make sure that revolutionary changes in the society do in fact end women's oppression.

RADICAL FEMINISM

What's This about Feminist Businesses?

Jennifer Woodul

It is time for feminist businesses to deal with questions and criticisms which are popping up within the women's movement. I've recently read several articles and participated in a well-attended community rap group on the subject of feminist businesses and the general economics of the women's community. The same issues come up over and over—vital ones for all of us to deal with more effectively than we've done in the past. As a member of the Olivia Records Collective, I'd like to respond here to the article which appeared in *off our backs,* Jan./Feb. 1976, by Hannah Darby and Brooke Williams: "God, Mom and Apple Pie: 'Feminist' Business as an Extension of the American Dream."

Invention, Not Solution

The gist of the problem as seen by Hannah and Brooke is that feminism and capitalism are antithetical; therefore, that *feminist business* is a *contradiction.* While it seems clear to me that the two above ideologies are indeed incompatible, I conclude that *feminist business* is an *invention.* Feminist business is an attempt to get power for women right now. It is not, and I don't think feminist business-women have ever claimed it was, a *solution* to the problem of woman-oppression, nor the final means of *taking* power.

One of my assumptions in writing this article is that capitalism is a patriarchal development. As such, it's been characterized by two elements which make it especially repugnant to feminists. They are: 1. exploitation of the labor workers that goes to the accumulation of profit that goes to an elite, providing them with living standards unavailable to workers, and 2. exploitation of the consumer by selling overpriced, low quality, useless, and unnecessary products. The basic process which supports this system of domination is the selling of goods or services at a price which affords a surplus of money, leading to accumulation of money. That's where we get interested as feminists: we do need money. Since it's not yet within our scope to do away with an oppressive system, is it possible to use the basics of that system to our own advantage, while avoiding 1 and 2 above? And, going even further, can we actually prepare ourselves for a feminist world at the same time?

Another assumption is that feminism presupposes a socialist economy of some kind. Communism was not invented by Marx, as we know. It has been an integral part of matriarchal society, and, in one form or another, is a continual guiding principle as feminists today decide what things we want to keep in our world. It is my firm contention that feminist businesses are not to be accused of revisionism with regard to long term goals and strategies.

Priorities

As political workers, there are a number of things that we should hold as priorities in any sort of plan that we put forth. Can this plan help women to change, to think politically, to identify themselves with the oppression of women globally? And can this plan concretely improve the lives of women at the same time—materially and psychologically? (For further development, see "Reform Tool Kit," Charlotte Bunch, in *Quest,* Volume I, number 1.) A major premise here is that the material improvement of the lives of women, the psychological improvement as well, represent CONTROL and that control means POWER. Over the past few years, we've discovered different ways to make our minds and bodies stronger—to take our personal power. Olivia and other feminist businesses believe that we now need to take our economic power. State power is a ways down the road, but just because we don't start with it, that doesn't mean we're not on the way to getting it.

First of all, I think it's important to point out that feminist businesses are not just "selling products which promote the idea of equality," as "God, Mom and Apple Pie" defines them, and they are not just "alternatives." Feminist businesses are the mainstream, the wave of the future. They are woman-designed to meet our own needs and to become what *we* want. They are superb inventions which test out our feminist principles in crises of the everyday decisions which are momentous because they have everything to do with our survival—politically and economically. Feminist businesses and feminist businesswomen are putting their lives and their livelihoods on the line in order to invent a way to gain actual power for women.

What makes a business feminist then? It should offer women something that they need, something relevant to their lives. However, as Brooke and Hannah point out, "products do not affect the nature of business as such." We agree. The nature of business will be changed by feminist operation of it. There should be structures for worker input, working toward meaningful worker control. Salaries should be set within a narrow range, with consideration of each woman's particular needs as well as her role in the company. Structures should be clear to all and determined on concrete bases. Decision-making methods should be set out, with the understanding that decision-making must presume responsibility. There must be a consciousness of accountability to the women's community. There must be a commitment to channel money back into the community or the movement. Finally, there must be a commitment to radical change—to the goals of economic and political power for women.

Choosing Isn't Easy

There are different ways to make the above things happen. Finding out what they are is what women's businesses are doing. As feminists trying to use capitalist procedures to our advantage, we are constantly walking a tightrope—trying to be sure that our decisions are made with the good of women in mind. The price of a record, for example, is a very heavy decision to make. The women who run Olivia are members of the feminist community. We know how little money many women have. We realize that if we're to depend on each other in order to make a strong economic community, we can't squeeze our own pockets too hard. At the same time, Olivia's survival is vital to the economic future of all of us; it must succeed. And we want this music to reach beyond the feminist community we're in touch with now. Both because we feel that music is an effective way of reaching other women, and because we're trying to make a big business, one that brings *new* money into the feminist community—not just circulates what we have among ourselves again and again. That means that the decision about record price must take into consideration the requirements of wholesale outlets. Where is the balance between these factors? The decision takes a long, thorough collective discussion. It's not based on simple evaluation of how high a price we can get.

Considerations of privilege and commitment—not just skills and qualifications—must go into decisions about hiring. Although it might be tempting to hire a woman who is highly skilled in some area by virtue of her past privilege—a woman who probably already has, or has access to, a good job—a better alternative might be to ask that woman to share her privilege by training a woman with less privilege, who needs that skill. And once women are hired, structures must be set to describe and/or provide means to share power. For example, although we tend to specialize in our Olivia work (bookkeeping, distribution, etc.) in the interest of efficiency, we've found that it's important that the sharing of information become systematic. Otherwise, the concentration of certain kinds of information in one head creates a power imbalance with regard to decisions we have to make in that area. Since all questions of power in a feminist business are ultimately contingent on responsibility, diverse levels of commitment should be faced squarely.

In order to build businesses which are truly feminist, we have to make energetic commitments to doing as much of our own work as possible. Olivia, for example, doesn't farm its product out to a fancy overground distribution company with loads of contacts and loads of money to promote records. After consultation with feminists who believed in the concept, Olivia started its own distribution network, which now employs (commissions) 58 women across the country. It's true that at this point, only a couple of those women are making a living from their Olivia work. But all of them believe, with us, that the absolutely essential requirement for building a women's economy is that we know it inside-out, and that we are as much in control of every part of it as we can be. We realize we're not in control of the whole thing yet, but we take one day at a time, with a vision of the whole.

It's from Scratch, but Start

"Women, lacking at the present time the access to and training in technology, as well as the necessary capital, cannot possibly hold economic power in a capitalistic system." It's certainly true that ALL WE HAVE IS OURSELVES. We haven't got control of many resources, factories, equipment, technical expertise, etc.—and we do need more money. But where should we get it? Shall we *wait* for it to show up? And certainly no one is going to come around and offer us training in technology. Right now, we're trying to get a few women trained, so they can train others. No one knows better than Olivia the headaches that come from the desperate need for technological knowledge. But we are getting it— slowly. We understand that knowledge of the processes of the recording industry, alone, is not the expertise that will shift the power balance in the United States. Happily, we are part of a growing concern of feminists—including a strong representation of feminists in business—who are making it their business to start learning everything and anything which might promote our collective strength.

The authors of "God, Mom, etc." contend that feminist businesses make feminism a commodity while creating a new market which can then be exploited by major industries. They argue that as major industries discover this new market to be profitable they will run our small businesses *out* of business. We think that whatever market feminist businesses "create," there is certainly a great demand for the things we are selling. And politically conscious women are not blind dolt consumers. There is a felt need which women express when they buy the products, and it is very often coupled with a strong desire to support a business that can be trusted. Many women won't buy "feminist" products created by male-controlled industries. Spending money with women's businesses has become for them a part of their own political commitment—and that involves a high level of trust. In turn, women's businesses have an obligation to be accountable to the women who support their efforts.

Counting & Accounting

The question of accountability pertains to the consumers, workers, and worker/owners of feminist businesses in exactly the same way that it does to any other political organization; feminist businesses committed to radical political and economic change are most definitely political organizations. Of course businesses are run to make a profit. The question is what happens to that money? Who gets it, or where does it go? Who decides that? Who can question who gets it? Of course, as Brooke and Hannah point out, the bigger you get the more danger there is of co-optation. That's why we try to make collective decisions and structures. That's why the feminist community should demand accountability.

"Feminism is concerned with women as a class. Business by its nature can only benefit a few women directly." It seems like an unproven assertion, but even so, *how many is enough?* If a business only affects 25 women's lives directly, should we fold it until it can hire everyone? How many women's lives can be affected by the music? How many women will change their lives, start their own businesses, do other political work, become lesbian-feminists, start seeing their entire lives as being inextricably involved with the struggle for women's liberation?

Brooke and Hannah suggest that our energies for dealing with the economy would be better spent in workplace organizing. What guilt-ridden condescension would lead middle-class women to go "organize" women in factories? Women, as we well know, are perfectly capable of organizing themselves whenever their consciousness tells them it's time. This kind of patronizing jive is middle-class bullshit that privileged leftists have been putting out for over 100 years. Let's concentrate our work on creating unoppressive jobs, so that *for once* this movement really has something to offer women who don't have the privilege to put their livelihood on the line everyday.

"The income of every business goes to its owners. They get the money and *they* decide what to do with it." Most of the income of businesses goes right back into expanding the business—whether that means more women's music, more political books, better food, etc. Some goes to support the owners and other workers. Women becoming self-sufficient and supporting themselves independently of working for the Man is GOOD. When the workers and the business have what they need, money should go to the movement, the community, more businesses, loans, etc. And someone must decide where that money goes, for sure. The women with the commitment to the business should have that final decision. At the same time, they should be accountable for those decisions. Women generally—especially those actively involved in the feminist movement—must take the responsibility to suggest where that money should go, and keep informed of any reports which the business makes to the community.

Control = Commitment

"Economic, social and even sexual exploitation have occurred in 'feminist' businesses. In fact, exploitation in alternative businesses is frequently more subtle and far-reaching than in straight businesses." Structures of accountability and collectivity should be the way to deal with the question of "exploitation" of any kind that occurs within the context of our businesses and our movement. However, we must be careful of what we call exploitation. We are trying to make a revolution; we must ask a lot of ourselves. Every woman who works for a feminist business should consider it a privilege. She should make an honest evaluation of her needs and her commitment. Perhaps she wants to work regular hours for a salary, but is not willing to put in the same kind of energy that it takes for the women who are ultimately responsible for the business. That's okay, but it should be made clear to everyone involved. If she is paid a salary and wants to be part of all decision-making processes, I expect her to put in the same kinds of hours that I do—long ones. We will all share in decision-making within the clear definitions of a structure which will allow all of us to control what we do. Final control and decision-making power will be shared as trust is built up. It's important to say that if there is no such structure or provision for sharing/acquiring real power, NO ONE SHOULD EXPECT THE COMMITMENT LEVELS TO BE THE SAME. And if a woman isn't willing to make that kind of commitment, SHE SHOULD NOT EXPECT TO SHARE CONTROL.

Inside Benefits

The question of hierarchy is not really any different in a feminist business than it is in any other feminist group or project. Any tendency toward top-dogism must be dealt with in specific and clear-cut terms. If we can manage to create good methods for acquiring, sharing, and checking power, it most definitely affects women in general and the women's movement in particular. The things that work, the things that allow us personal self-sufficiency and determination while making a self-sufficient business are the things that will help us run a feminist world—under whatever type of economy that we finally invent, as feminists.

". . . Power within a small business is not the same as decision-making power over the country." You bet. What can I say?

It's true, as Brooke and Hannah point out, that right now most feminist businesses cannot afford to provide many benefits for their workers. Naturally, it's important to feminist businesses that all workers have benefits that will deal with their needs. But again, we're making a revolution and this isn't going to come easy. The ideal thing will be that as we get stronger, and as other feminist businesses get stronger, together we'll be able to provide for the needs of all of us as workers. For example, why plug into establishment health care programs which are expensive and oppressive to women if we might be able to work out "insurance" programs with feminist health centers? Our creations need proceed directly from neither Marx nor General Motors.

Distortions

What other effects does feminist business have on the woman's movement? It's true that feminist businesses do have "power over determining the movement's public image and recruitment," as mentioned in "God, Mom, etc." So do individual women who get attention from the media. So do organizers of large demonstrations and actions. So do publications. So do large national organizations. The images which come out of feminist organizations of any kind must be watched carefully by all of us. We have the responsibility to protest when they are incorrect or objectionable. But it's also quite important to remember that the most harmful images of feminism come from distortions at the hands of male-controlled media, and not from any single category of women in the movement.

And can it really be true, as the authors suggest, that feminist publications feel pressured by feminist businesses around the issue of advertising? It seems pretty insulting to those women who work on newspapers across the country to imply that they would be seriously worried by Olivia's threatened withdrawal of an ad—even if we ever tried to apply that pressure. Most women in the movement are not jerks. It is further insulting to those of us who are involved in feminist businesses and who consider it part of our ongoing commitment to support the feminist press *whenever* we can through the purchase of ads—even though we know that frequently those ads come nowhere near paying for themselves in additional business. We would hope that women as actively involved in the movement as are the women who run our publications would be willing to speak up in protest of any undue pressure by feminist businesses. We certainly count on them to do so.

Pools of Money

"Feminist businesses can also have considerable financial clout. Very little of the money goes into the women's movement, because they both draw from the same pool of money, and most of the money stays within the business." It's true that at this point little money is going back into the movement *outside* of the businesses. We try to buy ads, give loans if we can, pay salaries, and certainly share our skills and information. Most of the money goes into the businesses, and that is the plan—to get the business in very strong shape so that it makes A LOT OF MONEY, not a little money. Back in the movement means back in the business for right now. Later it will mean spreading money around to other feminist organizations, businesses, and commitments. We have the goals of supporting individual women as well as supporting the movement in general. We see the two as being very much the same thing.

Delusion . . .

". . . Since feminist businesses offer the delusion of participation in the women's movement just by working in them, they militate against women participating in the women's (political) movement." Are women who work in feminist businesses "deluding" themselves that they are doing important political work? The premise we operate from is that Olivia Records will mean self-sufficiency for a lot of women, and a start towards a solid economic base for the movement (both because of payment of individual women and because of whatever money can be channeled into loans or gifts to other women's businesses and projects). Working at Olivia is participation in the movement, you bet. Every decision we make is made with as much consciousness of feminism (I'm presuming in the definition a priority of class, race consciousness as well as woman-oppression) as can be mustered by the *group* of women involved.

Diversion . . .

And I'm trying to think of an example of a feminist business that "provides similar services as, and diverts women from, political organizations with much less money." The letters we get at Olivia tell us that women who hear and are affected by the music that Olivia puts out frequently feel the need to become more and more involved with whatever feminist organizations are doing in their own communities. Many have felt compelled to become involved politically for the first time in their lives. My own reactions after reading political essays, novels, and poetry put out by women's publishing companies tell me the same thing: we get information and energy for our work from the fruits of feminist businesswomen's labor.

Subversion

But ". . . if universities can fund businesses, surely the potential exists for other outside agencies to create and fund businesses as well. Thus, businesses may possibly be used as instruments of external subversion of the women's movement." It seems silly to have to mention this, but anyone or any organization *may possibly* be funded by "outside agencies" and used as instruments of external subversion of the women's movement. We all have the responsibility to know our coworkers in the movement and keep an eye on where money to anyone is coming from and whether it may be coming with any strings.

Better Creations Than Ashes

Of course it's ironic that women who claim to be anti-capitalist are using capitalist strategies as a road to liberation. We are the first to agree with that. But it's also terribly creative. If we thought there were other ways to accumulate economic clout AT THIS TIME we might never feel the need to use capitalist strategies. We feel that until this movement doesn't have to depend on the good will of a few women with money any more, until the workers in the movement are freed from having to work for the Man, the movement will remain middle-class oriented and steered by middle-class women. Feminist businesses, by creating jobs with worker control and offering them to women with less class or race privilege are taking positive steps to change that balance of power. We feel that it's useless to advocate more and more "political action" if some of it doesn't result in the permanent material improvement of the lives of women.

Recently I read an article about a group of sewing machine operators in Thailand who tired of their oppressive work conditions and locked out the management. These women then proceeded to reorganize the company according to their own principles of worker/woman control. The result of their labor was that within a short time they tripled their individual wages and were able to sell the product at a lower price. They did *not* burn down the factory because it was capitalistic. That's the kind of thing Olivia wants to do—that many feminist businesses have in mind—not just following a capitalistic map and forming a carbon copy of the society that oppresses us. We want to take concrete steps toward creating *feminist structures that work*. We are part of a process of revolutionary change.

Down to Food and Shelter

In conclusion, I'd like to put out a call for more feminist businesses. With the exception of clinics, there are few women's businesses that deal with products or services that are *strictly* essential. Books aren't; records aren't. What we need is more women with the energy and access to capital (or willingness to search it out) who will put their feminist commitment and principles into owning and running apartment houses, operating food stores, repairing cars, etc.—with the understanding that each woman handling the money of other women has the strongest responsibility to be in every way accountable for the decisions she makes around it. Certainly this issue is not cut and dried. We need to continue to come up with creative feminist means of dealing with where we live and where we hope to be living in the future.

The demand for accountability is important. It is the key to making successful use of capitalist strategies for feminism. We join with Brooke and Hannah and the many other women who emphasize the importance of feminists requiring accountability from the women in feminist businesses, as well as from all feminist political organizations, as well as from individual feminists who are well-known and who speak (or sing) to many women. And we urge that women concerned about the economic future of women spend their money—if they have it, and when they can—to support feminist businesses that meet their needs.

SOCIALIST FEMINISM

Women as Workers under Capitalism

Staff of *Women*

. . . The subject, women as workers under capitalism, reaches into the guts of one of the major issues confronting the women's movement today: how a consciousness of women's oppression relates to a consciousness of capitalist/ imperialist oppression. The main questions we have to deal with are: what are the functions of women workers in this capitalist economy; what prevents women from identifying as workers; and how are all workers exploited through alienating work under capitalism.

Work and "Work"

Most women in our society do work, whether or not the society labels our functions "work." Our work both in and out of the home is vital to the maintenance of the capitalist economy. Ignoring the weariness and rage of millions of women who are scrubbing, waxing, ironing, dusting, cooking, diapering, even fucking away the best years of our lives, this society does not label these activities as work, but as "labors of love." (Of course, sometimes each of these is related to the most creative work women do; but sometimes each is a duty, performed to gain domestic bargaining power, or just to keep things running.) Although society doesn't pay us for this "non-work," we *do* it, and are made to feel that we are unloving if we don't love it! But our work in the home is not only important, but necessary: it provides for the creation, care and stabilization of the work force. In considering the role of housewives, we must also realize that the nuclear family inherently supports capitalism. As unpaid workers, women are dependent on the paid labor of others. But because society now is broken into family units, each requiring its own supply of goods, few people, paid or unpaid, can afford to risk losing their financial support by demanding control over their jobs.

The distinction of "work" is granted to women who, for personal or economic reasons, have jobs outside the home. In actuality, these women have two jobs, since usually their responsibilities within the home are not reduced. And the old saying, "last hired, first fired," aptly describes women, the surplus labor pool which must respond to the demands of the economy. For example, during the Christmas buying rush, women are encouraged to earn extra money by selling—money which is then returned to the employers when the women buy more expensive gifts—until January, when they are no longer needed in the jobs and are laid off.

Women are often sought to fill jobs with salaries too low to offer men, while men are threatened with being replaced by a woman who will work for less. Recent Labor Department statistics show that in 1969 the median wage for women was \$4,977/yr., compared to \$8,227/yr. for men. Not only does this indicate that women earn less in the same jobs as men, but we are still concentrated in lower-skilled, lower-status, lower-paying jobs. For example, 98% of all clerk typists are women, whereas—as of last fall—we were only 8.5% of all law students.

False Consciousness

Although most women understand the general facts of the exploitation of women workers, it would be naive to assume that we can all relate the idea of exploitation to our own work situations. There are many things which prevent us, first, from seeing our own oppression as women and as workers, and second, from working together to fight that oppression. Many women, particularly those who are educated and work in the "professions," are unable to perceive their oppression because of the myth of professional pride attached to many jobs, such as nurse, teacher, librarian, etc. To complain is considered impolite, unprofessional, and, of course, unladylike. The articles, "Ladies in the Lab" and "Teachers" in this issue discuss how professionalism supports an unhealthy individualism about the value of one's own work and makes women compete with other workers, thereby insuring that working conditions are kept relatively static. It is a further contradiction that such professional work often does not pay very much, frequently less than non-professional work; but the status and prestige that go along with certain jobs are supposed to make up for the lack of monetary reward. Thus a teacher, who usually earns less than the unionized skilled laborer, is able to feel superior to her/him because she speaks better English, may have traveled, and reads books. Because of the social (although not economic) class differences, the teacher is unlikely to demand more pay, and the teacher and laborer are unlikely to work together for change. On the other hand, many workers, particularly those involved in administrative bureaucracy, are paid fairly well and are thus bought off from seeing the essential meaninglessness of their work. And finally, the American work ethic insists that it is better to work than not to work (again using society's definition of work), implying that *doing* something, anything, is more important than *what* one does. Ultimately, this attitude supports the contention that if a person cannot survive on her/his own initiative, it is the fault of the individual not the system, and one is thought virtuous for the ability to survive alienating work and dehumanizing conditions.

There are other factors which promote the false consciousness women have of themselves as workers. First, since most women identify themselves primarily as wives and mothers and try to seek fulfillment in that sphere, we do not often expect or demand satisfying work outside the home. Also, the pattern of "woman's place" is established in the home, and extends as well to working situations. Often, a woman will view her job as fundamentally supportive of the work of her male boss. She may derive vicarious satisfaction and pride from being his invisible "right-hand-woman," as is the case with many secretaries. This kind of wife-role in the office causes her to ally with the boss (feeling that she has a stake in what *he* does, not in what in what is good for her), and perhaps even to side with him against other workers.

In an extension of their role as mothers, many women do social service and charity work. While such work is considered meaningful, the fact is that both its result and its purpose is to maintain the status quo: to keep society's rejects (the poor, unemployed, aged, sick) dependent on the more privileged people—and ashamed of their situation. The people who do social work, mostly women, feel that they are helping people, but in reality they are mainly serving the system which makes their jobs necessary.

Myths

There are a whole series of myths about female workers which are used to block us from equality and satisfaction in the work place. For example, it is popularly believed that women are bad hiring risks since they quit to marry and have children. Yet statistics show that 60% of all women in the labor force are married, and 20% are widowed, divorced, or separated; 1/3 of all mothers work, including 23% of mothers with husbands and with children under 6 years old, and 43% of mothers with children from 6–17 years old. Married women with husbands have an average work-life expectation at 35 of 24 more years, as compared to 28-1/2 years for men. Another myth is that women miss more work than men, yet a 1968 Public Health Survey shows that women lost an average of 5.3 days that year due to illness or injury, whereas men lost 5.4 days. And it is commonly thought that women are pin-money workers whose position or pay does not matter much. In reality, 40% of single, divorced, widowed, or separated working women are their own sole support. And of married working women, 60% need to work to give their families total incomes of at least $7,000. Still another prejudice against women stems from our total image: we are thought to be incompetent, unintelligent, and weak; we are often hired in order to be treated as sex objects and not taken seriously as responsible workers.

Alienation under Capitalism

Even if we could overcome all these barriers to our coming together to demand improvement of our working conditions, our demands would be meaningless within the present economic system. Work under capitalism is inherently alienating: workers sell their labor to employers and lose control over how that labor is used, what it produces, and what effect it has on society. Capitalism's overwhelming concern with profit works to the detriment of worker-consumers, who must contribute to the economy in order to survive. Beyond this lack of control, work is even more alienating because it is frequently wasteful—much of our work would be unnecessary if our economy were aimed at providing for people, instead of profiting from them.

Within a capitalist system, even the more creative jobs carry on the economic hierarchy fundamental to the economy. All levels of human interaction are tainted with the need for power over others (to compensate for the lack of power we each feel over our own lives). A capitalist economy could not survive without some classes oppressing others, one sex oppressing the other, one race oppressing another. Individuals are forced to fight for their own survival, encouraging divisions by class, race and sex among workers, so that we do not unite for our common good.

While we believe that all women are oppressed, we need to understand that because we are divided in these ways, some of us oppress other women because of our privileges. Although all classes of women do share in a similar oppressive socialization (often based on the economic exploitation of women as a caste), we must struggle with our sisters for an end to all economic exploitation if we are to achieve an end to sexual exploitation. How sensible but how unlikely it would be, for instance, for housewives to join the union of domestic workers at this time!

In trying to attain a new concept of work, we must be wary of the capitalist system's ability to coopt many of our demands within the current power structure. For example, in W.W. II, women were encouraged to work because the usual male labor force was fighting. Women were materially and psychologically rewarded for doing what was, and still is, considered "unladylike" work, because they were needed. This situation could give the illusion of meeting a demand of the women's movement—for the expansion of opportunities for women—when in reality it simply served the needs of the people in power.

We need to change the basic relationships of power within this society if we are to achieve our goals. We certainly do not want equality in the sense that women would be on top, filling the most oppressive roles alongside, or instead of, men. We see that men are also victims of economic exploitation in this country; we do not mean to call them our enemy, but to fight the system which manipulates all of us into playing the roles of oppressors and oppressed. We understand too that some goals, such as full employment of women, are impossible to achieve under capitalism. There are simply not enough jobs, not enough money, to pay workers decent wages without destroying profits. So a demand for meaningful work—work that is nonalienating and based upon real choice—is a revolutionary one if it stems from an analysis of how capitalism prevents its attainment. Furthermore, such work should provide the means whereby each one of us can live with dignity, with our work contributing to the good of society as well as paying enough to support everyone's needs.

Wages for Housework

Giuliana Pompei, Translated by Joan Hall

THE PROLETARIAN CONDITION OF WOMEN

Looking around ourselves as women, we discovered the home, the family structure, as a place of specific exploitation of our labour power. Inside the home we saw our *invisible work,* the enormous quantity of work that women are *forced* to perform every day in order to produce and reproduce the labour force, the invisible—because unpaid—foundation upon which the whole pyramid of capitalism rests.

This work, which consists of having children and taking care of them, feeding a man, keeping him clean and cheering him up after work, is never presented as such. It is presented as a mission whose fulfillment enriches the personality of the one who carries it out. A woman is a mother, a wife, a daughter; she is loved only if she is willing to work without grumbling in the service of others for hours and hours, Sundays, holidays, and nights. This labour relationship is seen always and only in personal terms: it is a personal affair between a woman and the man who has the right to appropriate her labour. It is explained continually to the woman that her world is the family and not society: within the family, therefore, she experiences the contradictions involved in the division of labour between men and women, which society imposes on her. The housewife has always been excluded from working class organizations, so all she can do is look for individual solutions.

As an individual, for instance, she has had to confront continual price increases. When her man's wages are no longer enough for meat she substitutes potato soufflé—which is equally nourishing but takes another hour of work; or she travels to markets and butcher shops far from home to save a few cents on housekeeping. Women, isolated in their homes, have had to bear the main brunt of inflation in terms of more work.

The material reality that binds us to this work is our dependence on a man's wage. This wage not only pays for many hours of his direct labour, it also commands other work which revolves around that wage: that of the woman in the domestic "factory." It is the woman who has to work like mad every day to put something resembling a full meal on the table. No matter what the income of the man she is dependent on, a housewife is in herself always a proletarian. Her social status can vary, but no one has ever thought that a slave was not a slave just because he had a rich master who could guarantee him a higher standard of living than other slaves.

There are very many women who, to escape the curse of inadequate wages and the isolation of their condition, decide to work outside the home *as well*. But their continued responsibility for the invisible work—within a patriarchal production relation—reveals the true face of the "emancipation of women through work." Only a part of this mass of housewives who "choose" double exploitation are taken into production, and then always at the lowest levels, for the lowest pay. And an outside job rarely takes away a woman's responsibility as a housewife. So against outside work women manage to organize only slowly and with enormous difficulty, because outside the factory or office there is another clock to punch: the child to be fetched, the shopping and the washing to be done.

Women's enormous quantity of unpaid labour lowers tremendously the cost for capitalism of producing that fundamental commodity which is labour power. It means capitalism can freely manipulate the labour market to suit its cyclic needs: in response to labour agitation it 1) creates a form of *unemployment* which goes uncontested because the woman expelled from socially organized production always has housework waiting, and 2) hurts the workers' capacity for struggle by cutting off or reducing the second family wage.

This will go on as long as housewives continue to function both as a part of the most exploited class and as persons who contain and control tensions and conflicts. Prices rise and women face the first consequences; sick people are inadequately cared for and women work to make up for the shortage of medical facilities. Neighborhoods turn into unlivable ghettoes and only women's work can make them bearable. Only women can absorb the lack of schools, shops, green spaces, and services in general without rebelling. Only they can mediate between society and members of the family to see that the men don't dismantle the factories and burn up the neighborhoods, to see that the old just grumble and don't go mad, that children don't end up institutionalized and that starvation wages go on feeding the family.

The only thing that can make women accept all this is constant blackmail: this is the only way of being a woman; those who rebel are going against their natural role. If one of us feels that she can't manage she is at once made to understand that this is a personal problem which she must solve for herself.

Even the task of assuring the renewal of the labour force is imposed on women as workers with no control over the process of production. For capital to be able to regulate the flow of potential labour, it is necessary to deprive women of control over their own bodies. The myth of maternity as a mission is the most effective ideological instrument for controlling women. Exalting its ideological appeal and masking its social uses, this myth continues to hide from women the reality of their condition. In 1970 painful childbirth and the dearth of effective contraceptives are signs of the backwardness to which women are relegated in capitalist development.

Women guarantee not only that labour power will be reproduced in the necessary quantity, but also that workers will grow up with characteristics suited to the development of the capitalist system. Children must be educated, at the most malleable age, for the division of labour; they must at once get it clear in their heads that everyone must sell his or her labour power to survive, and that there is no escape from this curse.

Through the mother, the child at once learns to accept all this as natural; this is the first step in an apprenticeship which later continues at school, in the propaganda of the mass media, etc.; it is meant to provide an adaptable labour force which will lend itself to the mechanisms of exploitation.

The Struggle against This Work

How can women's struggles fully express the revolutionary potential which is maturing as women find their position more and more unbearable?

We have already outlined a tentative answer: we've had enough of this work which suffocates us, deforms us, and blocks all our relationships with outside reality, this work that locks us in a woman's role.

We reject this work and we reject this role. We struggle for anything which will reduce our hours of work, which will give us a chance to meet, to organize and increase our strength, which will give us more freedom to start destroying our role in practice.

When we organize to achieve some objective, even a minimal one, we are already in practice rejecting housework: we must go out, we must join with other women, we must discover that our personal problems are everyone's problems and that only together can we find the strength to deal with them.

The cost—which up to now we have borne entirely alone—of running this domestic labour power factory should all be unloaded onto the system.

We want the system to assume the costs of maternity, while we ourselves decide and plan it, because we are sick of having it imposed on us as a "law of nature" within variable capitalist planning. We want the system to build and pay for nurseries, kindergartens, canteens, and centralized cleaning and laundry services, etc.

We want free housing—which means more than just removing the rent item from our already meager budgets. We want greenery, gardens, and parks in every part of the city—which means not spending two or more hours a day taking the children out to breathe and play. We want lower prices—which means less work cooking, going to distant markets to save a few pennies, etc.

All these are wage demands: we want a bigger share of real wealth—in terms of houses, green spaces, free services, etc.—not just what we manage to pay ourselves out of a man's wages. And this increased real wealth, this greater availability of goods and services which we demand as the minimum compensation for all the unpaid work we have on our shoulders, we intend to enjoy. What we want is not to go out working and be exploited better somewhere else, but to work less and to have more opportunity for social and political experience.

Precisely because the fight for free social services is already essentially a wage demand, in that it reduces our hours of work, we see no contradiction between this struggle and the struggle based on a demand for direct wages for housework, the work we are doing now and will go on doing whether or not we win our fight for a reduction in hours and workload.

Social services are not the ultimate objective of our struggle; still less do they offer a real alternative to the exploited situation we are immersed in. However, even these concessions will not be handed us on a platter— they can only be won by hard fighting at a high level of organization. And they should be seen as a victory: the conquest of our battleground and better conditions in which to broaden and build our struggle.

The Immediate Challenge

The right to be paid for work one does is something which immediately affects all women: even those who don't figure in the statistics as housewives, even those who are not wives or mothers: the girl living at home who studies or works but is always expected to "give a hand" at home, the "independent" woman with her own income who sooner or later is lumbered with the care of the old, the elderly woman who wears out the last years of her life looking after the children of a younger woman who is thus "freed" for factory work, the woman whose man is "understanding" and ready to help but always makes it clear that by rights she ought to be doing the work, and so on.

The demand for wages for housework is a demand for independence. No matter how many services we manage to win, no matter how much more free time we gain in this way, until we win our own incomes and thus break the bond of economic dependence on a man—whether husband or father—how can we form the relationships we want, decide if we want to get married or not, to have children or not? How can we control our own lives? How many women are unable to leave their husbands today and get divorced tomorrow because, although they have worked all their lives, they cannot support themselves and their children?

The demand for wages has in itself an ideological impact. We are looking at our work in a new way. We have been taught to see that work as an expression of our femininity, in which, we are told, our finest quality—generosity—is fully expressed in giving others security and serenity. The fact that we now see that work as a socially necessary activity, which must be paid for just like the work our fathers, husbands, and sons do outside the home, is already a big step towards achieving an attitude of detachment, towards destroying that naturally fixed role which society assigns us.

Women and Pay for Housework

Carol Lopate

Pay for housework is an idea which has been around for some time. Recently it has begun to receive serious consideration among feminist groups here, largely as a result of the publication in February 1973 of the English version of Maria Dalla Costa's pamphlet, *The Power of Women and the Subversion of the*

Community.[1] Dalla Costa's analysis comes out of the Italian women's movement and was first introduced to the American women's movement in her article, "Women and the Subversion of the Community," published in *Radical America* (January/February 1972, Vol. 6, no. 1).

Quite briefly, the pay-for-housework argument goes like this. Traditional analyses of the working class have excluded women because their work has not been considered "productive"—or, more commonly, has not been considered at all. These analyses have called women "oppressed" but not "exploited," because "exploitation" would imply that surplus value is extracted from their labor. In contrast, Dalla Costa and other feminists say that women's work in the home produces use value, rather than exchange value, and is thus a remnant of a pre-capitalist structure existing within capitalism. But, say these feminists, it is clear that women as housewives produce and reproduce capitalism to at least as great a degree as any other working sector. The work of women in the home forms the basis from which emanates all other labor, from which, in turn, surplus value is extracted. Women help reproduce capitalism both through childbirth and through socialization; they keep capitalism running smoothly by servicing its current (and future) workers with food, clothes and sex. Thus women in the home are part of the working class, but they are not recognized as such because they are unpaid. Producing only use value, they remain part of a pre-capitalist structure. To legitimize women as part of the working class, and to free them financially from men, they must produce exchange value. The subsequent demand proceeds directly from the analysis: pay women for housework.

The attraction of this theory is not difficult to understand. First, in a brief and efficient manner, women are analytically integrated into the working class. Second, a platform for concrete action flows directly from the analysis. Moreover, this demand can be readily understood as developing out of a comprehensive theoretical framework, a fact which might attract the large numbers of women who have not as yet been drawn into the women's movement despite the partial successes of the campaigns around such piecemeal feminist demands as abortion and childcare. Finally, given a capitalist society in which personal autonomy as well as status are gained through money, it may well be that women need to be wage-earners in order to achieve the self-reliance and self-esteem which are the first steps toward equality.

But the attraction of "pay for housework" is not unlike the attraction of union demands: better wages, shorter hours, increased benefits. All of these are far easier to conceptualize and communicate to workers than the demand to change the nature of work itself, a goal which, even when packaged as "workers' control," is comparatively utopian and hard for workers to visualize. Just as unions have generally pushed only quantitative demands and have become

---

[1]Published jointly by the Falling Wall Press, Ltd., 79 Richmond Rd., Montpelier, Bristol B56 5EP, England, and a group of individuals from the women's liberation movement in England and Italy.

reformist institutions for integrating workers into the system, feminist concentration on the pay-for-housework demand can only serve further to embed women (and men) in the clutches of capitalism.

Before going further, I want to make it clear that I am not against "reformist" demands as such, i.e., I'm not automatically opposed to demands whose goal is to ameliorate rather than change the basic structure and relations of society. For example, it is irrelevant to me that capitalism may have accepted abortion reform only because *its* need for workers no longer requires such a high birth rate. I support abortion reform because I believe that the right to decide whether or not to have a child *frees* women. In a similar vein, I am not opposed to pay for housework simply because it is a reformist, quantitative demand that the system could one day accept, but because instead of freeing women, it will serve to rigidify the sexual and other forms of oppression that we are already fighting against. In the following pages, I want to present a number of reasons why I am against women spending their energies on the pay-for-housework demand.

1 The women who support pay for housework say, quite rightly, that work outside the home is being glamorized and held out as a false carrot. But I do not believe that there has been a sufficient understanding of the quality of work and life inside the home. The lives and aspirations of most housewives have undergone major changes over the past thirty or so years. As men increasingly commute to work, women's daily lives have become more and more separate from those of their husbands. Moreover, the greatly accelerated geographic mobility among both blue- and white-collar workers has left women also bereft of continuity and community with neighbors and, with the decline of the extended family, without the support of relatives who once provided both friendship and assistance. The decrease in house size and the mechanization of housework has meant that the housewife is potentially left with much greater leisure time; however, she is often kept busy buying, using and repairing the devices and their attachments which are theoretically geared toward saving her time. Moreover, the trivial, manufactured tasks which many of these technological "aids" perform are hardly a source of satisfaction for housewives. Finally, schools, nurseries, daycare and television have taken away from mothers much of the responsibility for the socialization of their children; few women can feel that their children's upbringing is really in their hands.

Instead of simply paying women to do increasingly trivialized work, we need to look seriously at the tasks which are "necessary" to keep a house going and to make new evaluations. We need to investigate the time- and labor-saving devices and decide which are useful and which merely cause a further degradation of housework. We need to investigate the isolation of work done in the home and look for new, possibly communal, organizations for doing housework—even when living arrangements may not be communal.

2 The demand to pay for housework comes from Italy, where the overwhelming majority of women in all classes still remain at home. In the United States, over half of all women *do* work. The women who stay at home are predominately the very poor, usually welfare mothers who in a sense are already

being paid by the state to work in the home (or stay out of the labor market, however one wishes to conceive of it); and women of the upper-middle class. The wives of blue- and white-collar workers usually do not remain at home, even when they have children. They work. The project of bringing American women into the working class is therefore not merely a question of material conditions, but of ideology. Women who work in America are still seen in terms of their husband's or father's class designation; women themselves remain as if classless, no matter what they do or do not do for a living.

The proposal to pay women for housework does not deal with the fact that the ideological preconditions for working-class solidarity are networks and connections which arise from working together. These preconditions cannot arise out of isolated women working in separate homes, whether they are being paid for their work or not.

3 The financial aspects of payment for housework are highly problematical. Under our present system of corporate capitalism, pay for housework would not lead to any significant redistribution of income or wealth from the rich to the poor. Instead, the money to pay for housework would come from an already over-taxed working class, either through direct taxation or through special corporate taxes which would in turn be passed on to consumers. Moreover, since most men's incomes are at least partially determined on the basis of their being "family incomes," removal of all women from financial dependence on men would probably lower the income standards for male work. Concentration on the demand for pay for housework without acknowledgement of the effect on other segments of society would have the same devastating effect on any long-range strategy for alliance and solidarity between men and women workers as the demand for compensatory education and social welfare programs for blacks during the 1960s had on white-black relations. Workers knew that they, not the corporations, ended up paying for those programs.

The question of how one would evaluate what houseworkers ought to earn has provoked some almost funny alternatives, if one has a morbid sense of humor. For example, in Canada in the late 1960s, a plan, actually brought before the government, proposed that women be paid according to their educational background; that is, PhD's doing housework would get the highest rate and high-school drop-outs the lowest. The use of this salary scale for creating intra-class solidarity and inter-class antagonisms among women is not difficult to imagine. A second proposal which I have seen suggests that a composite of all the activities included in housework be made up with their respective average salaries (nursery care at X amount, sweepers at Y, dishwashers at Z, etc.), and that a final salary be based on the proportion of time generally spent in each of these activities. Since the only job on the list with any financial status is nursery teacher, houseworkers' wages would be very low. Finally, a third means of allocating payment might be to make housework competitive with what the woman (or man) could make on the outside. Naturally, this would again create a hierarchy of pay among women, with some women able to make $30 an hour for washing the dishes, while others would do their dishes for the minimum wage. Obviously, men would receive the highest wage for their work at home.

Another question is how houseworkers' work would be judged, and by whom. If the woman (or man) did not sweep behind the couch, would she (or he) be docked? Would there be increases for taking (or demerits for forgetting to take) the kids to the dentist? If the children cleaned their own rooms, would they get paid? Obviously, there would have to be some kind of institutionalized supervisor to investigate the cleanliness of homes and the health of children, since otherwise pay for housework would merely be welfare or a minimum standard income. But the vision of the visiting weekly supervisor smacks of yet another form of welfare investigator or inspector, of yet another arm reaching in from the state.

4   The elimination of the one large area of capitalist life where all transactions do not have exchange value would only serve to obscure from us still further the possibilities of free and unalienated labor. The home and family have traditionally provided the only interstice of capitalist life in which people can possibly serve each other's needs out of love or care, even if it is often also out of fear and domination. Parents take care of children at least partly out of love, and children are nourished by the knowledge that the care they are being given is at least partly on that basis. I even think that this memory lingers on with us as we grow up so that we always retain with us as a kind of utopia the work and caring which come out of love, rather than being based on financial reward. It seems to me that if a child grew up knowing that he cost the state more than his sister because he was a more difficult child, and so took more labor power to raise, that some of our last, ever more flimsy notions of humanity would be blown away like dust in a draught.

There are at least two strong counter-arguments against keeping the family, or whatever living group, in the private sphere: 1) The distinction between public and private should anyway be erased; and 2) This lovely domain of "free giving" that I am calling for has always been at the expense of women. I don't want to go into a long argument in favor of the private sphere. Let me say merely that I believe it is in our private worlds that we keep our souls alive, and that this is so not merely because we live in a capitalist world, but that we will also need private worlds if and when we live under socialism. The problem raised by capitalism is that it is so difficult to keep the private sphere alive when it is being constantly battered down by the commercialization of everyday life and the constant threats to it by the mass media. But we must fight this encroachment, and not simply abandon our last bastion under the guise of liberating women.

Women do not have to transform their labor into a commodity in order to be considered an intrinsic part of the working class or to be part of the struggle for human liberation. The commodity form is an alienated form and women will simply be perpetuating that alienation. The proposition that women must enter the commodity form in order to liberate themselves stems implicitly from a theory which regards capitalism as the inevitable transition stage between feudalism and socialism. Thus women must first be paid for their labor power if they are to move on to the next stage. But I believe there is no such inevitability in these stages. Moreover, to look at housework as a vestige of feudalism is to see it merely from one side. The separation between use value and exchange value is itself part of the capitalist stage of development. Unfortunately, in fact, attempts to bring underdeveloped sectors into the capitalist sector have done just that. Nothing more. The revolutionary project is quite another matter.

5   I have left for the end what I feel is the most obvious objection to the pay-for-housework demand: it does nothing to solve the sexual division of labor. Because I believe that feminist goals must be integrated into a total theory of revolution, I would not struggle for a feminist goal which sought to undermine the sexual division of labor if it did not at the same time seek to undermine the commodity form. But, conversely, I am not interested in revolutionary projects which do not include a constant attack on the sexual division of labor.

It is highly likely that the institution of pay for housework would solidify the nuclear family. It is difficult to conceive of the mammoth bureaucracy which would be required, whether public or private, allowing pay for communal houseworkers, pay for a man in a homosexual couple, pay for one of two women living together, or even pay for a man and a woman living in a nuclear situation but out of wedlock.

The demand for pay for housework is clearly an easier one to move on than is the call to abolish the sexual division of labor. The latter would involve a total restructuring of private work. Most of us women who have fought in our own lives for such a restructuring have fallen into periodic despair. First, there were the old habits—the men's and ours—to break. Second, there were the real problems of time: many of us have lived with men who work an eight- or ten-hour day, while we have found ourselves preferring or finding less consuming jobs, which have left us more time for housecare. Ask any man how difficult it is for him to arrange part-time hours, or for him to ask for special time schedules so that he can be involved equally in childcare! Finally, as we have argued and struggled with the men we have chosen to live with, we have found ourselves with little other than moral imperatives to bolster our side. I have noticed the relief of women in meeting when talking about the Dalla Costa analysis: it gives scientific validity to our struggle for equality; we need no longer resort to men's being "good" people.

But let us go back to the analysis of housework as production, from which the demand of pay for housework derived. There has been an argument in circles of left or Marxist feminists over whether the importance of woman's role within the family to capitalism lies in her role as producer/reproducer or as consumer. The argument for women as consumers is obvious, given the advertisements and commodities which are structured around the created needs of women. And yet, as most feminist Marxists like to point out, production is a more deeply essential category than consumption. The rhetorical battle goes back and forth, in my experience, with a lot of anger on each side. There is almost an unstated presupposition that if women can be shown to be the unrealized "producers," the spine of capitalism, then they will also be the "vanguard of the revolution."

I do not have my own analysis to propose; nor do I have a concrete, radical platform for feminist-socialist action. But I do have one insight which I hope can become part of a framework for analysis which I and others will do in the future and on which I and other women—and men—will act. This is that we women must stop borrowing categories from the Marxist world. We are not a class, since all individuals of a class have a specific relationship to the means of production, and we vary greatly in this respect. We are not a caste, as a caste is an endogamous (self-reproducing) group, often also characterized by a specific economic niche, and there is no way—as yet—that women can be endogamous. Even if we use sperm banks or other forms of mechanized reproduction, the sperm will come from the outside. Some of us may be doing work that has use value but that does not have exchange value, and many of us, including those who receive exchange value for our labor power, may be suffering from an ideology which still attributes to women the power and status of a second sex. The essential thing to remember is that we are a SEX. That is really the only word as yet developed to describe our commonalities. But what do the differences in our daily lives mean for theory and for practice? What does being female actually mean; what, if any, specific qualities necessarily and for all time adhere to that characteristic? I believe that if, as revolutionary feminists, we want to be clear about where we are going, we must also be clear about the terms we borrow from the Marxist analysis. It is a quick way to legitimate ourselves on the left, but it is not a long-range strategy. What we may, in fact, have to do is to devise our own new terms. We may have to decide that housework is neither production nor consumption. We may have to be hazy in our visions. After all, a total reordering of sex and sexual roles and relationships is not easy to describe.

SUGGESTIONS FOR FURTHER READING:
Part III, Work

Braverman, Harry: *Labor and Monopoly Capital: The Degradation of Work in the 20th Century,* Monthly Review Press, New York, 1976.

Dalla Costa, Mariarosa: *The Power of Women and the Subversion of the Community,* Falling Wall Press, Bristol, England, 1973.

Edmond, Wendy, and Suzie Fleming (eds.): *All Work and No Pay,* Falling Wall Press, Bristol, England, 1975.

Ehrenreich, Barbara, and Deirdre English: "The Manufacture of Housework," *Socialist Revolution,* October–December 1975.

Jenness, Linda: "Feminism and the Woman Worker," *International Socialist Review,* March 1974.

Lynd, Alice, and Staughton Lynd: *Rank and File,* Beacon Press, Boston.

Oakley, Ann: *Woman's Work,* Pantheon Books, New York.

Weinbaum, Batya, and Amy Bridges: "The Other Side of the Paycheck: Monopoly Capital and the Structure of Consumption," *Monthly Review,* July–August 1976.

"Who's Opposing the ERA?" *Dollars and Sense,* November 1976.

"Why Big Business Is Trying to Defeat the ERA," *MS,* May 1976.

FILLING IN THE FRAMEWORKS: FAMILY

It goes far to reconcile me to being a woman, that I reflect that I am thus in no danger of marrying one.

Lady Wortley Montagu

The point remains, however, that movement toward sex equality is restructured by the fact that our most intimate human relation is the heterosexual one of marriage. This places a major brake on the development of sex solidarity among women. . . .

Allice Rossi

The primary role of women is in the home and family . . . men still need a good mother to come to with their little troubles. Women should provide a place of refuge where the husband and children can return from a busy, confused and complex world.

Belle Spafford, President, Women's Auxiliary, Church of Jesus Christ of Latter-day Saints

Nowhere is woman treated according to the merit of her work, but rather as a sex. It is therefore almost inevitable that she should pay for her right to exist, to keep a position in whatever line, with sex favors. Thus it is merely a question of degree whether she sells herself to one man, in or out of marriage, or to many men.

Emma Goldman

The matter of life styles has been intensely debated since the mid-sixties. In part, this debate reflected the social changes already occurring (the "breakdown of the family," as shown in rising divorce rates, extramarital sexuality, communal living, etc.); in part, the debate began as a result of the New Left emphasis on the importance of so-called "cultural" issues (as opposed to "economic" ones); but above all it was probably due to the women's liberation movement and its exploration of the ways in which the personal is also the political. We believe that the various attitudes relative to domestic life style presuppose more fundamental philosophical positions. In this section we shall show how different conceptions of an appropriate type of living arrangement are generated systematically from different theories of the roots of women's oppression.

Although there are many different views about what might constitute a "liberated" life style, one thing that all the protagonists do agree on is that women's place in the family is central to the broader issue of women's liberation. Thus, the main complaint that conservatives make about feminism is that it will destroy the family, whereas all feminists believe either that women's position in the family must be radically changed as a precondition of liberation or that the family itself must be abolished.

CONSERVATISM

Given the biological determinist presuppositions of conservative theory, the conservative view of the family is easy to predict, at least in outline. It takes as biologically given the monogamous nuclear family; and it attempts to defend, on biological grounds, the traditional division of labor between the sexes, according to which the woman is responsible for domestic work and child care while the man's role is "to protect against the outside world and to show how to meet this world successfully." Note that the conservative takes for granted that the world is hostile and competitive.

Tiger and Fox argue that the healthy psychic development of a human individual requires that a strong mother-child bond should be established right at the start of a human infant's life, and that this bond should be maintained for a substantial part of childhood. Tiger and Fox's argument is biological in at least two respects. On the one hand, they believe that the necessity for a strong mother-child bond is "the ground rule of human biogrammar." To support this claim, they cite many examples of the abnormal behavior of animals that have been deprived of their mothers, and they also mention the unfortunate situation of children in orphanages. Leaving aside the questionability of arguments from analogy with animals, an obvious objection to Tiger and Fox's argument is that children in orphanages have been deprived of more than their mother: they have been deprived of a whole family context, including father, siblings, grandparents, etc. What justifies Tiger and Fox in claiming that the undoubted misery of many orphans is due specifically to maternal deprivation? To answer this question, Tiger and Fox have another biological argument: they claim that the mother's place as one term in this primary bond with the infant is determined by her ability to suckle and by the fact that she is "emotionally programmed to be responsive to the growing child." They imply that a man is not biologically equipped to enter into a primary bond with an infant. Hence, the kinds of social relations into which men and women may enter are determined in an important way by our biology.

Bruno Bettelheim also believes that men and women, respectively, should engage in very different sorts of relations with their children. For Bettelheim, the proper role of the mother is to provide emotional intimacy for the child and to take her or his side "no matter what"; the proper role for the father, on the other hand, is to set an example of "dedication to higher issues" which give "a meaning to life above and beyond the everyday experiences." In arguing for this division of psychic as well as physical labor, Bettelheim is wise enough to avoid arguments from analogies with animals, but he does, nevertheless, appeal to a biological argument very similar to that used by Tiger and Fox. That is to say, he claims that women are equipped for the physical and emotional work of child care as a result of the biological processes of pregnancy, birth, and breastfeeding. Unable to undergo these processes, men are not suited to child care: a man's function in society is "moral, economic, political." Despite the fact that his article purports to discuss the role of men, Bettelheim does not explain what specific biological capacities fit men for moral, economic, and political functions and what specific biological lacks make women ill equipped to perform them. An informed guess, however, suggests that Bettelheim would use a Freudian justification for his claim.

LIBERALISM

We know that liberals are skeptical of alleged biological determinations of human society, and hence we can predict a rejection of the sorts of arguments used by conservatives. In fact, one of the main sparks of the contemporary feminist movement was Betty Friedan's publication in 1964 of *The Feminine Mystique,* a slashing attack on the conservative view that women could and should find their supreme happiness and fulfillment in domesticity. Since that time, one of the main strands in the women's movement has been a critique of the assumption that women are uniquely suited for housework and child care.

Liberal feminists confront a dilemma when they criticize the contemporary definition of women as housewives. On the one hand, classical liberalism has traditionally made a sharp distinction between the public and the private spheres of an individual's life: the public sphere affects other persons and is therefore a proper subject for legal regulation; the private sphere is considered to affect no one but oneself and hence should be outside the realm of legal intervention. For classical nineteenth-century liberals, one's home and living arrangements fell within the private sphere. On the other hand, however, one of the important insights of the contemporary feminist movement has been that the personal is political, a claim which obliterates the traditional public/private distinction.

Twentieth-century liberal feminists attempt an uneasy compromise between the view that family life is private and the view that it is political. In line with the traditional liberal account of social relations as contractual, liberal feminists propose to define domestic arrangements in terms of a contract, imposing responsibilities on each party which should be enforced, perhaps legally; at the same time, however, liberals believe that individuals should be able to design whatever type of contract suits them best. Thus, liberals have no theoretical grounds for objecting to any particular type of living arrangement so long as it is chosen freely by the partners concerned. Living together, homosexual marriage, group marriage, open marriage, communal living, even traditional marriage are all acceptable to the liberal feminist, since different individuals will find fulfillment in different living arrangements, and since, for the liberal, an individual's domestic arrangements are ultimately her private concern.

This extreme tolerance may appear to conflict with the liberal feminist's condemnation of the traditional housewife role. To resolve the contradiction, we have to view the liberal as objecting, not to the role of housewife as such, but merely to the fact that women are channeled into it by the lack of equal opportunity in other fields. Once women have equal opportunity for paid jobs, liberals believe that we can be sure that any woman who elects to be a housewife is doing so out of free choice. Of course, we should recognize as equally valid the choice of a man to be a househusband.

Ann Crittenden Scott suggests that the viability of the occupation "houseworker" should be guaranteed by the payment of a wage to the houseworker. In evaluation of her arguments, it is important to notice that she does not suggest that the wage be paid by the state, as it would be according to some socialist-feminist proposals (see "Socialist Feminism" in the section "Filling in the Frameworks: Work"); instead, she recommends payment by the spouse. This would, of course, perpetuate the notion that a family's internal structure and, indeed, its survival are a matter only for the individuals concerned and not for society as a whole.

Alix Kates Shulman's example of a "marriage agreement" may seem to be a paradigm of the contractual liberal approach. We should note, however, one apparently nonliberal feature of the contract she presents. According to that contract, the allocation of tasks is not totally determined by the bargaining power of each of the contractees in the marriage market. In other words, the man is not allowed to use his greater earning power as a way of giving his job more importance and buying out of an equal share of the domestic work. To justify this restriction by liberal principles, we must assume that it is merely a temporary restriction on contracts necessary to compensate for past sexism. Past sexist practices have put men in a better position to compete in the labor market and have relegated women to domestic work. The liberal must argue that this pattern will be self-perpetuating if a limitation is not made on permissible contracts: men will continue to buy out of housework and women will never get a chance to compete in the labor market. But once a situation of equality of opportunity for the sexes has been established, the liberal would consistently have to drop this restriction on domestic contracts. To prohibit individuals from being houseworkers would go right against the fundamental liberal principles of individual choice and noninterventionism.

In our selections on liberalism, we have only discussions of heterosexual marriage, but it is easy to see how the same approach can also be used to set up many other types of domestic arrangements which would be equally justified on liberal principles.

TRADITIONAL MARXISM

We have seen in Part II of this book that traditional Marxism locates the roots of women's oppression in our place within the monogamous family. From this it would seem to follow that the traditional Marxist would recommend women's exit from the monogamous family as a precondition for our liberation. But this is true only in a rather special sense.

In ordinary usage, "monogamy" tends to have the meaning of emotional and sexual exclusivity. For Marx and Engels, however, it was a more technical term denoting the marriage of a man and woman *in which the man controls the family's wealth.* Hence, marriages between individuals who own no property (the proletariat) are not monogamous in this sense. This is what Marx and Engels mean when, in the piece we have excerpted from *The Communist Manifesto,* they talk about the "practical absence of the family among the proletarians." For Marx and Engels, then, so-called monogamous marriage is primarily an economic institution rather than an emotional or sexual one. From the very beginning, Engels says, "the sole exclusive aims of monogamous marriage were to make the man supreme in the family, and to propagate as the future heirs to his wealth, children indisputably his own."

From this account of monogamous marriage, we can see that when traditional Marxists propose to liberate women from monogamy, they are recommending the abolition of a certain kind of economic institution rather than of a certain kind of emotional or sexual arrangement. Hence, their criticism of the bourgeois family is not that this family is emotionally or sexually restrictive, but rather that it is founded on what Engels calls "the open or concealed domestic slavery of the wife." As Marx and Engels put it in *The Communist Manifesto,* "The bourgeois sees in his wife a mere instrument of production." In order to free women from this slavery, traditional Marxists believe that "the first condition for the liberation of the wife is to bring the whole female sex back into public industry." Lenin says:

> Notwithstanding all the laws emancipating women, she continues to be a *domestic slave,* because *petty housework* crushes, strangles, stultifies, and degrades her, chains her to the kitchen and the nursery, and she wastes her labour on barbarously unproductive, petty, nerve-racking, stultifying and crushing drudgery. The real *emancipation of woman,* real communism, will begin only where and when an all-out struggle begins (led by the proletariat wielding state power) against this petty housekeeping, or rather when its *wholesale transformation* into a large-scale social-ist economy begins. (V. I. Lenin, *On the Emancipation of Women,* Progress Publishers, Moscow, p. 61.)

Therefore, traditional Marxists have always argued for the industrialization and socialization of housework as a precondition of women's liberation. For an example of such an argument, see Margaret Benston's article in the "Traditional Marxism" part of the section "Filling in the Frameworks: Work."

Since capitalist society cannot accommodate the demand for the socialization of housework, the demand to bring women full-time into public production is often hailed as a revolutionary demand. But it is, of course, an economic demand, namely, the demand for "the abolition of the monogamous family as the economic unit of society." Traditional Marxists have no objection to heterosexual marriage as a *social* unit and usually take it for granted that people will continue to live in heterosexual couples both during and after the revolution. Hence, they see no need to liberate women or men from monogamy in its ordinary, nontechnical sense of emotional or sexual exclusiveness.

Turning to the traditional Marxist authors represented in this section, we see that, in the excerpt from *The Communist Manifesto,* Marx and Engels occupy themselves exclusively with an attack on the bourgeois family. Under capitalism, they argue, the ties between family members are really economic rather than emotional in nature; since the male controls the family wealth, the wives of the bourgeoisie are, in reality, prostitutes. For women to be equal with men in the family, Marx and Engels imply that the institution of private property, which gives males the real power, must be eliminated. They do not discuss in any detail the form of future living arrangements after class society has been abolished.

The contemporary piece by the Revolutionary Union (now the Revolutionary Communist Party) is concerned with defending the proletarian family as an emotional base for revolutionary activity. The Revolutionary Union emphasizes the strength of the proletarian family and is interested, not in transforming that family, but rather in drawing women into political struggle against capitalism. Note that the authors of this pamphlet urge men to "assist in lightening women's household burdens." These words imply that domestic work is still primarily women's responsibility.

Finally, in this section we have included some excerpts from the Cuban family code, which indicates the approach of one people struggling to build a socialist society. The Cuban code is obviously concerned with promoting the equality of the sexes in marriage, although there is some anomaly in its system for assigning a family name and in the fact that girls may marry at age 14 whereas boys may not do so until age 16. Apart from its egalitarianism, however, the code is remarkable for its strong insisitence on traditional family values.

Since traditional Marxism focuses primarily on the economic functions of the family, it has devoted little attention to the family's emotional and ideological functions. Our traditional Marxist selections on the family reflect this lack of interest in those aspects.

RADICAL FEMINISM

Radical feminists reject the premises of each of the views we have discussed so far: they reject the biological determinism of the conservatives; they reject the liberal belief that one's living arrangements are a matter of personal preference; and they reject the traditional Marxist belief that all that is wrong with heterosexual marriage is its economic context in capitalism. Unlike all the other theorists so far, radical feminists see heterosexual marriage as the primary institution for the oppression of women: hence, they believe that women's liberation is not possible so long as marriage survives in its present form.

This conclusion follows from Firestone's analysis of the roots of women's oppression as being embedded in the prehistoric biological family. (See Part II.) But radical feminists urge the abolition of marriage whether or not they accept Firestone's analysis. Hence, Sheila Cronan describes the contemporary institution of marriage as a form of slavery, while Rita Mae Brown proposes the establishment of all-woman communes. The all-woman commune would enable women to define ourselves independently of our relation to men at the same time that it would discourage the exclusivity and possessiveness which characterize any kind of marriage, heterosexual or homosexual. Not all radical feminists would agree with Brown that any permanent couple arrangement is undesirable, but all would agree that heterosexual marriage is bound to oppress women as long as it is situated in the context of an overwhelmingly sexist society. Only if sexism were eliminated could the possibility of reinstituting heterosexual marriage be considered.

SOCIALIST FEMINISM

The most deeply theoretical criticism of the functions of the contemporary family— economic, emotional, and ideological—has been undertaken by socialist feminists.

Indeed, it is precisely their focus on the importance of the family and "personal life" in general which distinguishes the social analysis of socialist feminists from that of classical Marxists. The foundation of the socialist feminist analysis is the explicit recognition that the family is in no way a "natural" institution outside the economy but instead must be understood as an inseparable part of the wider economic system. Eli Zaretsky's book, excerpted here, traces some of the ways in which, during the capitalist era, the family has responded to the needs of this wider economic system.

Not only do socialist feminists see the family as part of the wider economy, but many of them deny the classical Marxist assumption that the family is not structurally a part of the economic base of society. Eli Zaretsky, for example, argues that "sexuality and reproduction, like the production of food and shelter, are basic forms of 'economic' or material necessity in any society." Marx and Engels recognized this point explicitly in their work but failed to incorporate it into their developed social analysis. Consequently, socialist feminists believe that the special nature of women's oppression is not adequately expressed in traditional Marxist theory.

With the development of capitalism, production came to be defined as the production of commodities for sale on the market. Industrialization meant that this production of commodities no longer occurred in the home, and the home gradually ceased to be viewed as a productive unit of any kind. Instead, its function was thought to be primarily that of consumption. Therefore, insofar as women worked in the home, they were considered to be excluded from production, and their labor was thought to be quite outside the central arena of class conflict. Housewives were assigned their place in the class structure on the basis of their husbands' class position, and housework itself was seen as déclassé.

The tendency of Marxist theorists to ignore the importance of women's domestic labor was not helped by its definition as "unproductive." In classical Marxist terminology, "unproductive" labor is labor that does not contribute to the production of surplus value, that is, of capitalist profit. No judgment as to the social value of "unproductive" labor is implied. However, the belief that housework was outside "the economy," coupled with the familiar and distinctly pejorative nontechnical connotations of "unproductive," encouraged the thoughtless interpretation that housework is not real work.

In opposition to the traditional Marxist view, socialist feminists stress that women's work in the home is productive both in the nontechnical and in the technical Marxist senses. On the one hand, as we saw above in the quotation from Zaretsky, they point out that such work as child rearing, cooking, etc., is vital to any society and hence is certainly productive in the ordinary sense. On the other hand, socialist feminists point out that housework among the working class may be viewed as productive even in the technical Marxist sense of contributing to the production of surplus value. They argue that the invisible product of the working-class housewife is labor power. The housewife produces labor power not only in rearing children but in performing domestic labor for the male wage earner who would be forced to cut the time that he labors for capital if his food were not cooked and his clothes washed. Thus, socialist feminists claim that the wife of the male worker is, in fact, responsible for creating part of the surplus value that, in classical Marxist theory, he has been thought to produce alone.

We can now see the full rationale for the demand made by socialist feminists that housewives should be paid a wage. In the socialist feminist view, housework is not outside the class system; that is to say, working-class housewives belong to the working class, not solely in virtue of their relation to their husbands, but also by virtue of the work they do themselves. In order to emphasize this socialist feminist insight, we have placed our discussion of the socialist feminist demand for wages for housework in the context of the section "Filling in the Frameworks: Work." Note how different is the socialist feminist demand that wages should be paid by the state from the liberal feminist suggestion that a housewife should be paid by her husband. According to the latter suggestion, the housewife would become a domestic servant. However, if the housewife's wages were paid to her by the state, which for the Marxist is an agent of the ruling class, this payment would make clear that the housewife herself is a full member of the working class.

Socialist feminists see the contemporary family as supporting capitalism not merely through the production and reproduction of labor power. Socialist feminists point out many other ways in which the family helps to stabilize the capitalist economic system. Because of the "need" for each family to own expensive consumer goods, such as cars, refrigerators, televisions, and washing machines, coupled with the socially engendered ethos of competition, the contemporary family gives a much needed stimulus to the demand for the commodities produced by a prolific capitalist technology. Moreover, as is often pointed out, women's role as housewife within the family makes us a vital part of the "reserve army of labor" required by a capitalist economy. That is to say, because the role of housewife exists, women can be drawn into the active labor force when there is a need for workers and returned to the home when this need diminishes. For more discussion of this topic, see the section "Filling in the Frameworks: Work."

In addition to all this, socialist feminists have demonstrated the ideological function of the family which stresses the values of authority and competition and encourages jealousy and possessiveness among its members. These traits, of course, are all useful to capitalism. Most importantly, if Gayle Rubin is correct (see Part II), the family is the primary institution which imposes social gender on biological sex, creating the typical "masculine" and "feminine" personalities and thus laying what Rubin sees as the most basic foundations of women's oppression. For these and other reasons, therefore, the socialist feminist believes that the nuclear family must disappear. Unlike the classical Marxist, who thinks it is necessary merely to detach the family from its economic base in private property, the socialist feminist urges the elimination of the nuclear family also as a social and sexual unit.

The article by Barbara and Michael McKain offers concrete suggestions for an alternative to heterosexual marriage. The McKains believe that changes in our domestic arrangements cannot wait on a revolutionary change of the economic system. For them, it is vital to organize our households in such a way as to encourage our liberation from the possessiveness, dependence, and isolation of traditional marriage or couple arrangements. They emphasize that traditional couple arrangements will perpetuate the evils of the present: children who are nonsexist, independent, and able to establish close ties with more than one person will be able to develop only when they are free from the constraints of the traditional family.

The socialist feminist theory of society is characterized by an emphasis on the inextricable interconnectedness of home and work, private and public, personal and political, family and economic system, women's oppression and class society. It attempts to synthesize the important insights of both traditional Marxism and radical feminism while avoiding the inadequacies of both.

CONSERVATISM

Mother-Child Bonding

Lionel Tiger and Robin Fox

. . . Our first example of the bonding process was the mating, or "pair" bond. But there is an even more fundamental bond that all mammals at least have to respect—the bond between mother and child. Even in those mammalian species without pair bonds, where mating is brief and where the sexes part immediately after the mating season, the association of the young with the mother remains important. This is particularly true in all those species where the young are relatively dependent. Whether or not the pair bond will figure significantly in the social system seems to depend on factors associated with territoriality on the one hand, and the nature of the protection needed for the mother and young on the other. In some cases the mother and children can fend for themselves. The breeding season of the hamster, for example, lasts only about a week. During this time the males invade female burrows and then retire to their own. The mother and babies stay in the maternal burrow during the brief maturation period, after which the young disperse and the process starts all over again. With slower-maturing young this is not so easily arranged. Sometimes, as with wolves, pairs form and rear the young together. But with many ungulates, like the red deer, a group of females with their offspring, led by an older hind, form the ongoing social unit. Males associate with these "harems" only at the rutting period.

The reason behind the invariability of the mother-child bond in mammals—as compared with the extreme variability of the male-female bond—is very simple: suckling. Mammals after all are by definition the animals that suckle their young. With this evolutionary innovation the basis is laid for a greater development of sociality than can be found elsewhere in nature. This in turn follows from the longer period of dependency and immaturity in mammalian young. The young of an animal that mature quickly are fully formed both physically and socially at an early stage. Those that mature slowly have plenty of time to *learn* their sociality and incorporate greater variety into their behavior. As we go up the phylogenetic scale of mammals, we find several trends: life span increases; the gestation period becomes longer; the period of immaturity lengthens; the suckling period is extended; the size of the litter decreases until single births are most common. All these factors conspire to delay the maturity of the young animal as long as possible, to prevent his becoming fully formed too quickly.

In all these matters man is the supermammal. He does not achieve this by somehow overcoming or denying or surpassing his mammalian nature, but by exaggerating it. Of all mammals it is man who capitalizes most on the biological particularities of his order. This means that he exaggerates the *behavioral* characteristics—an increase in learning ability dependent on the greater size and complexity of the brain, an even more pronounced period of mother-child dependency, a greater emotional lability, a more elaborate sexuality, more complex play, more spectacular aggressivity, a greater propensity for bonding, a more extended system of communications, and so on. But all this rests on the bedrock of the mother-child bond, itself a product of the live-birth-and-suckling syndrome that is the defining characteristic of the zoological order to which we belong.

The mammalian mother has to suckle the child so that it can live, flourish, and eventually breed. But again, the higher we mount the scale of mammalian complexity, the more it becomes true that something other than simple feeding is involved in the mother-child relationship—particularly when, as with bottle-feeding, actual suckling is unnecessary. The further we move from the governance of primary instincts into the arena of learned abilities, the more it becomes essential for the slowly growing young animal to get its learning *right*. A great deal of its most important learning occurs early and involves those experiences that will provide the foundations for further learning. Since this is the time when the young will be intensively suckling, nature has no option but to make the mother-child bond the matrix for the basic learning processes of the maturing animal.

Simply on the basis of what we know about the social mammals in general, we can predict that if the mother-child bond does not go right, the unfortunate youngster may never get any of his *other* bonds right. The first instruction in the program says: "Form a close and emotionally satisfying bond with the mother; when completed, move on to form x number of bonds, in the following order." Ultimately the "nonbreeding" bond with the mother has to be transformed into a "breeding" bond with a member of the opposite sex. If the initial instructions are not properly followed, the rest of the program may be jeopardized and emerge in an attenuated or skewed form. At worst the wrongly programmed animal may not be able to breed at all and thus be lost to the gene pool; at best it may breed but put the programming of its own offspring in danger.

Sometimes nature tries to make sure of the bond by relatively mechanical means. These, like all instinctive mechanisms, have the advantage of sureness—but they can also go disastrously awry because of their otherwise advantageous rigidity. The idea of "imprinting" is now firmly established in both the ethological literature and the popular imagination. In some animals (*e.g.,* most species of duck) the young learn quickly and dramatically to associate with the first moving object of a given size and color that they see—or even more generally with any larger object that they encounter at a specific period in their development. They will follow and respond to this object in predictable and specified ways. The "object," of course, is almost always their mother, but if for some reason it is something else, the program is totally and irreversibly confused, and a duckling may become attached to a dog or an ethologist or a scientist's boot. The unfortunate creature accepts this object as of its own "species"; once the animal matures, the inexorably confused program instructs it to mate with the only other member of its "species," with comic and yet pathetic results. Zoo animals, to the distress of zoological societies and breeders, thus fixate on their keepers and fail to breed with their own kind. But this is rare. Usually the creature makes the appropriate fixation, and often this is ensured by such devices as having mother and child isolated for a period immediately after the birth. This is common in mammals and gives time for the bond to be formed exclusively with the mother animal, who will then be followed incessantly, turned to in danger, and generally used as a base providing security for forays into the outside world.

Ethologists, with some accuracy, have established "critical periods" during which various types of imprinting take place in various species. But even if the "learning" involved is not of this rather dramatic and rigid character—as is the case with higher mammals—it is nevertheless like it in that it must take place at certain times and in certain ways, and that its outcome determines to a large extent the future performance of the creature. For example, some infants for some reason may not take easily to food, and some mothers may be unwilling or temperamentally incapable of suckling or otherwise feeding them. As we have noted, these characteristics will simply not reproduce themselves in the gene pool if the infant dies or later cannot breed. And, again, the infant may be permanently damaged in a behavioral sense because it has not learned the first rule of the behavioral biogrammar that allows him or her to go on.

This sounds drastic, and it is. There is a striking similarity between behavioral "malnutrition" and food malnutrition. It is now absolutely clear that children deprived of good food—chiefly the substances contained in milk—when they are very young can never wholly recover. For one thing, their growth rates are adversely affected. This has evident consequences for other features of their development. Also, it has been shown recently that the lack of protein in the newborn's diet inhibits the little body's development of myelin, which is necessary if brain cells are to form in the appropriate sequence. Brain damage results as surely from deprivation in the first weeks and months of life as it does from a concussion later.

Development is also closely tied to social patterns, and there is a close connection between behavior and food—one without the other will not do. There is no point in going into an attractive restaurant staffed with capable and friendly waiters who do not serve food; it is just as unpleasant to eat good food in an environment in which one is harassed and abused. For the infant it is a far more desperate matter. Children in orphanages get the food but not the behavior; infants of loving but poor parents may get the behavior, but they will not get the food. In both cases, if the children live to become adults they will be less effective and more frail than their counterparts who were raised by competent mothers and given suitable food.

Our proposal is that the mother-infant bond precedes all others in time—which is obvious—and is the basis for the development of the other bonds that humans are "programmed" to be likely to have. What is the evidence for a statement both so simple and so portentous of complexities to come?

The maladjusted adult has frequently been traced back to the disturbed child, and the disturbed child to the unloved infant. Psychoanalysts argue among themselves about the most vulnerable period of the mother-child relationship. Some favor a late date, some argue for the first few months, some stress the moment of birth itself with its attendant traumas, while still others look into the darkness of the womb—which does in fact contain a living child capable of psychic upset. In any event, the child *is* born in a very "fetal" state—one of the means of extending its dependency and hence its maturation period. But all agree that basic disturbances in the early stages will adversely affect proper passage through the later ones. Many of these explanations and arguments seem overelaborate. A convergence of work in child psychiatry and the study of animal behavior suggests that something rather simple is behind all this, even if the simplicity is disguised by the jargon term "separation trauma." Nature intended mother and child to be together. It is at once as simple and as profound as that. If they are separated when the bond should be forming, it forms imperfectly, if at all. The child suffers a deep sense of loss and even physical distress. And though the mother may not be clear about what has happened to her, she too may suffer—from feelings of depression and inadequacy.

The mother is totally essential to the well-being of the child. Remove her, and its world collapses. This dependence is based on the suckling tendency of mammals, but it does not wholly hinge on food. It is largely a matter of emotional security, of which food is but a part. The human mother is a splendid mammal— the epitome of her order. Her physiology is more highly developed for suckling behavior—with permanent breasts, for example—than any of her cousins, except domesticated ungulates bred specially for milk-giving. But more than this, she is, like any other mammal, emotionally programmed to be responsive to the growing child. Her whole physiology from the moment she conceives is changed not only to accommodate the sheer business of parturition but also to cope with this physical extension of her body for years after the event. Animal experiments have shown that the softness and texture of the mother—and even her smell— are more important to the child than simply her milk supply, although without the latter, in most "wild" conditions, it would not live. Primate infants deprived of real mothers will adapt best to mechanical substitutes that are alike in *texture* to their real parent, in preference to those that simply provide milk but no warmth.

Whatever the value of the substitute, the young animal, psychically, is permanently damaged by the separation. The male may never learn to relate to females, with the consequence that his sexual identity will be confused. The female will almost certainly fail in her task as a mother by ignoring her own offspring, as she was ignored herself. Anyone who has seen the grief, the listlessness, the obvious and heartrending despair of infant monkeys deprived, in an experiment, of maternal care, will echo the sentiments of the man who performed the experiment. He declared: "Thank God we only have to do it once to prove the point."

The point is proved time and time again in human society. Brief separations of mother and child are bad enough, but excessive separations are devastating. Nature is ruthless about this. In the case of some animals, if the mother is not able to find the child immediately at birth, respond to its cries, and above all, lick it from head to foot, she will treat it as a stranger and refuse to suckle it when it is later presented to her. Yet in the name of sanitation we risk tampering with this delicate system by taking babies away from their mothers on the maternity wards moments after they are born. Monkey infants that lose their mothers develop all the characteristics of autistic children, even to the endless rocking and crouching—with little chance of becoming fully functioning adults. Our orphanages and nurseries are full of children wholly or partly so deprived who also rock and grieve and make only painfully insecure adjustments to the adult world.

The practice of taking infants from their mothers during the first five days of life is an example of the acceptance of hygiene and comfort as of greater importance than the possibility of behavioral disruption—if this is even considered. In some of the most sophisticated and admirable places on earth—the wards of excellent hospitals—newborn organisms emerge from their mothers' wombs in a demanding and exciting process to face a suddenly novel environment containing unmuted sounds, swirls of unfamiliar air, and the impressive movements of hands and bodies. Often the mother of such a confused and needy creature is drugged and will sleep for many hours after this first potential social encounter with her child. The neonate itself may be somewhat under the influence of her drugs and in any event will be quickly removed in a plastic basket from her presence to a ward of a dozen or two similar creatures, many crying, all under high light, and all handled by skilled nurses—part of whose professional skill must be that denial of the special treatment which seems to mark how women treat their own children as opposed to the children of others. The child will be labeled by a card on its container, and some mothers will confuse their own child with another, and the more naïve among them will question their competence as mothers: if they cannot even recognize their child, how can they possibly cope with it?

This plight has to be seen in the context of the improved health of mothers and infants. It is probably true that there are important advantages to having the mother rest after the single most trying of all predictable human actions. The question here is about the effects of systems—which are perhaps useful for mothers and certainly efficient for hospitals—on the essential bond between mother and infant. On theoretical and empirical grounds there is a real and disturbing possibility that—with effects difficult to measure—some human babies and their mothers encounter in the act of birth a fact of technology and custom that may make more uncertain the elaboration of a bond begun *in utero,* a bond severely interrupted at just that point when presumably some forceful recreation of the certainty and strength of uterine environment is most necessary.

The mother-child bond is the basic instruction in the human bonding program, and the ground rule of the human biogrammar. If this rule is not learned, the human may not learn to "speak" behaviorally, just as, if he does not learn the difference between subject and predicate, he will never be able to handle the verbal grammar. What he "learns," essentially, is the ability to make successful bonds in general. Bonds depend on feelings, and the mother-deprived child is most commonly described as "affectless"—lacking the motive power to love or care. It is here that the groundwork for "emotional maturity" is laid: that the child will eventually become an adult capable of the full sexual experience and of complete parental behavior. In general, he learns to be confident in his own ability to explore; he develops self-confidence and security. Young monkeys with mothers will move off to enjoy the pleasures of curiosity, whereas maternally deprived monkeys will be afraid to. Successful bonding in later life depends to a great extent on this tendency to explore. This program of security/exploration is so easily interfered with—especially in "advanced" societies—that a large number of people end up by making only partial adjustments in all these areas, to the detriment of their social relationships.

It is just as important to note that the instructions are also quite precise about the termination of the bond—which begins with the gross physiological act of weaning and ends with the transference of emotional ties onto peers and mates. If the mother ignores the instructions to terminate the bond, the results can be just as disastrous as if the child continues to talk baby talk into adulthood: its chances of communicating effectively with other adults are severely curtailed. "Maternal overprotection"—the continuation into adolescence of the relationship appropriate to childhood—extends the mother-child program to a time when the "child-child" and "child-other-adult" programs should be coming into play. . . .

Fathers Shouldn't Try to Be Mothers
Bruno Bettelheim

What is Father's job? What should he stand for in his children's eyes?

Once the answers were quite clear. Today they're not so simple.

A very popular German verse goes: "It's as easy to become a father as it is difficult to be one." And this is said of the German father, who was at all times master of the house, whose word was law for wife and children. If being a father was difficult for him, how much more tenuous is the modern American father's position!

Being one myself and having had intimate experience with the inner feelings of many other fathers, I know of the confusion and utter bafflement which the modern father often feels. He does more for his children and with them, than his father did. Nevertheless, instead of feeling more of a father he feels less so. Nor are matters helped much by the many comic strips, radio and TV programs that either frankly ridicule fathers or depict them as silly boys. These things are not only damaging to the way his wife and children see the father, but also to the way he sees himself.

In the old-fashioned family the father, through his work, provided for the family's physical existence and, he hoped, its emotional well-being. He set an example for standards of behavior and enforced them. He was the protector and the breadwinner—in a time when the bread was harder to win and the family knew it.

Nowadays, with earning and living conditions improved, most children know no fear of want. This security, desirable as it is in itself, tends to obscure the importance of a father's contribution both in his own eyes and in those of his children. Though well aware himself of how hard he works, he no longer finds the recognition at home that used to be the reward for his efforts.

This is not all. When the father comes home and is tacitly expected (or openly asked) to take over the care of the children; when he is received with an account of what went wrong during the day, as if nothing could possibly have gone wrong during his day at work; or with the request to do things around the house—the impression is conveyed to the child that he has been more or less loafing all day and Mother now expects him to start on the serious tasks. That the father accepts this as the right order of things supports other notions the child gets from his storybooks and primers where the father's work, if depicted at all, is with rare and laudable exceptions shown as easy pleasure. The text sometimes says he is hard-working but the pictures which make a much deeper impression on the child, don't show it. The storybook farmers or mail carriers hardly ever work in sleet or rain, nor does sweat run down their foreheads or soak their shirts though the sun burns down strongly. There are never work accidents or any layoffs.

Furthermore, whether or not the father was a good provider used not to be questioned in the child's mind. If he did not provide as much as he might, the child probably did not know it. Nowadays all this is changed. The mass media see to that. They harass the child with how desirable it is to have a new car or dishwasher and how easy these are to get.

In many other ways, too, and in many families, the father's importance as a breadwinner is undermined. The general panacea that modern psychology seems to offer is that we now have better parent-child relationships. But how is a father to relate to his children?

Today's father is often advised to participate in infant care as much as the mother does, so that he, too, will be as emotionally enriched as she. Unfortunately, this is somewhat empty advice because the male physiology and that part of his psychology based on it are not geared to infant care.

Not that there is anything wrong in a father's giving the baby a bottle. Far from it. He should certainly do so whenever the situation requires it or he enjoys it. What is wrong is to think that this adds to his parenthood. What is wrong is a thinking based on what I can best term division of labor rather than on inherent function; a thinking that disregards physiology, denies that our emotions have their deepest roots in it; a thinking that separates activities from the emotions we bring to them.

Nowadays women assume, or have had thrust upon them by technological and social change, many roles in society which until recently were masculine prerogatives. Perhaps that is why they now expect men to assume some of the tasks once reserved for women, and men have become ready to accept such demands. But infant care and child-rearing, unlike choice of work, are not activities in which who should do what can be decided independently of physiology.

For example, just reviewing the mother's function reveals some of the reasons why fathers have a much harder time with their fatherhood than mothers do with motherhood. I believe it is due to the essential difference in their biological roles.

Nine months of growth and profound physiological changes in the mother precede the arrival of a baby, permitting her to prepare not only *physiologically, but emotionally* for the coming child. The birth act itself, *the dramatic changes in her body, all impress upon her what a momentous event has taken place.* Great as a father's desire for a child may be, there are certainly no physiological changes within him to accompany the arrival of the new family member. And afterwards, he has no close relationship with a child that can compare with that of a nursing mother. For her, nursing creates a cycle of tension and relief, of need and fulfillment that is directly connected with her bodily functions and gives her a wonderful feeling of importance and well-being. The father, on the other hand, simply continues to pursue his normal occupation, may even feel a need to do better at it. But he undergoes no physiological and emotional changes comparable to the mother's, has no comparable feelings of contributing intimately and directly to the baby's welfare. Probably he is dimly aware that the physiological underpinning for getting his own satisfaction by administering intimately to the needs of the infant is lacking. When he tries to find greater fulfillment of his fatherhood by doing more for the child along the lines only mothers used to follow, the result is that he finds less rather than more fulfillment, not only for his fatherhood, but also for his manhood.

The completion of womanhood is largely through motherhood, but fulfillment of manhood is not achieved largely through fatherhood. The fulfillment of manhood is achieved by making a contribution to society as a whole, an impulse which is quickened when a responsible man becomes a father. Without a child, there seems little reason why a man should wish to perpetuate society, to plan beyond the reaches of his life; why he should plant trees, the fruits of which will not ripen while he can still enjoy them. But the relationship between father and child never was and cannot now be built principally around child-caring experiences. It is built around a man's function in society: moral, economic, political.

The father who read the Scriptures to his family, impressed on his child that his interest was concentrated on matters transcending daily toil, matters that gave a meaning to life above and beyond the everyday experiences. Though the child did not understand the content of the Scriptures, his father's concern with them, and what the child dimly felt they stood for, made a lasting impression on him. This example of a deep concern for matters beyond the day-to-day struggle made the head of the family a father just as much as his providing the wherewithal for the family. Thus the old-fashioned father influenced the personality of his child not so much through what he did with the child as through the importance of what he, the father, was concerned with. It was the depth of his dedication to higher issues which gave a broader scope to the child's life. This the modern father can still contribute. How? Today much of a father's positive relationship to his child is built up around playing games, working around the house, fixing the car or other leisure-time activities—and not around the father's function in society. When these activities remain mere enjoyment, though—as it is when advocated that father and child should enjoy each other—many modern fathers become play companions rather than parents. A meaningful parent is that father who manages to use such activities for conveying to the child what a man should be like in meeting life, in mastering it and its responsibilities.

When a father plays games and gets carried away by a childish desire to win, gets angry, upset or argumentative about rules, the child's confidence in him can be undermined. Also, in working together with their children, there are fathers who are more intent on getting done with the job than on using it to teach the child what it means to be a man.

For example, when a child watches his father slowly sawing through wood and even helps with his own little saw, the child may be daydreaming of how someday he will clear a large forest and build a city. The act of "doing together" shows the child the validity of his daydreams of future greatness because, while he dreamed them, something real was observed by his father. That the father's achievement required hard work, thinking, planning, is another important lesson that the child must learn, provided the work he has to do himself is not too hard.

So often it has been those men who have long and arduously daydreamed about a better world they would build who later become those best able to do it in reality. While those who were too soon made familiar with hardship as often as not learned to avoid it in later life, and to escape from it.

Contrary to such psychological facts, the opinion is widespread that hard work in childhood is the best training for meeting future hardships. The wish to get real work out of the child is often camouflaged behind high-sounding statements about its enhancing his self-respect. The child will recognize and resent our selfish motives.

These are some of the bad consequences of confused roles for the modern father who at one time is pal, at another the strict supervisor. The child can never be sure what attitude to expect. One of the most important factors contributing to the security of the child is the father's inner consistency. The father's attitude ought to be both strong and understanding, so that the child can afford to become angry and still feel secure nothing untoward will happen.

Provided such inner attitudes obtain, it is true that carefully planned and shared leisure-time activities—games, hikes, picnics, making things—can cement and add new enjoyment to a father and child relationship. They can be as satisfying for the father as the child. Although it has become fashionable for fathers to say they do not care what work their children choose to do when they grow up, many men hope that their sons will follow in their footsteps, take over the business, enter the same occupation, profession or company. Understandably, a father looks forward to the time when his child is grown enough so that he can teach him his craft. Unfortunately, a good many years are required by modern education, and by the time a child reaches the age at which he can learn a craft from his father, the child has also reached the developmental stage of late adolescence or early maturity, when his desire for independence from his parents stands in the way of such an undertaking. More often than not the father's dream that he will truly become a father by making a man out of his son through the handing down of a craft ends in deep disappointment for both of them. Actually no important teaching can take place once the child has reached maturity.

Most fathers realize this, at least to some degree. That is why we see efforts to build up a child's relation to his father at a much earlier age, and around paternal activities in which the child is better able to share. So intense has been the emphasis on "doing things together" that many fathers worry about the relatively short time they can spend with their children. This need not be a serious handicap. If a child sees his father for a few hours a day, he assumes that what his father is and how he acts during the time, is what he is and how he acts when he is away. When a father feels deeply for his child during the few hours he is with him the child is convinced he feels that way all the time. If the father is able to answer the child's questions about life, the child assumes he can answer all important questions. If the father remains calm and in command of himself in the small emergencies around the house the child will feel that, come hell or high water, his father can always control an emergency. And this gives the child the security he needs to meet life—a security far more important than just the act of playing ball or checkers or soldiers with his father.

The issue, as I see it, in this question of the modern father's role, is that in our society fathers have assumed too much the role of an "also ran." No longer is there one central figure in the home—the mother—whose sole or at least major function is to provide physical, physiological, emotionally intimate satisfaction to the members of the family and another equally important person—the father— whose role is clearly to protect against the outside world and to teach how to meet this world successfully. Since both parents try to do both, neither parent is experienced by the child as a secure haven for either. We all need both: someone who always takes our side and sees things our way, no matter what; and also someone who, though definitely on our side, can be relied on to give us sound advice even if it goes against our wishes, who responds to our needs by seeing them in a broader perspective.

Fathers will have to accept and be satisfied with the fact that their contribution will be less immediately obvious to the young child than the mother's. But how important to the child to have a father whose greater objectivity can be trusted in all emergencies just because he is not so immediately involved in the picayune squabbles; to be able to rely on the judgment of a father who is known to think beyond the problems of the moment to their far-reaching implications and consequences.

The child's view of the world and himself will be deeply influenced by the father's quiet confidence; the inner security which permits him freely and graciously to admit an error, which gives him the freedom not to think poorly of himself if a colleague earns more money, which permits him not to blame his difficulties on others or to become defensive about them. In this matter of being a father, as in everything, it is not the externals that count, but the inner convictions and the ability to put them into practice.

LIBERALISM

A Marriage Agreement

Alix Kates Shulman

When my husband and I were first married a decade ago, "keeping house" was less of a burden than a game. We both worked full-time jobs and we each pretty much took care of ourselves. We had a small apartment which stayed empty most of each day so that taking care of it was very little trouble. Every couple of weeks we'd spend a Saturday morning cleaning and taking our laundry to the laundromat. Though I usually did the cooking, our meals were casual and simple. We shopped for food together after work; sometimes we ate out; we had our breakfast at a diner near work; sometimes my husband cooked; there were few dishes. In the evenings we went for long walks and weekends we spent in Central Park. Our domestic life was beautifully uncomplicated.

Then our first child was born. I quit my job to stay home with him. Our domestic life was suddenly very complicated. When our second child was born, domestic life, the only life I had any longer, became a tremendous burden.

Once we had children, we totally accepted the sex-roles society assigns. My husband worked all day in an office and I was at home, so the domestic burden fell almost entirely on me. We had to move to a larger apartment to accommodate the children. Keeping it minimally livable was no longer a matter of an hour or two a week but took hours of every day: children make unbelievable messes. Our one meal a day for two people turned into a half a dozen meals a day for anywhere from one to four people at a time, and everyone ate different food. To shop for this brood—or even just to run out for a quart of milk—became a major project. It meant putting on snowsuits, boots, and mittens, getting strollers or carriages up and down stairs, and scheduling the trip so it not interfere with someone's feeding or nap or illness or some other domestic job. Laundry turned from a weekly to a daily chore. And all this tumult started for me at six in the morning and didn't let up until nine at night, and *still* there wasn't time enough to do everything.

But even more burdensome than the physical work of child-rearing was the relentless responsibility I had for the children. There was literally nothing I could do or even contemplate without having to consider first how the children would be affected. Answering their questions alone ruled out for me such a minimum of privacy as a private *mental* life. They were always *there*. I couldn't read or think. If there ever was a moment to read, I read to them.

My husband's job began keeping him at work later and later, and sometimes took him out of town. If I suffered from too much domesticity, he suffered from too little. The children were usually asleep when he got home and I was too exhausted to talk. He became a stranger. Though he had sometimes, when we were first married, cooked for the two of us, that was no longer possible. A meal had become a major complicated production, in which timing counted heavily and someone might be crying in the background. No longer could we decide at the last moment what we felt like having for supper. And there were always dishes in the sink.

As the children grew up, our domestic arrangement seemed increasingly odious to me. I took free-lance work to do at home in order to keep some contact with the world, but I had to squeeze it into my "free" time. My husband, I felt, could always change his job if the pressure was too great, but I could never change mine. When I finally began to see my situation from a women's liberation point of view, I realized that the only way we could possibly survive as a family (which we wanted to do) was to throw out the old sex roles we had been living by and start again. Wishing to be once more equal and independent as we had been when we had met, we decided to make an agreement in which we could define our roles our own way. We wanted to share completely the responsibility for caring for our household and for raising our children, by then five and seven. We recognized that after a decade of following the traditional sex roles we would have to be extremely vigilant and wary of backsliding into our old domestic habits. If it was my husband's night to take care of the children, I would have to be careful not to check up on how he was managing; if the baby sitter didn't show up for him, it would have to be *his* problem.

When our agreement was merely verbal, it didn't work; our old habits were too firmly established. So we made a formal agreement instead, based on a detailed schedule of family duties and assignments. Eventually, as the old roles and habits are replaced, we may be able to abandon the formality of our arrangement, but now the formality is imperative. Good intentions are simply not enough.

Our agreement is designed for our particular situation only in which my husband works all day at a job of his choice, and I work at home on a free-lance basis during the hours the children are in school (from 8:30 till 3:00). If my husband or I should change jobs, income, or working hours, we would probably have to adjust our agreement to the altered circumstances. Now, as my husband makes much more money than I do, he pays for most of our expenses.

MARRIAGE AGREEMENT

I Principles

We reject the notion that the work which brings in more money is the more valuable. The ability to earn more money is already a privilege which must not be compounded by enabling the larger earner to buy out of his/her duties and put the burden on the one who earns less, or on someone hired from outside.

We believe that each member of the family has an equal right to his/her own time, work, value, choices. As long as all duties are performed, each person may use his/her extra time any way he/she chooses. If he/she wants to use it making money, fine. If he/she wants to spend it with spouse, fine. If not, fine.

As parents we believe we must share all responsibility for taking care of our children and home—not only the work, but the responsibility. At least during the first year of this agreement, *sharing responsibility* shall mean:

1 Dividing the *jobs* (see "Job Breakdown" below); and
2 dividing the *time* (see "Schedule" below) for which each parent is responsible.

In principle, jobs should be shared equally, 50-50, but deals may be made by mutual agreement. If jobs and schedule are divided on any other than a 50-50 basis, then either party may call for a re-examination and redistribution of jobs or a revision of the schedule at any time. Any deviation from 50-50 must be for the convenience of both parties. If one party works overtime in any domestic job, she/he must be compensated by equal extra work by the other. For convenience, the schedule may be flexible, but changes must be formally agreed upon. The terms of this agreement are rights and duties, not privileges and favors.

II Job Breakdown

A Children

1 Mornings: Waking children; getting their clothes out, making their lunches; seeing that they have notes, homework, money, passes, books, etc.; brushing their hair; giving them breakfast; making coffee for us.

2 Transportation: Getting children to and from lessons, doctors, dentists, friends' houses, park, parties, movies, library, etc. Making appointments.

3 Help: Helping with homework, personal problems, projects like cooking, making gifts, experiments, planting, etc.; answering questions, explaining things.

4 Nighttime: Getting children to take baths, brush their teeth, go to bed, put away their toys and clothes; reading with them; tucking them in and having night-talks, handling if they wake and call in the night.

5 Babysitters: Getting babysitters, which sometimes takes an hour of phoning.

6 Sickcare: Calling doctors, checking out symptoms, getting prescriptions filled, remembering to give medicine, taking days off to stay home with sick child; providing special activities.

7 Weekends: All above, plus special activities (beach, park, zoo, etc.).

B Housework

8 Cooking: Breakfasts; dinners; (children, parents, guests).

9 Shopping: Food for all meals; housewares; clothing and supplies for children.

10 Cleaning: Dishes daily; apartment weekly, bi-weekly, or monthly.

11 Laundry: Home laundry; making beds; drycleaning (take and pick up).

III Schedule

(The numbers on the following schedule refer to Job Breakdown list.)

1 Mornings: Every other week each parent does all.

2 and **3** Transportation and Help: Parts occurring between 3:00 and 6:30 pm, fall to wife. She must be compensated (see 10 below). Husband does all weekend transportation and pickups after 6:00. The rest is split.

4 Nighttime (and all Help after 6:30): Husband does Tuesday, Thursday, and Sunday. Wife does Monday, Wednesday, and Saturday. Friday is split according to who has done extra work during the week.

5 Babysitters must be called by whoever the sitter is to replace. If no sitter turns up, the parent whose night it is to take responsibility must stay home.

6 Sickcare: This must still be worked out equally, since now wife seems to do it all. (The same goes for the now frequently declared school closings for so-called political protest, whereby the mayor gets credit at the expense of the mothers of young children. The mayor only closes the schools, not the places of business or the government offices.)

7 Weekends: Split equally. Husband is free all of Saturday, wife is free all of Sunday, except that the husband does all weekend transportation, breakfasts, and special shopping.

8 Cooking: Wife does all dinners except Sunday nights; husband does all weekend breakfasts (including shopping for them and dishes). Sunday dinner, and any other dinners on his nights of responsibility if wife isn't home. Breakfasts are divided week by week. Whoever invites the guests does shopping, cooking, and dishes; if both invite them, split work.

9 Shopping: Divide by convenience. Generally, wife does local daily food shopping, husband does special shopping for supplies and children's things.

10 Cleaning: Husband does all the house-cleaning, in exchange for wife's extra childcare (3:00 to 6:30 daily) and sick care. Dishes: same as 4.

11 Laundry: Wife does most home laundry. Husband does all dry cleaning delivery and pick up. Wife strips beds, husband remakes them.

After only four months of strictly following our agreement, our daughter said one day to my husband, "You know, Daddy, I used to love Mommy more than you, but now I love you both the same."

The Value of Housework

Ann Crittenden Scott

. . . According to economists at the Chase Manhattan Bank, housewives are doing gratis work worth at least $257.53 a week on the current labor market, and they are performing a dozen or so tasks, any one of which, outside the home, would be an independent profession with its own salary. (See chart.)

Chase's calculations don't even include some of the most important tasks performed by women who work at home. Aside from their daily "jobs," they act as teachers for their children and as hostesses and frequently secretaries for their husbands. And tying all these roles together, balancing time and allocating energies, is a managerial skill that, according to one economist, is equivalent to the functions performed by an independent entrepreneur of a small fairly complex business.

In fact, if the job weren't considered "woman's work," there is little doubt that its challenges, its variety, and its flexibility would appeal to many men. For

Woman's Work

Job	Hours per week	Rate per hour	Value per week	Job	Hours per week	Rate per hour	Value per week
Nursemaid	44.5	$2.00	$89.00	Laundress	5.9	$2.50	$14.75
Dietitian	1.2	4.50	5.40	Seamstress	1.3	3.25	4.22
Food buyer	3.3	3.50	11.55	Practical nurse	.6	3.75	2.25
Cook	13.1	3.25	42.58	Maintenance man	1.7	3.00	5.10
Dishwasher	6.2	2.00	12.40	Gardener	2.3	3.00	6.90
Housekeeper	17.5	3.25	56.88	Chauffeur	2.0	3.25	6.50
				TOTAL	$257.53 or $13,391.56 a year*		

*Considerably more than what 83.8 percent of all American workers were able to earn in 1970
Source: Chase Manhattan Bank, 1972.

many individuals, these rewards more than outweigh the long hours—sometimes 13 to 14 hours per day—and the hard, often routine work. But what man would want a position that guarantees no independent income, no Social Security, not even a living wage? And worse, which has, in this male-dominated culture, in spite of all propaganda to the contrary, almost no status at all?

For the truth is, although the housewife may take justifiable pride in the home she works so hard to maintain, housework is not viewed as dignified or respected employment. The housewife is the subject of endless jokes and social put-downs; she is patronized, condescended to, and considered unemployed. All too often, the woman who has chosen to be a housewife and stays home with her children is looked upon as lazy, untalented, or someone who "doesn't really work." . . .

Some economists maintain that housewives' services are excluded from the GNP because it is impossible to impute a value to them, but a number of other nonmarket items are figured into the accounts—the value of agricultural commodities produced and consumed by a family, for instance, or the value of owner-occupied dwellings. Although it might not be easy to set a price for unpaid housework, it would surely be within the capability of interested economists. And it might help correct the impression that those 30 million Americans are living off the fat of the land.

According to Gardner Ackley, Chairman of the President's Council of Economic Advisers under President Johnson, the "failure to recognize the value of these productive services is a source of serious bias in the national product." Under the existing method of accounting, for example, every time a woman leaves home to take a job, the move is counted as an addition to the GNP, instead of simply a shift in the type of work being done. Since more women have been entering the job market in recent years, this makes the GNP look as though it is growing faster than it really is. Conversely, by leaving housework out of the GNP, economists have vastly underestimated the total amount of productive work being done. By one calculation, housewives' services probably amount to about one-fourth of the current level of GNP, or $250 billion—and that's not even counting all the unpaid volunteer work that women perform for hospitals, charities, political candidates, and other worthy causes. . . .

One of the main reasons the housewife's bearing and caring for children, her cooking, cleaning, chauffeuring, and shopping are scoffed at, ignored, or taken for granted, is because it is work being done by a woman. Men who cook are chefs; women are just cooks. Men who handle finances are accountants; woman are simply bookkeepers. Men who plan and order supplies are purchasing agents; women who do the same are only consumers. Not so long ago when men were secretaries and bank tellers, the jobs were the training grounds for executive positions. When performed by women, those tasks are likely to be dead-end jobs.

An explicit downgrading of the work done by women is found in the *Dictionary of Occupational Titles,* a Labor Department publication that defines some 22,000 occupations and serves as a standard reference for government and industry. Each occupation is rated on a skill scale from a high of 1 to a low of 887. Listed at the 878 level are homemakers, foster mothers, child-care attendants, home health aides, nursery school teachers, and practical nurses. A marine mammal handler, on the other hand, has a ranking of 328, a hotel clerk 368, and a barber 371. Obviously, "woman's work" doesn't measure up. Ultimately, the only way to achieve any real equality between the sexes is to abolish sex roles altogether; to put an end to woman's work and man's work, and to develop the concept and value of human work.

One way to achieve this might come from making marriage a true partnership, legally and financially, as well as personally. Both partners, for example, should have equal rights to all income and property acquired during marriage, as well as to its management and control. If one partner works outside the home, then half of his or her salary should by law belong to the other party, and the partners could decide between themselves how the household expenses should be handled. . . .

Another proposal giving credence to the idea of equality between the sexes would have the law assure the wife a salary for the housework she performs. This salary would reflect the value of her individual services, what she could be earning in the labor market, or the official minimum wage. She could receive a percentage of her husband's salary to be paid by him or paid directly by his employer in the same way as the military sends allotment checks to the wives of servicemen who are stationed overseas. If she is paid by her husband, her salary would not be subject to tax, since it was already taxed once when the husband received it. Since the husband would in fact be the "employer," he would be expected to pay the basic household expenses of food, clothing, and shelter, allowing his wife to spend her salary as she chose, on her own personal needs, on her family, savings, or investment. If she worked outside the home and did all the housework, too, she would get paid for both jobs. If a husband and wife each did half of the housework, they would receive no household salary, or they could split a salary. A husband who refused to pay his wife for housework could be taken to domestic court for a determination of her proper salary. . . .

Still, the idea of a salary for housewives arouses strong opposition—and sometimes among housewives themselves. Many feel that they receive payment enough in the love and affection from their families. "No amount of money could make you do some of the things you have to do," says one Dallas suburbanite. "You only do it for love." Others resent the notion of trying to place a crass, monetary value on that labor of love. "How could you place a value on some of the functions of mothering, of being there when people need you, of making sure that everything in the household happens smoothly and on time?" asks New York economist Alfred Eichner. "It wouldn't be a realistic exercise. What makes a household a home is people sacrificing themselves. No money could buy a comparable commitment, just as money can't buy a good soldier."

That may be, but because a service is invaluable seems a poor reason to turn it into servitude, and it's a little late to be romanticizing a housewife's martyrdom on the altar of love. Elizabeth Janeway, in her book, *Man's World, Woman's Place,* has some astute things to say about the dangers of being paid in emotional capital alone. As she sees it, women who work at home have no objective means of judging their own value or skills. They must become "managers of emotions," in Kenneth Keniston's phrase, who keep their successes on a private and personal level, and live vicariously on the praise and success of others. The situation can all too often turn normal family encounters into opportunities for emotional manipulation and blackmail.

A more practical argument against salaries for housework is simply this: in most families, after all the basic bills are paid, there is no money left over for a salary for anybody. A household wage might therefore benefit only the more affluent wives. And many feminists worry that the idea would only reinforce the association of housework with "woman's work," and make the eventual goal of abolishing sex roles more difficult than ever to achieve. "The husband would just be employing his wife as a servant," complains one activist, "and who wants that?"

Some advocates overcome this objection by suggesting that the salary need not be actually paid unless the marriage is dissolved. At that time the wife's "back wages" could be awarded to her as a sort of "severance pay." Others have suggested that the portion of the family income allotted to the wife as salary be used to buy an annuity or pension, payable if the marriage went aground—a sort of forced savings against the possibility of divorce. And in that event, instead of receiving alimony, with all its connotations of charity, the wife would receive accrued income, or reparations, for the labor she had put into the job of marriage. The New York Chapter of NOW is extending that idea by pushing for family insurance. In cases of divorce, such an insurance policy would guarantee the homeworking wife an income, determined by number of children and length of marriage.

Today, housewives still don't enjoy basic rights and safeguards that workers in factories and offices have long taken for granted. "The rights to support of women and children are much more limited than is generally known," stated a recent report by the Labor Department. "A married woman living with her husband can, in practice, only get what he chooses to give her." In all but eight states, for example, a husband's earnings are his separate personal property and his wife has no legal claim on them, or on any property accumulated in his name.

Nor does she have any right to compensation for the labor she may have put into the marriage. He can make and spend his own money, build up his own estate, without her participation or knowledge of what is happening.

Another way for a housewife to collect her well-earned salary might be to place housework in the category of jobs covered by the Social Security system. A similar proposal was recently made by the West German government, after a poll revealed that 86 percent of the population was in favor of housewives receiving their own pension. Under the proposed law, all houseworkers would register for Social Security as individuals, so that they could take their own pensions into marriage, and out of it again if divorce occurred. Whatever their work pattern, they could collect a full pension. During marriage, if the houseworker had no other income, the other spouse would contribute to the plan for both. In justifying the proposed change, the West German government declared that "to be a housewife is a full job . . . as much a career as any other. . . . Economists agree that the work done at home contributes to the family income, for if it were done professionally, unmanageable costs would be added to the household's budget."

The inequities of the current Social Security system in the United States are a result of the fact that housewives are considered "nonworking" women. Because the system is based on contributions from employer and employee, and she has neither employer nor salary, she gets no benefits from the system except Medicare. Everything is dependent on her husband's pension. If she is widowed and at least 62, she receives only 82½ percent of the benefits he had earned. If she is divorced, she receives nothing unless she was married at least 20 years and can show that he is contributing or was ordered to contribute to her support. And if she has worked outside the home for a time, as most women do, she must choose, upon retirement, either her own benefit or half of her husband's, whichever is larger. She can't receive both, even though both have been earned. That means the government benefits from their marriage by retaining more cash than it would have done had this man and woman remained single.

There has been some agitation in Congress to correct these inequities in the Social Security system, but virtually no initiatives have been taken to grant women full pensions, or any kind of salaries for housework.

But, in an unorganized way, things are changing. At least 50 percent of American women 18 years and over (and almost 40 percent of women with children under 18) are in the labor force, and who-knows-how-many men are in the kitchen. The growth of child-care centers and businesses supplying household services also suggests a new fate for housework in the future. But these trends are not change enough.

Nothing will be enough until the working woman—wherever she works—is free to earn a living in any way that she chooses. "Occupation: Houseworker" is a viable and respectable choice for anyone, male or female, provided it is treated as such, socially and economically. If it were, the houseworker could at last be recognized as a professional member of the American labor force, paid for her or his labor, time, and skills.

TRADITIONAL MARXISM

The Family
Friedrich Engels

. . . Abolition of the family! Even the most radical flare up at this infamous proposal of the Communists.

On what foundation is the present family, the bourgeois family, based? On capital, on private gain. In its completely developed form this family exists only among the bourgeoisie. But this state of things finds its complement in the practical absence of the family among the proletarians, and in public prostitution.

The bourgeois family will vanish as a matter of course when its complement vanishes, and both will vanish with the vanishing of capital.

Do you charge us with wanting to stop the exploitation of children by their parents? To this crime we plead guilty.

But, you will say, we destroy the most hallowed of relations, when we replace home education by social.

And your education! Is not that also social, and determined by the social conditions under which you educate, by the intervention, direct or indirect, of society, by means of schools, etc.? The Communists have not invented the intervention of society in education; they do but seek to alter the character of that intervention, and to rescue education from the influence of the ruling class.

The bourgeois clap-trap about the family and education, about the hallowed co-relation of parent and child, becomes all the more disgusting, the more, by the action of Modern Industry, all family ties among the proletarians are torn asunder, and their children transformed into simple articles of commerce and instruments of labour.

But you Communists would introduce community of women, screams the whole bourgeoisie in chorus.

The bourgeois sees in his wife a mere instrument of production. He hears that the instruments of production are to be exploited in common, and, naturally, can come to no other conclusion than that the lot of being common to all will likewise fall to the women.

He has not even a suspicion that the real point aimed at is to do away with the status of women as mere instruments of production.

For the rest, nothing is more ridiculous than the virtuous indignation of our bourgeois at the community of women which, they pretend, is to be openly and officially established by the Communists. The Communists have no need to introduce community of women; it has existed almost from time immemorial.

Our bourgeois, not content with having the wives and daughters of their proletarians at their disposal, not to speak of common prostitutes, take the greatest pleasure in seducing each others' wives.

Bourgeois marriage is in reality a system of wives in common and thus, at the most, what the Communists might possibly be reproached with, is that they desire to introduce, in substitution for a hypocritically concealed, an openly legalised community of women. For the rest, it is self-evident that the abolition of the present system of production must bring with it the abolition of the community of women springing from that system, *i.e.,* of prostitution both public and private. . . .

The Nuclear Family

The Revolutionary Communist Party

. . . The women's liberation movement, because of its basic class outlook, did not and could not attract large numbers of working class women, either white or third world.

Take the question of the nuclear family. Because of the fact that under capitalism, the monogamous family (the "nuclear family," consisting of husband, wife and children) is an instrument for the oppression of women, many in the women's liberation movement saw the nuclear family as the chief evil that had to be combatted in order for women to be liberated.

The justified indignation many petty bourgeois women felt at being confined to deadening household chores, burdened with attending to the personal needs of both children and husband, unable to work outside the home or to go to school (or continue schooling), came to be directed both at men in general and the nuclear family as an institution. As a result, many working class women generally got the impression that women's liberation was man-hating and anti-family.

While it is true that the nuclear family in bourgeois society generally serves to confine women to the sphere of home and family, while allowing somewhat more flexibility for the man—flexibility in that, in general, he can get out and sell his labor power more easily and does not have household chores and child care responsibilities limiting both his outlook and his time—the nuclear family is not the enemy.

In fact, for many working people, the family provides one of life's few bright spots. Despite the many difficulties of raising children under capitalism, including financial hardships and real fears for their health and safety, the proletariat loves its children and does all it can to enable them to "have a better life than I did."

The present welfare system actually helps break up families, forcing husbands and fathers to leave their families in order for the women and children to get a grant. The demand of the working class is not to break up the family, but, rather, to fight the attacks on it—high prices, unemployment, poor medical care, and most recently, the energy freeze, everything that makes raising a family increasingly difficult.

Instead of being a weapon used by the bourgeoisie to try to keep the proletariat weak and divided, the single family unit can and must be turned into *a weapon for the proletariat,* a fighting unit in which husband and wife are equals. Men and women must come to understand equally the necessity not only for a particular economic struggle, such as a strike, but, most importantly, for political struggle against the capitalist system. And the men, in particular, must understand that women's participation in struggle is vitally necessary if the working class is to win, and that they must assist in lightening women's household burdens.

Cuban Family Code (excerpts)

Article 1　This Code regulates judicially the institutions of the family—marriage, divorce, parent-child relations, obligation to provide alimony, adoption and tutelage—with the main objectives of contributing to:

- the strengthening of the family and of the ties of affection and reciprocal respect between its members;
- the strengthening of legally formalized or judicially recognized marriage, based on absolute equality of rights between men and women;
- the most effective fulfillment by parents of their obligations regarding the protection, moral upbringing and education of their children so they can develop fully in every field as worthy citizens of a socialist society;
- the absolute fulfillment of the principle of equality of all children.

TITLE I　MARRIAGE

Chapter I　Marriage in General

Section One　Marriage and its establishment

Article 2　Marriage is the voluntarily established union between a man and a woman who are legally fit to do so, in order to live together.

Marriage will have a legal effect only when it is formalized or recognized in keeping with the rules established in this Code.

Article 3　Women and men who are more than 18 years old are authorized to marry. Those who are less than 18 years old are not.

In spite of the contents of the above paragraph, under exceptional circumstances and for justified reasons the parents or other relatives in lieu of them, or in other cases, the court, can grant permission to those who are under 18 to formalize their marriage, as long as the girl is at least 14 and the boy at least 16 years old.

This exceptional permission must be granted by:

1　the father and mother on a joint basis, or the one which has *patria potestas;*

2　the maternal or paternal grandparents, without distinction, in lieu of the parents, with preference given to those who live in the same dwelling as the minor;

3 the person or persons who adopted the minor—in case of adoption;
4 the tutor, if the minor was subject to tutelage;
5 the court, if for reasons contrary to the norms and principles of socialist society, one of the above refuses to give permission.

In this case, one or both interested parties or a brother or sister of age, with the aid of a district attorney, can call on the competent regional people's court to grant the required permission. The court, after having heard the opinions of the interested parties and taking into account the interests of society and those of the interested parties, will summarily decide what is best.

Article 4 The following people will not be able to marry:

1 those who are mentally unfit to give their consent;
2 those who have been joined in a formalized or judicially recognized marriage;
3 girls under 14 and boys under 16. . . .

Chapter II Relations between Husband and Wife

Section One Rights and duties between husband and wife

Article 24 Marriage is established with equal rights and duties for both partners.

Article 25 Partners must live together, be loyal, considerate, respectful and mutually helpful to each other.

The rights and duties that this Code establishes for partners will remain in effect as long as the marriage is not legally terminated, even if the partners do not live together for any well-founded reason.

Article 26 Both partners must care for the family they have created and each must cooperate with the other in the education, upbringing and guidance of the children according to the principles of socialist morality. They must participate, to the extent of their capacity or possibilities, in the running of the home, and cooperate so that it will develop in the best possible way.

Article 27 The partners must help meet the needs of the family they have created with their marriage, each according to his or her ability and financial status. However, if one of them only contributes by working at home and caring for the children, the other partner must contribute to this support alone, without prejudice to his duty of cooperating in the above-mentioned work and care.

Article 28 Both partners have the right to practice their profession or skill and they have the duty of helping each other and cooperating in order to make this possible and to study or improve their knowledge. However, they must always see to it that home life is organized in such a way that these activities are coordinated with their fulfillment of the obligations posed by this Code.

Section Two The economic basis of matrimony

Article 29 The economic basis of matrimony will be joint property of goods as contemplated in this Code.

This will prevail from the moment a marriage is formalized or from the date a union is initiated in the cases covered by Article 19 and it will cease when the marriage is terminated for any reason.

Article 30 In line with the bases mentioned in the above article, the following will be considered joint property:

1   the salaries or wages, retirement pensions, benefits and other pensions or other income obtained by one or both partners during the marriage as a result of work done or from the social security fund;

2   the goods and the rights acquired by virtue of a purchase made during the marriage with common funds, regardless of whether the purchased item is for joint use or for one of the partners;

3   the benefits, rents or interests received or acquired during the marriage from goods or items which are considered joint property or those which are the individual property of either partner.

Article 31 The goods in possession of the partners will be presumed to be common property as long as it is not proven that they are the sole property of one or the other.

Article 32 The following items are the property of the partners individually:

1   those purchased by either one prior to the marriage;

2   those they purchased during the marriage with money derived from inheritance, in replacement or substitution of another item which is their property, and for commercial purposes. In cases of donations and onerous payment made with funds which are common property, a deduction will be made;

3   those which were purchased with the money of one of the partners;

4   the money collected by one or the other partner in periods during the marriage which is the result of an amount or credit in his or her favor previous to the marriage and payable in a specific number of installments;

5   those which are for the exclusive use of each of the partners.

Section Three   Responsibilities and obligations involved in joint property of goods

Article 33 The joint property of goods will involve the following responsibilities:

1   support of the family and meeting of the expenses resulting from the education and upbringing of children of both or one of the partners;

2   all debts and obligations arising during the marriage which were taken on and assumed by either partner, except in the cases when the consent of both was required to assume them;

3   the rent or interests derived during the marriage from the obligations to which the goods which were the property of the individual partners and those which are joint property are subject;

4   minor repair work or upkeep of individual property during the marriage.

Article 34 The payment of the debts assumed by either partner before marriage will not have to be covered by joint property.

Section Four   Administration of joint property

Article 35   The partners are the ones who must administer their joint property and either of them may be in charge of administration and the purchase of goods which, due to their nature, are destined for ordinary use or consumption by the family.

Article 36   Neither partner may have control over goods which are joint property without the consent of the other except when it is to satisfy a demand posed by the community.

Article 37   In all cases not covered in this Code, the joint property of goods will be governed by the general provisions which cover the joint property. . . .

Section Four   Divorce

Article 49   Divorce will result in the dissolution of the matrimonial ties and all the other effects mentioned in this section.

Article 50   Divorce can only be obtained by means of a judicial decree.

Article 51   Divorce will take effect by common agreement or when the court determines that there are factors which have led the marriage to lose its meaning for the partners and for the children and, thus, for society as a whole.

Article 52   For the purposes of this law it is understood that marriage loses its meaning for the partners and for the children and, thus, for society as a whole when there are causes which create an objective situation in which the marriage is no longer, or cannot be in the future, the union of a man and a woman in a manner adequate to exercise the rights, fulfill the obligations and obtain the objects mentioned in Articles 24–28 inclusive.

Article 53   Either one of the partners can take action to obtain a divorce.

Article 54   The divorce action can be taken at any time as long as the situation which motivated it exists.

Article 55   The divorce will have the following effects between the partners:

1   termination of their marriage, as of the day the court decree becomes definitive;
2   separation of property of the partners, following liquidation of the joint property of goods, which is to be carried out in keeping with the rules established in Section Five, Chapter II, Title I of this Code;
3   termination of the right of succession among the partners.

Article 56   If the partners have lived together for more than a year or if children have been born during their marriage, the court, when handing down the decree of divorce, will grant an alimony for one of them in the following cases:

1   the partner who does not have a paying job and lacks other means of support. This will be temporary and it will be paid by the other partner for six months if there are no minor children in his or her care and guardianship, or for a year if there are, so the beneficiary can obtain a paying job;
2   the partner who because of age, disability, illness or other insurmount-

able obstacle is unable to work and lacks other means of support. In this case the alimony will continue as long as the obstacle exists.

Article 57   In the decree of divorce the court will grant *patria potestas,* establishing as a rule that both parents shall retain it over their minors.

However, the court may grant it to the parent whom it feels should have it, when this is required by the interests of the minors, outlining the reasons why one or the other is deprived of it.

Likewise, the court may determine, outlining its basis for doing so, the negation of *patria potestas* to both parents when this is necessary for the interests of the children, in which case the children will be placed under tutelage.

Article 58   In the decree of divorce the court must determine which of the parents will have guardianship and care over the children born during the marriage and will take the necessary measures so the children can maintain adequate communication with the parent that is not entrusted with their guardianship and care.

For the purposes of the provisions in the previous paragraph, the court will be guided by the rules established in Articles 88, 89 and 90.

Article 59   Support of minors is a duty of both parents even if they do not have *patria potestas* over them or even if the children are not under their guardianship and care or even if they are enrolled in an educational institution. In accordance with this norm, the court, in its decree of divorce, will set the amount of alimony to be paid by the parent who does not have the minors under his or her guardianship and care.

Article 60   The amount of alimony for minors will be determined by their normal expenses and the income of the parents, in order to determine the responsibility of the latter in a proportionate manner. . . .

TITLE II   RELATIONS BETWEEN PARENTS AND CHILDREN

Chapter I   Recognition of paternity

Section One   Recognition and registration

Article 65   All children are equal and they have equal rights and duties with regard to their parents, regardless of the latter's civil status.

Article 66   In the case of a formalized or judicially recognized marriage, the registration of the birth of a child in the Civil Register by one of the parents will have legal standing with respect to both.

Article 67   The registration of the birth of a child and the recognition of paternity by parents who are not married must be done by both, either together or separately.

Article 68   In the case of the previous article, when only the mother seeks to have the birth of a child registered and she states the name of the father, he will be summoned to appear before the head of the Civil Register and notified that if he does not appear within 30 days to accept or deny paternity the child will be registered as his. Following this period and if there is no challenge to the paternity, the registration will become binding and once this has been done the challenge can only be carried out by means of the corresponding procedure, within a year.

If there is a denial of paternity the child will be registered without mentioning the name of the father, the latter may recognize paternity at a later date, provided the mother agrees. If not, they must proceed in the manner outlined in the final paragraph of the previous article.

Article 69   When the mother appears to have the child registered without mentioning the name of the father, the latter may recognize paternity at a later date, provided the mother agrees. If not, they must proceed in the manner outlined in the final paragraph of the previous article.

Article 70   Recognition of paternity of an offspring who is of age requires his consent.

Article 71   Paternity of children can only be proven by a certification of the registration of their birth, issued with the due formalities by the Civil Register.

Any genuine document, public document, writ or unappealable sentence in which paternity is recognized or declared will be binding only when it is included in the corresponding Civil Register.

Article 72   In cases of registrations of births in which the parents are not present, the persons who do this can indicate the name of the parents but this will not be proof of paternity.

Article 73   The first last name of the children will be that of the father and the second last name the first last name of the mother.

If the name of only one parent appears on the birth certificate of a child born outside the framework of the situation described in Article 66, he will have the last names of that parent or repeat the last name in case of one last name only. . . .

Chapter II   Relationship between parents and children

Section One   *Patria potestas* **and its exercise**

Article 82   Minors are under the *patria potestas* of their parents.

Article 83   The exercise of *patria potestas* corresponds jointly to both parents.

It will correspond solely to one of them as a result of the death of the other or as a result of suspension or deprivation of its exercise.

Article 84   The children are obliged to respect, show consideration for and help their parents and to obey them while under their *patria potestas*.

Article 85   *Patria potestas* entails the following rights and duties of the parents:

1   keeping the children under their guardianship and care; making every possible effort to provide them with a stable home and adequate nourishment; caring for their health and personal hygiene; providing them with the means of recreation fitting their age which are within their possibilities; giving them the proper protection; seeing to their good behavior and cooperating with the authorities in order to overcome any situation or environmental factor that may have an unfavorable effect on their training and development;

2   seeing to the education of their children; inculcating them with the love for learning; seeing to it that they attend school; seeing to their adequate technical, scientific and cultural improvement in keeping with their aptitude and vocation and the demands posed by the country's development; and collaborating with the educational authorities in school programs and activities;

3   training their children to be useful citizens; inculcating them with the love for their country, respect for the country's symbols and their country's values, the spirit of internationalism, the standards of coexistence, and socialist morality; respect for social property and the property and personal rights of others; arousing the respect of their children by their attitude toward them; and teaching them to respect the authorities, their teachers and every other person;

4   administering and caring for their children's property; seeing to it that their children use and enjoy in a proper manner whatever property they have; and not to sell, exchange or give any such property except in the interest of the children and pursuant to the requisites of this Code;

5   representing their children in every judicial action or arrangement in which they are involved; giving their authorization in those cases where full capacity for taking action is required; and taking action opportunely and in due fashion to defend the children's interests and property.

Article 86   The parents are invested with the authority to reprimand and set straight adequately and moderately those children under their *patria potestas*.

RADICAL FEMINISM

Marriage

Sheila Cronan

Marriage has been a subject which has generated considerable controversy in the Women's Movement. So far as I know, no group other than The Feminists has publicly taken a stand against marriage, although I'm sure it has been a topic of discussion in most. . . .

The Feminists decided to examine the institution of marriage as it is set up by law in order to find out whether or not it did operate in women's favor. It became increasingly clear to us that the institution of marriage "protects" women in the same way that the institution of slavery was said to "protect" blacks—that is, that the word "protection" in this case is simply a euphemism for oppression.

We discovered that women are not aware of what marriage is really about. We are given the impression that love is the purpose of marriage—after all, in the ceremony, the wife promises to "love, honor, and cherish" her husband and the husband promises to "love, honor, and protect" his wife. This promise, which women believe to be central to the marriage contract, is viewed as irrelevant by the courts. For example, in a well-known case here in New York State, a woman attempted to obtain an annulment on the grounds that her husband had told her that he loved her prior to the marriage and then afterward admitted that he did not and never would. This was held *not* to give grounds for annulment,[1] despite the fact that the man committed fraud, which is normally grounds for nullifying any contract.

There is nothing in most marriage ceremonies specifically referring to sex, yet the courts have held that "the fact that a party agrees to and does enter into the marriage implies a promise to consummate the marriage by cohabitation, so that failure to do so gives grounds for annulment on the basis of fraud in the inducement.[2] An annulment was granted a New York man on the grounds that his wife was unable to have sex with him due to an incurable nervous condition.[3]

But then, one might ask, how is this particularly oppressive to women? After all, men also enter into marriage with the understanding that love is central. Many of us, in examining our personal histories, however, have suspected that "love" has a different meaning for men than it does for women. This has been substantiated by a study done by a man, Clifford R. Adams of Penn State University, who spent thirty years researching the subconscious factors involved in mate selection, studying 4000 couples. His conclusion was:

> When a man and a woman gaze into each other's eyes with what they think are love and devotion, they are not seeing the same thing. . . . For the woman, the first things she seeks are love, affection, sentiment. She has to feel loved and wanted. The second is security, then companionship, home and family, community acceptance, and sixth, sex. But for the man sex is at the top of the list, not at the bottom. It's second only to companionship. The single category of love-affection-sentiment is *below* sex.[4]

Sex is compulsory in marriage. A husband can legally force his wife to have sexual relations with him against her will, an act which if committed against any other woman would constitute the crime of rape. Under law, "a husband cannot be guilty of raping his own wife by forcing her to have sexual intercourse with him. By definition, the crime [of rape] is ordinarily that of forcing intercourse on someone other than the wife of the person accused."[5] Thus the threat of force is always present even if it is not necessary for the man to exert it—after all, most women are aware of the " 'right' of the husband to insist on and the 'duty' of the wife to 'submit' "[6] to sexual intercourse.

[1]*Schaeffer v. Schaeffer,* 160 AppDiv 48, 144 NYS 774.
[2]Eugene R. Canudo, *Law of Marriage, Divorce and Adoption* (Gould Publications, 1966), p. 20.
[3]*Hiebink v. Hiebink,* 56 NYS(2) 394, aff'd 269 AppDiv 786, 56 NYS(2) 397.
[4]Reported in *Glamour Magazine,* November, 1969, p. 214.
[5]Harriet F. Pilpel and Theodora Zavin, *Your Marriage and the Law* (New York: Collier Books, 1964), p. 215.
[6]*Ibid.,* p. 64.

It is clear that the compulsory nature of sex in marriage operates to the advantage of the male. The husband theoretically has the duty to have intercourse with his wife also, but this normally cannot occur against his will. Furthermore, as far as the enjoyment of the sex act is concerned, figures show that men (with the exception of impotent men who generally cannot have sex at all) nearly always experience orgasm when they have sex. Women, however, are not so fortunate. Surveys have shown that:

> fifteen to twenty percent of all [American] married women have never had an orgasm. About fifty percent reach orgasm on a "now and then" basis, meaning that they experience full culmination about one sex act out of three. Thirty to thirty-five percent of American wives say that they "usually" reach orgasm, meaning that they get there two out of three times or thereabouts. Only a very few women can claim that they have an orgasm every time they take part in sexual activities.[7]

Thus sex as practiced in American marriages clearly benefits the male far more than the female. Despite the emphasis that has recently been put on the husband's duty to give pleasure to his wife, this is not happening most of the time, and we all know that intercourse without orgasm is at best a waste of time. From the above figures we see that 70 percent of American wives have this boring and often painful experience over two-thirds of the time.

> In Alabama's legal code of 1852 two clauses, standing in significant juxtaposition, recognized the dual character of the slave.
> The first clause confirmed his status as property—the right of the owner to his "time, labor and services" and to his obedient compliance with all lawful commands. . . .
> The second clause acknowledged the slave's status as a person. The law required that masters be humane to their slaves, furnish them adequate food and clothing, and provide care for them during sickness and in old age. In short, the state endowed masters with obligations as well as rights and assumed some responsibility for the welfare of the bondsmen.[8]

The following is a description of marital responsibilities:

> The legal responsibilities of a wife are to live in the home established by her husband; to perform the domestic chores (cleaning, cooking, washing, etc.) necessary to help maintain that home; to care for her husband and children.
> The legal responsibilities of a husband are to provide a home for his wife and children; to support, protect and maintain his wife and children.[9]

The word "slave" is usually defined as a person owned by another and forced to work without pay for, and obey, the owner. Although wives are not bought and

[7]L. T. Woodward, M.D., *Sophisticated Sex Techniques in Marriage* (New York: Lancer Books, 1967), p. 18.
[8]Kenneth M. Stampp, *The Peculiar Institution* (New York: Vintage Books, 1956), p. 192.
[9]Richard T. Gallen, *Wives' Legal Rights* (New York: Dell Publishing Co., 1967), pp. 4–5.

sold openly, I intend to show that marriage is a form of slavery. We are told that marriage is an equitable arrangement entered into freely by both husband and wife. We have seen above that this is not true with regard to the sexual aspect of marriage—that in this respect marriage is clearly set up to benefit the male. It also is not true with regard to the rest of the marital responsibilities.

Women believe that they are voluntarily giving their household services, whereas the courts hold that the husband is legally entitled to his wife's domestic services and, further, that she *cannot be paid* for her work.

> As part of the rights of consortium, the husband is entitled to the services of his wife. If the wife works outside the home for strangers she is usually entitled to her own earnings. But domestic services or assistances which she gives the husband are generally considered part of her wifely duties. The wife's services and society are so essential a part of what the law considers the husband is entitled to as part of the marriage that it will not recognize any agreement between the spouses which provides that the husband is to pay for such services or society. In a Texas case David promised his wife, Fannie, that he would give her $5000 if she would stay with him while he lived and continue taking care of his house and farm accounts, selling his butter and doing all the other tasks which she had done since their marriage. After David's death, Fannie sued his estate for the money which had been promised her. The court held that the contract was unenforceable since Fannie had agreed to do nothing which she was not already legally and morally bound to do as David's wife.[10]

Whereas the legal responsibilities of the wife include providing all necessary domestic services—that is, maintaining the home (cleaning, cooking, washing, purchasing food and other necessities, etc.), providing for her husband's personal needs and taking care of the children—the husband in return is obligated only to provide her with basic maintenance—that is, bed and board. Were he to employ a live-in servant in place of a wife, he would have to pay the servant a salary, provide her with her own room (as opposed to "bed"), food, and the necessary equipment for doing her job. She would get at least one day a week off and probably would be required to do considerably less work than a wife and would normally not be required to provide sexual services.

Thus, being a wife is a full-time job for which one is not entitled to pay. Does this not constitute slavery? Furthermore, slavery implies a lack of freedom of movement, a condition which also exists in marriage. The husband has the right to decide where the couple will live. If he decides to move, his wife is obligated to go with him. If she refuses, he can charge her with desertion. This has been held up by the courts even in certain cases where the wife would be required to change her citizenship.[11] In states where desertion is grounds for divorce (forty-seven states plus the District of Columbia), the wife would be the "guilty party" and would therefore be entitled to no monetary settlement.

The enslavement of women in marriage is all the more cruel and inhumane

---

[10]Pilpel and Zavin, *op. cit.*, p. 65. For a New York case similar to the Texas one cited, *see* *Garlock v. Garlock*, 279 NY 337.

[11]Gallen, *op. cit.*, p. 6.

by virtue of the fact that it appears to exist with the consent of the enslaved group. Part of the explanation for this phenomenon lies in the fact that marriage has existed for so many thousands of years—the female role has been internalized in so many successive generations. If people are forced into line long enough, they will begin to believe in their own inferiority and to accept as natural the role created for them by their oppressor. Furthermore, the society has been so structured that there is no real alternative to marriage for women. Employment discrimination, social stigma, fear of attack, sexual exploitation are only a few of the factors that make it nearly impossible for women to live as single people. Furthermore, women are deceived as to what the nature of marriage really is. We have already seen how we are made to believe that it is in our interest. Also, marriage is so effectively disguised in glowing, romantic terms that young girls rush into it excitedly, only to discover too late what the real terms of the marriage contract are.

The marriage contract is the only important legal contract in which the terms are not listed. It is in fact a farce created to give women the illusion that they are consenting to a mutually beneficial relationship when in fact they are signing themselves into slavery. . . .

While wives are "owned" by their husbands in the same sense that slaves are owned by their masters—that is, that the master is entitled to free use of the slave's labor, to deny the slave his human right to freedom of movement and control over his own body—the scarcity of slaves resulted in their monetary value. Any man can take a wife and although he is legally required to support her, there is very little anyone can do if he is unable to fulfill this responsibility. Thus many women are forced to work outside the home because their husbands are unemployed or are not making enough money to support the family. This in no way absolves us from our domestic and child care duties, however.[12]

Since marriage constitutes slavery for women, it is clear that the Women's Movement must concentrate on attacking this institution. Freedom for women cannot be won without the abolition of marriage. Attack on such issues as employment discrimination is superfluous; as long as women are working for nothing in the home we cannot expect our demands for equal pay outside the home to be taken seriously.

Furthermore, marriage is the model for all other forms of discrimination against women. The relationships between men and women outside of marriage follow this basic pattern. Although the law does not officially sanction the right of a man to force his sweetheart to have sex with him, she would find it very difficult to prove rape in the courts, especially if they have had a regular sexual relationship. Also, it is not unusual for a man to expect his girl friend to type his term papers, iron his shirts, cook dinner for him, and even clean his apartment. This oppressive relationship carries over into employment and is especially evident in the role of the secretary, also known as the "office wife."

One of the arguments in the Movement against our attacking marriage has been that most women are married. This has always seemed strange to me as it is

---

[12]Gallen, *op. cit.,* p. 7.

like saying we should not come out against oppression since all women are oppressed. Clearly, of all the oppressive institutions, marriage is the one that affects the most women. It is logical, then, that if we are interested in building a mass movement of women, this is where we should begin.

Another argument against attacking marriage has been that it is dying out anyway. The evidence cited for this is usually the growing rate of divorce. But the high rate of remarriage among divorced persons shows that divorce is not evidence for the decline of marriage. We have seen that divorce is in fact a further abuse so far as women's interests are concerned. And the fact is that marriage rates have been on the increase. From 1900 to 1940 approximately one half of all American women over twenty years of age were married at any given time. After 1940 the figure began to rise noticeably: by 1960 it had reached the rate of two-thirds of all women over twenty.[13]

The Women's Movement must address itself to the marriage issue from still another point of view. The marriage relationship is so physically and emotionally draining for women that we must extricate ourselves if for no other reason than to have the time and energy to devote ourselves to building a feminist revolution.

The Feminists have begun to work on the issue of marriage. It is only a beginning, however; all women must join us in this fight.

Living with Other Women
Rita Mae Brown

It is the primacy of women relating to women, of women creating a new consciousness of and with each other which is at the heart of women's liberation, and the basis for the cultural revolution. Together we must find, reinforce and validate our authentic selves. As we do this, we confirm in each other that struggling incipient sense of pride and strength, the divisive barriers begin to melt, we feel this growing solidarity with our sisters. We see ourselves as prime, find our centers inside of ourselves. We find receding the sense of alienation, of being cut off, of being behind a locked window, of being unable to get out what we know is inside. We feel a real-ness, feel at last we are coinciding with ourselves. With that real self, with that consciousness, we begin a revolution to end the imposition of all coercive identifications, and to achieve maximum autonomy in human expression.

from *The Woman-Identified Woman*

Before the dawn of the woman-identified woman, back in the Age of Spermatic Oppression, women did love and live with other women. Two women met, fell in love, married and lived ever after. The women were forced to lead a double life if they were to economically and socially survive. It was a high price to pay but countless women paid it and are paying it still because life with another woman allows greater freedom for self-knowledge and far more emotional support. This

---

[13]*American Women: Report of the President's Commission on the Status of Women,* 1963, p. 6.

kind of life, which I will call old gay, is another version of that great Amerikan
lie, the Individual Solution. The Individual Solution means that you and your
lover can stay aloof from the problems of others, work hard, save your money,
budget wisely and lead the "good life." Lesbians had no choice in staying away
from the problems of other people, they were never welcome. For old gay
women the Individual Solution was the only road available to them. Along with
the lie of the Individual Solution hung the albatross of love oppression. Women
of the pre-woman-identified woman era were love drugged. Love was the
answer. It solved all problems and if allowed to flow free it could solve the
problems of the world. All a woman had to do was find that four letter word,
love, and that other four letter word, life, just opened up and bloomed with
eternal joy. Of course, you had to work to make love work—it was your life's
work. Old gay women were just as oppressed by the love definition applied to
women as heterosexual women because the definition makes women into a
function (lover, comforter, companion) rather than a person. Since women were
neither seen nor treated as persons, as full-fledged individuals, few women had a
sense of self but only a sense of function.

Lesbians, although more independent by virtue of being free from a man,
had internalized along with love oppression many other values of the establishment, and these were reflected in how they lived. For instance, old gay, like
other forms of oppression, imitated the values of the dominant culture (the white,
rich, heterosexual male) with few improvements. Class and race lines were more
fluid but the standard was that of materialism and status within the system. In
other words, you could move "up" much more easily in the old gay world than in
the straight world but the values were much the same. Women who were married
set up house together. Women who were unattached continued to look for
someone to love and marry. It was all conducted underground so there was a
taste of excitement to it and if you lived in one of the big cities, a taste of glamor.
But it was the same pattern as the rest of society where you isolate yourself from
others who share your oppression and try to "make it" on your own or in
tandem.

Before the Women's Liberation Movement, old gay lesbians had organized
into the Daughters of Bilitis. This nationwide organization did not and does not
have radical politics. Its purpose was to promote greater understanding of the
lesbian way of life, and hopefully, to allow lesbians to participate in the mainstream of society. In the late 1960's as Women's Liberation began to gather
strength many old gay women became interested in the movement but remained
outside it because of the theme of this issue: How we live and with whom. Old
gay women knew from bitter experience that heterosexual women neither understood the lesbian living situation nor desired to understand it. The heterosexual
women had accepted the male definition of women to such an extent that the idea
of a woman living with and loving another woman was too threatening even
though there was similarity in how they both lived. The early movement blatantly
discriminated against the lesbian, in some cases expelling women who were
lesbians. A few women refused to be repulsed. At the same time other old gay

women helped found and shape the Gay Liberation Movement. As the lesbians in Women's Liberation became increasingly dissatisfied over their treatment at the hands of heterosexual women, the lesbians in Gay Liberation became dissatisfied with their treatment at the hands of homosexual men. These women came together and tried to define what had been their lives and what their lives were now becoming due to some heavy changes in consciousness. Their effort became the paper, *The Woman-Identified Woman*.

Woman-Identified Woman moved beyond the definition of old gay and the traditional definition of women toward a concept of women defining themselves. It sounds so simple and it is; yet, women are just beginning to define themselves. A woman-identified woman is one who defines herself in relationship to other women and most importantly as a self apart and distinct from other selves, not with function as the center of self, but being. In other words, only you can identify yourself; only you know who you are. As long as you accept male values you cannot accept yourself. The entire Women's Liberation Movement has proved time and time again that those values never granted woman a self, only a service. A woman can best find out who she is with other women, not with just one other woman but with other women, who are also struggling to free themselves from an alien and destructive culture. It is this new concept, that of woman-identified woman, that sounds the death knell for the male culture and calls for a new culture where cooperation, life and love are the guiding forces of organization rather than competition, power and bloodshed. This concept will change the way we live and who we live with.

The women who wrote *Woman-Identified Woman* and the women who have come to understand it are in a transition period. We must move out of our old living patterns and into new ones. Those of us who believe in this concept must begin to build collectives where women are committed to other women on all levels—emotional, physical, economic and political. Monogamy can be cast aside, no one will ''belong'' to another. Instead of being shut off from each other in overpriced cubicles we can be together, sharing the shitwork as well as the highs. Together we can go through the pain and liberation of curing the diseases we have all contracted in the world of male dominance, imperialism and death. Women-identified collectives are nothing less than the next step towards a Women's Revolution.

None of us are there yet. Few of us are even in collectives much less woman-identified collectives. But at least we know what has to be done. This time of transition is a time of reaching out in the dark and hoping another sister's hand will reach back and connect. Knowing what has to be done makes it harder in some ways as we are more impatient for the collectives to materialize. It can be a time of anguish because we may be ready to try to build a woman-identified collective and find that no one else is ready to build with us. A collective, like a revolution, cannot be built by one woman. But it will come to pass. And when it does we will look back on our various lives as some old discarded rocket boosters and fully realize just how much we were compromised and strung out by a very basic matter: How we live and with whom.

SOCIALIST FEMINISM

Building Extended Families

Barbara and Michael McKain

In a society of scarcity and overt political and economic oppression, the building of a new society and a new man must wait on the seizure of power. But in a society of surplus, where oppression takes the form of psychological and social manipulation, the development of a new man seeking a new society is in itself the first necessary response of socialist revolution. Regardless of when the political/ economic revolution occurs, unless there has been a change in personal relationships, the way human beings look at and treat one another, we have failed. It is unlikely that a change for the better in interpersonal relations will evolve naturally with other revolutionary changes. This is something that must be consciously developed along with the other changes.

The present basis of man's interpersonal relations antidates man himself. Our distant ancestor existed on the basis of what property (women, children, tools, animals, and lands) he could hold for his exclusive use in a war of survival against his entire environment, from wild beasts to competing neighbors, to the elements. Accordingly, it is of little wonder that man has come to identify himself with his property and to define whatever he could as property, including himself and his family.

Two institutions which are based in and perpetuate these "people-as-property" attitudes are marriage and family. Heretofore the radical community has accepted the basic male-female, parent-child relationships as they exist in today's society. These two institutions have never been seriously attacked on the same intense, highly publicized basis that other oppressive institutions have been. Although draft files have been burned, free schools set up, corporations picketed and harassed, the oppressive institutions of marriage and family remain untouched and unexamined as we separate ourselves into couples, discipline and feed our own children and close the door of our own apartment or house against the rest of the world. But it must be faced: the institutions of marriage and family in America today have failed. A nurturing atmosphere for the intellectual and emotional development of its members is impossible while the family remains largely a property relationship with the "my husband," "my wife," "my children" syndrome, which is characterized by a feeling of ownership.

The Western myth of romantic love begins with the one man for one woman and vice versa. Present male-female relationships are based largely on the belief that the human being's ability to love is finite rather than infinite and that only one intense relationship at a time is possible. But is intense emotional involvement with only one person conducive to the freedom and growth of the two individuals involved? Sexual fidelity seems to be more an attribute that enslaves the people involved rather than one which encourages or promotes their individual freedom. It is ridiculous to assume that because a man or a woman is involved with one partner that all others of the opposite sex cease to be sexually, emotionally, or intellectually attractive. And yet in a couple relationship, a man or a woman tends to cut off leads to further involvement with others because of the feeling of being owned by the partner. And in turn, that fidelity is a claim of ownership on the other partner.

In addition to the sexual aspect of human beings, the couple relationship causes other restrictions and frustrations. For instance, consider the role of the woman. When a man returns to the couple relationship after a day of work and/or political involvement, one of two things usually happens. The woman submerges her problems, identity and needs in order to provide a peaceful nest to which the hard-working male can return. This way at least one person is reasonably content. Or, she demands sharing of the shit work involved in homemaking, rights in terms of her own involvement in the outside world and expansion of her own identity. Then anger and bitterness occur again and again, making both people unhappy. Usually it is the man's work, meetings, etc., which are considered the most important. If a babysitter is needed and can't be found, it is the woman who is expected to stay home. It would seldom even occur to the male that a woman's political role could be more important or more relevant than his own. Thus the woman sits at home and waits unless it is convenient for her to go. Within a couple relationship, it may be nearly impossible for the woman to lead even a reasonably independent existence. Women too often fall prey to seeking their identity as part of a couple and a supporting rather than active part at that, rather than defining themselves for themselves.

Another ownership problem is that of the parent-child relationship. Most parents, including many radicals, find it hard to deal with their children as separate individuals. Most mothers are not prepared to live a life of their own outside of their family. Consequently they cling to their children and in the process, smother them. Just as they are oppressed, women in turn oppress their children by limiting their identity. The nuclear family is additionally limiting as it restricts the choice of adult behavior patterns with which the child may identify. As children have only their parents as guides for emotional responses, they become limited to those responses when they themselves become adults. In fact, many adults who have broken away from the intellectual attitudes of their parents, find themselves acting out the very same emotional attitudes which they found so abhorrent in their parents.

What is necessary is the dissolution of marriage and family as institutionalized relationships and the building of extended families based not on contracts, insecurity and ties of blood, but on mutual convenience, concern and respect. Some of the problems of the nuclear family, its dissolution, and the development of an extended or corporate family are explored in fiction by Robert Rimmer in *Proposition 31*. An extended family is a community of adults committed to each other with common concerns, goals and ideals. People enter the community as individuals rather than as couples. The dependence on one person decreases.

Responsibility increases as it extends to the whole community. The loss of identity that a woman feels in a couple relationship is less likely to occur when she is in a group. Here she will have to stand on her own merits as an individual rather than being accepted because she is so and so's wife. Also, one partner is incapable of fulfilling all the needs, potentialities and interests of another person. The extended family is more likely to enable the individual to use and develop his/her potentialities and interests simply because there are a variety of individuals of both sexes involved and therefore more attitudes, interests and experiences available to the individual. By providing more leeway and flexibility in personal relationships, the extended family would enable us to express those attitudes which we would like to have toward one another.

The extended family might also enable us to explore a very touchy area— the heterosexual morality that society has given us. Today's society publically pushes heterosexuality, condemns homosexuality, and ignores completely the concept of bisexuality. The extended family can give us the necessary forum in which to deal with the entire area of human sexuality.

The concept of the group raising children is perhaps more acceptable than the implications of group marriage. The kibbutz, Skinner's *Walden Two* and other utopian communities have spelled out ways of how to raise children in a group. And as the studies of the kibbutz continue to come out, it seems that this way of raising children produces some very desirable traits that the nuclear family does not necessarily produce.

In any case, having children raised by the group tends to break down the ownership identification that parents have toward children. It also tends to free the adults involved. Children growing up in an extended family would have a larger, stronger emotional base. This is extremely important when attempting to raise children in a society that has a different and hostile set of values. Each extended family would probably have a slightly different method of raising children, but undoubtedly they would all be more beneficial to both parent and child than the present family situation.

Then too, revolution is a twenty-four hours a day job that applies to all areas of one's life. Being a political radical is not enough. One must have an open mind and be willing to examine and criticize all phases of one's life. To do this, a person needs a strong, secure emotional, social and economic base. The couple relationship seems unable to provide this security. Even political radicals, both males and females, tend to turn to their couple relationships with the same exploitative, possessive attitudes as the rest of today's society and thus take out their anxieties and insecurities on one another. Somehow, it seems impossible for that atmosphere to exist which enables one to criticize positively with the intention of helping, a criticism without hostility and animosity that includes a great deal of sensitivity and warmth so that the person does not feel as if he/she has been brutally and personally attacked by a loved one. The concept of criticism and self-criticism is badly needed among radicals today. Hopefully, through the extended family it can be developed; for there lies the necessary reservoir of trust and security. Certainly as we explore new ways of relating to one another with our personal, social, sexual human needs, some tool is needed to keep our eyes on our goals and our commitment to one another.

We must build our new life, our radical communities, within the present society with the intention of living in the sight of all, viable enriching alternatives to the present society which we find so abhorrent. This is not to say that the extended family is the be all and end all of everyone's dream or the easy road to utopia. Nor is this a guarantee of the liberation of women, an end to racism or the freeing of all from economic and political oppression. It is a call for all men and women, black and white, to begin to build a new, better way of living with each other, inviting those who can accept our new freedom to join us and by doing so, bring the new world closer to today.

However, a big problem that many of us face is that we are already too strongly imprisoned. We all have our stake, our property, by which we define ourselves. That property may be a job, a home, a husband, a wife, a child. We must choose. To make that start at building a new life and a new identity is, in fact, the revolution.

Capitalism, the Family, and Personal Life
Eli Zaretsky

. . . The organization of production in capitalist society is predicated upon the existence of a certain form of family life. The wage labour system socialized production under capitalism is sustained by the socially necessary but private labour of housewives and mothers. Child-rearing, cleaning, laundry, the maintenance of property, the preparation of food, daily health care, reproduction, etc. constitute a perpetual cycle of labour necessary to maintain life in this society. In this sense the family is an integral part of the economy under capitalism. . . .

. . . In pre-capitalist society the family performed such present functions as reproduction, care of the sick and aged, shelter, the maintenance of personal property, and regulation of sexuality, as well as the basic forms of material production necessary to sustain life. There were forms of economic activity that were not based upon family units—such as the building of public works, and labour in state-owned mines or industries. But they do not compare in extent or importance to peasant agriculture, labour based upon some form of the family, or upon the village, an extension of one or several families. In the most "primitive" societies—those in which production is least developed socially—the material necessity of the family, its role in sustaining life, was overwhelming. Even putting aside the dependence of children, adults in "primitive" society had no option but to rely upon the cooperative work of the household and particularly on the sexual division of labour, which by restricting tasks to one sex or the other insured their reciprocal dependence. In such societies, widows, orphans, and bachelors are scorned or pitied as if they were witches or cripples: their survival is always in doubt.[1]

It is only under capitalism that material production organized as wage labour and the forms of production taking place within the family, have been separated so that the "economic" function of the family is obscured. . . . Only with the emergence of capitalism has "economic" production come to be understood as a "human" realm outside of "nature." Before capitalism, material production was understood, like sexuality and reproduction, to be "natural"—precisely what human beings shared with animals. . . . Before capitalism the family was associated with the "natural" processes of eating, sleeping, sexuality, and cleaning oneself, with the agonies of birth, sickness, and death, *and* with the unremitting necessity of toil. It is this association of the family with the most primary and impelling material processes that has given it its connotation of backwardness as society advanced. Historically, the family has appeared to be in conflict with culture, freedom, and everything that raises humanity above the level of animal life. Certainly it is the association of women with this realm that has been among the earliest and most persistent sources of male supremacy and of the hatred of women.[2]

Capitalism, in its early development, distinguished itself from previous societies by the high moral and spiritual value it placed upon labour spent in goods production. This new esteem for production, embodied in the idea of private property and in the Protestant idea of a "calling," led the early bourgeoisie to place a high value upon the family since the family was the basic unit of production. While in feudal society the "personal" relations of the aristocracy were often highly self-conscious and carefully regulated, the domestic life of the masses was private and unexamined, even by the church. Early capitalism developed a high degree of consciousness concerning the internal life of the family and a rather elaborate set of rules and expectations that governed family life. This led to a simultaneous advance and retrogression in the status of women. On one hand, women were fixed more firmly than ever within the family unit; on the other hand, the family had a higher status than ever before. But the feminist idea that women in the family were outside the economy did not yet have any basis. As in pre-capitalist society, throughout most of capitalist history the family has been the basic unit of "economic" production—not the "wage-earning" father but the household as a whole. While there was an intense division of

---

[1]Claude Lévi-Strauss described "meeting, among the Bororo of central Brazil, a man about thirty years old: unclean, ill-fed, sad, and lonesome. When asked if the man were seriously ill, the natives' answer came as a shock: what was wrong with him?—nothing at all, he was just a bachelor. [Since] only the married status permits the man to benefit from the fruits of women's work, including delousing, body-painting, and hair-plucking as well as vegetable food and cooked food . . . a bachelor is really only half a human being." "The Family," p. 57.

[2]H. R. Hays, in *The Dangerous Sex: The Myth of Feminine Evil,* New York, 1972, gives a historical overview of male supremacy that indicates not only its persistence but the recurrence of identical themes. Almost, but not quite, universally, women are portrayed as dirty, bad-smelling, unhealthy, unspiritual, driven by sensuality and instinctual needs, weak, unreasoning and, in general, under the sway of brute necessity. Early myths such as those of Eve and Pandora also link women with both sexuality and the necessity of labour.

labour *within* the family, based upon age, sex, and family position, there was scarcely a division *between* the family and the world of commodity production, at least not until the nineteenth century. Certainly women were excluded from the few "public" activities that existed—for example, military affairs. But their sense of themselves as "outside" the larger society was fundamentally limited by the fact that "society" was overwhelmingly composed of family units based upon widely dispersed, individually owned productive property. Similarly, women had a respected role within the family since the domestic labour of the household was so clearly integral to the productive activity of the family as a whole.

But the overall tendency of capitalist development has been to socialize the basic processes of commodity production—to remove labour from the private efforts of individual families or villages and to centralize it in large-scale corporate units. Capitalism is the first society in history to socialize production on a large scale. With the rise of industry, capitalism "split" material production between its socialized forms (the sphere of commodity production) and the private labour performed predominantly by women within the home. In this form male supremacy, which long antedated capitalism, became an institutional part of the capitalist system of production.

This "split" between the socialized labour of the capitalist enterprise and the private labour of women in the home is closely related to a second "split"— between our "personal" lives and our place within the social division of labour. So long as the family was a productive unit based upon private property, its members understood their domestic life and "personal" relations to be rooted in their mutual labour. Since the rise of industry, however, proletarianization separated most people (or families) from the ownership of productive property. As a result "work" and "life" were separated; proletarianization split off the outer world of alienated labour from an inner world of personal feeling. Just as capitalist development gave rise to the idea of the family as a separate realm from the economy, so it created a "separate" sphere of personal life, seemingly divorced from the mode of production.

This development was a major social advance. It is the result of the socialization of production achieved by capitalism and the consequent decline in socially necessary labour time and rise in time spent outside production. Personal relations and self-cultivation have always, throughout history, been restricted to the leisure classes and to artists, courtiers, and others who performed the rituals of conversation, sexual encounter, self-examination, and physical and mental development according to well-developed and socially shared codes of behaviour. But under capitalism an ethic of personal fulfillment has become the property of the masses of people, though it has very different meanings for men and for women, and for different strata of the proletariat. Much of this search for personal meaning takes place within the family and is one reason for the persistence of the family in spite of the decline of many of its earlier functions.

The distinguishing characteristic of this search is its subjectivity—the sense of an individual, alone, outside society with no firm sense of his or her own place in a rationally ordered scheme. It takes place on a vast new social terrain known as "personal" life, whose connection to the rest of society is as veiled and obscure as is the family's connection. While in the nineteenth century the family was still being studied through such disciplines as political economy and ethics, in the twentieth century it spawned its own "sciences," most notably psychoanalysis and psychology. But psychology and psychoanalysis distort our understanding of personal life by assuming that it is governed by its own internal laws (for example, the psychosexual dynamics of the family, the "laws" of the mind or of "interpersonal relations") rather than by the "laws" that govern society as a whole. And they encourage the idea that emotional life is formed only through the family and that the search for happiness should be limited to our "personal" relations, outside our "job" or "role" within the division of labour.

Thus, the dichotomies that women's liberation first confronted—between the "personal" and the "political," and between the "family" and the "economy"—are rooted in the structure of capitalist society. . . . The means of overcoming it is through a conception of the family as a historically formed part of the mode of production.

The rise of capitalism isolated the family from socialized production as it created a historically new sphere of personal life among the masses of people. The family now became the major space in society in which the individual self could be valued "for itself." This process, the "private" accompaniment of industrial development, cut women off from men in a drastic way and gave a new meaning to male supremacy. While housewives and mothers continued their traditional tasks of production—housework, child-rearing, etc.—their labour was devalued through its isolation from the socialized production of surplus value. In addition, housewives and mothers were given new responsibility for maintaining the emotional and psychological realm of personal relations. For women within the family "work" and "life" were not separated but were collapsed into one another. The combination of these forms of labour has created the specific character of women's labour within the family in modern capitalist society. . . .

Personal Life and Subjectivity in the Twentieth-century United States

As capitalism developed the productive functions performed by the family were gradually socialized.[3] The family lost its core identity as a productive unit based upon private property. Material production within the family—the work of housewives and mothers—was devalued since it was no longer seen as integral to the production of commodities. The expansion of education as well as welfare, social work, hospitals, old age homes, and other "public" institutions further eroded the productive functions of the family. At the same time the family

[3]Although much of the following also applies to black and other "third world" families, there are also enormous differences that I do not discuss. A good starting place for such a discussion is Angela Davis, "Reflections on the Black Woman's Role in the Community of Slaves," *Black Scholar*, December 1971.

acquired new functions as the realm of personal life—as the primary institution in which the search for personal happiness, love, and fulfilment takes place. Reflecting the family's "separation" from commodity production, this search was understood as a "personal" matter, having little relation to the capitalist organization of society.

The development of this kind of personal life among the masses of people was a concomitant of the creation of a working class in capitalist society. Peasants and other pre-capitalist labourers were governed by the same social relations "inside" and "outside" work; the proletarian, by contrast, was a "free" man or woman outside work. By splitting society between "work" and "life," proletarianization created the conditions under which men and women looked to themselves, outside the division of labour, for meaning and purpose. Introspection intensified and deepened as people sought in themselves the only coherence, consistency, and unity capable of reconciling the fragmentation of social life. The romantic stress on the unique value of the individual began to converge with the actual conditions of proletarian life, and a new form of personal identity developed among men and women, who no longer defined themselves through their jobs. Proletarianization generated new needs—for trust, intimacy, and self-knowledge, for example—which intensified the weight of meaning attached to the personal relations of the family. The organization of production around alienated labour encouraged the creation of a separate sphere of life in which personal relations were pursued as an end in themselves.

But the creation of a separate sphere of personal life was also shaped by the special problems of the capitalist class in the early twentieth century. Increasing proletarianization, along with deepening economic crises, created increasing labour unrest and class conflict, as well as the growth of the socialist movement. Beginning in the early twentieth century a significant minority of American capitalists saw the possibility of integrating labour within a capitalist consensus through raising its level of consumption. Besides expanding the market for consumer goods, such a strategy would divert the working class from socialism and from a direct assault on capitalist relations of production. Edward Filene, for example, a Boston department store owner, urged his fellow capitalists to recognize unions and raise wages as a way of extending "industrial democracy" and "economic freedom" to the working class. "The industrial democracy I am discussing," he explained, "has nothing to do with the Cubist politics of class revolution." Instead, he urged that workers be free to "cultivate themselves" in the "school of freedom" which the modern marketplace constituted. "Modern workmen have learned their habits of consumption . . . in the school of fatigue," but mass production was transforming the consumer market into a "civilizing" experience for the working class. The emphasis on consumption was an important means through which the newly proletarianized, and still resisting, industrial working class was reconciled to the rise of corporate capitalism, and through which the enormous immigrant influx of the late nineteenth and early twentieth centuries was integrated with the industrial working class.

The extraordinary increases in the productivity of labour achieved during the nineteenth century, along with increasing American dominance within the world market, made it possible for capitalists to pursue this course. By the 1920s many firms had acceded to the sustained demand for a shorter work-day. This demand, probably the most persistent trade union demand of the nineteenth century, was the necessary pre-requisite to the establishment of personal life among the proletariat: it freed life-time from the immediate demands of capital. In the nineteenth century, socialists had emphasized the eight-hour day, since it would free the working class for self-education and political activity. But with the decline of American socialism after World War I, this issue receded. In the 1930s the eight-hour day and the forty-hour week became the standard in mass-production industry. Work time has been fixed at these levels ever since, in spite of subsequent technological progress. The capitalist class has extended "leisure" to the proletariat, but only within the limits set by the capitalists' need to retain control of the labour force.

Similarly, the capitalist class has raised wages in accord with its overall interests. Monopoly control of the market made it possible for capitalists to "compensate" themselves for wage increases by simultaneously raising prices. Beginning in the 1930s state programmes such as welfare and unemployment insurance financed a minimum level of consumption among the entire working class by taxing its better-paid sectors. Along with these measures corporate capitalists created a sales force and employed the new media of radio and television to spread the ethic of consumerism into every home.

The family, no longer a commodity-producing unit, received a new impor-tance as a market for industrial commodities. Mass production forced the capitalist class to cultivate and extend that market, just as it forced it to look abroad for other new markets. As a result, American domestic and personal life in the twentieth century has been governed by an ethic of pleasure and self-gratification previously unknown to a labouring class. Working people now see consumption as an end in itself, rather than as an adjunct to production, and as a primary source of both personal and social (i.e., "status") identity. This is often expressed within the "middle class" as "lifestyle," a word that is used to defend one's prerogatives regardless of the demands of "society."

The rise of "mass consumption" has vastly extended the range of "per-sonal" experience available to men and women while retaining it within an abstract and passive mode: the purchase and consumption of commodities. Taste, sensibility, and the pursuit of subjective experience—historically reserved for leisure classes and artists—have been generalized throughout the population in predetermined and standardized forms by advertising and other means. This is reflected in the modern department store in which the wealth, culture, and treasures of previous ruling classes now appear in the form of cheap jewellery, fashions, and housewares.

On one hand there has been a profound democratization of the idea that it is good to live well, consume pleasurably, and enjoy the fruits of one's labour. On the other hand, "mass consumption"—within the context of capitalism—has meant the routinization of experience and the deepening of divisions within the proletariat. The deep material deprivation that still characterizes the lives of most

Americans—bitter inadequacies of housing, food, transportation, health care, etc.—has taken on added emotional meanings. The "poor" feel personally inadequate and ashamed, while the more highly educated and better-paid sectors of the working class experience guilt toward the "less fortunate."

In developed capitalist society, the enhancement of personal consumption has been closely related to the devaluation of labour. Like the rise of mass consumption, the idea that labour is worthless results from its vastly expanded productivity. Expanded production of necessary goods—for example, food, clothing, and housing—without expanding the labour time spent in such production, began in agriculture after the Civil War and in manufacturing during the 1920s. As a result, the sphere of necessary goods production has shrunk in relation to other spheres of production. To counteract the effects of this tendency—particularly rising unemployment—and to maintain a level of "scarcity" in consumer goods, corporate capitalism has fostered inflation, waste, planned obsolescence, and under-utilization of productive capacity. It has vastly expanded "non-productive" industries such as advertising and finance, and used the state to subsidize the production of useless or destructive goods, such as armaments. A great amount of labour time in capitalist society is spent in activities that have the purpose of perpetuating capitalist relations of production, rather than producing necessary goods. This deepening irrationality of capitalist production has obscured the place of production within our society.

. . . Most people see no meaning or value in their work. In addition, marginal employment and unemployment characterize major groups in American society—youth, housewives, "hippies," the black "lumpenproletariat." Within these groups, which are themselves marginal to the sphere of commodity production, the idea has developed that production is itself marginal to social life. . . .

The combination of waste, under-employment, and rationalization has come close to destroying people's understanding of their part in an integrated system of social production. It has reinforced the tendency to look to personal life for meaning, and to understand personal life in entirely subjective terms. The isolation of so much of modern life from the sphere of necessary goods production gives it its "abstract" character. Both "society" and personal life are experienced as formless, with no common core, in inexplicable disarray. . . .

Increasingly cut off from production, the contemporary family threatens to become a well of subjectivity divorced from any social meaning. Within it a world of vast psychological complexity has developed as the counterpart to the extraordinary degree of rationalization and impersonality achieved by capital in the sphere of commodity production. The individualist values generated by centuries of bourgeois development—self-consciousness, perfectionism, independence—have taken new shape through the insatiability of personal life in developed capitalist society. The internal life of the family is dominated by a search for personal fulfilment for which there seem to be no rules. Much of this search has been at the expense of women.

Already in the late nineteenth century American women were consumed with a sense of their own diminished role and stature when compared with their mothers and grandmothers, women who laboured within the productive unity of the family defined by private property. In a letter to Jane Addams in the early twentieth century, Charlotte Gilman described the married woman's sense of living secondhand, of getting life in translation, of finding oneself unready and afraid in the "face of experience." By 1970 this fear had become a desperate sense of loss. Meredith Tax describes the "limbo of private time and space" of the housewife:

> When I am by myself, I am nothing. I only know that I exist because I am needed by someone who is real, my husband, and by my children. My husband goes out into the real world . . . I stay in the imaginary world in this house, doing jobs that I largely invent, and that no one cares about but myself. . . .. I seem to be involved in some sort of mysterious process.

Just as the rise of industry in the eighteenth and nineteenth centuries cut women off from men and gave a new meaning to male supremacy, so the rise of mass education has created the contemporary form of youth and adolescence. The "generation gap" is the result of the family lagging behind the dominant tendencies of the culture and of the transformation of productive skills which children learn in school and through the media. Parents now appear "stupid" and "backward" to their children, representing, as they do, an earlier stage of capitalist development. Beginning in the early twentieth century the family began to appear to young people as a prison cut off from reality.

At the same time, in the form of "public opinion," the imperatives of capitalist production have been recreated within the family, particularly in the "expectations" through which parents bludgeon themselves and their children into submission. Fathers, like school teachers or policemen, appear to stand for the whole bourgeois order. Hence, the split between the public and the private is recreated within the family. As in the "outside world," people feel they are not known for themselves, not valued for who they really are.

While serving as a refuge, personal life has also become depersonalized; subjective relations tend to become disengaged, impersonal, and mechanically determined. Introspection has promised to open a new world to men and women, but increasingly the inner life reverberates with the voices of others, the imperatives of social production. This is inevitable because the expansion of inner and personal life has been as integral to capitalist expansion in the modern epoch as has the spread of capitalism throughout the world.

But this process has also given shape to the revolutionary possibilities of our time. In previous centuries only a handful of individuals were prized for their special qualities of mind or character; the mass of men and women were ground down to an approximate sameness in the general struggle for existence. What distinguishes developed capitalist society is that the stress on individual development and uniqueness has become a tendency characterizing all of society.

The bourgeoisie made its revolution on behalf of a specific property form—

private property—which it already possessed. But the only "property" that the proletariat possesses lies within itself: our inner lives and social capabilities, our dreams, our desires, our fears, our sense of ourselves as interconnected beings. Reflecting the "separation" of personal life from production, a new idea has emerged on a mass scale: that of human relations, and human beings, as an end in themselves.

This idea as it currently prevails is ideological. It presents human beings as an end in themselves only insofar as they are abstracted from the labour process. These ideas flourish within the worlds of modern art, psychology, and communes, and in such utopian authors as Norman O. Brown who envision a society passing totally beyond the realm of necessity. But in themselves they cannot supply the basis for a transformation of society, since a new society—whether socialist, communist, or anarchist—would necessarily be based upon a new organization of labour and a new mode of production.

But these ideas also express what is realistic: the possibility of a society in which the production of necessary goods is a subordinate part of social life and in which the purposes and character of labour are determined by the needs of the individual members of society. It is appropriate that the family, in which so many of the most universal and impelling material processes of society have so far taken place, should also indicate the limited ability of capitalism to subordinate human needs to its own empty aggrandizement. The latest and most democratic form of an old hope can be discerned in the often tortured relations of contemporary personal life: that humanity can pass beyond a life dominated by relations of production. In varying forms this hope has given shape to radical and revolutionary movements since the nineteenth century.

SUGGESTIONS FOR FURTHER READING:
Part III, Family

Caulfield, Mina Davis: "Imperialism, the Family, and Cultures of Resistance," *Socialist Revolution,* No. 20, 1974.

Chodorow, Nancy: "Family Structure and Feminine Personality," in Michelle Zimbalist Rosaldo and Louise Lamphere (eds.), *Women, Culture and Society,* Stanford University Press, Stanford, Calif., 1974.

Cuban Family Code, effective March 8, International Women's Day, 1975. Available from The Center for Cuban Studies, 220 East 23rd St., New York 10010.

Davis, Angela: "The Black Woman's Role in the Community of Slaves," *Black Scholar,* December 1971.

Ehrenreich, Barbara, and Deirdre English: "The Manufacture of Housework," *Socialist Revolution,* October–December 1975.

Friedan, Betty: *The Feminine Mystique,* Dell, New York, 1970.

Gordon, Linda: "The Functions of the Family," *Women: A Journal of Liberation.*

Gordon, Michael (ed.): *The American Family in Social-Historical Perspective,* St. Martins Press, New York, 1973.

Gough, Kathleen: "The Origin of the Family," in Rayna Reiter (ed.), *Toward an Anthropology of Women,* Monthly Review Press, New York, 1975.

Komarovsky, Mirra: *Blue Collar Marriage,* Random House, New York, 1964.

Lundberg, Ferdinand, and Maryia S. Farnham: *Modern Woman: The Lost Sex,* Harper & Row, New York, 1947.

Stack, Carol: "Sex Roles and Survival Strategies in an Urban Black Community," in Michelle Zimbalist Rosaldo and Louise Lamphere (eds.), *Women, Culture and Society,* Stanford University Press, Stanford, Calif., 1974.

Weinbaum, Batya, and Amy Bridges: "The Other Side of the Paycheck: Monopoly, Capital and the Structure of Consumption," *Monthly Review,* July–August 1976.

FILLING IN THE FRAMEWORKS: SEXUALITY

Pin up on your bed, your mirror, your wall, a sign, lady, until you know it in every part of your being: We were designed to delight, excite, and satisfy the male of the species.

Real *women know this.*

"J"
The Sensuous Woman

The bride should be advised to allow her husband's sex drive to set their pace and she should attempt to gear her satisfaction to his. If she finds after several months or years that this is not possible, she is advised to consult her physician as soon as she realizes there is a real problem.

Novak's *Textbook of Gynecology,* 1970

I am your best fantasy and your worst fear.

Sign at a Gay Rights demonstration

The liberated orgasm is any orgasm you *like, under any circumstances* you *find comfortable.*

Barbara Seaman
Free and Female, Coward, McCann & Geoghegan, New York, 1972, p. 67.

Perhaps no area of our personal lives is more problematic for most of us than dealing with our sexuality. The widespread availability of contraceptives during the recent past has made it possible for women to significantly minimize the risk of unwanted pregnancies, and some say that this has led to sharp increases in sexual activity. The women's movement has raised our consciousness in this area, leading us to question old assumptions and old forms of behavior. The questions that confront us are many: What kinds of relationships and practices enhance our personhood? Who, if anyone, shall we choose as our sexual partner(s)? How safe are most female contraceptives, and whose sexual freedom have they promoted? What is the best way of integrating sexuality into our lives? As one might expect, the alternative theoretical frameworks we have been examining in this volume offer very different interpretations of the basis for sexual relationships and different criteria according to which we are urged to evaluate our own sexuality.

CONSERVATISM

Conservative views on sexuality make numerous references to biology. They appeal both to behavior among lower animals and insects and to human physiology. According to their reading of it, biology dictates a sexually active and aggressive role for the man and defines the woman as sexually passive. Anthony Storr cites as evidence for this view the "fact" that "spermatozoon swim actively, whilst the ovum passively awaits its penetration." Further, we are told that the structure of the female and male sex organs dictates this relation. Man must conquer and woman must submit. Her sexuality has as its goal fulfillment through pregnancy, while his aims and needs focus on pleasure and sexual release. Aggression is portrayed as a necessary part of male sexuality and its frustration is considered dangerous. Taken to its logical conclusion, the conservative view of male sexuality offered by Anthony Storr seems to justify male sexual behavior bordering on rape.

As a corollary of the view that sex roles are rigidly determined by biology, the conservative warns us that deviation from these roles is sure to produce discord and trauma. In the selection by David Allen we consider a contemporary conservative assessment of the damage done by emphasis on women's rights. Allen argues that the contemporary redefinition of women's role has seriously undermined male/female relations. Increased freedom for women has tipped the natural balance in relations between the sexes and has done tremendous damage to the self-image of men in contemporary society.

While a deviation in the proper male/female roles is seen as dangerous, conservatism regards any alternative sexual combinations as abnormal. The structure of the vagina and the penis are interpreted as clear indications that heterosexual intercourse is the only "natural" and therefore "normal" form of sex. Lesbianism and male homosexuality are rejected as abnormal and unhealthy.

LIBERALISM

Rejecting conservatism's preoccupation with biologically determined sex roles, liberal theory stresses the rights of both parties to self-expression and fulfillment. As is clear from the portion of the introduction to Alex Comfort's book which is excerpted here, the liberal denies any attempt to attribute an exclusively active or passive role to either sex and urges equal opportunity in this as well as all other areas of life. Comfort urges us to take time to develop our sexuality just as we might spend time learning to paint, ski, or dance. The only rule he urges us to adopt is that we engage in only those forms of sexual activity that we enjoy and that we attempt to learn and then satisfy our partner's needs.

At the heart of the liberal position on sexuality is the view that one's private life should not be subject to regulation by society. Sexuality is a private concern, and individuals should be free to pursue sexual fulfillment in any way they choose as long as they do not harm anyone else. Regarded in this way, the choice to earn one's living through prostitution might be defended by the liberal theorist on the grounds that, as long as the choice is made freely, society has no right to interfere. It is interesting to recognize, by way of comparison, that what the liberal would regard as a free choice in this case the Marxist would criticize as resulting from economic coercion. The difference in their analyses results from the liberal's acceptance of the public/private distinction and her failure to analyze society in terms of fundamental power differentials based on wealth. The Marxist view, on the other hand, analyzes individual choices within the context of class society where vast inequalities in wealth, power, and opportunities limit real freedom of choice.

In general, the liberal, unlike the conservative, tends to adopt an attitude of tolerance toward lesbianism and male homosexuality as long as these practices are carried out by consenting adults in privacy. Some liberal theorists adopt a position like the one argued here by Albert Ellis. Ellis thinks that an exclusive preoccupation with any form of sexual activity is unhealthy. In addition, he is suspicious of the choice made by the male homosexual and lesbian to engage in sexual activity for which they will be penalized by their society. On the other hand, he argues that failure to engage in homosexuality under conditions where a member of the opposite sex is not available for long periods of time would be equally a form of maladjustment.

In general, liberalism places its emphasis on individual fulfillment through varied experimentation and on equal opportunity to pursue pleasure without the strictures of highly defined sex roles.

TRADITIONAL MARXISM

In many cases the traditional Marxist theorist's position on sexual expression is more a reflection of the prejudices of his or her society than an extension of Marxist theory. Engels's position is a case in point. Classical writers tended to condemn sexual activity that went beyond recognized forms of heterosexual interaction; but insofar as Marxist theory focuses its analysis on the individual as a wage laborer struggling against exploitation by the ruling class, no developed position on sexual preferences or expression is likely to emerge. The area of sexuality and other pursuits and relationships that would be classified as forms of "personal" life simply do not receive recognition or attention. This is not because of anything like the liberal bias, which regards these areas as "private," but simply because within a traditional Marxist framework these areas of concern are not regarded as significant.

The position on sexual fulfillment most consistent with traditional Marxist theory is that taken by Engels when he maintains that a definition of nonexploitative, mutually fulfilling sexual relationships must await the time when differences in power and wealth no longer separate women and men.

RADICAL FEMINISM

Radical feminism portrays the choice of one's sexual partner(s) as a matter of political importance for feminism. Although all institutions of society are regarded as reflecting a struggle for power between women and men, many radical feminists argue that the core of women's oppression is the popular belief that love and sexual fulfillment for women are possible only in relationships with men. Given the way that women have traditionally been defined as primarily sexual beings, the belief that heterosexual intercourse is the norm for sexual activity points to the conclusion that emotional and sexual relationships with men provide the most important opportunities for fulfillment in women's lives. It is clear how this belief is oppressive to women insofar as it encourages us to define our achievement in terms of our success in being attractive to and pleasing men.

We have already looked at the radical feminist analysis of marriage as an institution for enslaving women. In this section we shall see how, according to the radical feminist, the norm of heterosexual intercourse itself functions as a mechanism for forcing women to submit to male control and domination. In arguing that heterosexual intercourse should not be the norm of sexual activity, radical feminists draw support from the new popular acceptance of the fact that for most women orgasm requires direct clitoral stimulation of the kind that is not ordinarily provided during heterosexual intercourse. Hence, radical feminists conclude that the only reason for society's emphasis on heterosexual intercourse must be to attempt to make women dependent on men for sexual satisfaction. It does this by encouraging women to define their sexual role in terms of men's pleasure while ignoring their own sexual needs.

Far from considering this dependency to be natural, the radical feminist often maintains that within the context of sexist society, female sexuality is most fully developed when it is explored through a lesbian relationship. This is true, she feels, both because a genuinely loving relationship is possible only between equals and because the unique quality of female sexuality can best be understood by another woman.

Some radical feminists hold that a broader definition of what it means for women to love women is also compatible with radical feminist theory. According to this broader understanding, intimate relationships between women need not entail either sexual intimacy or sexual exclusivity. In contrast to other views we have considered, all radical feminists agree that how we choose to define and explore our sexuality is a matter of extreme personal *and* political importance.

SOCIALIST FEMINISM

The socialist feminist insists that an analysis of sexuality must take explicit account of the fact that sexual interaction occurs within the context of a society which not only is male-dominated but is one in which those who control the wealth exercise disproportionate power. Rejecting traditional Marxism's failure to recognize the importance of our nonworking lives, socialist feminism maintains that how we define our sexuality is highly political. Further, in opposition to liberalism, it argues that the choice is not ours to make freely. In fact, most socialist feminists argue that the much talked-about new sexual freedom and the seeming permissiveness of contemporary American society are illusions. They grow out of the needs of a society organized around the profit motive and the preservation of male privilege. These interests provide the context in which society allows us to define ourselves. Under such conditions the liberal's emphasis on equal freedom and opportunity to explore our sexuality is deceptive. Capitalist society teaches us to define freedom in terms of depersonalized sexuality which encourages us to buy cosmetics, cars, clothing, perfume, dishware, etc., to make ourselves sexually desirable. Socialist feminism exposes and rejects the commoditization of sexuality by contemporary capitalism.

Some socialist feminists believe that male privilege is so pervasive in contemporary society that loving sexual relationships with men are difficult if not impossible. They see this antagonism as a historical phenomenon which can be altered through a revolutionary restructuring of society and of relations between and among the sexes. Rather than talking about the need for equal sexual freedom and rights, socialist feminists stress the need to redefine our sexual identities. One ideal held up is that of androgyny. By this they mean that it is necessary to go beyond the traditional sex roles assigned to women and men and redefine ourselves as complete human beings, all of whom are capable of independence and dependence, tenderness and strength, giving and receiving. For those who accept Gayle Rubin's account of the roots of women's oppression, the genderless society is at least as necessary to women's liberation as is the classless society.

In short, the goal of socialist feminism is to transcend sex role stereotyping and commercialized, degraded, and alienating forms of sexuality offered to us by movies, books, and advertisements in an effort to sell more coffeepots and stereos. Once differences in wealth and power are eliminated from society, say the socialist feminists, it will be possible to achieve a genuinely liberated sexuality which has no goal or purpose other than the enrichment of human existence.

CONSERVATISM

Aggression in the Relations between
the Sexes

Anthony Storr

. . . In the relation between the sexes, the spermatozoon swims actively, whilst the ovum passively awaits its penetration. The anatomy of the sexual organs itself attests the differentiation of the sexual role; and although culture and ontogenetic development may obscure the psychological dichotomy, anatomy and physiology form the inescapable substratum upon which the emotional difference between the sexes stands firm. In simpler creatures than ourselves, it is possible to stimulate the various drives concurrently or separately. Thus, in cichlids, aggression, fear and sexual behaviour can be elicited by appropriate stimuli, or more than one drive set in motion at once. In female cichlids, aggression inhibits sexuality, whereas fear has no such effect. In male cichlids, aggression and sexuality can march together, but fear prevents the male from exercising his sexual function.

It is dangerous to press the analogy too far; but, in ourselves, the parallel is close. Male sexuality, because of the primitive necessity of pursuit and penetration, does contain an important element of aggressiveness; an element which is both recognized and responded to by the female who yields and submits. Moreover, it is impossible for the male human who is frightened of women either himself to become fully aroused or to awake a corresponding response in the female. Impotence in men, whether partial or complete, is invariably the result of fears which may be, and often are, unconscious.

In women, however, the reverse is more generally true. Although women who suffer from excessive fear of the sexual act may also be frigid, it is the aggressive woman who resents the male and who is unconsciously competing with him who constitutes the commoner problem in our culture. A complete and fully satisfying sexual relationship implies emotional commitment on either side. There are many people who, because of the vicissitudes of their childhood development, are unable to achieve this; who cannot trust themselves to love without reserve, and who cannot trust another to love them unequivocally. The emotional insecurity which underlies this lack of faith in other human beings tends to cause different forms of behaviour in the two sexes. Insecure men are frequently less dominant and aggressive than their more confident counterparts. Insecure women commonly display a greater degree of aggressiveness and competitiveness than their more secure sisters.

Moreover, Christianity has for so long taught us to conceive of love in terms of self-sacrifice and gentleness that there are many couples who have never experienced the full splendour of sexuality. Innumerable manuals have instructed husbands to be so restrained, or so careful in their love-making that they have inhibited the aggressive component in sexual congress with the result that their wives cannot fully respond to them, and they themselves fail to gain complete satisfaction.

The role of aggression in the relation between the sexes may be further underlined by a glance at the so-called sexual deviations. Insecure people who have been unable to achieve complete sexual happiness commonly have sexual phantasies of which they are often deeply ashamed, but which contain, albeit in exaggerated form, the elements of erotic passion which are missing from their actual sexual lives. These phantasies are generally, though not invariably, sado-masochistic in content; that is, concerned with male dominance and female submission in extreme degree. It is significant that there is a difference between the sexes in the type of phantasy which appeals to each. The idea of being seized and borne off by a ruthless male who will wreak his sexual will upon his helpless victim has a universal appeal to the female sex. It is the existence of this phantasy which accounts for the wide popularity of such figures as *The Sheik,* Rhett Butler, or even King Kong. A *frisson* of fear of the more dominant male reinforces rather than inhibits erotic arousal in females; and the phobias of men under the bed or hidden in dark corners which are so common in adolescent girls, invariably contain an element of concealed sexual excitement as well as fear. On the other hand, women, however forceful they may actually be, seldom have phan-tasies of dominating or humiliating men, although they may take part in erotic activities which involve this in order to please the men who demand it of them.

In contrast to women, men very frequently have sexual phantasies in which they behave sadistically; and a vast erotic literature exists in which women are bound, restricted, rendered helpless or beaten. There is generally a wide gap between phantasy and reality, in that men who find themselves the prey of sadistic imaginations seldom actually hurt their partners, whom they wish to enjoy the role of helpless victim. Psychopathic or psychotic persons may act out sadistic phantasies without regard to the feelings of their partners; but most men who are possessed by such thoughts are actually over-considerate, less demanding and less aggressive than is generally expected of the male.

For those unfamiliar with this area of human experience it is less easy to understand why men also may have masochistic phantasies in which they are at the mercy of dominant females. The explanation is that the regressive wish to be cared for by a powerful figure is common to both sexes. For we all start life as helpless infants, and so both retain the memory, and may pursue the illusion, of an erotic relationship in which we are helpless in the hands of a powerful parent. The female is more prone to regress in this way because of her greater need for a protective figure. It is well recognized that women have a greater need for security than men; that is, for a home in which they can bring up their children, safe in the knowledge that a man will provide and care for them. Men tend to feel restricted by the same situation; caught, and used by the female for her own purposes, and it is of course this difference which accounts for a large part of the battle between the sexes. . . .

The Price of Woman

David Allen

If there is one thing the biological approach to human behavior clearly demonstrates, it is the intricacy of the mesh between males and females. If the male and female are not designed to function in a complementary way, then we know nothing about biology.

The degree and complexity of the interlock is something to marvel at. There has been a deliberate design here, which has been undergoing constant refinement over the millennia. The two sexes are meant to function as one whole. Each is dependent upon the other in critical ways. There is more than romantic and poetic meaning to this thought. From the basic, locking, design of the sexual parts, up through the morphology of the body, to the morphology of the mind, and beyond the body to the different but complementing roles they play in society, each sex is incomplete without the other. Only a couple is immortal; the single sex perishes.

Therefore, if one finds an area in which the sexes do not mesh, where they are not functionally complementary, one is entitled to the legitimate suspicion that something isn't working right. If complementarity and harmony are the evolutionary goals, as they obviously are, the lack of complementarity and harmony must be regarded as abnormal and dysfunctional. And if one finds a failure to mesh in a crucially important area, one must consider the dysfunction a serious one.

There is one such area in contemporary life in which the sexes are not in harmony, and that is in their sexuality. The sexes are not meshing well sexually. This failure is bad in itself as well as bad for what it implies for the whole relation between the two sexes which is built on it. I believe that this lack of mesh in sexual relationships is a socially caused abnormality which is by that very reason controllable, even though marriage counselors have always accepted it as part of the given facts. Millions of years of evolution have made the sexes mesh like fine gears at the biological level; it seems unthinkable, therefore, that this abnormality should be biological and unalterable. But if it is not innate it must be social, and within our power to change. In this it is like feminine immaturity, which we have always taken as biologically immutable, rather than as a sign of a socially caused neurosis which it was in our power to correct.

The dysfunction which strikes me as a major proof of the seriously maladjusted relationship between the sexes shows up in the curve of the sexual drive of adults. Biology calls for them to be in harmony, but in fact they are not. The adult male has a downward curve while the adult female curve is rising. In other words, while the male is experiencing decreased sexual desire with advancing age, the female is experiencing increased desire as she gets older. The male peaks at about age 18, the female at about age 35. Something is wrong here.

This is not to say that males on a downward curve cannot successfully copulate with females on an upward one; obviously, they can. But the differences either deny the principle of biological harmony or point to a maladjustment in social roles. I take the latter to be the case. I believe that excessive responsibility is suppressing male desire, and that insufficient responsibility leading to an unhealthy fantasy life is overstimulating female sexual desire. Life has pushed male and female out of step with each other. Let us review what we know and try to find out where things are going wrong, in order to pinpoint corrective action.

We know that up to adolescence, the central nervous system of the human female develops faster than the male's. We interpret this to mean that nature has programmed the female to perform her most important task, reproduction, as early as possible, before she has a chance to get killed off. As the time draws near for her to perform this task, the male suddenly experiences a spurt in the growth of his nervous system so that he too is ready to play his part. His spurt shows up as an increase in mental agility, a desire to set up on his own, and a drive to copulate. The female has been made ready and receptive. He is driven by increased aggression to take the initiative. His drive is greater than hers at this point, but that is all right. Although she is experiencing no increased tension, she, too, is ready.

At this point, we can accept a difference in sexual drive as normal. But from here on, why should her drive increase while his declines? Why do they not both decline, having presumably accomplished their reproductive tasks?

It is in the cards that his should decline somewhat. Having impregnated a female he now turns his attention to safeguarding her during her period of defenselessness. But since she has already been fertilized, why should she experience more rather than less desire now? As can be seen in the housecat, her mothering instincts decline after the first litter. Having completed her task she no longer has need for a strong maternal drive. Nonetheless, she grows more sexy while he grows less so. What has happened?

I think two things have happened simultaneously: The male sex drive is depressed even more than we should expect by the demands of fatherhood, while the release from responsibility stimulates the female's sexual appetite sufficiently to reverse the natural biological decline. In this overstimulation of the female and oversuppression of the male I see, in capsule form, the present social disequilibrium of the emotional economy. What biology harmonized, society has antagonized.

There are both long-term and short-term causes for this situation. In the short run we are experiencing the overzealousness of females determined to redress the balance of many generations of sexual denial. The pendulum of history has swung to the other extreme. For the first time in history, the female has been freed from the fear of untimely pregnancy by the pill. Simultaneously with her new freedom, she has become aware that the aberrations of Puritanism were responsible for cheating her out of sexual pleasure. In addition to these two factors, the feminists have made women suspicious in general concerning the sufficiency of their share of the spoils; as a result, we have the spectre of the female sex gourmand—a creature determined to "get hers" come what may. Until the pendulum settles down again, female excess will be the norm.

There is another reason for this female excess: Getting a husband is the most critical challenge in her life, even in our modern world, because a husband is the ticket to the cop-out. You can't goof off without a man to foot the bills. Success requires self-discipline. This is one time in a woman's life when she actively enforces such self-discipline. If this period is unduly prolonged, if she experiences difficulty in getting a husband, she may build up quite a head of resentment against males for having forced her to undergo such a trial. Once she has run the gauntlet and survived, she is likely to spend the rest of her life exacting revenge from the unwitting unfortunate she has married. Two of the ways in which she will do this are to find him sexually inadequate, and lacking in earning power.

But most women are not motivated by a desire for vengeance. Once she has passed her test, the average woman simply relaxes and forgets about it. Now, freed from all future worries about the feeding and shelter of herself and her infants, she is in a position to become playful—and that is precisely the way she gets. Though she appears to have more cares than ever, she moves toward irresponsibility. Not having to submit to the chastening embrace of reality, she can and does live in fantasy. In that fantasy world—exacerbated by the mass media—she dwells on the pleasures of sex, and comes to expect a level of performance that a reality-dwelling man cannot deliver. Thus, the female soars along on a constantly rising sex curve.

But the error is not all on her side. The male curve is also skewed down further than it ought to be. Upon marriage, the male experiences a dramatic increase in sexual inhibition, which comes as much as a surprise to him as it does to his spouse. As a bachelor, he had thought that in marriage he would have it made. Instead, her new spontaneity is matched by his loss of it. Her new freedom has become his surprising loss of freedom. Her irresponsibility has become his responsibility. The key word is *responsibility*. The key concept is its movement to a new location. In the modern world, marriage liberates the female and enslaves the male, in a way and to a degree unprecedented in history.

In Paleolithic days, marriage made no changes in the life of the hunter, except to enrich it. He went about his business just as though he were a bachelor. Hunting was still as much a sport as a chore. The share of meat the female got would have gone into the community pot anyway, primitives being natural communists.

The same cannot be said of hunting's modern equivalent work, and its corollary, responsibility. Modern man's work load and responsibility load are the most effective sexual depressants ever invented. Few marriage counselors have ever understood the full significance of the effect work, responsibility, and worry have on the sexual drive, although every married male is privately aware of it. It is one of those common experiences which have been taken for granted tacitly for so long that their full significance is not grasped.

Not that any kind of work or responsibility necessarily acts as a sexual depressant. Indeed, some kinds of work under certain kinds of conditions are powerful sexual stimulants. What I am asserting is that work and responsibility in our modern technological society are sexual depressants for two reasons. The first one, that males accept self-serving feminine values as their own, I have already discussed. The second, that man is oppressed by a massive bureaucracy from which there is no escape, is important enough to warrant separate analysis, which follows in the next chapter.

At this point I should like to discuss in a general way how it is possible for work and responsibility to act as sexual depressants.

Any number of things can turn off the sex switch. Humans may be sexually active to a far greater extent than other creatures, but they still experience even more powerful drives, and when these collide with sex, sex loses out. Hunger, thirst, fatigue, danger, fear, worry, absorption in thought or study, are some of the stimuli that turn off the sexual apparatus. In general, any stimulus of a crisis nature will eliminate all competing stimuli, in order that all bodily energy can be focused on the challenge. Man's adrenaline pattern clearly shows that meeting crisis is his biological specialty, to the extent that a generalist has a specialty. Our crisis-meeting mechanisms are also our hangup.

Hunting was our earliest racial experience of crisis, and our crisis-meeting mechanisms evolved out of this collective experience. Work also evolved out of hunting. But the hunting crisis and the work crisis are two different things. The insecurity and uncertainty of the modern work experience, and distorting pressures exerted by the competitive rat race, act as extended crises which turn man off sex, despite medical plans, accident plans, retirement plans, and all other cradle-to-grave security plans. For the same reasons he is also turned off culturally, artistically, emotionally, and philosophically. The hunting crisis was of short duration and this is the type of crisis we are programmed for. The work crisis is permanent, and we have not been programmed for it. Having to face it nonetheless, our response is trancelike. We rivet our attention on the crisis and stay riveted for the duration with all other stimuli shut out. Man, at this point in history, lives his entire adult life in a condition of permanent crisis, and is more or less permanently turned off, sexually speaking. Not only do his worries and responsibilities leave little room for the lighter side of his nature, but every orgasm is accompanied by the penis-shrinking knowledge that he may just have forged another $1,500-per-year link in his chain. It costs, as of the latest 1970 estimates, $30,000 to rear one child to age 18—without the frills, just for meat and potatoes and protection from the rain. If one throws in the frills that are commonplace among middle-brow families, and throws in the cost of college at the rate of $5,000 per year, we can see that we are seriously underestimating the bite. Few lectures on sin or venereal disease can match this for effectiveness, in inhibiting the male sex urge! Little wonder that 75% of the 100,000 people per year now seeking sterilization are men.

It does nothing to assuage man's growing sense of entrapment to understand that while he is being alienated from his deepest self, his wife is discovering the full depth of her soul; or that, while he is becoming imprisoned, she is gaining freedom. A woman has some twenty-five to thirty opportunities in her life to prove her femininity by bearing children. Some women have to be restrained from using them all. But there are few men so economically successful that they can bear with equanimity more than two $1,500-per-annum permanent increases in overhead. In plain fact, most men worry about their ability to support children.

Women are not so burdened. They leave that worry to him, and see no connection between it and his sexual coolness. . . .

The gulf that separates the boy from the adult male world can never have been so difficult to cross as it is today. The boy must view the chasm with great anxiety, for never has the development of competence been so trying. With the possible exception of warrior cultures like the Sioux, who lived on poor land, or the Eskimo, there may never have been a culture which demanded so much from its young males as does ours.

At first sight this seems rather exaggerated. One of the tests a little Sioux boy had to pass was to run five miles through the hot desert with a mouthful of water without swallowing a drop. This test separated the men from the boys so well that the Sioux were obliged to invent a male squaw role, not so much for their homosexual boys, as for their heterosexual boys who couldn't pass the warrior tests.

The young American boy may be spared the physical agonies of such puberty rites, but the psychological gauntlet he runs is just as fearsome. The Sioux boy was a Stone Age boy. When his tests were over he fit into a Stone Age culture. The modern boy comes into the world a Stone Age baby, just like the Sioux boy, but when his rites of passage are over he must fit himself into the 20th century.

In all cultures, the fear that little boys will not grow up to be men is more severe than that little girls will not grow up to be women. Among warrior cultures, as well as in modern American culture, this fear is pervasive. It is no wonder that some Sioux boys copped out and became squaws, or that more and more American boys become homosexual. The little boy sees he will have to put out to join the world of men. The little girl knows she will coast into the adult world of women without a ruffle. The boy will pass through a psychological crucible on the way to manhood, and when he reaches it, he will have to prove it over and over again. Yesterday's feats do not excuse tomorrow's failures. In the test of his manhood, he is never a winner.

Even the sexual role of the male is more challenging than the female's. He must produce an erection to copulate; she can fake her way through. Failure to produce an erection at the appointed moment is for him tantamount to failure as a man—in front of the woman. Yet a worried man cannot get an erection or arouse a female. The fear of not being able to perform on cue is one of the chief fears of the homosexual hankering after heterosexuality. Dr. Bieber of the New York Medical College concludes that homosexuals avoid intercourse with women because "they have developed overwhelming fears of their sexual capacity," which means, of getting an erection at the right time. Psychiatrist Harry Hershman says, "A woman poses a tremendous problem to him, for only she can expose him as defective in the role of a man."

The homosexual is not the only one disconcerted by the female. According to both Packard and Brenton, the heterosexual male is too. Her aggressiveness in matters sexual, instead of delighting the male whose sex fantasies have now come down to earth, alarm him. Modern women are becoming "critical consumers of male performance." Theodore Reik declared himself amazed at the way "women, more and more, are taking over the active role in sex." Man's sexual performance is increasingly being judged in terms of his ability to give sexual pleasure, not to impregnate. Considering that recent research has shown that woman is capable of practically unlimited orgasms, and coming at a time when responsibility is depressing his sexual capacity, this is a situation wide open to abuse. It may be appropriate to judge prostitutes on their ability to deliver sexual pleasure, but not anyone else. The male does not need this cross to bear in addition to the ones already laid on his back. Especially is this true when the same research that demonstrated woman's unlimited orgasmic capacity also showed that her best source of sexual pleasure is self-masturbation, followed, secondly, by a male masturbating her. Third and last as her source of pleasure is the male penis. Under these circumstances, one must question a woman's fitness to be a judge of sexual capacity, her own or anyone else's. This unlimited quality to current feminine sexuality is explained by the fact that her fantasies are unencumbered by the tempering quality of an encounter with reality. She lives in a pornographic state of mind. . . .

LIBERALISM

On Advanced Lovemaking

Alex Comfort

All of us who are not disabled or dumb are able to dance and sing—after a fashion. This, if you think about it, summarizes the justification for learning to make love. Love, like singing, is something to be taken spontaneously. On the other hand, the difference between Pavlova and the Palais de Danse, or opera and barber-shop singing, is much less than the difference between sex as the last generation came to accept it and sex as it can be.

At least we recognize this now (so that instead of worrying if sex is sinful, most people now worry whether they are "getting satisfaction"—one can worry about anything, given the determination). There are now enough books about the basics: the main use of these is to get rid of worries over the normality, possibility, and variety of sexual experience. The people who go to Masters and Johnson are getting over hangups so basic that in past generations the folk tradition would have taken care of them. At least the "permissive" scene in publishing removed some of this cover-up. Our book is slightly different, in that there are now enough people who have the basics and really need hard information (not simply reassurance).

Chef-grade cooking doesn't happen naturally: it starts at the point where people know how to prepare and enjoy food, are curious about it and willing to take trouble preparing it, read recipe hints, and find they are helped by one or two detailed techniques. It's hard to make mayonnaise by trial and error, for instance. Cordon Bleu sex, as we define it, is exactly the same situation—the extra one can get from comparing notes, using some imagination, trying way-out or new experiences, when one already is making satisfying love and wants to go on from there. . . .

This book is about love as well as sex as the title implies: you don't get high quality sex on any other basis—either you love each other before you come to want it, or, if you happen to get it, you love each other because of it, or both. No point in arguing this, but just as you can't cook without heat you can't make love without feedback (which may be the reason we say "make love" rather than "make sex"). Sex is the one place where we today can learn to treat people as people. Feedback means the right mixture of stop and go, tough and tender, exertion and affection. This comes by empathy and long mutual knowledge. Anyone who *expects* to get this in a first attempt with a stranger is an optimist, or a neurotic—if he does, it is what used to be called love at first sight, and isn't expendable: "skill," or variety, are no substitutes. Also one can't teach tenderness. . . .

. . . Most people now know that man's "sexuality" starts at birth and runs continuously from mother-child to man-woman relations, that it involves some periods of programmed anxiety about the genitals ("castration fears") which probably served originally to stop young apes from falling foul of their fathers, but which, in man, are building stones for a lot of other adult behaviors; and that the wide range of human sex needs of all kinds controlled by this unique developmental background—long childhood, close mother-child contact but a taboo on mother-child or father-child sex, close pair-bonding which centers in sexual play, the way bird pair-formation centers in nest-building and display (this is the phenomenon more often described as love), and so on. . . .

A little theory makes sex more interesting, more comprehensible, and less scarey—too much is a put-down, especially as you're likely to get it out of perspective and become a spectator of your own performance. If you have really troublesome hangups you need an expert to hold the mirror for you and go personally into what they mean—self-adhesive labels are actively unhelpful. All humans are sadistic, narcissistic, masochistic, bisexual and what have you—if you stuck on all the labels you would look like a cabin trunk. What matters is whether any of the behaviors in which you engage are bothering you or other people—if so, they are a useful pointer to what the problem is, but no more than that. . . .

. . . There are two modes of sex, the duet and the solo, and a good concert alternates between them. The duet is a cooperative effort aiming at simultaneous orgasm, or at least one orgasm each, and complete, untechnically-planned let-go. This in fact needs skill, and can be built up from more calculated "love-play" until doing the right thing for both of you becomes fully automatic. This is the basic sexual meal. The solo, by contrast, is when one partner is the player and the other the instrument; the aim of the player is to produce results on the other's pleasure experience as extensive, unexpected and generally wild as his or her skill allows—to blow them out of themselves. The player doesn't lose control, though he or she can get wildly excited by what is happening to the other. The instrument *does* lose control—in fact, with a responsive instrument and a skillful performer, this is the concerto situation—if it ends in an uncontrollable ensemble, so much the better. All the elements of music and the dance get into this scene—rhythm, mounting tension, tantalization, even actual aggression: "I'm like the executioner," said the lady in the Persian poem, "but where he inflicts intolerable pain I will only make you die of pleasure." There is indeed an element of aggression or infliction in the solo mode, which is why some lovers dislike it and others overdo it, but no major lovemaking is complete without some solo passages.

The antique idea of the woman as passive and the man as performer used to ensure that he would show off playing solos on her, and some marriage manuals perpetuate this idea. In a more liberated scene she is herself the soloist par excellence, whether in getting him excited to start with, or in controlling him and showing off all her skills. In fact there is only one really unmusical situation, and that is the reverse of a real solo, where one uses the other to obtain satisfaction, without any attempt at mutuality. True, one may say, "Do it yourself this time," as a quick finish, but it is no more than that. . . .

Solo devices are not, of course, necessarily separate from intercourse. Apart from leading into it there are many coital solos—for the woman astride, for example—while mutual masturbation or genital kisses can be fully-fledged duets. Nor is it anything to do with "clitoral" versus "vaginal" orgasm (this is only a crass anatomical way of trying to verbalize a real difference), since the man feels the same distinction, and you can get a roaring solo orgasm from the skin of the fingertips, the breasts, the soles of the feet, or the earlobes of a receptive woman (less commonly extra-genitally in the man). Coition which ought to be mutual but gives a solo feeling (to her) is what people who talk about "clitoral orgasm" are trying as a rule to verbalize. Solo-response can be electrifyingly extreme in the quietest people. Skillfully handled by someone who doesn't stop for yells of murder, but does know when to stop, a woman can get orgasm after orgasm, and a man can be kept hanging just short of climax to the limit of human endurance. . . .

In writing descriptively about sex it is hard not to be solemn, however unsolemnly we play in bed. In fact, one of the things still missing from the "new sexual freedom" is the unashamed ability to use sex as play—in this, psychoanalytic ideas of maturity are nearly as much to blame as oldstyle moralisms about what is normal or perverse. We are all immature, and have anxieties and aggressions. Coital play, like dreaming, is probably man's programmed way of dealing acceptably with these, just as children express their fears and aggressions in games. If they play at Indian tortures, out of jealousy of their little brother or the opposite sex, we don't call that sadism: adults are unfortunately afraid of playing games, of dressing up, of acting scenes. It makes them self-conscious: something horrid might get out.

Bed is the place to play all the games you have ever wanted to play, at the play-level—if adults could become less self-conscious about such "immature" needs we should have fewer deeply anxious and committed fetishists creating a sense of community to enable them to do their thing without feeling isolated. We heard of a frogman who used to make his wife sleep in rubber bedsheets; he had to become a frogman for real, because dressing in a diving-suit for kicks was embarrassing and made him look odd. If we were able to transmit the sense of play which is essential to a full, enterprising and healthily immature view of sex between committed people, we would be performing a mitzvah: people who play flagellation games and are excited by them bother nobody, provided they don't turn off a partner who finds the scenario frightening. People who enact similar aggressions outside the bedroom are apt to end up at My Lai or Belsen. . . .

There are after all only two "rules" in good sex, apart from the obvious one of not doing things which are silly, antisocial or dangerous. One is "don't do anything you don't really enjoy," and the other is "find out your partner's needs and don't balk them if you can help it." In other words, a good giving and taking relationship depends on a compromise (so does going to a show—if you both want the same thing, fine: if not, take turns and don't let one partner always dictate). . . .

Sexual Perversions

Albert Ellis

. . . Although the usual definitions of sexual deviation would seem to be preju-diced and parochial, and none of them can be *absolutely* upheld, there seems to be one that holds up fairly well for people living in our own society as well as for most individuals in most societies: namely, a psychosocial approach to deviation.

This definition starts with the assumption, which I first stated in *The American Sexual Tragedy* (1963e), that an individual who has no sexual defects (such as an injured penis or neuromuscular deficiencies) may be considered to be sexually deviated if he can *only*, under *all* circumstances, enjoy one special form of sexual activity: or if he is obsessively-compulsively fixated on a given mode of sex behavior; or if he is fearfully and rigidly bound to one or two forms of sexual participation.

This definition of sexual deviation—or sexual neurosis—is the only one that seems to be consistent with that which is usually given of a non-sexual deviation or neurosis. A non-sexual neurotic is an individual who, out of some kind of illogical fear, favors one kind of behavior (such as staying alone in his room) and disfavors another kind (such as going to social functions or riding on trains). A sexual neurotic or deviant, similarly, may be said to be an individual who, out of irrational anxiety, rigidly refrains from one kind of behavior (such as heterosex-uality) and adheres exclusively to another kind (such as homosexuality or masturbation).

By the same token, a non-sexual neurotic often becomes obsessively-compulsively attached to a given form of conduct—such as touching picket fences, keeping his room inordinately clean and tidy, or remaining thoroughly attached to his mother. And a sexual neurotic or deviant becomes obsessively-compulsively attached to a given form of sex conduct—such as copulating with women who have small feet, or who wear bloomers, or who whip him.

This does not mean that individuals cannot *logically* favor or prefer one kind of sexual (or non-sexual) conduct to another. They can (Kepner, 1959). Thus, it is possible for a woman to prefer staying by herself to attending social functions or prefer being a Lesbian to being heterosexual—provided that she has, for a reasonable length of time, unprejudicedly *tried* both alternatives (that is, tried sociality *and* asociality or heterosexuality *and* Lesbianism) and then merely decided that she likes one mode better than the other.

If, however, this same woman rarely or never tries, say, social functions or heterosexuality and still insists that they are worthless, pleasureless activities, we can only surmise that she has some irrational fear of these kinds of acts and that she is compulsively attached to other activities because of her fear. Under these circumstances, we would have to think of her as being neurotic.

Moreover: even if this woman tries social functions and heterosexuality and finds them relatively unsatisfactory as compared to staying at home and being homosexual, it would be suspicious if she *always,* under *all* circumstances, rigidly sticks to her preferences. Granted that she usually may dislike social affairs, why should she always find them distasteful—especially, say, when something is to be gained, such as a job promotion, by attending one? And granted that she prefers Lesbians, why should she, in the face of suffering possible grave penalties for being homosexual, always engage in Lesbian acts and refuse more safely available, albeit somewhat less satisfactory, heterosexual affairs?

If we forget about sex for a moment and transpose the problem of deviance and neurosis into, say, the analogous problem of eating, the core attitudes behind deviation will probably become much clearer.

Suppose, for instance, that an individual who is in good physical health and has no special allergic reactions tries all kinds of foods, eats at different hours, and uses several types of crockery. He finally decides that he prefers meat and potatoes to all other foods, that he likes to eat one large meal a day, at three in the morning, and that blue plates are best for him. Under these circumstances, many of us might think this individual peculiar; but we would have no scientific grounds for calling him neurotic or deviated.

Suppose, however, this same individual insists, after little or no experimentation, that he will eat *nothing* but meat and potatoes; or that he *only* will eat at three in the morning, even if he is starving; or that he must eat *exclusively* on blue plates and cannot eat on dishes of any other color. Or suppose, if meat and potatoes are arbitrarily banned in his community and a stiff jail sentence is given to anyone discovered eating them, he *still* insists on ingesting only this kind of food and refuses to touch any other kind of easily available victuals. Or suppose that he is utterly revolted by every other kind of food except meat and potatoes and winces with disgust every time he sees others eating other foods.

Such an individual, obviously, has a distinct, illogical *fear* of most foods, or of different eating times, or of non-blue plates. From a psychological standpoint, he is clearly abnormal, fixated, compulsive, or neurotic.

Suppose—to use an opposite example—that a person enjoys many kinds of foods but that, without really ever having tried meat and potatoes, or after trying them once or twice and finding them mildly unsatisfying, or after trying them only *after* he has convinced himself that they cannot be appetizing, he insists that these foods *must be* utterly revolting and he either never tries them again or occasionally tries them with great prejudice and keeps insisting that they are tasteless or disgusting. From a psychological standpoint, again, this person would have to be classed as distinctly phobic or neurotic.

So, too, are sexually fixated or compulsively driven people neurotic. Irrationally ignoring the *many* possible kinds of sex participation, they rigidly adhere to a single mode or two. Or, in some instances, they try a variety of sex acts (such as masturbation, homosexuality, exhibitionism, and peeping) but fearfully refrain from other common modes (such as heterosexuality).

If these people, without fear and after a fair trial, simply *preferred* one kind of sex behavior and *preferred* to eliminate another kind, that would be one thing. But when they are thoroughly *fixated* on one mode and *phobic* toward another, they are clearly afflicted with sexual deviation or neurosis (Ollendorf, 1966). . . .

If we eliminate unscientific and vague definitions of deviation, it should be clear that a human being's engaging in many acts which have frequently been labeled as "unnatural" or "perverse" may or may not constitute his being deviated.

Thus, if a male engages in homosexual activity during his teens, becomes heterosexually oriented by the time he is an adult, but occasionally (especially when he is isolated from females) re-engages in homosexual acts, we cannot justifiably call him a homosexual or a deviant.

A fixed homosexual is one who, after reaching adulthood, *exclusively* or *mainly* lusts after members of his own sex and has little or no desire for members of the other sex.

A fixed homosexual is a deviant not because he engages in inverted acts but because, out of an irrational fear of heterosexuality, he does not desire heterosexual activities. If he were truly bisexual or ambisexual and had spontaneous, non-compulsive desires for members of both sexes he would not necessarily be sexually deviant or neurotic. He might, on other counts, however, be emotionally disturbed not for having but for giving in to his bisexual desires, just as a person might be neurotic not merely for having but chronically giving in to the desire to steal when he lived in a community which severely punished thieves.

Our typical Greenwich Village type homosexuals are deviant or neurotic because they not only engage in inverted sex acts, but usually are (a) compulsively homosexual; (b) irrationally afraid of or disgusted by members of the other sex; (c) rebelliously insistent on flouting their homosexuality, in spite of the legal penalties and other difficulties which are attendant upon such flouting; and (d) exceptionally defensive about their homosexuality, usually will not admit that it is limited or neurotic, and often contend that they are better off than or superior to heterosexuals. The deviation of these homosexuals consists not in the kind of sex act they perform but the fearful and hostile *manner* in which they perform it. . . .

Once we define sexual deviation in the psychological manner in which we are now doing, we must be consistent and objective about whom we label as deviant. Just as we may call a person deviant because he is a fixed homosexual, so we may also, at times, have to term him deviant because he is a fixed and invariant heterosexual.

Thus, we have the cases of many heterosexuals who under *no* circumstances would consider forgoing their usual heterosexual activities for masturbatory or homosexual acts—even, for example, if they were imprisoned only with members of their own sex for thirty years. And we have many other heterosexuals who, in their marital relations, will adhere *only* to one form of activity, such as coitus with the male surmounting the female, and will under no conditions resort to petting, kissing, or other coital positions.

Such individuals, obviously, have some arbitrary or irrational *fear* of non-heterosexual or non-coital relations. Therefore, even though the form of their sex activity is perfectly "normal" their general sex outlook is deviated or abnormal.

Are we to conclude, then, that the only individual in our society who is perfectly normal sexually is one who engages in *all* kinds of activity, including heterosexual, homosexual, and animal relations?

Naturally not: any more than we would contend that anyone who did not thoroughly enjoy *all* kinds of food would be abnormal.

A *reasonable* restriction or constriction of one's sex desires and acts, in accordance with personal individualization, is only to be expected; and a reasonable channelization is also to be expected—especially in a country, such as our own, where the laws and mores actively propagandize the citizens against certain sex practices, such as homosexual activities, and in favor of other practices, such as heterosexual participations.

The fact remains, however, that when an individual in our society *completely,* under *all possible* circumstances restricts himself to one, and only one, quite specialized form of sex behavior, and when he does so not out of mere preference, after first engaging in considerable experimentation, and not because of some unusual physical anomaly but out of an arbitrary, illogical, or fear-induced notion, then he is sexually deviated or neurotic.

By the same token, an individual who utilizes several kinds of sexual outlets but who will under no circumstances even try another common kind of outlet (such as masturbation, coitus, petting, or genital kissing), is to some extent deviated, though perhaps to a lesser degree than the person who rigidly adheres to a single outlet.

If the mode of sex behavior to which a deviant rigidly is attached is a broad one, as well as one which is socially approved in the community in which he resides, then he may be relatively little deviated or neurotic.

Thus, an individual in our society who only engages in heterosexual relations, including kissing, petting, and several different coital positions but who under no conditions will ever consider masturbating or having homosexual relations, may be considered a minor deviant.

By the same token, a person who masturbates, pets, and has several kinds of heterosexual coitus but who will under no circumstances try oral-genital relations (which today are becoming acceptable among educated persons) with his or her mate is also deviated; but probably to a minor degree.

On the other hand, an individual in our society who, under normal conditions, refuses to try sex relations with members of his own sex or with animals can hardly be called deviated: since these are still highly frowned upon and legally penalized activities. At the same time, if this individual refuses, under quite *abnormal* conditions (say, on a desert island, where there is no sexual alternative) to consider having homosexual or animal relations, then we may justifiably call him a deviate—though a minor one. . . .

TRADITIONAL MARXISM

Sexual Love

Friedrich Engels

We thus have three principal forms of marriage which correspond broadly to the three principal stages of human development: for the period of savagery, group marriage; for barbarism, pairing marriage; for civilization, monogamy supplemented by adultery and prostitution. Between pairing marriage and monogamy intervenes a period in the upper stage of barbarism when men have female slaves at their command and polygamy is practiced.

As our whole presentation has shown, the progress which manifests itself in these successive forms is connected with the peculiarity that women, but not men, are increasingly deprived of the sexual freedom of group marriage. In fact, for men group marriage actually still exists even to this day. What for the woman is a crime entailing grave legal and social consequences is considered honorable in a man or, at the worst, a slight moral blemish which he cheerfully bears. But the more the hetaerism of the past is changed in our time by capitalist commodity production and brought into conformity with it, the more, that is to say, it is transformed into undisguised prostitution, the more demoralizing are its effects. And it demoralizes men far more than women. Among women, prostitution degrades only the unfortunate ones who become its victims, and even these by no means to the extent commonly believed. But it degrades the character of the whole male world. A long engagement particularly is in nine cases out of ten a regular preparatory school for conjugal infidelity.

We are now approaching a social revolution in which the economic foundations of monogamy as they have existed hitherto will disappear just as surely as those of its complement—prostitution. Monogamy arose from the concentration of considerable wealth in the hands of a single individual—a man—and from the need to bequeath this wealth to the children of that man and of no other. For this purpose, the monogamy of the woman was required, not that of the man, so this monogamy of the woman did not in any way interfere with open or concealed polygamy on the part of the man. But by transforming by far the greater portion, at any rate, of permanent, heritable wealth—the means of production—into social property, the coming social revolution will reduce to a minimum all this anxiety about bequeathing and inheriting. Having arisen from economic causes, will monogamy then disappear when these causes disappear?

One might answer, not without reason: far from disappearing, it will on the contrary begin to be realized completely. For with the transformation of the means of production into social property there will disappear also wage labor, the proletariat, and therefore the necessity for a certain—statistically calculable—number of women to surrender themselves for money. Prostitution disappears; monogamy, instead of collapsing, at last becomes a reality—also for men.

In any case, therefore, the position of men will be very much altered. But the position of women, of *all* women, also undergoes significant change. With the transfer of the means of production into common ownership, the single family ceases to be the economic unit of society. Private housekeeping is transformed into a social industry. The care and education of the children becomes a public affair; society looks after all children alike, whether they are legitimate or not. This removes all the anxiety about the "consequences," which today is the most essential social—moral as well as economic—factor that prevents a girl from giving herself completely to the man she loves. Will not that suffice to bring about the gradual growth of unconstrained sexual intercourse and with it a more tolerant public opinion in regard to a maiden's honor and a woman's shame? And finally, have we not seen that in the modern world monogamy and prostitution are indeed contradictions, but inseparable contradictions, poles of the same state of society? Can prostitution disappear without dragging monogamy with it into the abyss?

Here a new element comes into play, an element which at the time when monogamy was developing existed at most in embryo—individual sex love.

Before the Middle Ages we cannot speak of individual sex love. That personal beauty, close intimacy, similarity of tastes and so forth awakened in people of opposite sex the desire for sexual intercourse, that men and women were not totally indifferent regarding the partner with whom they entered into this most intimate relationship—that goes without saying. But it is still a very long way to our sexual love. Throughout the whole of antiquity, marriages were arranged by the parents, and the partners calmly accepted their choice. What little love there was between husband and wife in antiquity is not so much subjective inclination as objective duty, not the cause of the marriage but its corollary. Love relationships in the modern sense only occur in antiquity outside official society. The shepherds of whose joys and sorrows in love Theocritus and Moschus sing, the Daphnis and Chloe of Longus, are all slaves who have no part in the state, the free citizen's sphere of life. Except among slaves, we find love affairs only as products of the disintegration of the old world and carried on with women who also stand outside official society, with *hetaerae*—that is, with foreigners or freed slaves: in Athens from the eve of its decline, in Rome under the Caesars. If there were any real love affairs between free men and free women, these occurred only in the course of adultery. And to the classical love poet of antiquity, old Anacreon, sexual love in our sense mattered so little that it did not even matter to him which sex his beloved was.

Our sex love differs essentially from the simple sexual desire, the Eros, of the ancients. In the first place, it assumes that the person loved returns the love; to this extent the woman is on an equal footing with the man, whereas in the Eros of antiquity she was often not even asked. Secondly, our sex love has a degree of intensity and duration which makes both lovers feel that non-possession and separation are a great, if not the greatest, calamity; to possess one another, they risk high stakes, even life itself. In the ancient world this happened only, if at all, in adultery. And finally, there arises a new moral standard in the judgment of a sexual relationship. We do not only ask, was it within or outside marriage, but also, did it spring from love and reciprocated love or not? Of course, this new standard has fared no better in feudal or bourgeois practice than all the other standards of morality—it is ignored. But neither does it fare any worse. It is recognized, like all the rest, in theory, on paper. And for the present more than this cannot be expected.

At the point where antiquity broke off its advance to sexual love, the Middle Ages took it up again—in adultery. We have already described the knightly love which gave rise to the songs of dawn. From the love which strives to break up marriage to the love which is to be its foundation there is still a long road, which chivalry never fully traversed. Even when we pass from the frivolous Latins to the virtuous Germans we find in the *Nibelungenlied* that although in her heart Kriemhild is as much in love with Siegfried as he is with her, yet when Gunther announces that he has promised her to a knight he does not name, she simply replies: "You have no need to ask me; as you bid me, so will I ever be; whom you, lord, give me as husband, him will I gladly take in troth." It never enters her head that her love can be even considered. Gunther asks for Brünhild in marriage and Etzel for Kriemhild, though they have never seen them. Similarly, in *Gutrun,* Sigebant of Ireland asks for the Norwegian Ute, whom he has never seen, Hetel of Hegelingen for Hilde of Ireland, and finally Siegfried of Morland, Hartmut of Ormany and Herwig of Seeland for Gutrun—and here Gutrun's acceptance of Herwig is for the first time voluntary. As a rule, the young prince's bride is selected by his parents if they are still living or, if not, by the prince himself with the advice of the great feudal lords, who have a weighty word to say in all these cases. Nor can it be otherwise. For the knight or baron, as for the prince of the land himself, marriage is a political act, an opportunity to increase power by new alliances; the interest of the *house* must be decisive, not the wishes of an individual. What chance then is there for love to have the final word in the making of a marriage?

The same thing holds for the guild member in the medieval towns. The very privileges protecting him, the guild charters with all their clauses and rubrics, the intricate distinctions legally separating him from other guilds, from the members of his own guild or from his journeymen and apprentices, already made the circle narrow enough within which he could look for a suitable wife. And who in the circle was the most suitable was decided under this complicated system most certainly not by his individual preference but by the family interests.

In the vast majority of cases, therefore, marriage remained up to the close of the middle ages what it had been from the start—a matter which was not decided by the partners. In the beginning, people were already born married—married to an entire group of the opposite sex. In the later forms of group marriage similar relations probably existed, but with the group continually contracting. In the pairing marriage it was customary for the mothers to settle the marriages of their children; here, too, the decisive considerations are the new ties of kinship which are to give the young pair a stronger position in the gens and tribe. And when, with the preponderance of private over communal property and the interest in its bequeathal father right and monogamy gained supremacy, the dependence of marriages on economic considerations became complete. The *form* of marriage by purchase disappears; the actual practice is steadily extended until not only the woman but also the man acquires a price—not according to his personal qualities but according to his property. That the mutual affection of the people concerned should be the one paramount reason for marriage, outweighing everything else, was and always had been absolutely unheard of in the practice of the ruling classes; that sort of thing only happened in romance—or among the oppressed classes, who did not count.

Such was the state of things encountered by capitalist production when it began to prepare itself, after the epoch of geographical discoveries, to win world power by world trade and manufacture. One would suppose that this manner of marriage exactly suited it, and so it did. And yet—there are no limits to the irony of history—capitalist production itself was to make the decisive breach in it. By changing all things into commodities, it dissolved all inherited and traditional relationships, and in place of time-honored custom and historic right, it set up purchase and sale, "free" contract. And the English jurist H. S. Maine thought he had made a tremendous discovery when he said that our whole progress in comparison with former epochs consisted in the fact that we had passed "from status to contract," from inherited to freely contracted conditions—which, in so far as it is correct was already in *The Communist Manifesto* [Chapter II].

But a contract requires people who can dispose freely of their persons, actions, and possessions and meet each other on the footing of equal rights. To create these "free" and "equal" people was one of the main tasks of capitalist production. Even though at the start it was carried out only half-consciously, and under a religious disguise at that, from the time of the Lutheran and Calvinist Reformation the principle was established that man is only fully responsible for

his actions when he acts with complete freedom of will, and that it is a moral duty
to resist all coercion to an immoral act. But how did this fit in with the hitherto
existing practice in the arrangement of marriages? Marriage according to the
bourgeois conception was a contract, a legal transaction, and the most important
one of all because it disposed of two human beings, body and mind, for life.
Formally, it is true, the contract at that time was entered into voluntarily;
without the assent of the persons concerned, nothing could be done. But
everyone knew only too well how this assent was obtained and who were the real
contracting parties in the marriage. But if real freedom of decision was required
for all other contracts, then why not for this? Had not the two young people to be
coupled also the right to dispose freely of themselves, of their bodies and organs?
Had not chivalry brought sex love into fashion, and was not its proper bourgeois
form, in contrast to chivalry's adulterous love, the love of husband and wife?
And if it was the duty of married people to love each other, was it not equally the
duty of lovers to marry each other and nobody else? Did not this right of the
lovers stand higher than the right of parents, relations, and other traditional
marriage brokers and matchmakers? If the right of free, personal discrimination
broke boldly into the Church and religion, how should it halt before the intolerable claim of the older generation to dispose of the body, soul, property, happiness, and unhappiness of the younger generation?

These questions inevitably arose at a time which was loosening all the old
ties of society and undermining all traditional conceptions. The world had
suddenly grown almost ten times bigger; instead of one quadrant of a hemi-
sphere, the whole globe lay before the gaze of the West Europeans who hastened
to take the other seven quadrants into their possession. And with the old narrow
barriers of their homeland fell also the thousand-year-old barriers of the prescribed medieval way of thought. To the outward and the inward eye of man
opened an infinitely wider horizon. What did a young man care about the
approval of respectability or honorable guild privileges handed down for generations when the wealth of India beckoned to him, the gold and the silver mines of
Mexico and Potosi? For the bourgeoisie it was the time of knight-errantry; they,
too, had their romance and their raptures of love, but on a bourgeois footing and,
in the last analysis, with bourgeois aims.

So it came about that the rising bourgeoisie, especially in Protestant countries where existing conditions had been most severely shaken, increasingly
recognized freedom of contract also in marriage, and carried it into effect in the
manner described. Marriage remained class marriage, but within the class the
partners were conceded a certain degree of freedom of choice. And on paper, in
ethical theory and in poetic description, nothing was more immutably established
than that every marriage is immoral which does not rest on mutual sexual love
and really free agreement of husband and wife. In short, the love marriage was
proclaimed as a human right, and indeed not only as a *droit de l'homme,* one of
the rights of man, but also, for once in a way, as *droit de la femme,* one of the
rights of woman.

This human right, however, differed in one respect from all other so-called
human rights. While the latter in practice remain restricted to the ruling class (the

bourgeoisie) and are directly or indirectly curtailed for the oppressed class (the proletariat), in the case of the former the irony of history plays another of its tricks. The ruling class remains dominated by the familiar economic influences and therefore only in exceptional cases does it provide instances of really freely contracted marriages, while among the oppressed class, as we have seen, these marriages are the rule.

Full freedom of marriage can therefore only be generally established when the abolition of capitalist production and of the property relations created by it has removed all the accompanying economic considerations which still exert such a powerful influence on the choice of a marriage partner. For then there is no other motive left except mutual inclination.

And as sexual love is by its nature exclusive—although at present this exclusiveness is fully realized only in the woman—the marriage based on sexual love is by its nature individual marriage. We have seen how right Bachofen was in regarding the advance from group marriage to individual marriage as primarily due to the women. Only the step from pairing marriage to monogamy can be put down to the credit of the men, and historically the essence of this was to make the position of the women worse and the infidelities of the men easier. If now the economic considerations also disappear which made women put up with the habitual infidelity of their husbands—concern for their own means of existence and still more for their children's future—then, according to all previous experience, the equality of woman thereby achieved will tend infinitely more to make men really monogamous than to make women polyandrous.

But what will quite certainly disappear from monogamy are all the features stamped upon it through its origin in property relations; these are, in the first place, supremacy of the man and secondly, the indissolubility of marriage. The supremacy of the man in marriage is the simple consequence of his economic supremacy, and with the abolition of the latter will disappear of itself. The indissolubility of marriage is partly a consequence of the economic situation in which monogamy arose, partly tradition from the period when the connection between this economic situation and monogamy was not yet fully understood and was carried to extremes under a religious form. Today it is already broken through at a thousand points. If only the marriage based on love is moral, then also only the marriage is moral in which love continues. But the intense emotion of individual sex love varies very much in duration from one individual to another, especially among men, and if affection definitely comes to an end or is supplanted by a new passionate love, separation is a benefit for both partners as well as for society—only people will then be spared having to wade through the useless mire of a divorce case.

What we can now conjecture about the way in which sexual relations will be ordered after the impending overthrow of capitalist production is mainly of a negative character, limited for the most part to what will disappear. But what will there be new? That will be answered when a new generation has grown up: a generation of men who never in their lives have known what it is to buy a woman's surrender with money or any other social instrument of power; a generation of women who have never known what it is to give themselves to a man from any other considerations than real love or to refuse to give themselves to their lover from fear of the economic consequences. When these people are in the world, they will care precious little what anybody today thinks they ought to do; they will make their own practice and their corresponding public opinion about the practice of each individual—and that will be the end of it.

Let us, however, return to Morgan, from whom we have moved a considerable distance. The historical investigation of the social institutions developed during the period of civilization goes beyond the limits of his book. How monogamy fares during this epoch, therefore, only occupies him very briefly. He, too, sees in the further development of the monogamous family a step forward, an approach to complete equality of the sexes, though he does not regard this goal as attained. But, he says:

> When the fact is accepted that the family has passed through four successive forms and is now in a fifth, the question at once arises whether this form can be permanent in the future. The only answer that can be given is that it must advance as society advances, and change as society changes, even as it has done in the past. It is the creature of the social system, and will reflect its culture. As the monogamian family has improved greatly since the commencement of civilization, and very sensibly in modern times, it is at least supposable that it is capable of still further improvement until the equality of the sexes is attained. Should the monogamian family in the distant future fail to answer the requirements of society . . . it is impossible to predict the nature of its successor [1963: 499].

Lenin on Sexual Love
Clara Zetkin

. . . "I was also told that sex problems are a favourite subject in your youth organisations too, and that there are hardly enough lecturers on this subject. This nonsense is especially dangerous and damaging to the youth movement. It can easily lead to sexual excesses, to overstimulation of sex life and to wasted health and strength of young people. You must fight that too. There is no lack of contact between the youth movement and the women's movement. Our Communist women everywhere should cooperate methodically with young people. This will be a continuation of motherhood, will elevate it and extend it from the individual to the social sphere. Women's incipient social life and activities must be promoted, so that they can outgrow the narrowness of their philistine, individualistic psychology centred on home and family. But this is incidental.

"In our country, too, considerable numbers of young people are busy 'revising bourgeois conceptions and morals' in the sex question. And let me add that this involves a considerable section of our best boys and girls, of our truly promising youth. It is as you have just said. In the atmosphere created by the aftermath of war and by the revolution which has begun, old ideological values, finding themselves in a society whose economic foundations are undergoing a radical change, perish, and lose their restraining force. New values crystallise slowly, in the struggle. With regard to relations between people, and between man and woman, feelings and thoughts are also becoming revolutionised. New boundaries are being drawn between the rights of the individual and those of the community, and hence also the duties of the individual. Things are still in complete, chaotic ferment. The direction and potentiality of the various contradictory tendencies can still not be seen clearly enough. It is a slow and often very painful process of passing away and coming into being. All this applies also to the field of sexual relations, marriage, and the family. The decay, putrescence, and filth of bourgeois marriage with its difficult dissolution, its licence for the husband and bondage for the wife, and its disgustingly false sex morality and relations fill the best and most spiritually active of people with the utmost loathing.

"The coercion of bourgeois marriage and bourgeois legislation on the family enhance the evil and aggravate the conflicts. It is the coercion of 'sacrosanct' property. It sanctifies venality, baseness, and dirt. The conventional hypocrisy of 'respectable' bourgeois society takes care of the rest. People revolt against the prevailing abominations and perversions. And at a time when mighty nations are being destroyed, when the former power relations are being disrupted, when a whole social world is beginning to decline, the sensations of the individual undergo a rapid change. A stimulating thirst for different forms of enjoyment easily acquires an irresistible force. Sexual and marriage reforms in the bourgeois sense will not do. In the sphere of sexual relations and marriage, a revolution is approaching—in keeping with the proletarian revolution. Of course, women and young people are taking a deep interest in the complex tangle of problems which have arisen as a result of this. Both the former and the latter suffer greatly from the present messy state of sex relations. Young people rebel against them with the vehemence of their years. This is only natural. Nothing could be falser than to preach monastic self-denial and the sanctity of the filthy bourgeois morals to young people. However, it is hardly a good thing that sex, already strongly felt in the physical sense, should at such a time assume so much prominence in the psychology of young people. The consequences are nothing short of fatal. Ask Comrade Lilina about it. She ought to have had many experiences in her extensive work at educational institutions of various kinds and you know that she is a Communist through and through, and has no prejudices.

"Youth's altered attitude to questions of sex is of course 'fundamental,' and based on theory. Many people call it 'revolutionary' and 'communist.' They sincerely believe that this is so. I am an old man, and I do not like it: I may be a morose ascetic, but quite often this so-called 'new sex life' of young people—and frequently of the adults too—seems to me purely bourgeois and simply an extension of the good old bourgeois brothel. All this has nothing in common with free love as we Communists understand it. No doubt you have heard about the famous theory that in communist society satisfying sexual desire and the craving for love is as simple and trivial as 'drinking a glass of water.' A section of our youth has gone mad, absolutely mad, over this 'glass-of-water theory.' It has been fatal to many a young boy and girl. Its devotees assert that it is a Marxist theory. I want no part of the kind of Marxism which infers all phenomena and all changes in the ideological superstructure of society directly and blandly from its economic basis, for things are not as simple as all that. A certain Frederick Engels has established this a long time ago with regard to historical materialism.

"I consider the famous 'glass-of-water' theory as completely un-Marxist and, moreover, as anti-social. It is not only what nature has given but also what has become culture, whether of a high or low level, that comes into play in sexual life. Engels pointed out in his *Origin of the Family* how significant it was that the common sexual relations had developed into individual sex love and thus became purer. The relations between the sexes are not simply the expression of a mutual influence between economics and a physical want deliberately singled out for physiological examination. It would be rationalism and not Marxism to attempt to refer the change in these relations directly to the economic basis of society in isolation from its connection with the ideology as a whole. To be sure, thirst has to be quenched. But would a normal person normally lie down in the gutter and drink from a puddle? Or even from a glass whose edge has been greased by many lips? But the social aspect is more important than anything else. The drinking of water is really an individual matter. But it takes two people to make love, and a third person, a new life, is likely to come into being. This deed has a social complexion and constitutes a duty to the community.

"As a Communist I have no liking at all for the 'glass-of-water' theory, despite its attractive label: 'emancipation of love.' Besides, emancipation of love is neither a novel nor a communistic idea. You will recall that it was advanced in fine literature around the middle of the past century as 'emancipation of the heart.' In bourgeois practice it materialised into emancipation of the flesh. It was preached with greater talent than now, though I cannot judge how it was practised. Not that I want my criticism to breed asceticism. That is farthest from my thoughts. Communism should not bring asceticism, but joy and strength, stemming, among other things, from a consummate love life. Whereas today, in my opinion, the obtaining plethora of sex life yields neither joy nor strength. On the contrary, it impairs them. This is bad, very bad, indeed, in the epoch of revolution.

"Young people are particularly in need of joy and strength. Healthy sports, such as gymnastics, swimming, hiking, physical exercises of every description and a wide range of intellectual interests is what they need, as well as learning, study and research, and as far as possible collectively. This will be far more useful to young people than endless lectures and discussions on sex problems and the so-called living by one's nature. *Mens sana in corpore sano.* Be neither monk nor Don Juan, but not anything in between either, like a German philistine. You know the young comrade X. He is a splendid lad, and highly gifted. For all that, I am afraid that he will never amount to anything. He has one love affair after another. This is not good for the political struggle and for the revolution. I will not vouch for the reliability or the endurance of women whose love affair is intertwined with politics, or for the men who run after every petticoat and let themselves in with every young female. No, no, that does not go well with revolution."

Lenin sprang to his feet, slapped the table with his hand and paced up and down the room.

"The revolution calls for concentration and rallying of every nerve by the masses and by the individual. It does not tolerate orgiastic conditions so common among d'Annunzio's decadent heroes and heroines. Promiscuity in sexual matters is bourgeois. It is a sign of degeneration. The proletariat is a rising class. It does not need an intoxicant to stupefy or stimulate it, neither the intoxicant of sexual laxity or of alcohol. It should and will not forget the vileness, the filth and the barbarity of capitalism. It derives its strongest inspiration to fight from its class position, from the communist ideal. What it needs is clarity, clarity, and more clarity. Therefore, I repeat, there must be no weakening, no waste and no dissipation of energy. Self-control and self-discipline are not slavery; not in matters of love either. . . ."

RADICAL FEMINISM

Radical Feminism and Love
Ti-Grace Atkinson

Radical feminism is a new political concept. It evolved in response to the concern of many feminists that there has never been even the beginnings of a feminist analysis of the persecution of women. Until there is such an analysis, no coherent, effective program can be designed to solve the problem. The OCTOBER 17th MOVEMENT was the first radical feminist group begun and has spent a great deal of its first five months working out the structure and details of a causal class analysis.

The analysis begins with the feminist *raison d'être* that women are a class, that this class is political in nature, and that this political class is oppressed. From this point on, radical feminism separates from traditional feminism. . . .

Since it is clear that men oppress women, and since this oppression is an ongoing process, it was clear to radical feminists that women must understand the *dynamics* of their oppression. Men are the *agents* of the oppression of individual women, and these agents use various means to achieve the subordination of their counter-class. But over thousands of years, men have created and maintained an inclosure of institutionalized oppression to fortify their domination of women by using many institutions and values as vehicles of oppression, e.g., marriage, family, sexual intercourse, love, religion, prostitution. Women are the victims of this oppression. . . .

I propose that the phenomenon of love is the psychological pivot in the persecution of women. Because the internalization of coercion must play such a key functional part in the oppression of women due to their numbers alone, and because of the striking grotesqueness of the one-to-one political units "pairing" the oppressor and the oppressed, the hostile and powerless, and thereby severing the oppressed from any kind of political aide, it is not difficult to conclude that women by definition must exist in a special psycho-pathological state of fantasy both in reference to themselves and to their manner of relating to their counter-class. This pathological condition, considered the most desirable state for any woman to find herself in, is what we know as the phenomenon of love.

Because radical feminists consider the dynamics of their oppression the focal point of their analysis, it is obvious that some theory of "attraction" would be needed. Why do women, even feminists, consort with the enemy? For sex? Very few women ever say that; that's the male-role reason. What nearly all women mutter in response to this is: for love.

There has been very little analytic work done on the notion of "love."[1] This is remarkable, considering the importance of it in ethics and political philosophy. Philosophers usually skirt it or brush it aside by claiming it's irreducible, or irrational. Or they smile and claim it's the sine qua non. All these things may be true and are clues to the political significance of "love": it's basic; it's against individual human interest; a great deal rests upon it.

Any theory of attraction could begin with the definition of the verb to attract: the exertion of a force such as magnetism to draw a person or thing, and susceptibility in the thing drawn. Magnetism is caused by friction or conflict, and the primary relationship between men and women of class confrontation or conflict certainly suffices for the cause of magnetism. Usually the magnetized moves towards the magnet in response to the magnet's power, otherwise the magnetized is immobile.

The woman is drawn to→ attracted by→ desirous of→ in love *with*→ the man. She is power*less,* he is power*ful.* The woman is instinctively trying to recoup her definitional and political losses by fusing with the enemy. "Love" is the woman's pitiful deluded attempt to attain the human: by fusing, she hopes to blur the male/female role dichotomy, and that a new division of the human class might prove more equitable: she counts on the illusion she has spun out of herself in order to be able to accept the fusion, to be transferred to the whole and, thus, that the new man will be garbed now equally in her original illusion. Unfortu-nately, magnetism depends upon inequity: as long as the inequity stands, the fusion may hold (everything else relevant remaining the same); if the inequity changes, the fusion and the magnetism fall with the inequity. A woman can unite with a man as long as she is a woman, i.e., subordinate, and no longer. There's no such thing as a "loving" way out of the feminist dilemma: that it is as a *woman* that women are oppressed, and that in order to be free she must shed what keeps her secure.

---

[1] I distinguish between friendship and love. Friendship is a rational relationship which requires the participation of two parties to the mutual satisfaction of both parties. Love can be felt by one party; it is unilateral by nature, and, combined with its relational character, it is thus rendered contradictory and irrational.

THE OCTOBER 17TH MOVEMENT recently devoted one of its meetings to a discussion of "love" and tried to analyze together how this phenomenon operated. The main difficulty was, and was left at, understanding the shift from the woman desiring an alliance with the power*ful* to the woman being *in love with* the man. It's clear that love has to do with some transitional or relational factor. But why, exactly? She is going from the political, the power*less* identification, to the individual, one-to-one unit. She is disarming herself to go into the enemy camp. Is love a kind of hysterical state, a *mind*less state therefore a *pain*less state, into which women retreat when the contradiction between the last shreds of their human survival and the everyday contingencies of being a woman becomes most acute?

Is love a kind of frenzy, or something like a Buddhist immolation, to unite with the One? The love women feel for men is most akin to religious love.

But hysteria might be a more useful paradigm for us since it's limited almost exclusively to women (the word "hysterical" derives from the Greek word for "uterus") and the condition is marked by certain characteristics strikingly similar to those of "love": anxiety converted into functional symptoms of illness, amnesia, fugue, multiple personality.

Coming Out

Coletta Reid

In the winter of 1969–70, I joined a consciousness raising group and a newly formed women's newspaper. My life had been typical of a well-socialized American female. I had interrupted college at twenty to marry a man both older and above me in social class. I supported him through graduate school, then went back to school myself to get a degree. I started graduate school, dropped out when my first child was an infant, returned to school then dropped out again. Finally, I got pregnant a second time because I didn't know what else to do.

Graduate school had been all too depressing. I never had a woman teacher; one teacher even boasted that he would refuse to teach in a department with a woman. Another upon meeting me suggested I do my thesis with him, after staring at my legs for five minutes. I had become unable to complete my work, an "erratic underachiever," they said. It was becoming clear that there were no teaching jobs available for women in my field; the possibilities of work were the same ones I had already been through: waitress, nurses' aide, secretary, admitting clerk in a hospital. My husband was angry at my long periods of depression and what he called "my low level of functioning"—"I don't see why you can't have this apartment clean and dinner fixed when I get home. You have nothing else to do all day."

Thus at 27, pregnant and with a toddler, I came to the women's movement. I had never been in a political movement before. I tended toward the conservative end of liberalism, I suppose. After all, I *had* married "up," the system had been good to me. I was extremely naive about power. I remember clearly the first time I realized my husband wasn't in total sympathy with the movement. I brought home a newspaper account of women sitting-in at a male-only university karate course. He said that women only wanted to be violent like men. I asked whether defending yourself against rape was being violent like a man. He countered that rape was hardly a big enough reason to train yourself to become a potential killer. From then to the end only took nine months.

For the month before I asked him to leave, I had a recurring dream: I was a leaf in the wind being tossed and turned to and fro endlessly. To stop the dream I had to wake myself up. I realized that I had never really imagined myself without a man. I had always assumed I would get married. I had never *really* thought I would have to support myself and/or my children by myself all of my life. I was suddenly scared to death of the lack of structures in my life: no marriage, no family, no job, no reason to be living in the city I was in. (I had come there for my husband's job.) I now had to do everything for myself, make my own life choices, deal with the world myself. I found that I had no center to myself; my center had always been my husband, or my husband/children.

How had I come to such a frightening decision? Through working with women for the liberation of women. At first my husband became irrelevant; he wasn't nearly as exciting and provocative as the women I was working with. He had very little to say about my oppression; he wasn't interested in putting all his time and energy in on behalf of women. Later he became a hindrance; his needs had always come first in the marriage and to change that was a constant battle.

Almost everything I was reading at the time led me toward lesbianism. If "The Myth of the Vaginal Orgasm" was true, then intercourse was not necessary or even relevant to *my* sexual satisfaction. If "Sexual Politics" was right that male sexuality was an expression of power and dominance, then I was choosing my own oppression to stay in a relationship with a man. If sex roles were an invention of society, then women—not just men—were possible people to love, in the fullest sense of that word. If I could hug and kiss a woman I loved, why couldn't I touch all of her body? Since my husband really thought men were superior, then wasn't my needing to be in a relationship with someone superior to me, self-hating and woman-hating? The conclusion seemed inescapable. I asked my husband to leave; he took our son and I kept our daughter.

Lesbian Oppression

Deciding that a course of action is best and carrying it out are two different cans of worms. I had some sense of the tremendous changes in my own psychology becoming a lesbian would require; I had no conception of the roadblocks society would throw up. Telling my family was my first shock; I said that I was getting divorced in order to become independent. My parents were furious; how could I break up my family for such a selfish and self-centered reason. I was just trying to shirk my responsibilities. I was lucky to have such a nice husband. He never beat me; he didn't drink; he didn't have a mistress; he supported me well. I was ungrateful; I didn't realize how lucky I was. My father yelled at my mother. She had failed in raising me. My mother blamed herself; she didn't understand where she had gone wrong. I clearly had become a "bad woman." My mother stopped being sympathetic; my father withdrew in hurt and anger. My mother said my father felt I had been mean to *him*. How? Because I had divorced Bob. Men stick together to the end.

That was only the beginning. I was getting my initiation into lesbian oppression. Most of the women I worked with were surprisingly non-committal. I had expected joy and jubilation, since I was choosing myself, other women, and strength. The non-committal attitude turned into outright hostility whenever I discussed the political implications of my choice. It might have been ok if I had said that my choice was purely personal, that it had no relevance to any other feminist's life. But to suggest that becoming a lesbian might be a happier, more whole way of life for any feminist was too much. In a newspaper article my politics were identified with those of Norman Mailer—sexual fascism: Mailer required all women to be heterosexual and I required them all to be lesbian. Of course, it was ignored that Mailer had every institution in society on his side making heterosexuality the only choice even imaginable to 90% of the women in America. To compare that to one woman's voice with no power behind it except perhaps a glimmer of truth was and is ludicrous.

The full range of attitudes and prejudices came out in the course of a meeting of a daycare center I had helped found and worked in for nine months. One woman expressed misgivings about me or my friends being around her daughter since I had become a lesbian. She evidently thought I would molest her little precious; she had no similar qualms about my being around her son when I was heterosexual. Nor had she any qualms about the heterosexual men being around her daughter which is strange since 100% of the child molestation cases reported in D.C. last year were committed by men. Another woman said she thought lesbians were too hostile, angry and man-hating to be around children who needed love and good vibes. Someone expressed regret at my husband's leaving since he was one of the few men she could relate to. Better to have a man around to relate to than have a fellow sister grow and become strong. The sexism inherent in almost all the responses was glaring. Some of the men at the daycare center were outrageously piggy toward the children but they were never called on the carpet at a meeting or put in the position of having to defend themselves as I was. In general the parents agreed that they were open to their children becoming bi-sexual but they certainly didn't want them encouraged to become little dykes and faggots.

I slowly left the women's movement or more accurately I was slowly pushed out. I had never envisioned myself a lesbian/separatist when I left my husband. The women's movement had given me the ideas, strength and support to do something I thought best for me and womankind; I had no idea it would reject me once I had done it.

Heterosexual Privilege

I had heard the term "heterosexual privilege" before, but I never really understood how it worked. Now I knew. When I was heterosexual I was accepted as normal by my family, friends, acquaintances, and contacts. But once I started putting myself and other women *first* in my life I was variously seen as: unnatural, immoral, perverted, disgusting, sick or a sexual fascist. In general, heterosexual feminists felt themselves superior to lesbians since they were involved in natural relationships. If I was honest about my lesbian relationship, I was flagrant. When they met their men at the door with kisses, that was normal. They were willing to accept my lesbianism only if it was secreted and viewed as minor to my life. They kept telling me it didn't make any difference who I personally loved. But I knew it made a tremendous difference. I was beginning to get the feeling that lesbianism was of crucial importance to feminism. Otherwise, why was I being oppressed so much for it, why was it so threatening to both men and women.

As I tried to live as an open lesbian I began to see the privileges I had taken for granted when married. My husband had been able to make more money than my lover and I together. There were no daycare centers for children under three since, of course, mothers should stay home and let their husbands work. But my lover couldn't make enough money as a waitress to support us both. My husband had taken the car; I was unable to get a loan for another one. I had no credit as it was all in my husband's name. Landlords wanted to rent houses to families; I had to pretend I was straight to get a job.

I realized that when I was married I had been bought off. I had accepted being subservient, sexually available, and keeper of his home in return for some degree of economic security and social acceptance. I had become a fat hen who gave up her freedom for regular corn. Being a bird who could fly was risky; and you ended up not nearly as well-fed. At some point in my life I had sold out as a form of survival.

The saddest revelation was that feminists still had a stake in being fat hens. They primarily wanted the farmer to treat them a little better. My co-workers at the newspaper were threatened by my becoming a lesbian. If I could do it, they could do it. They could stop co-operating in their oppression. They could choose to be lesbians, lesbians weren't born, they were made. I wasn't a rich artist who lived in Paris, I was an ordinary housewife with two kids and no skills, who with the help of women's liberation had taken her life into her own hands. And they could too. Even in the women's movement, women punish other women who stop accepting their role as weak, passive and dependent. Women who step out of line are threatening because they offer that choice as a possibility to others.

Myths about Lesbians

Most women accept the male myths about lesbians without questioning the use of those myths to keep women apart. Lesbianism is threatening to male social power because it represents the spectre of women united in their own interests. It is threatening to individual male power because it represents the loss of a personal servant, plus an always available sperm receptacle. It is quite inconceivable to most men that women could actually prefer female company and bodies to their own. The male ego is closely linked to his sense of superiority over women; he is outraged to think a "mere" woman could be thought his equal.

The most common myth accepted was that lesbians wanted to be men; they were unhappy male egos trapped in female bodies; they had confused sexual identities. In fact, lesbians don't even like men and the world they've made. Why would anyone want to be rapists, perpetrators of wars and sexual and racial oppression, pollutors and capitalists? Certainly no self-respecting woman. Lesbians do, however, want many of the freedoms men have reserved for themselves. They want self-determination over their own bodies and children. They want access to the many areas men have forbidden them: governing the society through decision-making at all levels, physical strength and athletic ability, knowledge and skills from plumbing to bio-chemistry. Lesbians see the whole world as their province and aren't content to be restricted to woman's place.

The second myth is that lesbians embody in exaggerated form all the despicable qualities of men. They are always "on the make," they rape women, molest children, and view other women as "sexual objects." In fact, men have taken those very qualities women fear them for and have projected them onto lesbians. Thus women end up fearing lesbians more than men. By making lesbians "bogeywomen" men have kept women from loving and respecting each other, thereby robbing us of our greatest strength and potential for unity.

The third most common myth is that lesbians are just as involved in role-playing as are heterosexual couples—everybody knows about butch and femme. The aim of roles is not simply to divide all behavior, dress, jobs, etc. into two separate spheres. The aim is to make one set the superior role, to give one role power over the other. When two women are involved in a relationship, neither of them has the real social power behind a role to fall back on. Even if there is a "butch," she cannot marshall social pressure of family, friends and acquaintances to keep her femme dependent. She can't legally rape her (in marriage there is no rape); she can't leave her with five kids and no job; she has no church, marriage contract, or legal structures on her side. Behind the male role is social power, economic clout and physical strength. There is no such reality behind a butch.

Lesbians, in fact, are women and as such, they have all been socialized to be women. Most are actively involved in trying to overcome that female-training; they want to be what straights call "butches." They want to be physically strong enough to defend themselves; they want to be psychologically able to put their own needs and growth first; they want skills and jobs so they can support themselves and take care of themselves and each other. They want to be women who can establish relationships with each other out of mutual love, respect and equality—not out of desperate need and economic necessity. Lesbians do not sit and passively wait for a female knight in shining armor to come take them away to bliss. They are not looking for a love partner whom they can take care of, live through, and dedicate their lives to, secure in a role. Together, they *are* engaged in a fight to build positive, active, aggressive selves who can take control of their lives.

One stereotype concerns lesbians wearing male clothing. Lesbians wear male clothing because it's more comfortable, better made, more durable, cheaper and doesn't immediately brand you as a potential "sex object" to all men. Female clothing, just like female hair styles, and "feminine mannerisms" are all aimed at making the differences between men and women readily apparent. If men and women dressed and acted alike only *very* large men and *very* small women would be easily recognizable. How would men know who to treat as inferior, who to hire as secretaries, who to rape? Female clothing keeps women less mobile and more physically vulnerable. Ever try to escape from or fight a rapist in tight baggies and stacked heels?

Lesbianism and the Feminist Analysis

When I left marriage and the family, I was uncertain about the connection between the liberation of women and lesbianism. I only knew that becoming a lesbian was tremendously significant to my life. As I encountered the oppression that society heaps on lesbians I sensed that lesbianism must be, in some way, crucial to ending the exploitation of women.

The feminist analysis of women's condition asserts the exploitation of women as a *sex*—women are exploited by men because they are women, because they have different genitals. Women's biology dictates that new generations of people be produced via women's bodies; in other words women provide *necessary* social labor just by being women. Through the process of becoming impregnated, carrying a child, and giving birth, woman performs an absolutely socially necessary task. Men have taken this biological fact and turned it into an ideology about woman's place.

Because some women must give birth each generation, men have constructed an ideology which says that:

1 The aim of all women's lives is to give birth. (Motherhood)
2 Because vaginal intercourse is necessary to impregnation, all sexual activity must have vaginal intercourse as its end. (Heterosexuality)
3 Because male impregnation is necessary to birth, women must bind themselves for life to the man who impregnates them. (Marriage)
4 All women must not only birth but also raise children. Women have a necessary relation to providing for children's day-to-day needs. (The Family)
5 Because women take care of children and are married, they must also take care of their men, which they cannot do properly if they leave the home to work. If they leave the home to work, it must be for the preservation of the home and they must still meet their husband's and children's daily needs. (Housewifery)
6 If women work outside the home, it should only be in the capacity of meeting men's needs (waitresses, secretaries) or children's needs (teachers, nurses). Because it is less important than men's work (the primary work), it can be paid less. (Job discrimination)

Men have taken the natural fact that woman reproduces the species and constructed an ideology that says that motherhood, heterosexuality, marriage, the family, housewifery and a secondary place in the job market are natural. In early feminist analysis, all of those "natural" constructs were challenged except heterosexuality. Early feminism took for granted that "natural sexuality" was heterosexuality; that "natural sexual relations" was vaginal intercourse; that female sexuality must be directed toward men. In other words, feminists still felt themselves to be "naturally" dependent on men for sexual satisfaction.

Women's sexuality *per se* is in no way naturally or necessarily connected to penises or penile penetration. Fucking *once* is necessary to getting pregnant once, that's all. Female orgasm originates in the clitoris whose stimulation is only peripherally involved in intercourse. Many other forms of clitoral stimulation are more effective than penile interpenetration. In fact, the vagina's only function is as a passageway between the external organs of sensual satisfaction (clitoris, labia, plevic floor, etc.) and the reproductive organs (uterus, fallopian tubes, etc.). The vagina has sensory nerves only at its entrance. This is not to deny that the vagina contracts during orgasm, so does the uterus; but orgasm originates in the clitoris and is dependent on clitoral stimulation. So, although it's possible for women to experience orgasm during intercourse; intercourse isn't necessary or even the "best way" for women to achieve sexual satisfaction.

However, men seem to think that it is the best way for men to achieve sexual satisfaction. So they have used female sexuality in service of their own. They have placed their own sexual interests ahead of women's during the course of which they have totally distorted female sexuality: "Men need sex more than women; women are naturally masochistic (they get pleasure from pain); if women don't enjoy fucking, they're frigid; the only orgasm is vaginal; if women don't have orgasm during intercourse, it's their own fault, etc." Male sexuality then has become a matter of male imposition of his supposed sexual needs upon women, with a mythology developed to justify it.

In other words, heterosexuality as an institution operates for the benefit of men. It is in men's interests for women to think that they "need" men for sexual pleasure, to think that vaginal intercourse is the only "natural" expression of female sexuality. Heterosexuality keeps women thinking that without a man in their lives they have to become asexual. Women are taught that the only way to get physical affection and sexual satisfaction is to be heterosexual. Thus women have seemingly "chosen" heterosexuality—and generally think that women who haven't are a deviant minority.

In the context of the institutional nature of enforced heterosexuality, lesbianism is an act of individual rebellion. The lesbian refuses to make the male's sexual "needs" primary. She sets out to reclaim her own sexuality, discover her own sexual needs and aggressively pursue them with other like-minded women. Female sexual passivity is central to heterosexuality. Women wait for men to make a date, make the first move, and finally to "get it up." Men are "turned off" by women who are aggressive and pushy about what they want and need. It is no accident that the "missionary" position is the favored one in advanced patriarchy. The man is "on top" in bed just as he is in the economy and politics. The woman is pinned down, can hardly move, and has the least chance of having an orgasm. If marriage is legalized prostitution, then heterosexuality is socially approved rape.

Thinking that your sexuality has to be directed toward men is analogous to thinking that your life must be directed toward men. Both are part of an ideology aimed at making and keeping women dependent. If women continue to lend their bodies to men to be used and entered for male pleasure, they are going to find it very hard to keep from lending their lives to men to be used for their ends.

In a world devoid of male power and, therefore, sex roles, who you lived with, loved, slept with and were committed to would be irrelevant. All of us would be equal and have equal determination over the society and how it met our needs. Until this happens, how we use our sexuality and our bodies is just as relevant to our liberation as how we use our minds and time.

SOCIALIST FEMINISM

Sex in a Capitalist Society
The Staff of *Women*

What We've Been Taught about Sex

Society has done little to make us secure about our sexuality. Throughout our lives we are bombarded with myths about our bodies and our nature. As females, we are told from infancy to be passive and submissive. During childhood we are taught that bodies are "possessions" to be guarded and hidden. Our "private parts" are places we must not look at, touch or think about. To touch another person is dirty and sinful. We become so alienated from our bodies, because of this conditioning, that puberty, the time of our greatest physical development, is the most embarrassing and awkward stage in our lives. As young women, we begin to hear tales of the "over-sexed" half of the human race: "Watch out for the boys! All they want is your body." We also learn early that we must be sexually attractive by society's fixed standards or we are worth little. The double message is, "Be sexy, but don't indulge until it's proper."

After 18 years of such teachings, we find ourselves waiting for the man of our dreams to come along with the key to our sexuality and happiness—the magic words, "I love you. Will you marry me?" On that day alone, we can forget about the "dirty" aspects of sex and prepare for the most "romantic" experience of our lives: copulation. Our bodies are no longer private—they are owned by that man and he can *have* us. According to the myth, we are ready to settle down to a life of bliss—ever faithful to the one we love because sex with anybody else is still dirty. When the experience isn't all we expected it to be, we worry that we're frigid. We're caught in another double bind: we've been told we have less potential for enjoying sex, and less need for it, yet we're supposed to dig sex with our husband, taking care to fulfill his greater needs.

Prostitution and Rape

Prostitution and rape are logical extensions of our society's attitudes toward sexuality. Prostitution relies on misconceptions about both the prostitute and her customers. Since society so severely limits the sexuality of its "good" women, those who become prostitutes are held to be "bad," i.e. sexually deviant. In reality, prostitutes are often forced into their occupation out of economic need and limited opportunities. The prostitute's customer, so the myth goes, visits her primarily out of unsatisfied sexual needs. Actually, men frequently visit prostitutes for other reasons: proof of sexual power, compensation for failures in other relationships, lack of political power, contempt for women and for sex. In its treatment of women as commodities, prostitution represents the complete objectification of women's bodies. Prostitution should be eliminated from society. For the present, however, all laws which make prostitution a crime should be revoked. We oppose the legalization of prostitution or any steps which suggest that prostitution be a legitimate social institution.

Like prostitution, rape has been justified, or at least tolerated, because modern mythology tells us that men are driven by uncontrollable sexual desires. Actually, men commit rape for the same reasons that they go to prostitutes. Rapists have internalized our cultural equation of sex, power, and violence.

Why Sexual Myths Exist

Historically, the doctrines of religion and morality have been repressive to both male and female sexuality. Our Judeo-Christian culture has always degraded the body and praised the soul or mind. Yet even in the most sexually repressive times, men's sexual needs have at least been acknowledged, though healthy expression of them has been denied. Recently, society has progressed to toleration and then to encouragement of men's sexuality.

Many people believe that sexual liberation was accomplished for women with "the pill" and the "sexual revolution" of the 1960's. Of course, birth control does improve the quality of women's lives by decreasing the risk of pregnancy. However, despite the sexual revolution, the double standard continues: birth control is almost exclusively the responsibility of women; and in the hip culture "free love" means that women are available sexually for any man.

These sexual myths continue to exist in our society because, first of all, they are ideally suited to shoring up the institution of marriage. If we believe that women naturally desire an exclusive sexual relationship and don't have much sex drive anyway, then we are easily convinced to settle into a monogamous marriage. In a society based on private property, marriage fulfills an important function. It insures that fathers will know their children and thereby upholds the patriarchal system of inheritance. Society's vested interest in maintaining the institution of marriage overrides any progressive attitudes towards women's sexuality. Although modern methods of contraception no longer require strict sexual fidelity to one man as a means of determining paternity, women are not encouraged to question the monogamous, patriarchal system which controls their lives. The myths remain to insure that we will continue to choose marriage, and to hide the economic reality that, in fact, we have little other choice. In the nuclear family, our basic economic unit, the man is financially responsible for his wife and children. Under this arrangement, women do not do productive work for pay and, therefore, are not financially independent.

The sense of privacy and exclusiveness that is built up about our sexuality has another effect. Privitization fosters insecurity and competition over what each of us owns sexually, just as privacy about financial matters encourages competition over material possessions. We each imagine that everyone else has more money, better sex, more beautiful bodies than we do.

Where Are We Now?

In working on this issue of the Journal, we tried not only to analyze underlying social attitudes and institutions, but also to assess the effects of these on our personal lives. Our consciousness-raising was very difficult, so difficult in fact, that one question we asked is why it's so hard to talk about our sexuality. We all admitted that we feel judged and are wary of revealing inadequacies in such a competitive area. If we are in a monogamous sexual relationship, we wonder if we're "repressed"; if we're maintaining more than one sexual relationship, we often feel "promiscuous." Because we do not talk openly enough with other women about our sexual experiences and feelings, we fall into the trap of thinking our problems are unique.

We talked about our socialization into passive roles in sexual relationships. This has alienated us from our potential as sensuous, sexual, aggressive and vigorous human beings, not only in relationship to sex, but also to sports, self-defense, health care and sensuous activity.

We questioned the limited roles society allows us for sexual expression. Most of us are involved in or just moving out of monogamous heterosexual relationships. We realize that the basic assumption of monogamy—that all our needs for love and security can be met by one person—is impossible, but most of us are having difficulty coping with the hurt and insecurity resulting from the breakdown of sexual monogamy.

In discussing lesbian relationships, some of us said we feel more comfortable with women precisely because an overtly sexual dimension is lacking. We are fearful of dealing with the jealousy and possessiveness, now present in our heterosexual relationships, in our relationships with women. This is not to deny our own socialized fears of a lesbian relationship. We acknowledge hang-ups in that area and are continuing to challenge ourselves.

Our Hopes for the Future

Through our discussions, we realized, first of all, the benefits of breaking down the walls of privacy. Talking about our sexuality has liberated us from judgements we had feared. We discovered that we all had problems, that none of us were sexual "freaks." Some of us realized that even though we had "liberated" theories about our sexuality—like seeking our own pleasure—we found it hard to put them into practice. But with the support of one another we are beginning to take our sexual needs more seriously and are finding encouragement that they can be fulfilled.

We have also inspired each other to search for a more total body awareness. We would like to see genital sex as only one aspect of an expanded sensual awareness. Being more sensual can mean touching our bodies or another person's without this leading to genital sex. Sensuality includes sense awareness of the world around us, through stroking a cat or smelling a flower. Being with children is a very sensual experience for many of us, probably because we feel freer to express our feelings and to be physical with them. Being in touch with our bodies through dancing, swimming, and exercising is also a sensual experience.

For some of us, being expressive of our feelings has led to deep emotional relationships with other women. Because society termed them lesbian, these feelings were repressed in us. Many of us also want to grow in sensual expression and emotional closeness in our heterosexual relationships. For all of us, a free society would allow us to respond to women and men, lovingly, with our total selves.

We want to emphasize the importance of non-sexual relationships, and we want to take our commitments to other women seriously. For those of us who are not ready to share our sexual relationships, making strong, though non-sexual, commitments to others is the first step in breaking down the possessiveness of monogamy.

Progress in all these directions is slow, but we would never have gotten started if we hadn't sat down together and talked as honestly as we could about our sexuality.

Concluding Remarks

As radical women, we want to understand the relationship between our sexual lives and the political/economic system under which we live. We know it is a privilege to spend time and energy on the psychological dimension of our lives. It is necessary, first of all, to be fed, housed and clothed, which is not the condition of most people in the world. But we also know it is important to demonstrate that sexuality is more than a personal matter. Monogamy has long been the backbone of our patriarchal system. The availability of birth control and abortion is not controlled by women whose lives are affected most personally. Prostitution and rape are outgrowths of a society that is sexually sick and sexist, where women are treated as property, where people are sexually repressed, and where choice of work is severely limited by economic realities.

But women are beginning to demand self-determination through birth control and abortion and are exposing the hypocrisy and corruption at the heart of rape and prostitution in America. We are acquiring knowledge about how our bodies work. We are challenging power relationships as they affect us most intimately, i.e. within sexual relationships. For this power relationship is but a reflection of other power relationships—between boss and worker, rich and poor, black and white—which permeate our society.

It is a myth that people can find totally satisfactory solutions to their personal problems, including sexual problems. The questions raised and discussed in this issue are closely related to broad social problems. . . .

Imperialism and Sexuality

Sheila Rowbotham

. . . A similar imperial onslaught on sexuality, particularly female sexuality, has further eroded the traditional notions women had of their value. The cosmetics industry has mushroomed and created needs as well as products. The female who is the cosmetic ideal is more or less unattainable, no sooner captured she appears in another form. Playing on insecurity and anxiety the advertisers market goods which actually create new fears. Vaginal deodorants make people anxious about sexual odour. Acting on the assumption that women regard themselves through men's eyes as objects of pleasure, advertising and the media project a haunting and unreal image of womanhood. The persistent sense of dislocation between the unrealized female self and the projected female stereo-types has contributed to a feeling of failure. Women are not brought up to cope with the male world of production, work, ideas, power. They find their own preserved world threatened, their value reduced and depreciated, and are given an ideal of femininity which is foisted onto them by ever more powerful forms of the mass media.

The media have considerable power to throw back to us a version of ourselves which is presented as the "norm." This "norm" is not unaffected by changes in society. Women's liberation has brought a sprinkling of adverts which attempt to appeal to dissatisfaction. However, the images of freedom are still completely male-defined. Either girls step out in freedom bras towards a man, or they simply become male fantasies of freedom. Girls replace men behind the wheels of fast sports cars. Advertising has a vested interest in presenting the sexual roles between men and women as clearly defined. But it has also to respond, however bizarrely, to changes in the consciousness of women. It reflects very clearly the production relations general in society. In order to sell commodities women are themselves reduced to commodities. However, if a section of middle-class women manage to alter their position in society through agitation there is no reason why adverts should not present these women with a spurious sense of liberation by inverting male-female roles in certain cases, and presenting men as commodities.

The visual impact of advertisements played a large part in awakening women to their own reflection in advanced capitalism. Immediate images on film and television make explicit areas of experience which have previously existed only in our subterranean selves. The very act of communication makes these sensations and experiences assume a shape, whereas before they were only implicit. New forms of consciousness are offered up by the marketing of new commodities and the mass communication of news and events. As a result, many aspects of life which were considered private and personal before become part of what is normally seen.

Sexual relations between men and women, or between men and men, and between women and women, are very clearly no longer exempt from the penetration of the market and the exposure of the sexual sell. This means that sexuality as the symbol of the natural assumes an importance beyond itself. It also means that political resistance to capitalism has to take on new forms, because the tendency for capitalism to distort all areas of human experience is no longer merely an abstract idea, it is an everyday happening.

Within advanced capitalism the maintenance of the separation of male and female conditioning has also assumed a new acuteness. This is partly because the existing sexual division of labour is still necessary to capitalist production. But also because of the deep and long-established nature of female subordination, and the hold it has over both men's and women's notions of their very identities, any challenge touches on deep and intensely personal areas of consciousness. The idea of romantic love, itself a creation of the bourgeoisie, has undergone innumerable transformations and permutations since it originated. Sexual love has assumed immense significance in containing many aspects of social relations incompatible with the work-discipline of commodity production. Here lurk affection, tenderness, passion, violence, satisfaction, fulfilment, excitement, imagination, religion, madness, fantasy, beauty, sensation, cruelty, transcendence, communion, escape. Weighed down with such unrealizable expectations, and surrounded by such an intolerable state of affairs elsewhere, sexuality has been as incapable as the family of providing a genuine alternative to the wasteland.

Sexual pleasure has an elusive and often exhausted quality. It is unable to compensate for everything denied to human beings in normal life. Not surprisingly it has assumed bizarre and distorted forms under the prevailing production for private profit. Belief in property, possession, domination does not stop at the factory gates. But like the family, sex represents the hope of an alternative. It has become the new "sigh of the oppressed creature, the sentiment of a heartless world, and the soul of soulless conditions." Like religion, which it rivals and replaces, sexuality now "is the fantastic realisation of the human being in as much as the human being possesses no true reality."[1] Love and orgasmic explosion have no proper place in a society in which the end of life is the production of goods, in which work discipline as a thing in itself becomes the guardian of morality. Consequently sexual sensation is packaged, and delivered confined and synthesized in prevailing notions of sexuality—sugar sweet or black leather and net. Sex roles of dominator and dominated are part of the sexual sell. Such notions determine the structure of human fantasy—they are the symbol of everything which is not possible in everyday life.

Sexuality is communicated in the media in a series of images. A hand stroking hair, legs walking into summer, clean-washing-crisp housewives, children with cereal spoons and oral brand satisfactions, the power of money and class selling cigars, motor cars, pale ale—these become the visible shell for accumulated unrealizable desire. The loving emotion and physical excitement in

---

[1]Marx and Engels, *Gesamtausgabe*, I, I, i, quoted in Karl Marx, *Selected Writings in Sociology and Social Philosophy*, ed. T. B. Bottomore and M. Rubel, Watts, 1956, pp. 26–7. See also Christopher Caudwell, "A Study of Changing Values: Love," in *The Concept of Freedom*, Lawrence & Wishart, 1965.

sex become loaded with the great weight of this accumulation. Sexual relations between people start to sag, drop into odd places, assume fantastic shapes, in pornographic fetish, the rituals of desire, or the complacency of hypocritical virtue. Any challenge to the prevailing order of fantasy is a political struggle, just as the criticism of religion in the nineteenth century was political.

It would be foolish not to recognize the resilience of the subterranean imagination. The desecration of capitalism's sanctuaries, where pain and domination, grotesque imagination, masochism and guilt, emotional blackmail, and the thwarted ego have a hothouse life of their own, needs, as Wilhelm Reich understood, a conscious commitment to sexual alternatives in the revolutionary movement. Women's liberation attacked from the start the way in which women were presented in the media. By doing this the whole image of the family, of children, of manliness, became very obvious as well as the distortion of sexuality. The distortions appeared clearly because the old moral taboos were being eroded. Instead of the ethic of thrift, abstinence, and sacrifice which came out of the early stages of capital accumulation, capitalism needs now people who can regulate themselves precisely and on their own initiative at work and spend and consume without repression during their leisure. Though these long-term needs are temporarily contradicted by the creation of new forms of labour-intensive work which need the old kind of openly authoritarian supervision, and by short-term economic problems which involve cutting back on demand, they have already had a considerable social influence.

Much of the talk of permissive society and sexual liberation means merely permission to consume. However, this changing climate has a very important effect on the position of women. For the first time in human society it is possible for women to choose when they become pregnant. This with the panic about population explosion means that the persistent connection between sex and procreation, and the fear in male-dominated society of female sexual pleasure, and often of any sexual act which is not likely to produce children, lose their force to contain women—and men. The implications of these for both women's liberation and gay liberation are apparent.

Contraception, like other technological advances in capitalism, has a dual nature. By immeasurably increasing the possibilities of sexual relationship without fear of pregnancy, contraceptives contribute to a loosening of moral coercion to the "permissive" society. Within such a society the carrot replaces the stick as the prime inducement to cooperation, though the stick is kept for the last resort. As long as sexuality, thus liberated, is confined to a small elite group, who are not within the discipline of commodity production, or as long as the kind of sexuality which is permitted retains, in however bizarre a form, the structure of dominance and abnegation, self-disgust and self-destruction, which within capitalism hold down and limit the human consciousness, it can be accommodated. But whenever the notion of pleasure takes off into a questioning of the need to produce people only to produce things it becomes subversive. Nasty, dirty hippy sex exults in its opposition to commodity production. It parades itself dancing in the streets, becomes gleefully transvestite, many coloured, confuses sexual roles, makes love every day. Then capitalism thinks "how nice," not like those old-fashioned revolutionaries, and sells them a few clothes. The market flourishes and the fashion spreads. Nudity proliferates in the underground papers first, and then in the popular press. But despite its ambiguities, and particularly its ambiguities towards women, the emphasis in the underground on sexual pleasure still contains a threat to commodity production. When it seems to spread to the young working classes capitalism suddenly remembers morality, and in its zealous puritan disguise flays out against the sexuality it had formerly encouraged.

That the cult of free sex contains many distortions and much mystique and illusion is not surprising; what is surprising is the tendency for conservative supporters of capitalism to blame these on contraception, and look back longingly to the romantic nonsense of a mythical former unity, when pregnancy followed pregnancy, when childbirth frequently brought the mother's death, and infant mortality was high. The source of mystique and illusion comes from the mess outside, not from the technology of diaphragm, pill and safe abortion. Contraception, like any other kind of knowledge, is not accumulated in a social vacuum. The course of research by private firms, experiments with poor Third World women, the lack of concern about the effects on women psychologically and physically, reflect a bias which is profit-oriented, imperialist and male-biased. Women's liberation has consistently demanded abortion and contraception as means of control for women, not as part of a social engineering plan to keep population down to avoid the discontent of the poor. None the less, contraceptives lay the basis for a great explosion in the possibility of female pleasure. The release of the female orgasm from the fatalism, fear and shame of millennia is one of the triumphs of bourgeois technology. The social expression of this release and the shape it assumes in consciousness will depend on the activity of revolutionary human beings in history. Its integration is not impossible within capitalism. The glossy women's magazines are already pushing their own version of sexual liberation. How to undress in front of your husband, how to package yourself for all his sexual fantasies. In a popular book on sex technique published recently women are urged to work like the devil to accent their good features and hide the bad. They are shown how to package themselves for the market and check their tone and volume, to remember they are training their body to become a superb instrument of love. Passivity is rebuked, enthusiastic participation and a close check on "Maintenance, Reclamation and Salvage" recommended.[2] But while increasing female participation in the sexual act is convenient as a compensatory feature of advanced capitalism, the notion of female power to control equally in bed upsets the conditioning of men to dominate and females to acquiesce. This is rather like the unresolved contradiction of how to educate people to work with initiative, and get them to continue to obey orders. Hysteria so long contained in the womb leaps exulting up from under. The female orgasm explodes and scrawls itself generously over the women's lavatory at Willesden railway station, "We are all the same, good or bad, slag or vergin."

[2] "J," *Sensuous Woman*, London, 1971, pp. 37–9. I owe this reference to Jenny Moss.

SUGGESTIONS FOR FURTHER READING:
Part III, Sexuality

Barbach, Lonnie Garfield: *For Yourself: The Fulfilment of Female Sexuality,* Doubleday Anchor, New York, 1976.

Bengis, Ingrid: *Combat in the Erogenous Zone,* Bantam Books, New York, 1973.

The Boston Women's Health Book Collective, *Our Bodies, Ourselves,* Simon and Schuster, New York, 1973.

Brownmiller, Susan: *Against Our Will: Men, Women and Rape,* Simon and Schuster, New York, 1975.

Ehrenreich, Barbara, and Deirdre English: *Complaints and Disorders: The Politics of Sickness,* The Feminist Press, New York, 1973.

Frankfort, Ellen: *Vaginal Politics,* Bantam Books, New York, 1973.

Seaman, Barbara: *Free and Female,* Coward, McCann & Geoghegan, New York, 1972.

Sherfey, Mary Jane: *The Nature and Evolution of Female Sexuality,* Vintage Books, New York, 1973.

Acknowledgments

Adams, Phyllis: "With an Eye to the Future." Copyright © 1976 by Janice-Lynn, Inc., P.O. Box 124, Morris Plains, N.J. 07950. Reprinted by permission of Janice Lynn and Jerry Russo.

Allen, David: *The Price of Women,* Jarrow Press, San Francisco, 1971, pp. 153–158 and 161–162. Reprinted with permission of Jarrow Press, a division of The Anchor Society, Inc., San Francisco.

Atkinson, Ti-Grace: "Radical Feminism and Love" from *Amazon Odyssey,* Links Books, New York, 1974.

Babcox, Deborah: "The Liberation of Children," *Up From Under,* vol. 1, no. 1, May-June 1970, pp. 43–46.

Bem, Sandra L., and Daryl J. Bem: "Homogenizing the American Woman" from *Beliefs, Attitudes, and Human Affairs* by D. J. Bem, Brooks/Cole Publishing Company, Monterey, Calif., 1970, pp. 89–99.

Benston, Margaret: "The Political Economy of Women's Liberation," *Monthly Review,* September 1969, pp. 13–25. Copyright © 1969 by Monthly Review, Inc., New York. Reprinted by permission of Monthly Review Press.

Berkeley, Joyce Maupin: "Older Working Women," *WOMEN: A Journal of Liberation,* vol. 4, no. 2, 1975, p. 14. Copyright © 1975 by WOMEN: A Journal of Liberation, 3028 Greenmount Ave., Baltimore, Md. 21218.

Bettelheim, Bruno: "Fathers Shouldn't Try to Be Mothers," *Parents' Magazine,* October 1956, pp. 40 and 126–129. Copyright © 1956 by Parents' Magazine, New York.

Brown, Rita Mae: "Living with Other Women," *WOMEN: A Journal of Liberation,* vol. 2, no. 2, 1971, pp. 63–67. Copyright © 1971 by WOMEN: A Journal of Liberation, 3028 Greenmount Ave., Baltimore, Md. 21218.

Bunch, Charlotte: "Lesbians in Revolt" from *Lesbianism and the Women's Movement,* Diana Press, Oakland, Calif., 1975, pp. 29–37.

Comfort, Alex: "On Advanced Lovemaking" from *The Joy of Sex,* Crown Publishers, Inc., New York, 1972, pp. 8–15. Copyright © 1972 by Mitchell Beazley Publishers, Ltd. Used by permission of Crown Publishers, Inc.

Cronan, Sheila: "Marriage," *Notes from the Third Year: Women's Liberation,* pp. 62–66. Copyright © 1971 by Notes From the Second Year, Inc., P.O. Box AA, Old Chelsea Station, New York, N.Y. 10011.

Cuban Family Code, Law #1289. (The complete Family Code and other original Cuban documents can be obtained from the Center for Cuban Studies, 220 E. 23 St., New York, N.Y. 10010.)

Ellis, Albert: "Sexual Perversions" from *The Art and Science of Love,* Bantam Books, Inc., New York, 1969, pp. 194–205. Copyright © 1960 and 1966 by The Institute of Rational Living, Inc. Published by arrangement with Lyle Stuart.

Engels, Friedrich: *The Origin of the Family, Private Property and the State,* International Publishers Company, Inc., New York, 1942, 1970, pp. 53, 54, 71, 87–146.

Firestone, Shulamith: *The Dialectic of Sex,* William Morrow & Company, Inc., New York, 1970, pp. 1–14. Copyright © 1970 by Shulamith Firestone. Adapted by permission of William Morrow & Company, Inc.

Freud, Sigmund: "Femininity" from *New Introductory Lectures on Psychoanalysis,* W. W. Norton & Company, Inc., New York, 1933, pp. 158–184. Translated and edited by James Strachey. Copyright © 1965, 1964 by James Strachey. Copyright 1933 by Sigmund Freud. Copyright renewed 1961 by W. J. H. Sprott. Reprinted by permission of W. W. Norton & Company, Inc.

Charlotte Perkins Gilman Chapter: *A View of Socialist Feminism,* Charlotte Perkins Gilman Chapter, New American Movement, 110 N. Estes Drive, Chapel Hill, N.C. 27514.

Goldberg, Steven: *The Inevitability of Patriarchy,* William Morrow & Company, Inc., New York, 1974, pp. 103–114. Copyright © 1973, 1974 by Steven Goldberg. Adapted by permission of William Morrow & Company, Inc.

Gould, Robert E.: "Measuring Masculinity by the Size of a Paycheck," *Ms. Magazine,* June 1973, pp. 18–21. Copyright © 1973 by Ms. Magazine Corp. Reprinted with permission.

Hariton, E. Barbara: "The Sexual Fantasies of Women," *Psychology Today,* March 1973, pp. 39–44. Copyright © 1973 by Ziff-Davis Publishing Co. Reprinted by permission of Psychology Today Magazine.

Lenin, V. I.: "Women and Society" from *The Woman: Selections from the Writings of Marx, Engels, Lenin and Stalin,* International Publishers Company, Inc., New York, 1938, pp. 62–63.

Litewka, Jack: "The Socialized Penis," *Liberation Magazine,* vol. 18, March-April 1974. Copyright © 1974 by Liberation Magazine. Reprinted by permission.

Lopate, Carole: "Women and Pay for Housework," *Liberation Magazine,* June 1974, pp. 8–11. Copyright © 1974 by Liberation Magazine. Reprinted by permission.

Mainardi, Pat: "The Politics of Housework" from *Sisterhood Is Powerful,* Vintage Books, New York, 1970, pp. 447–454.

Schulman, Alix Kates: "A Marriage Agreement," *Up From Under,* vol. 1, no. 2, Fall 1970, pp. 5, 6, 8.

Scott, Ann Crittenden: "The Value of Housework," *Ms. Magazine,* vol. 1, no. 1, July 1972, pp. 56–59. Copyright © 1972 by *Ms.* Magazine Corp. Reprinted with permission.

Sexton, Patricia Cayo: "Workers (Female) Arise!" *Dissent,* Summer 1974, pp. 380–388.

Storr, Anthony: "Aggression in the Relations between the Sexes" from *Human Aggression,* Atheneum Publishers, New York, 1968, pp. 69–72. Copyright © 1968 by Anthony Storr. Reprinted by permission of Atheneum Publishers.

Tiger, Lionel, and Robin Fox: "Give and Take" and "Mother-Child Bonding" from *The Imperial Animal,* Holt, Rinehart and Winston, Inc., New York, 1971, pp. 60–67 and 142–146. Copyright © 1971 by Lionel Tiger and Robin Fox. Reprinted by permission of Holt, Rinehart and Winston, Inc.

Women Staff: "Women as Workers under Capitalism," *WOMEN: A Journal of Liberation,* vol. 2, no. 3, inside cover. Copyright © 1971 by WOMEN: A Journal of Liberation, 3028 Greenmount Ave., Baltimore, Md., 21218.

Women Staff: "Sex in a Capitalist Society," *WOMEN: A Journal of Liberation,* vol. 3, no. 1, inside cover. Copyright © 1972 by WOMEN: A Journal of Liberation, 3028 Greenmount Ave., Baltimore, Md., 21218.

"Women in the Work Force: Five Tables":The Female Labor Force (page 23) from Peter Gabriel Filene, *Him/Her Self Sex Roles in Modern America,* Harcourt Brace Jovanovich, Inc., New York, 1974, p. 219; pages 23 to 25 from Research Group One Report No. 13 (rev.), *Women and Men: A Socioeconomic Factbook,* Vacant Lots Press, Baltimore, 1975.

Woodul, Jennifer: "What's This about Feminist Businesses?" *Off Our Backs,* June 1976, vol. 6, no. 4, pp. 24–26. Reprinted by permission of Off Our Backs, 1724 20th St., N.W., Washington, D.C. 20009.

Zaretsky, Eli: *Capitalism, the Family and Personal Life,* Harper & Row, Publishers, Incorporated, New York, 1976, pp. 23–35 and 65–77, Harper Colophon edition. Copyright © 1976 by Eli Zaretsky. Reprinted by permission of Harper & Row, Publishers, Incorporated.

Zetkin, Clara: "Lenin on Sexual Love" from *The Emancipation of Women,* International Publishers Company, Inc., New York, 1934, 1938, 1951, 1966, pp. 104–108.

Index

Index